Value for Money

Measuring the Return on
Non-Capital Investments

Analytics in Action

ROI Case Studies
Volume I

Patricia Pulliam Phillips, Ph.D.
and
Jack J. Phillips, Ph.D.

With the Assistance of Hope Nicholas

ROI INSTITUTE®

P.O. Box 380637
Birmingham, AL 35238-0637
www.roiinstitute.net
info@roiinstitute.net

The case studies presented in this book have been previously published in the following publications and are reprinted here with permission.

Chapter 8, 18, and 25
> Phillips, P.P., Phillips, J. J., Ray, R., Measuring the Success of Employee Engagement (ATD, Alexandria, VA, 2016)

Chapters 13
> Phillips, P.P., Phillips, J.J., and Edwards, L.A. *Measuring the Success of Coaching* (ASTD, 2012)

Chapter 14
> Phillips, P.P., Zuniga, L., Phillips, J.J., *Measuring the Success of Organizational Development* (ASTD, 2013)

Chapter 15, 16, and 19
> Phillips, P.P., Phillips, J.J, Ray, R., *Measuring the Success of Leadership Development* (ATD, 2015)

Chapter 17 and 21
> Elkeles, T., Phillips, P.P., Phillips, J.J., *Measuring the Success of Learning Through Technology* (ASTD, 2014)

Chapter 20
> Phillips, J. J., Phillips, P.P., *Proving the Value of HR, 2nd ed.* (SHRM, 2012)

Chapter 22, 23, and 24
> Phillips, P.P., Phillips, J.J., Robinson, R., *Measuring the Success of Sales Training*, (ASTD, 2013)

ISBN-13: **978-0-9790285-5-7**
ISBN-10: **0-9790285-5-8**

Printed by AGS, an R.R. Donnelley & Sons Company
Published by Business Writers Exchange Press
Distributed by ROI Institute, Inc.
Cover Design by Hannah O'Toole
Edited by Hope Nicholas, Director of Publications, and Katelyn Parmley, Client Relatationship Manager, ROI Institute.

PO Box 380637
Birmingham, AL 35238-0637

Table of Contents
Volume 1

Preface

This collection of ROI case studies represents the use of the Phillips ROI Methodology™ in a broad range of applications in the human resources, learning and development, and performance improvement fields. Each case follows the methodology and describes in detail how it was used to show the value of a particular project, program, or initiative.

These case studies have been selected for use in ROI workshops, briefings, and in the Certified ROI Professional (CRP) certification processes. They are designed to be teaching tools. Most cases were originally published in another document, either for The Association for Talent Development (ATD, Alexandria, VA), The Society for Human Resource Management (SHRM, Alexandria, VA), or Wiley. Special thanks go to these publishers for allowing us to reprint these useful studies in this special edition for use in our learning process.

The ROI Methodology

The ROI Methodology is now the most used evaluation system in the world, adopted by 5,000 organizations in 65 countries. Over two-thirds of the Fortune 500 companies, 26 federal governments, and many large NGOs such as the United Nations are using it. Over 100 universities are using this, along with 300 healthcare-delivery organizations funded by both public and private entities. The methodology is appropriate for all types of human capital programs and particularly soft skills programs.

Target Audience

This book should interest anyone involved in human resources, learning and development, organization development, change management, consulting, and performance improvement. The primary audience is practitioners who are struggling to determine the value of programs and projects and to show how they contribute to the strategic goals of the organization. These practitioners are the ones who request more real-world examples. This same group also expresses concern that there are too many models, methods, and theories with too few examples to show if any of them has really made a difference. This publication should satisfy practitioners' needs by providing successful examples of the implementation of comprehensive evaluation processes.

Readers should find this casebook entertaining and engaging. Questions are placed at the end of each case to stimulate additional thought and discussion. One of the most effective ways to maximize the usefulness of this book is through group discussions, using the questions to develop and dissect the issues, techniques, methodologies, and results.

The Cases

The case studies we selected met specific guidelines. Each case study includes data that can be converted to monetary values so that ROI can be calculated. The selected case studies provide a method of isolating the effects of the program. The isolation step is necessary the true value of a program. The methodologies included in the case studies presented in this book are control groups, trend line analysis, forecasting, and participant and manager estimates.

Although there was some attempt to structure cases similarly, they are not identical in style and content. It is important for the reader to experience the programs as they were developed and identify the issues pertinent to each particular setting and situation. The result is a variety of presentations with a variety of styles. Some cases are brief and to the point, outlining precisely what happened and what was achieved. Others provide more detailed background information, including how the need for the program was determined, the personalities involved, and how their backgrounds and biases created a unique situation.

Acknowledgments

We would like to acknowledge the clients who allowed us to publish these case studies. We greatly appreciate the opportunity to learn from these clients as we have worked together in applying this methodology. In addition, we were assisted in the development of some of these cases by Dianne Hill (Chapter 1); Tim Renaud (Chapter 2); Al Pulliam (Chapter 4); Patrick Whalen (Chapter 5); Lizette Zuniga (Chapter 14); John Kmiec, Sandra Dugas, Cyndi Gaudet, Heather Annulis, Mary Nell McNeese, and Susan Bush (Chapter 21); Emma Weber (Chapter 22); Claude MacDonald and Louis Larochelle (Chapter 23); and Matgorzata Mitoraj-Saroszek (Chapter 24) all of whom are, or have been, associates or clients of ROI Institute.

For a variety of reasons, many of the clients have elected not to include their names or the names of their organizations. In today's competitive world and in situations where there is an attempt to explore new territory, it is understandable why an organization would choose not to be identified.

Identification should not be a critical issue, however. These cases are based on real-world situations faced by real people.

We want to acknowledge the outstanding work of the ROI Institute Publishing Team. Hope Nicholas, director of publications, provided guidance and direction on the project, as well as much of the initial work. Hope is amazing as she managed our publishing program. Anita Azeta assisted with the project through editing and production. Katelyn Parmley provided the finishing touches. Without the excellent work of Hope, Anita, and Katelyn, this book would not have become a reality. Thanks for your enormous contribution.

Suggestions

We welcome your input. If you have ideas or recommendations regarding presentation, case selection, or case quality, please send them to us. Contact us with your comments and suggestions at ROI Institute, P.O. Box 380637, Birmingham, AL 35238-0637, www.roiinstitute.net., info@roiinstitute.net.

Patti and Jack Phillips
ROI Institute, Inc.

About the Authors

Patti P. Phillips, Ph.D. is president and CEO of ROI Institute, Inc., the leading source of ROI competency building, implementation support, networking, and research. A renowned leader in measurement and evaluation, she helps organizations implement the ROI Methodology in 65 countries around the world. She serves as Principal Research Fellow for The Conference Board, Chair of the Institute for Corporate Productivity's People Analytics Board, board member of the Center for Talent Reporting, and ATD CPLP Certification Institute Fellow. Patti also serves on the faculty of the UN System Staff College in Turin, Italy; The University of Southern Mississippi's PhD in Human Capital Development program; and Escuela Bancaria y Comercial in Mexico City, Mexico. Her work has been featured on CNBC, EuroNews, and over a dozen business journals.

Patti's academic accomplishments include a Ph.D. in International Development and a master's degree in Public and Private Management. She is a certified in ROI evaluation and has been awarded the designations of Certified Professional in Learning and Performance and Certified Performance Technologist.

She, along with her husband Jack Phillips, contributes to a variety of journals and has authored over fifty books on the subject of measurement, evaluation, analytics, and ROI. Patti Phillips can be reached at patti@roiinstitute.net.

Jack J. Phillips, Ph.D. is a world-renowned expert on accountability, measurement, and evaluation. Phillips provides consulting services for Fortune 500 companies and major global organizations. The author or editor of more than 75 books, he conducts workshops and presents at conferences throughout the world.

Former bank president, Phillips has received several awards for his books and work. The Society for Human Resource Management presented him an award for one of his books and honored a Phillips ROI study with its highest award for creativity. The American Society for Training and Development gave him its highest award, Distinguished Contribution to Workplace Learning and Development for his work on ROI. His work has been featured in the *Wall Street Journal*, *BusinessWeek*, and *Fortune* magazine. He has been interviewed by several television programs, including CNN.

Dr. Phillips regularly consults with clients in manufacturing, service, and government organizations in over 70 countries in North and South America, Europe, Middle East, Africa, Australia, and Asia.

Dr. Phillips has undergraduate degrees in electrical engineering, physics, and mathematics; a master's degree in Decision Sciences from Georgia State University; and a Ph.D. in Human Resource Management from the University of Alabama. He has served on the boards of several private businesses—including two NASDAQ companies—and several nonprofits and associations, including the American Society for Training and Development, the National Management Association, and the International Society for Performance Improvement, where he served as president. He is chairman of ROI Institute, and can be reached at jack@roiinstitute. net.

THE ROI METHODOLOGY

The ROI Methodology is the most recognized approach to ROI evaluation. Implemented in a variety of organizations in over 70 countries, the ROI Methodology provides organizations a process that can cut across organization boundaries, linking programs, processes, and initiatives to bottomline measures.

The ROI Methodology has sustained its position as the leading approach to program evaluation because it:

- Reports a balanced set of measures;
- Follows a methodical, step-by-step process; and
- Adheres to standards and philosophy of maintaining a conservative approach and credible outcomes.

A Balanced Set of Measures

The concepts of cost-benefit analysis and ROI have been used to show the value of programs, processes, and initiatives for centuries. Cost-benefit analysis is grounded in welfare economics and public finance; ROI in business accounting and finance. Together the two are the ultimate measures of contribution of programs, processes, and initiatives. But alone, they are insufficient. While cost-benefit analysis and ROI report the financial success of programs, they omit critical evidence as to how the financial impact is achieved. By balancing financial impact with measures that address individuals' perspectives and the systems and processes that support the transfer of learning, a complete story of program success can be presented.

The ROI Methodology categorizes evaluation data into five levels as shown in Table 1. These five levels tell the ultimate story of program success:

Table 1. The ROI Methodology Five-Level Evaluation Framework

Level	Measurement Focus
1. Reaction & Planned Action	Measures participant reaction to the program and captures planned action
2. Learning	Measures changes in knowledge and skills
3. Application & Implementation	Measures changes in behavior and specific actions on-the-job
4. Business Impact	Measures changes in business impact measures
5. Return on Investment (ROI)	Compares the monetary benefits to the cost of the program

Level 1: Reaction and Planned Action

This initial level of evaluation is the most commonly used; reaction and planned action data are usually collected by an end-of-course questionnaire. This is the questionnaire typically offered to participants at the end of all programs. Although criticized by researchers because of the limited relationship between participant reaction and the use of the knowledge and skills, when used appropriately, the Level 1 reaction questionnaire is a source of data that predicts actual use of skills and knowledge. Level 1 evaluation answers five questions:

1. Is the program relevant to participants' needs?
2. Is the program important to participants' success?
3. Do participants intend to use what they learned in the program?
4. Are participants willing to recommend the program to others?
5. Did the program provide participants with new information?

All five of these measures usually show a significant correlation with application.

Level 2: Learning

Participant learning of new knowledge and skills in a program is necessary to change behavior and apply what they learn on the job. Learning measurement takes place during the program through a variety of techniques such as tests, facilitator assessment, peer assessment, self-assessment, observation, reflective thinking, and documentation. Learning measurement answers two critical questions:

1. Do participants know what they are supposed to do and how to do it?
2. Are participants confident to apply their newly acquired knowledge and skills when they leave the program?

Level 3: Application and Implementation

Executives and administrators often make this comment, "It's not what the employees learn, it's what they do with what they learn that's important." Organizations invest millions in learning and development initiatives, yet there is still limited evidence as to what is gained through those initiatives. Measuring application and implementation provides evidence that the learning is transferring to the workplace; that employees are doing something different because of the learning.

Success in application and implementation is measured after participants have applied the knowledge and skills on a routine basis, although it can be forecasted using a variety of techniques. Data are collected through surveys, questionnaires, interviews, focus groups, observations, action plans, and performance contracts. A critical component of application and implementation measurement is the determination of enablers supporting the transfer of learning and the barriers preventing the transfer of learning. Measurement at Level 3 provides the richest source of data of any of the five levels. Five key questions are answered when measuring success at Level 3:

1. To what extent are participants applying their newly acquired knowledge and skills?
2. How frequently are participants applying their newly acquired knowledge and skills?
3. How successful are participants with the application?
4. If they are applying their knowledge and skills, what is supporting their effort?
5. If they are not applying their knowledge and skills, why not?

Level 4: Business Impact

Measuring business impact connects the program to important business measures. Improvement in productivity, quality, cost, and time is critical in any organization. Other measures of success such as customer satisfaction, employee satisfaction, and innovation are also important in achieving organizational goals. Level 4 Business Impact measures are defined as the consequence of applying skills and knowledge from the program. Measuring these consequences answers one important question with regard to the program: This level of evaluation is the number 1 data set for executives. Two key questions are answered at Level 4:

1. What is the consequece of application?
2. What is the change in the business measures connected to the program?

Level 5: Return on Investment (ROI)

The ultimate measure of financial success of a program, process or initiative is ROI, which compares the monetary benefits to the costs of the program. To calculate ROI, six steps of cost-benefit analysis are taken:

Step 1 Identify the improvements in impact measures
Step 2 Isolate the amount of improvement to the program

Step 3 Convert the improvements to monetary value
Step 4 Tabulate the fully-loaded costs of the program
Step 5 Identify the intangible benefits linked to the program
Step 6 Compare the monetary benefits to the cost in an ROI calculation

The first step, improvements in business measures, are taken when evaluating at Level 4. The amount of improvement connected to the program is identified (step 2). These improvements are then converted to monetary value (step 3). A fully-loaded cost profile is developed (step 4) and intangible benefits are defined (step 5). Finally, the monetary benefits of the program (Level 4 measures converted to monetary value) are compared to the fully-loaded costs of the program to calculate an ROI (step 6). Measurement at Level 5 answers one critical question:

1. Do the monetary benefits of the program meet or exceed the costs of the program?

When fully developed, these five levels of evaluation plus the intangible benefits represent a chain of impact that occurs when participants attend a program, learn, apply their learning, and improve impact measures. Figure 1 depicts this chain of impact. As shown in Figure 1, the chain of impact represents the five levels of evaluation along with a step to isolate the effects of the program.

Figure 1. The Chain of Impact Tells the Complete Story of Program Success.

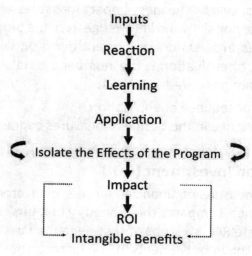

The process answers the question:

1. How do you know it was caused by the program?

Not all programs are evaluated at all the levels. Only certain programs require such a comprehensive evaluation. Those programs include very expensive programs, programs that have a long life cycle, programs that have a very broad reach, comprehensive programs, and programs that instill significant change in the organization. Other variables such as the need for the program, the purpose of the evaluation, and the stakeholders' needs often drive the level to which a program is evaluated.

ROI Methodology Process

The ROI process includes ten steps to ensure the appropriate data are collected from the proper sources at the right time. As shown in the figure 2, the evaluation of a program begins with identifying program objectives and planning the evaluation. This section provides an overview of each step of the ROI process.

Figure 2. ROI Methodology™ Process

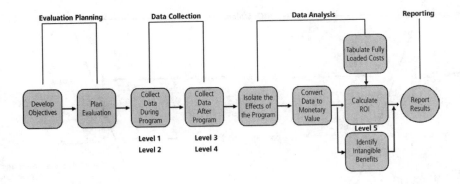

The ROI Methodology follows a step-by-step process beginning with developing program objectives and planning the evaluation. Data are collected at two different time frames, during the program and after the program. Improvements in key impact measures are isolated to the program. When appropriate, these improvements are converted to monetary value and compared to the fully-loaded costs of the program.

Data Collection Procedures

The data collection process includes four primary elements: 1) defining the program objectives and measures to determine if the objectives have been achieved; 2) determining the data collection methods; 3) identifying the sources of data; and 4) determining the timing of data collection.

Program Objectives and Measures

Program objectives are typically derived from a formal needs assessment. The needs assessment identifies the gaps in performance. The gaps can come from excessive costs and inefficiencies, behavior, knowledge, skills, and even individual perceptions. When these gaps or needs are identified, a solution is developed to solve the problem. To ensure that the solution designer, facilitator, and participant involved in the process know the expected outcomes, SMART objectives are defined. The solution is then evaluated against those objectives. Figure 3 depicts this connection among the needs, objectives, and evaluation. The needs assessment drives program objectives, which then drive the evaluation.

Figure 3. Program Alignment

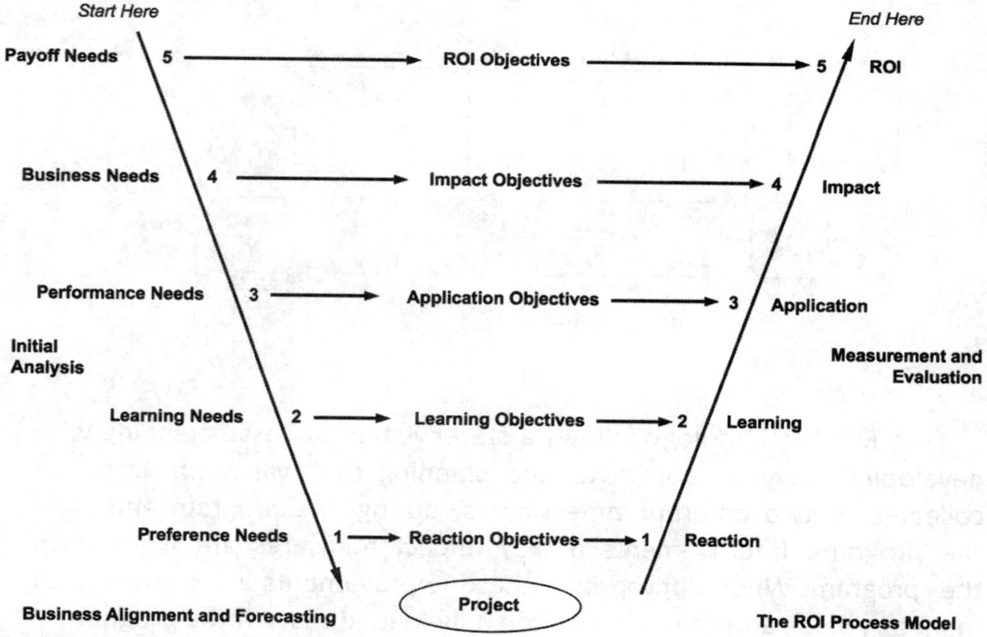

Data Collection Methods

A variety of data collection methods are considered when planning an evaluation. These methods include tests, surveys, questionnaires, interviews, observation, focus groups, action plans, and organization records.

Data Sources and Timing

Selecting the data source is a critical step in data collection because the source drives the credibility and validity of the study. The fundamental question asked when selecting data sources is: Who knows best about the measures being taken?

Data are usually collected in two different time frames: 1) Level 1 and 2 data are collected during the program and 2) Level 3 and 4 data are collected after participants have had time to apply knowledge and skills on a routine basis.

Data Analysis Procedures

Data analysis begins with isolating the effects of each initiative from other influences that may positively or negatively impact Level 4 measures. When ROI is calculated, the benefits of the program (Level 4 Impact measures) are converted to monetary value then compared to the Fully-Loaded costs of the program. This section presents options for data analysis.

Isolating the Effects of the Program

A variety of techniques are available for isolating the effects of a program:
- Control group arrangement
- Trend line analysis
- Forecasting methods
- Estimations
- Previous studies/experts
- Subordinate report of other factors
- Calculating/estimating the impact of other factors
- Use of customer input

Appropriate techniques to use in a survey are determined during the evaluation planning phase.

Converting Data to Monetary Value

Data conversion takes place only when the ROI is pursued. This step is dependent on the Level 4 business impact measures that improve due to the program. Not all Level 4 measures need to be converted to money; some will be reported as intangible benefits.

The techniques that can be used to convert measures to monetary value include:

- Using standard values for
  - Output
  - Quality
  - Employee's time (calculate the value using)
- Locating internal and external experts
- Data from external databases
- Securing estimates from
  - Participants
  - Supervisors/managers
  - Learning staff
- Linking with other measures

This step in the process will be considered as important business impact measures are identified through evaluation planning and data analysis.

Tabulating Fully-Loaded Costs

The final data necessary to calculate ROI is to determine the fully-loaded costs. These costs include needs assessment, design/delivery costs, facilitation, participation, and evaluation costs, representing a fully-loaded cost profile necessary to ensure a conservative estimate of program costs.

ROI Calculation

The ROI calculation is the standard financial equation developed through finance and economics:

$$BCR = \frac{\text{Program Benefits}}{\text{Program Costs}}$$

$$ROI = \frac{\text{Net Program Benefits}}{\text{Program Costs}} \times 100$$

The net program benefits is the program benefits minus the program costs.

Intangible Benefits

Along with the ROI calculation, intangible benefits of each initiative will be identified. In many cases, these intangible benefits, those benefits not converted to monetary value, are more important to an organization than a positive ROI. Intangible benefits may include enhanced job satisfaction and commitment, customer satisfaction, teamwork, images, stress and job engagement.

Throughout the evaluation of each initiative, value will be assessed at every level. Data will be provided to the client to ensure that improvements to the initiatives are implemented. A comprehensive report will be developed that describes in full the value of each initiative.

Scope and Use of ROI Methodology

The scope and use of the ROI Methodology has grown tremendously. The methodology had its beginnings in the learning and development area and quickly grew into other applications. The process has also expanded to all types of projects and programs in all types of organizations including non-profits, NGOs, and the public sector.

This process captures a balanced set of data. It is systematic and user-friendly and brings business evaluation to major programs. The process is supported by a tremendous amount of research with practical usage and application. It is estimated that 3,000-5,000 studies are conducted each year. The conservative standards make it executive friendly. This has become the most documented evaluation system in the world, with books in 38 languages and case books developed in at least a dozen countries.

The Benefits of ROI

As listed in Figure 4, the payoffs of the ROI Methodology are numerous. This approach satisfies the desire to have a credible process and shows the contribution of important programs. Perhaps the four most important reasons are: to improve programs (process improvement versus performance evaluation for the program team is critical), gain support for the programs, build relationships with key executives and administrators (who often fund the programs) and provide funding for programs in the future.

Figure 4. Benefits of Using ROI Methodology: The Payoff

- Align programs to organizational needs
- Show contributions of selected programs
- Earn respect of senior management/administrators
- Build team morale
- Justify/defend budgets
- Improve support for programs
- Enhance design and implementation processes
- Identify inefficient programs that need to be redesigned or eliminated
- Identify successful programs that can be implemented in other areas

How to Use this Casebook

These cases present a variety of approaches to evaluating human resources, learning and development, and performance improvement training programs. The cases focus on evaluation at the ultimate level— return on investment (ROI). Collectively, the cases offer a wide range of settings, methods, techniques, strategies, and approaches and represent manufacturing, mining, financial services, hospitality, healthcare, retail stores, technology, construction, utilities, service, and governmental organizations. Target groups for the programs vary from all employees to managers to technical specialists. As a group, these cases represent a rich source of information about the strategies of some of the best practitioners, consultants, and researchers in the field.

Although most of the case studies represent excellent role models, some cases do not necessarily represent the ideal approach for the specific situation. In almost every case it is possible to identify areas that might benefit from refinement or improvement. That is part of the learning process—to build on the work of others. The questions at the end of each case provide a hint at possible weaknesses. Although the implementation processes are contextual, the methods and techniques can be used in other organizations.

Table 1 represents basic descriptions of the cases in the order in which they appear in the book. This table can serve as a quick reference for readers who want to examine the evaluation approach for a particular type of program, audience, or industry.

Using the Cases

There are several ways to use this book. It will be helpful to anyone who wants to see real-life examples of the return on investment of specific programs. The authors recommend the following four uses:

1. This book will be useful to professionals as a basic reference of practical applications of measurement, evaluation, and analytics. A reader can analyze and dissect each of the cases to develop an understanding of the issues, approaches, and, most of all, possible refinements or improvements.

2. This book will be useful in group discussions where interested individuals can react to the material, offer different perspectives, and draw conclusions about approaches and techniques. The questions at the end of each case can serve as a beginning point for lively and entertaining discussion.

3. This book will serve as a supplement to other textbooks. By providing the extra dimensions of real-life cases that show the outcomes of human resources, learning and development, and performance improvement programs.
4. Finally, this book will be extremely valuable for managers who do not have primary responsibility for human resources, learning and development, or performance improvement. These managers provide support and assistance to the staff, and it is helpful for them to understand the results that their programs can yield.

This book offers a variety of approaches and provides an arsenal of tools from which to choose when evaluating programs. It is important to remember that each organization and its program implementation are unique. We do not recommend attempting to replicate a case study for a similar problem. What works well for one, may not work well for another, even if they are in similar settings. The key is to use the ROI framework and methodology.

Follow-Up

Space limitations necessitated that some cases be shorter than the authors would have liked. Some information concerning background, assumptions, strategies, and results had to be omitted. If additional information on a case is needed, we are pleased for you to contact us directly at patti@roiinstitute.net or jack@roiinstitute.net.

Table 1. Overview of Case Studies

Case	Industry	Program	Target Audience
Healthcare	Healthcare	Sexual Harassment Prevention	First-and-Second Level Supervisors, Managers, All Employees
Canadian Valve Company	Manufacturing	New Employee Training	Machine Operators
Midwest Electric, Inc.	Electric Utility	Stress Management	Work Teams
National Steel	Manufacturing	Safety Incentives	Production Employees
United Petroleum International	Energy	e-Learning – Sales	Sales Engineers
Cracker Box, Inc.	Restaurant	Performance Management Training	Store Manager Trainees
Retail Merchandising Company	Retail Stores	Interactive Selling Skills	Sales Associates

Southeast Corridor Bank	Banking	Employee Engagement	Branch Employees
Federal Information Agency	Public Sector – Federal	Internal MS Degree Program	Technical Specialists
Metro Transit Authority	Public Sector - City	Absenteeism Reduction	Bus Drivers
Global Car Rental	Car Rental	Leadership Development	First-Level Managers
TechnoTel Corporation	Telecommunications	Effective Meeting Skills	Project Leaders
Nations Hotel	Hospitality	Business Coaching	Executives
Agua Manufacturing Company	Manufacturing	Organization Culture Change	Managers/Teams
Fashion Stores Incorporated	Retail Stores	Leadership for Performance for Store Managers	Store Managers
Global Bank Inc.	Banking	Selection and Onboarding Program for New Leaders	MBA Recruits
Transoft Inc.	Software Industry	Upgrade Selling Program: Mobile Learning	Sales Associates
International Premium Hotel Group	Hospitality	New Selection Process	New Employees
Global Engineering and Construction Company	Commercial Construction	Safety Leadership for Construction Project Leaders	Project Safety Leaders
Family Mutual Health and Life Insurance	Health and Life Insurance	Work-at-Home Program	Claims Processors, Claims Examiners
PolyWrighton	Manufacturing	Employee Engagement	Supervisors
Multinational Automotive Company	Automotive Industry	Sales Training Program	Sales Executives
Future-Tel	Telecommunications	Simulation-Based Sales Training	Sales Professionals
McArthur Sp. z.o.o.	Retail Stores	Selling Skills for Retail Sales Assistants	Sales Staff
Home Furnishings, Inc.	Retail Stores	Employee Engagement	All Employees

Additional Publications on the ROI Methodology from ROI Institute Executives, Partners, and Associates

- *The Bottomline on ROI* 3rd Ed. (HRDQ, 2017)

- *The Business Case for Learning: Using Design Thinking to Deliver Business Results and Increase the Investment in Talent Development.* (HRDQ and ATD Press, 2017)

- *The Chief Talent Officer: Driving Value Within A Changing Organization Through Learning and Development* 2nd Ed. (Routledge, 2016)

- *Accountability in Human Resource Management: Connect HR to Business Results,* 2nd edition. (Routledge, 2016)

- *Real World Evaluation Training: Navigating Common Constraints for Exceptional Results* (ATD Press, 2016)

- *Handbook of Training Evaluation and Measurement Methods,* 4th Ed. (Routledge, 2016)

- *Measuring the Success of Employee Engagement: A Step-by-Step Guide for Measuring Impact and Calculating ROI* (ATD Press, 2016)

- *High-Impact Capital Strategy: Addressing the 12 Major Challenges Today's Organizations Face* (AMACOM, 2015)

- *Maximizing the Value of Consulting: A Guide for Internal and External Consultants* (Wiley, 2015)

- *Performance Consulting: A Strategic Process to Improve, Measure, and Sustain Organizational Results,* 3rd Ed. (Berrett-Koehler, 2015)

- *Measuring the Success of Leadership Development: A Step-by-Step Guide for Measuring Impact and Calculating ROI* (ATD, 2015)

- *Making Human Capital Analytics Work: Measuring the ROI of Human Capital Processes and Outcomes* (McGraw-Hill, 2015)

- *Measuring ROI in Environment, Health, and Safety* (Scrivener, 2014)

- *Measuring the Success of Learning Through Technology: A Step-by-Step Guide for Measuring Impact and ROI on E-Learning, Blended Learning, and Mobile Learning* (ASTD Press, 2014)

- *Measuring the Success of Organization Development: A Step-by-Step Guide for Measuring Impact and Calculating ROI* (ASTD Press, 2013)

- *Measuring the Success of Sales Training:* A Step-by-Step Guide for Measuring Impact and Calculating ROI (ASTD Press, 2013)

- *Survey Basics: A Complete How-to Guide to Help You: Design Surveys and Questionnaires, Analyze Data and Display Results, and Identify the Best Survey Tool for Your Needs* (ASTD Press, 2013)

- *Measuring Leadership Development: Quantify Your Program's Impact And ROI On Organizational Performance* (McGraw-Hill, 2012)

- *Proving the Value of HR: How and Why to Measure ROI.* 2nd Ed. (SHRM, 2012)

- *The Bottomline on ROI: Benefits and Barriers to Measuring Learning, Performance Improvement, and Human Resources Programs.* 2nd Ed. (HRDQ, 2012)

- *Measuring ROI in Healthcare: Tools and Techniques to Measure the Impact and ROI in Healthcare Improvement Projects and Programs* (McGraw-Hill, 2012)

- *Measuring the Success of Coaching: A Step-by-Step Guide for Measuring Impact and Calculating ROI* (ASTD Press, 2012)

- *Measuring ROI in Learning and Development: Case Studies from Global Organizations* (ASTD Press, 2012)

- *10 Steps to Successful Business Alignment* (ASTD Press, 2011)

- *The Green Scorecard: Measuring the Return on Investment in Sustainability Initiatives* (Nicholas Brealey, 2011)

- *Project Management ROI: A Step-by-Step Guide for Measuring the Impact and ROI for Projects* (John Wiley, 2011)

- *Measuring for Success: What CEOs Really Think About Learning Investments* (ROI Institute, ASTD Press, 2010)

- *The Consultant's Guide To Results-Driven Proposals. How To Write Proposals That Forecast The Impact And ROI* (McGraw-Hill, 2010)

- *Beyond Learning Objectives: Develop Powerful Objectives that Link to the Bottom Line* (ASTD Press 2008)

- *Return on Investment in Meetings & Events: Tools and Techniques to Measure the Success of All Types of Meetings and Events* (Butterworth-Heinemann, 2008)

- *ROI in Action Casebook* (Pfeiffer, 2008)

- *The Measurement and Evaluation Series – ROI Fundamentals1, Data Collection 2, Isolation of Results 3, Data Conversion 4, Costs and ROI 5, Communication and Implementation 6* (ROI Institute, Pfeiffer, 2008)

- *The ROI Field Book: Strategies for Implementing ROI in HR and Training* (Elsevier Butterworth-Heinemann, 2007)

- *The Value of Learning: How Organizations Capture Value and ROI and Translate Them Into Support, Improvement, and Funds* (Pfeiffer, 2007)

- *Show Me the Money: How to Determine ROI in People, Projects, and Programs* (Berrett-Koehler, 2007)

- *Proving the Value of Meetings & Events: How and Why to Measure ROI* (ROI Institute, MPI, 2007)

- *The Chief Learning Officer: Driving Value Within A Changing Organization Through Learning and Development* (Butterworth-Heinemann, 2007)

- *Return on Investment Basics: A Complete, How-to Guide to Help You: Understand and Apply Basic Principles and Practices, Select Appropriate Programs to measure, and Communicate Results and Sustain Momentum* (ASTD Press, 2005)

- *ROI at Work: Best Practice Case Studies from the Real World* (ASTD Press, 2005)

- *The Leadership Scorecard (Improving Human Performance Series)* (Elsevier Butterworth-Heinemann, 2004)

- *Return on Investment in Training and Performance Improvement Projects, 2nd Ed.* (Elsevier Butterworth-Heinemann, 2003)

- *How to Measure Training Results: A Practical Guide to Tracking the Six Key Indicators* (McGraw-Hill, 2002)

- *Measuring ROI in the Public Sector: In Action Case Study Series* (ASTD Press, 2002)

- *Measuring Return on Investment: Volume 3 (In Action)* (ASTD, 2001)

- *The Human Resources Scorecard: Measuring Return on Investment* (Elsevier Butterworth-Heinemann, 2001)

Chapter 1

Measuring ROI in Sexual Harrassment Prevention

Healthcare

by Diane Hill

Most organizations have sexual harassment prevention programs, but few are subjected to accountability up to and including a return-on-investment (ROI) analysis. In the setting in this case, a large healthcare chain conducted a sexual harassment prevention workshop involving first-level managers and supervisors. Meetings followed workshops with all employees, conducted by the same managers and supervisors. In all, seventeen workshops were presented, and the monetary impact was developed. Several unique issues are involved in this case, including the techniques to isolate the effects of training and convert data to monetary values. The analysis used a traditional ROI model and yielded significant and impressive results that surprised the evaluation team and senior managers.

BACKGROUND

Healthcare is a regional provider of a variety of healthcare services through a chain of hospitals, HMOs, and clinics. Healthcare has grown steadily in the last few years and has earned a reputation as an aggressive and financially sound company. Healthcare is publicly owned, with an aggressive management team poised for additional growth.

The healthcare industry in the USA continues to operate in a state of tremendous transformation and transition. The concern about healthcare costs, the threat of additional government regulation, and the implementation of new technology and healthcare delivery systems are radically transforming the healthcare field. HI is attempting to take advantage of these challenges and carve out a significant market share in its regional area of operation.

Events Leading to Program

In the USA, sexual harassment continues to grow as an important and significant employee relations issue. Sexual harassment claims throughout the USA and in the healthcare industry continue to grow, sparked in part by increased public awareness of the issue and the willingness of the victims to report harassment complaints. Healthcare has experienced an increasing number of sexual harassment complaints, with a significant number of them converting to charges and lawsuits. The company record was considered excessive by executives and represented a persistent and irritating problem. In addition, Healthcare was experiencing an unusually high level of turnover, which may have been linked to sexual harassment.

Senior management, concerned about the stigma of continued sexual harassment complaints and the increasing cost of defending the company against claims, instructed the HR vice president to take corrective and preventive action to significantly reduce complaints and ultimately rid the workplace of any signs of harassment. The HR vice president instructed the HRD staff to develop a workshop for employees or managers or both, but only if a lack of understanding and knowledge of the issue existed.

In response to the request, the HRD staff conducted interviews with the entire EEO and affirmative action staff in which the magnitude of the problem and the potential causes were explored. Most of the staff indicated that there seemed to be a significant lack of understanding of the company's policy on sexual harassment and what actually constituted inappropriate or illegal behavior. In addition, the complaints for the last year were examined for issues and patterns. Exit interviews of terminating employees for the last year were reviewed to see if there was a linkage to sexual harassment. Approximately 11 percent of terminating employees identified sexual harassment as a factor in their decision to leave HI. Because of the request to proceed with this program, the HRD staff members did not conduct a full-scale needs assessment. Instead, they augmented the input from the EEO/AA staff with the exit interviews conducted with ten randomly selected first-level supervisors to explore the level of understanding of the policy, inappropriate and illegal behavior, and the perceived causes of the increased complaint activity.

From an analysis of complaints, the typical person accused of sexual harassment was a supervisor and male. The typical victim of harassment was non-supervisory and female. The analysis also revealed that the type of sexual harassment typically experienced at HI was in the category, defined by the EEOC as "an individual making unwelcome sexual advances or other verbal or physical conduct of a sexual nature with the purpose of, or that creates the effect of, unreasonably interfering with an individual's work performance or creating an intimidating, hostile, or offensive working environment." This type of harassment should be minimized by developing a clear understanding of Healthcare's policy regarding harassment and by teaching managers to identify illegal and inappropriate activity. As part of Healthcare's policy, supervisors and managers were required to conduct a limited investigation of informal complaints and to discuss issues as they surfaced.

The Program: Design, Development, and Implementation

Armed with input from ten interviews and with detailed input from the EEO/AA staff, the major causes of the problem were identified. There was an apparent lack of understanding of (1) the company's sexual harassment policy and (2) what constituted inappropriate and illegal behavior. In addition, there was an apparent insensitivity to the issue. As a result, a one-day sexual harassment prevention workshop was designed for all first- and second-level supervisors and managers. The program had the following objectives. After attending this program, participants should be able to:

- Understand and administer the company's policy on sexual harassment.
- Identify inappropriate and illegal behavior related to sexual harassment.
- Investigate and discuss sexual harassment issues.
- Conduct a meeting with all direct reports to discuss policy and expected behavior.
- Ensure that the workplace is free from sexual harassment.
- Reduce the number of sexual harassment complaints.

Because of the implications of this issue, it was important for the information to be discussed with all employees so that there would not be any misunderstanding about the policy or inappropriate behavior. Each supervisor was asked to conduct a meeting with his or her direct employees to discuss this topic.

The program design was typical of Healthcare programs, using a combination of purchased and internally developed materials. The one-day program was implemented and conducted during a 45-day period, with 17 sessions involving 655 managers. HR managers and coordinators served as program facilitators.

Why ROI?

HR/HRD programs usually targeted for an ROI calculation are those perceived to be adding significant value to the company, closely linked to the organizational goals and strategic objectives. Then, the ROI calculation is pursued to confirm the added value, and based on the results of the ROI analysis, these programs may be enhanced, redesigned, or eliminated altogether if the ROI is negative. The sexual harassment prevention program is different. If the ROI analysis yields a negative value, the program would not be discontinued. It might be altered for future sessions but only if the behavior changes were not occurring at Level 3.

At Healthcare, this program was chosen for an ROI calculation for two reasons. First, the HR and HRD departments were interested in the accountability of all programs, including sexual harassment programs. Second, a positive ROI would clearly show management that these types of programs, which are preventive in nature, can significantly impact the bottom line when implemented throughout the organization and supported by management.

ROI PLANNING

Data Collection Plan

Figure 1-1 shows the completed data collection plan for the sexual harassment training program. A pre/post-test was administered to measure knowledge of Healthcare's sexual harassment policy and of inappropriate and illegal behavior. The 20-item questionnaire was evenly split on policy and behavior issues.

Figure 1-1. Evaluation Plan: Data Collection

Program: <u>Preventing Sexual Harassment</u>   Responsibility: _____   Date: _____

Level	Program Objective(s)	Evaluation Method	Timing	Responsibilities
I. Reaction, Satisfaction, and Planned Actions	• Obtain a positive reaction to program and materials • Obtain input for suggestions for improving program • Identify planned actions	• Reaction questionnaire	• End of session	• Facilitator
II. Learning	• Knowledge of policy on sexual harassment • Knowledge of inappropriate and illegal behavior • Skills to investigate and discuss sexual harassment	• Pre/post-test • Skill practices	• Beginning of session • End of session • During session	• Facilitator
III. Job Application	• Administer policy • Conduct meeting with employees • Ensure that workplace is free of sexual harassment	• Self-assessment questionnaire (1) • Complete and submit meeting record • Employee Survey (25% sample)	• 6 months after program • 1 month after program • 6 months after program	• Program evaluator • HRIS staff • Employee communication
IV. Business Results	• Reduce internal complaints • Reduce external complaints • Reduce employee turnover	• Performance monitoring • Self-assessment questionnaire (1)	• Monthly for 1 year before and after program • 6 months after program	• Program evaluator

To measure the success of program application, three data collection methods were used. First, a meeting record was required of each supervisor and manager to document the actual meeting with employees, recording the time, duration, topics, and participants. Although, this form did not address the quality of the meeting, it provided evidence that the meeting was conducted.

The second data collection method was a survey of the nonsupervisory employees, the typical target group for harassment activity. Although the entire team could have been surveyed, it was felt that it was more important to examine behavior change from the perspective of those who were more likely to be victims of harassment. The survey was planned for administration six months after the program was completed. It provided post-program data only; and therefore, each questionnaire had to be worded to capture change since the training was conducted. The 15-item survey examined specific behavior changes and environmental changes related to harassment activity, including actions that might be considered inappropriate or offensive. Figure 1-2 shows some typical questions.

Figure 1-2. Sample of Questions

	Strongly Disagree	Disagree	Neutral	Agree	Strongly Agree
I have noticed less offensive language at work.	☐	☐	☐	☐	☐
I am certain that the company will take swift action against those who are found guilty of sexual harassment.	☐	☐	☐	☐	☐

The third data collection method was a self-assessment questionnaire completed by supervisors and managers. This questionnaire captured actions, behavior change, and results linked to the program. Although there were a variety of other data collection possibilities, including focus groups, interviews, and third party observation, it was felt that, given the time and cost considerations, these three methods provided sufficient data to capture behavior change and show that the program had succeeded.

Business results measures included several items. Initially, it was planned that internal complaints, lodged formally with the HR division, would be monitored along with external charges filed with various agencies (primarily the EEOC). Because of the lag time between changes in behavior and a reduction in complaints, data would be collected for one year after the program and compared with data from one year before the program to determine specific improvements. Also, as alternative information, litigated complaints would be tracked along with the direct costs, including legal fees, settlements, and losses. In addition, because of the perceived link between a hostile work environment and turnover, annual employee turnover would be examined for the same time period.

ROI Analysis Plan

To develop the ROI calculation, several other issues needed to be addressed to plan for the Level 5 evaluation. The specific method(s) to isolate the effects of the program from other influences would have to be selected and implemented. The various ways in which data are converted to monetary values would need to be pinpointed. Each specific program cost element would have to be identified along with other issues that might influence the reduction in complaints and litigation expenses. Finally, intangible benefits expected from the program needed to be itemized and the communication targets established.

Figure 1-3 shows the completed document for the ROI analysis plan. Because of the relatively short timeframe required to implement the program and the desire from top management to implement it throughout the organization quickly, a control group arrangement was not feasible. However, because historical data are available for all complaint measures, a trend line analysis was initially planned. Complaint activity would be projected based on 12 months of data prior to the program. Actual performance would be compared with the projected value, and the difference would reflect the actual impact of the program on that measure. In addition to trend line analysis, participants' estimation was planned to compare with trend line data. In this type of situation, supervisors and managers (participants) are asked to indicate the extent to which the program influenced the changes in the number of complaints.

For turnover, trend line analysis could not be used because of the other initiatives implemented to reduce turnover. Therefore, a type of forecasting was used in which the percentage of turnover related to sexual harassment is developed for the 12-month period prior to the program. The same percentage is developed for the post program period.

In regard to converting the data to monetary values, the cost of

Figure 1-3. Evaluation Strategy: ROI Analysis

Program: Preventing Sexual Harassment   **Responsibility:** _____   **Date:** _____

Data Items	Methods of Isolating the Effects of the Program	Methods of Converting Data	Cost Categories	Intangible Benefits	Other Influences/ Issues	Communication Targets
Formal internal complaints of sexual harassment	• Trend line analysis • Participant estimation	• Historical costs with estimation from EEO/AA staff	• Needs assessment • Program development/ acquisition • Coordination/ facilitation time • Program materials • Food/ refreshments • Facilities • Participant salaries and benefits • Evaluation	• Job satisfaction • Absenteeism • Stress reduction • Image of HI • Recruiting	• Several initiatives to reduce turnover were implemented during this time period	• All employees (condensed info.) • Senior executives (summary of report with detailed backup)
External complaints of sexual harassment	• Trend line analysis • Participant estimation	• Historical costs with estimation from EEO/AA staff			• Must not duplicate benefits from both internal and external complaints	• All supervisors and manager (brief report)
Employee turnover	• Forecasting using percent of turnover related to sexual harassment	• External studies within industry				• All HR/RD staff (full report)

complaints would be derived both from historical data, when available, and from estimates for other factors, such as the actual time used for harassment complaints. The estimates would be developed with input from the EEO/AA staff. For turnover, industry data would be used because Healthcare had not calculated the actual cost of turnover for any employee groups. The specific cost items, intangible benefits, other influences, and communication targets were all identified and are presented in Figure 1-3.

RESULTS

Reaction and Learning Data

A typical end-of-program questionnaire was used to capture reaction data. Overall, the participants reacted positively to the program and perceived it to be timely and useful. A composite rating of 4.11 out of a possible 5 was achieved. The vast majority of the participants (93 percent) provided a list of action items planned as a result of the program.

For a Level 2 evaluation, the pre-program test scores averaged 51 and the post-program scores averaged 84, representing a dramatic increase of 65 percent. These results were significant and exceeded the expectations of the program developers. Two important points were underscored with the Level 2 measures. First, the low scores on pre-program testing provided evidence that the program was necessary. The participants did not understand the organization's policy, nor did they recognize what constituted inappropriate and illegal behavior. Second, the dramatic improvement in scores provided assurance that the content of the program was appropriate for both key issues, as the participants learned much about policy and behavior. As part of the Level 2 evaluation, participants were involved in skill practices for issues involving administering policy.

Application

One of the initial actions required of participants was to conduct a meeting with his/her employees to discuss sexual harassment issues, review Healthcare's policy on sexual harassment, and discuss what constitutes inappropriate and illegal behavior. Handouts and visual aids were provided to each supervisor and manager to assist with the meeting. A meeting record form had to be completed and submitted to the HR department as evidence that the meeting was conducted. The time of the meeting, the duration, the participants by name, and the specific topics covered were noted on the form. Within one month of the program, 82 percent of the participants had completed the meeting record.

Ultimately, 96 percent completed it. Some managers did not conduct meetings because they did not have direct reports.

Six months after the program was conducted, an anonymous survey was conducted with a 25 percent sample of non-supervisory employees. A total of 1,720 surveys were distributed, and 1,100 were returned for a response rate of 64 percent. The survey yielded an average score of 4.1 on a scale of 1 to 5. The rating represents the extent to which the behavior had changed in the six months since the program was conducted. Overall, the survey results indicated that significant behavior change had occurred and the work environment was largely free of harassment.

A follow-up questionnaire was administered directly to all participants six months after the program was conducted. A total of 571 questionnaires were returned, representing a response rate of 87 percent. The questionnaire probed the extent to which program materials were used and specific behavior changes had been realized. In addition, participants estimated the amount of improvement in sexual harassment complaints that was directly attributable to this program. Although the input from participants (managers and supervisors) may be biased, significant changes were reported. With regard to actions completed, 92 percent reported that some actions were completed, while 68 percent reported that all actions were completed.

Business Impact

Figure 1-4 shows the complaint and turnover data for one year prior to the program and one year after the program. In the six-month follow-up questionnaire, participants were provided the six-month averages from before and after the program and were asked to estimate the percent of improvement actually caused by this program. The average percentages from all participants are included in the right column. The results also show the turnover rate for the non-supervisory employees for the 12 months preceding the program and for the 12 months after the program.

Figure 1-4. Complaint and Turnover Data

Business Performance Measure	One Year Prior to Program	One Year After Program	Factor for Isolating the Effects of the Program
Internal Complaints	55	35	74%
External Charges	24	14	62%
Litigated Complaints	10	6	51%
Legal Fees and Expenses	$632,000	$481,000	
Settlement/Losses	$450,000	$125,000	
Total Cost of Sexual Harassment Prevention, Investigation, and Defense*	$1,655,000	$852,000	
Turnover (Non-Supervisory) Annualized	24.2%	19.9%	

*Includes legal fees, settlement/losses, portion of EEO/AA staff assigned to sexual harassment, management time for this activity, printed materials, and miscellaneous expenses.

Figure 1-5 shows a plot of the formal internal complaints of sexual harassment 12 months prior to the program and 12 months after the program. Prior to the program, there was an upward trend of complaints and senior managers felt this would continue if they took no action to improve the situation. Also, no other initiatives were undertaken to focus attention on sexual harassment. The magnitude of the program, involving 17 training sessions with 655 managers and meetings with all employees, focused significant attention on the issue. Therefore, it was felt that the trend line analysis might be an effective tool for isolating the effects of the training.

The turnover rate showed a dramatic improvement during this same timeframe. However, because of the serious problem with turnover, other initiatives were undertaken to help reduce the departure rate of employees. Recruiting processes were enhanced, entry-level salaries were increased, and more effective selection techniques were employed during the same time period. All these actions were initiated to develop a better match between the employees and the culture at Healthcare. Therefore, the trend line forecast for the turnover rate would be accurate because of the influence of these factors on the turnover rate.

Figure 1-5. Formal Internal Complaints of Sexual Harassment

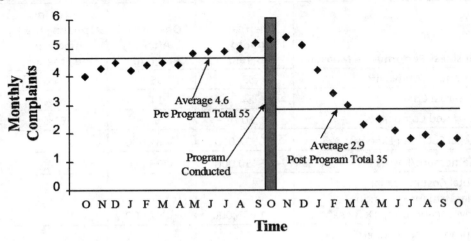

To estimate the percent of turnover reduction directly related to this program, a special version of the forecasting process was considered. During the needs assessment, the exit interview files were reviewed for evidence of sexual harassment as a factor in the decision to leave. In these cases, 11 percent of the actual turnovers had mentioned sexual harassment. Employees are often reluctant to indicate the presence of sexual harassment, although this issue may be the reason for their departure. Therefore, it was felt that this 11 percent figure was a conservative estimate of the number of terminations related to a hostile work environment. A 12-month review of exit interviews, on a post-program basis, revealed that only 3 percent of the interviewees mentioned sexual harassment or a hostile work environment as a reason for their departure. The percent of employees leaving because of sexual harassment dropped from 11 to 3 percent of terminations. The target group for the turnover reduction was non-supervisory employees, which represented an average of 6,844 on a post-program basis and 6,651 on a pre-program basis. For the 12-month period after the program, the employment levels at Healthcare averaged 7,540, including 655 for the target group for training and 41 senior managers who did not participate directly in the training program. The average non-supervisory salary for the post-program period was $27,850, and for the pre-program period, it was $26,541. Several industry studies on the cost of turnover were briefly discussed, which showed ranges from 110 percent to 150 percent of annual salaries. The evaluation team felt that 75 percent of annual salaries would be a conservative estimate.

Program Costs

Program costs are fully loaded and include the cost of the needs assessment ($9,000), design and development ($15,000), and evaluation ($31,000). The needs assessment cost was an estimate based on the direct time and expenses involved in the process. The development costs were low because of the availability of materials for purchase. The evaluation costs include an estimate of all internal and external costs associated with the follow-up evaluation, including the ROI. Participants' salaries and benefits were included, although it was not HI's policy to include salaries and benefits as a training expense for a one-day program for supervisors and managers.

Figure 1-6 shows the salary profile of participating supervisors and managers. The time necessary for program coordination was estimated along with the time for facilitator preparation and delivery. When considering the average salaries plus benefits for these individuals, a value of $9,600 was estimated. Travel and lodging for coordination and facilitation was a minor factor, estimated at $1,520. Program materials cost $12 per participant, and food and refreshments during the workshop cost $30 per participant. The estimated value of the conference rooms used for the program was $150 per day.

Figure 1-6. Salaries and Benefits of Participants

Management Level	Number Participating in Program	Salary Midpoint Value
7	41	$32,500
8	435	43,600
9	121	54,300
10	58	66,700

Employee benefits costs as a percent of payroll = 39%.
Managers work an average of 47 weeks per year.

Monetary Benefits from Program

Figure 1-7 shows the calculation for the monetary benefits from the sexual harassment program. For the reduction of complaints, the value could be based on reducing internal complaints, external charges, or litigated complaints, but not all three. The value for each measure is shown in the exhibit. Taking the total cost of sexual harassment prevention, investigation, and defense from Figure 1-4 and dividing it by each of these three measures develops the values. The total value of the reduction for each measure (indicated in Figure 1-4) was developed, leaving the decision of which measure to use. Because of the interest in tracking internal complaints, the evaluation team decided to use it as the unit of improvement in the analysis. Therefore, the value of one internal complaint was placed at $24,343. If one complaint could be avoided, Healthcare would save that amount. The lower value is used to be conservative. Another approach is to examine the total cost of sexual harassment, including prevention, investigation, and defense, and use a value equal to the reduction in cost. However, because there is a lag between measures of complaints and actual losses and legal expenses, the reduction may not reflect the actual cost savings.

Although the total improvement is 20 internal complaints, the improvement related directly to the program is 74 percent of that figure, or 14.8 complaints. The 74 percent is an estimate from the supervisors and managers taken directly from the questionnaire, as they were asked to indicate the extent to which the reduction in complaints was related directly to the program and the confidence of the estimate. The value of the improvement is $360,276. Figure 1-7 shows these calculations.

The value for the turnover reduction was developed in a similar manner. The unit of improvement is one turnover statistic. The 24.2 percent turnover rate represents 1,610 employees who, before the program, left voluntarily or were forced to leave because of performance. According to the exit interviews, 11 percent of those were related to sexual harassment. Therefore, 177 terminations were related to sexual harassment. On a post-program basis, the 19.9 percent turnover represents 1,362 employees. Post-program exit interviews revealed that 3 percent were related to a hostile work environment. Therefore, 41 employees left because of sexual harassment. The improvement related directly to the program is 136 terminations, a significant number when the cost of turnover is included. Although there was sufficient evidence to use the annual salary as a cost of turnover, to be conservative the team used 75 percent of the annual salaries, representing $20,887 as a cost of one turnover statistic. The 136 yielded a staggering $2,840,632 as the savings generated by the reduction in turnover that was caused by sexual harassment.

Figure 1-7. Monetary Benefits from Program

Complaint Reduction		
	Pre-Program	Post-Program
Average Cost of Internal Complaint	$30,090	$24,343
Average Cost of External Complaint	$68,958	$60,857
Average Cost of Litigated Complaint	$165,500	$142,000

Unit of Improvement = One Internal Complaint
Value of One Internal Complaint = $24,343 Total
Improvement: 55 – 35 = 20
Improvement Related to Program: 20 x 74% = 14.8
Value of Improvement = 14.8 x $24,343 = $360,276

Turnover Reduction
Unit of Improvement = One Turnover Statistic (Termination)
Turnover Pre-Program = 6,651 x 24.2% = 1,610
Turnover, Pre-Program, Related to Hostile Environment: 1,610 x 11% = 177
Turnover, Post-Program: 6,844 x 19.9% = 1,362
Turnover Post-Program Related to Hostile Environment: 1,362 x 3% = 41
Improvement Related to Program: 177 – 41 = 136
Cost of One Turnover: 75% of Annual Salary = $27,850 x .75 = $20,887
Value of Improvement: 136 x $20,887 = $2,840,632

Figure 1-5, presented earlier, shows the trend line projections for the internal complaint data. The trend, established prior to the program, was projected for the evaluation period. As the projection shows, the impact of the program is even more dramatic than illustrated in the above calculations because of the upward trend of the data. Instead of a value of 14.8 (20 x 74%), a value of 32 could be used in the analysis. However, the team thought that there must be another factor causing the results. The trend line is no more conservative than the participants' estimates. Because the impact is more conservative using the participants' estimates, this figure was used in the analysis. Therefore, the actual calculations represent an understatement of actual performance.

Program Cost Summary

Figure 1-8 shows the detail of the program cost categories. Most of the cost items were straightforward and taken from actual cost statements or from estimates given by those closely involved in the process. Participants' salaries and benefits were developed using midpoint values for the managers in each classification. The managers' midpoint salary data were converted to a daily rate by dividing by 235 (the number of days actually worked), and this was multiplied by the number of managers at that grade level attending the program. Participants' salaries and benefits greatly overshadow the other cost elements.

Figure 1-8. Program Costs

Needs Assessment (Estimated Cost of Time)	$ 9,000
Program Development/Acquisition	15,000
Program Coordination/Facilitation Time	9,600
Travel and Lodging for Facilitation and Coordinators	1,520
Program Materials (655 @ $12)	7,860
Food/Refreshments (655 @ $30)	19,650
Facilities (17 @ $150)	2,550
Participant Salaries and Benefits ($130,797 x 1.39)	181,807
Evaluation	<u>31,000</u>
	$277,987

ROI Calculation

Figure 1-9 shows the benefit-cost ratio and ROI calculations for these values. Benefits, based entirely on complaint reduction and turnover reduction, are used in the benefits-cost ratio to yield 11.5:1. Therefore, for each $1 spent on the program, $11.50 was returned. The ROI calculation, which uses net benefits, shows a return of 1,052 percent, an impressive and staggering amount.

Figure 1-9. ROI Calculation

$$BCR = \frac{Benefits}{Costs} = \frac{\$360,276 - \$2,840,632}{\$227,987} = \frac{\$3,200,908}{\$227,987} = 11.5.1$$

$$ROI = \frac{Net\ Benefits}{Costs} = \frac{\$360,276 - \$2,840,632}{\$227,987} = 1,052\%$$

Questions for Discussion

1. Was the needs assessment appropriate for this situation? Please explain.
2. Should this program be evaluated at Levels 4 and 5? If so, what specific measures should be used for Level 4 data?
3. What specific method(s) should be used to isolate the effects of the program?
4. What are the most appropriate ways to convert the Level 4 data to monetary values?
5. Critique the Level 2 and Level 3 results. Was the employee survey necessary? Explain.
6. Which Level 4 complaint measure is most appropriate? Why?
7. Project the trend line for internal complaints and estimate the impact of the program on the number of complaints. Use the average of the last three months for comparison.
8. Is the ROI lower or higher than you expected? Please comment.
9. Do you consider this estimate realistic?
10. How could this process be improved?
11. How would you present these data to management? To all employees?

Chapter 2

Forecasting ROI in
Machine Operator Training

Canadian Valve Company

by Timothy P. Renaud

Before funds can be allocated for major training programs, management sometimes needs information on the forecasted return-on-investment (ROI). In this case, which involves the training of machine operators, the proposed program included significant capital expenditures and the creation of a training facility. Prior to pursuing the project, an ROI was developed using a small-scale pilot effort. The ROI was developed using methods typically reserved for post-program evaluation. The results of the process can apply to almost any type of setting in which a major training expenditure is under consideration.

BACKGROUND

Canadian Valve Company (CVC) has enjoyed a long and profitable history as a family-owned business, serving the international industrial valve market. CVC machines, polishes, and assembles valves to be shipped to the worldwide market from several strategically located plants. The company has enjoyed tremendous growth in recent years, much of it is in foreign markets.

The company's growth and persistent employee turnover have always left a critical need for new machine operators. Unfortunately, the skilled labor market was unable to adequately supply trained machine operators, and CVC had to develop its own training program. Machine operators work various equipment including lathes, drill presses, and milling machines. New employees recruited for the machining area were usually untrained, inexperienced operators who received on-the-job training by their supervisors using the regular production equipment. This approach had created problems because new trainees were not productive during initial employment, and production machines were virtually out of service during training. Production management considered the traditional on-the-job training methods not very effective, and the training time to prepare new operators appeared excessive. In addition, the problems of high scrap and excessive machine down time were often by-products of ineffective initial training provided to new employees. Too often a new machine operator, in the midst of frustration, left the company and became a turnover statistic.

The production division, led by Bob Merkle, was concerned about the approach to training and wanted some changes. The human resources manager, Jim Gates, thought that a separate area for training was needed along with a comprehensive training program. In an initial conversation, Merkle concluded that a structured training program taught by an experienced instructor away from the pressures of production should reduce costs, increase productivity, and improve the training process. Jim Gates saw an excellent opportunity to make a significant impact with training, and he wanted to use the resources of the Ontario Training and Adjustment Board (OTAB).

Jim Gates and the Opportunity

A 10-year employee with Canadian Valve, Jim Gates had worked in production before taking on the job of human resource development manager. He understood the company's business and was anxious to help the company solve problems. He had earned an excellent reputation for producing effective programs and saw the comprehensive program to train new machine operators as an excellent opportunity to show the benefits of training and boost his own career opportunities at CVC. He was becoming convinced that if there was any area of training and development in which a cost-benefit analysis could be forecasted, it would be with the machine operator training and he was very interested in pursuing this project.

Bob Merkle and the Challenge

A task-oriented production manager with an engineering degree, Bob Merkle joined CVC as a management trainee 20 years earlier and progressed to vice president of production. Most of his job assignments were in the production area. He was very concerned about the bottom line and took great pride in his cost-control methods and strategies to improve efficiency.

In all his years in production, Merkle was never completely convinced that training was worth the time and effort. He had supported it primarily because the president had a strong commitment to training and development. Although his employees had always participated in programs, both on and off the job, he was skeptical of the results they produced. He felt training was best accomplished on the job by the immediate supervisor.

In recent months, however, his own production supervisors had complained about the approach to training new machine operators and the problems that new recruits created for the various departments. The production supervisors wanted to hire experienced operators and often could not understand why they were not available. The employment office had tried unsuccessfully to find experienced machine operators, using a variety of recruiting strategies. The production departments had to settle with unstructured on-the-job training with inexperienced operators.

Gates had initially approached Bob Merkle about the idea of a separate training area utilizing off-the-job training. On a pilot basis, they borrowed a production machine from one department and prepared it for training. A relief supervisor was assigned the task of training new recruits. Gates and the supervisors were pleased with the experimental effort and the reaction from the union was positive. Consequently, they took the proposal to Merkle to consider establishing a comprehensive training program.

The Project

After listening to the initial proposal from Gates, Merkle seemed to be interested in pursuing the process. Finally he said to Gates, "Jim, prepare a detailed analysis of the savings that this new approach to training would generate. Contact the Ontario Training and Adjustment Board to see if funding assistance is available to help with this type of program. Be sure to include a labor representative on your team. Calculate the benefits of this approach in terms of an expected return-on-investment. Based on the analysis we will go forward with it." Merkle knew the president would support the project if the payback were sufficient.

Gates was pleased with the assignment and added, "This is an excellent project. We know we can deliver a top-notch training program that we all can be proud of, and one that will bring significant improvements. With the help of OTAB, we will complete the task and have the full proposal in two weeks." Gates assembled a task force to work on the project.

A major issue in developing the program was the question of where the training should take place. The task force concluded that training should take place out of the production environment where the trainee could learn under the close supervision of a professional instructor who was experienced with all the machines. As a result, Gates explored the possibility of locating a separate area in a remote section of the main production area. In his view, this assignment had three major tasks:

1. Develop a complete training plan detailing the type of training program duration, training outlines, training structure, and training organization.
2. Design a preliminary layout of the area planned for training and determine how to procure machines for training.
3. Estimate the expected benefits and costs for the proposed program.

Although challenging, the tasks were feasible and could be completed in about two weeks. Gates was very excited about this opportunity.

John McIntosh

Gates contacted John McIntosh, a consultant for the Ontario Skills Development Office (OSDO), who was assigned to a local college near Canadian Valve's main location. McIntosh provides training and development consulting services to local clients from this location. Having worked in a variety of training and manufacturing companies before joining the ODSO program, he is always eager to help his clients with training plans. Because of the sheer number of clients, however, he was limited with the amount of time he could spend with them to develop a cost-benefit analysis (CBA).

PROGRAM RESULTS

Although small in scale, the experimental pilot project revealed surprising results. Trainees were able to reach target levels of productivity much faster than expected, and their error rates were much lower than anticipated. In addition, the trainees seemed to be more satisfied with their jobs. In a brief meeting with McIntosh, Gates and his staff identified several areas for potential cost savings. Most of these were developed after an analysis of the performance of the employees in the pilot training program when compared to the performance of the employees who had not participated in the training. Gates and McIntosh decided that they would drive the project evaluation with several important performance improvement measures. Other benefits could be identified as additional reasons for moving forward with the project. The expected improvements in productivity, scrap rates, safety, and maintenance expense. Other benefits were not so obvious. Previously, trainees had become frustrated when supervisors did not have time to work with them on a one-on-one basis to develop skills. The frustration led to a turnover statistic. The following performance measures were isolated:

- Reduction in time to reach a standard proficiency level (training time)
- Improvement in the scrap rate for new employees
- Improvement in the employee safety record (first-aid injuries)
- Reduction in equipment maintenance expense
- Reduction in turnover of new employees

These tangible benefits were to be used in the analysis. Gates and McIntosh could see other benefits. Low tolerance production could be performed in the training area as practice work for the trainees. Limited small-scale research and development projects could also be performed there. Although these benefits would be monitored, there would be no attempt to place a monetary value on them. They would be listed as intangible benefits.

Employees in training make mistakes and sometimes do not meet with friendly responses from their supervisors, so they were always frustrated during their initial stages of employment. This training program, if implemented properly, should improve employee satisfaction and engagement. Another benefit was improved absenteeism. When employees are frustrated and having difficulty on a job, they sometimes remove themselves from the frustration and take a day off. The anxiety or frustration may cause problems, leaving employees thinking they are actually sick when they are not. Finally, another advantage is a reduction in training responsibility for supervisors. With an influx of new employees in the shop, many supervisors have complained that they do not have time to train them. Consequently, they neglect other duties. This new approach to training should free supervisors to perform what they do best—plan and coordinate the work of machine operators and keep them motivated. Because of the difficulty of measuring these additional intangible benefits, Gates decided not to use them in calculations of cost savings. Instead, he would rely on the improvements in the five tangible measurement factors listed earlier.

Converting Data to Monetary Values

One of the most difficult tasks in completing an ROI evaluation is estimating the expected benefits from the program. This calculation is more difficult to do than a post-program evaluation, where the results can be compared to a before-and-after situation. With this assignment, Gates had to estimate the benefits, relying on two sources of information. First, the pilot program, which was conducted quickly, presented some measurable improvements, and this information was used in each of the five tangible benefit areas. As part of the analysis of the pilot results, Gates asked the relief supervisor, who was responsible for the training, and his department manager if there had been other factors that had contributed to the results. The answer was negative.

Next, Gates and McIntosh consulted production supervisors who were involved in early discussions of the concept of the program. In a focus group format, they discussed the benefits of the new approach to training and provided estimates of the extent of potential improvements When combined, these two approaches formed the basis for estimating the potential improvements that would be related directly to the new approach to training.

Training Time

As a standard practice, supervisors recorded the production shortfall with new employees until they reached the standard rate for a machine. These losses were essentially lost production as a result of trainees taking time allowed to learn to operate a machine at a standard rate. Company records indicated that more than $65,000 was charged to trainee losses in the machining areas during the previous year. The pilot program showed a 64 percent reduction, and the supervisors estimated that trainee losses could be reduced by 50 percent with a structured training program in a separate area. The lower value was used, resulting in a projected savings of $33,000.

(Note that all dollars are in Canadian funds.)

Turnover

The turnover rate in the machining area was eight employees per month. Because of the smaller numbers of employees involved in the brief pilot program, there was no turnover. Because of this short period, turnover reduction data were inconclusive. The supervisors felt that a significant percentage of the overall turnover was directly related to ineffective or insufficient training, or both, and they estimated that a new approach to training could reduce this turnover rate by at least 30 percent. This value was used in the analysis. The turnover of eight employees per month translates to 96 employees per year. The estimated cost to recruit and train a new employee was $4,000, representing a total annual cost of $384,000. A 30 percent savings would be $115,200.

This estimate was considered conservative. The $4,000 cost to recruit, employ, and train a new employee includes unproductive time in the first week of employment. On average, new employees who left the company during the training program worked longer than one week. Therefore, the cost to the company was probably greater than $4,000, because some lost production occurred after the first week

Safety

Most accidents in the machining area were not lost-time injuries, but were first-aid injuries treated in the company's medical facility. First-aid injuries were used in the analysis. The pilot program reflected a 25 percent reduction. The supervisors estimated that accidents could be reduced by 30 percent with an effective training program that emphasized safety practices. The number of first-aid injuries in the machining area was 86 the previous year, with the majority of them involving new employees. The total cost of these accidents (including outside medical costs, workers' compensation, and first aid) was $57,000. The 25 percent value resulted in an annual savings of $14,250. The 30 percent value is $17,000. The lower value was used.

Maintenance Expense

Effective training of new employees should result in reduced maintenance on production machines. A part of the current, unscheduled machine downtime is caused by new employees improperly operating equipment during their training period. The pilot program showed a dramatic reduction of 45 percent. However, the supervisors estimated that the unscheduled maintenance expense could be reduced by 10 percent each year with the implementation of the training program. The lower value was used. Last year, the unscheduled maintenance costs for the machining areas were $975,000. The annual savings would be $97,500. This estimate was considered very conservative.

Savings Summary

The total projected annual savings are as follows:

	Pilot Results ($)	Supervisor Estimate ($)
Training time	41,600	33,000 √
Machining scrap	76,500	45,000 √
Turnover	N/A	115,200 √
Accidents	14,250	17,100 √
Maintenance expense	438,750	97,500 √
Total	$571,100	$304,950

The values with the check (√) were used in the benefits calculation, resulting in a total of $304,950. To ensure that top management bought into the process, Gates and McIntosh reviewed the benefits analysis and the assumptions, including the logic, with all the supervisors and the managers in the machining area and with the accounting manager. Collectively, they felt the estimates were conservative and supported the projected savings.

Program Costs

The cost for the proposed program involved the acquisition of the necessary equipment, the salaries and expenses of two instructors, and the additional administrative overhead expenses connected with the training program. The most efficient approach was to use space in a remote, currently unused part of the plant. A nominal rent of $10,000 per year was to be charged to the project. The initial program development cost was estimated to be $15,000. This amount was spread over two years. The equipment cost less than expected. Most of the equipment planned for the new facility was surplus from the production line that was modified and reconditioned for use in training. The total equipment cost was estimated at $95,000. This figure included $7,000 initial installation expenses. The cost included the equipment for staffing two cubicles for the instructors and providing them with various training aids, including audiovisual. This investment was prorated over a five-year period. The salaries of two instructors plus benefits and expenses were estimated to be $80,000 per year. The overhead costs, which include normal maintenance, were estimated to be $15,000 each year.

The total annualized costs are as follows:

Equipment (prorated)	$19,000
Space (rental)	10,000
Program development (prorated)	7,500
Instructors	80,000
Maintenance	15,000
	$131,500

Although there may be other costs, Gates and McIntosh thought that these were the most significant ones and covered what would be necessary in the proposal. As with the benefits, cost figures were reviewed with production managers as well as the finance and accounting staffs to ensure complete support for the numbers. With minor adjustments, they were ready to move forward and calculate the return.

As part of the funding assistance available from OTAB, a reimbursement of one-third of the development costs and instructor costs was available. However, to ensure that the costs are fully loaded, this reimbursement was not considered in the analysis.

Calculating the Expected Return on Investment

A comparison of costs with the savings yields the following calculations. The benefit-cost ratio (BCR) is:

$$BCR = \frac{\$304,950}{\$131,500} = 2.32$$

The first-year net savings are as follows:

Annual gross savings	$304,950
Less program costs	131,950
Net savings	173,450

The expected ROI for the first year is:

$$\text{ROI} = \frac{\$173,450}{\$131,500} \times 100 = 132\%$$

The investment in the equipment and the program development was spread over several years (five years and two years, respectively). This approach assumes a useful life of five years for the building, equipment, and program development.

This estimate of BCR and ROI seemed to be a little high but was expected in this case. Gates attributed high value of this ratio to the following reasons:

- The equipment costs were low, using the salvage value plus costs for reconditioning. New equipment would cost much more but have a longer useful life.
- There was no additional investment in a new facility, which would have added to the start-up costs.

However, several items make a case for the BCR and the ROI to be undervalued:

- The cost savings were probably understated because the lower value was used when two values were available. Pilot program results were usually greater.
- The reimbursement of a portion of the costs from OTAB was not considered in the analysis. Thus, the actual project costs are overstated.
- The potential monetary benefits from the intangible measures could add to the cost savings.

Presentation of Results

With calculations developed, the project was ready for presentation. The training program details had been designed with input from production supervisors and the training staff. Both Gates and McIntosh contributed to the final arrangement for the proposal. The engineering department assisted in the layout and workflow. Gates set up a meeting with Merkle and the production managers and presented the proposal in the following order:

- Program design
- Equipment procurement and layout
- Program benefits
- Costs
- Expected return-on-investment and cost-benefit analysis
- Intangible benefits

Although there were a few questions, the methodology, assumptions, and calculation were fully supported. The managers were particularly impressed with the conservative approach used in the analysis and the involvement of the supervisors. The project was approved in the meeting.

As Gates left the meeting, he felt a great sense of accomplishment in demonstrating the potential benefits of training on a forecasted basis. He knew that now the challenge was up to his group to show that the project would realize the benefits forcasted. He would use a comprehensive measurement system to track the performance measures used to estimate cost savings and would report on results in six months.

Questions for Discussion

1. How credible is the process? Explain.
2. Without the information from the pilot program, would the ROI be credible? Explain.
3. How would you critique the methods used in converting data to monetary values?
4. An important part of any ROI calculation is to account for other factors that may influence output measures. How is this issue addressed in this case?

5. Are projected program costs reasonable? Explain.
6. How realistic are the values for BCR and ROI. Explain.
7. How helpful is the role of OTAB in this process?
8. How important are the intangible benefits? Could other intangible benefits be identified? Should they be converted to monetary benefits?

Chapter 3

Measuring ROI in Stress Management

Midwest Electric Inc.

by Jack J. Phillips

This case study begins by describing how the needs for a stress management program were determined and how an organization development solution was evaluated through ROI. The comprehensive approach includes the use of the StressMap® to measure learning, as well as the use of control groups to isolate the effects of the program. A description of how the ROI was measured is included. The specific forms, issues, and processes make this a practical case study for organizations interested in a comprehensive, balanced approach to evaluation.

BACKGROUND

Midwest Electric Inc. (MEI) is a growing electric utility serving several midwestern states. Since deregulation of the industry, MEI has been on a course of diversification and growth. Through a series of acquisitions, MEI has moved outside its traditional operating areas and into several related businesses.

MEI had been experiencing significant workplace changes as it transformed from a bureaucratic, sluggish organization into a lean, competitive force in the marketplace. These changes placed tremendous pressure on employees to develop multiple skills and perform additional work. Employees, working in teams, had to constantly strive to reduce costs, maintain excellent quality, boost productivity, and generate new and efficient ways to supply customers and improve service.

This case was prepared to serve as a basis for discussion rather than to illustrate either effective or ineffective administrative and management practices. The authors, dates, places, names and organizations may have been disguised at the request of the author or organization.

As with many industries in a deregulated environment, MEI detected symptoms of employee stress. The safety and health function in the company suggested that employee stress lowered productivity and reduced employee effectiveness. Stress was also considered a significant employee health risk. Research had shown that high levels of stress were commonplace in many work groups and that organizations were taking steps to help employees and work groups reduce stress in a variety of ways. The vice president of human resources at MEI asked the safety and health department, with the help of the training department, to develop a program for work groups to help them alleviate stressful situations and deal more productively and effectively with job-induced stress.

Needs Assessment

Because of its size and sophisticated human resource systems, MEI had an extensive database on employee-related measures. MEI prided itself as being one of the leaders in the industry in human resources issues. Needs assessments had been routinely conducted at MEI, and the HR vice president was willing to allow sufficient time for an adequate needs assessment before proceeding with the stress management program.

The overall purpose of the needs assessment was to identify the causes of a perceived problem. The needs assessment would:

- Confirm that a problem did exist and provide an assessment of the actual impact of this problem.
- Uncover potential causes of the problem within the work unit, company, and environment.
- Provide insight into potential remedies to correct the problem.

The sources of data for the needs assessment included company records, external research, team members, team leaders, and managers. The assessment began with a review of external research that identified the factors usually related to high stress and the consequences of high stress in work groups. The consequences uncovered specific measures that could be identified at MEI.

This external research led to a review of several key data items in company records, including attitude surveys, medical claims, employee assistance plan

(EAP) use, safety and health records, and exit interviews. The attitude survey data represented the results from the previous year and were reviewed for low scores on the specific questions that could yield stress-related symptoms. Medical claims were analyzed by codes to identify the extent of those related to stress-induced illnesses. EAP data were reviewed to determine the extent to which employees were using provisions and services of the plan perceived to be stress-related. Safety records were reviewed to determine if specific accidents were stress-related or if causes of accidents could be traced to high levels of stress. In each of the above areas, the data were compared with data from the previous year to determine whether stress-related measures were changing. Also, where available, data were compared with expected norms from the external research. Finally, exit interviews for the previous six months were analyzed to determine the extent to which the stress-related situations were factors in an employee's decision to voluntarily leave MEI.

During MEI's needs assessment process, a small sample of employees was interviewed (10 team members) to discuss their work-life situations and to uncover symptoms of stress at work. Also, a small group of managers (five) was interviewed with the same purpose. To provide more detail about this input, a 10 percent sample of employees received a questionnaire to explore the same issues. MEI had 22,550 employees with 18,220 non-supervisory team members.

Summary of Findings

The needs assessment process uncovered several significant findings:

- There was evidence of high levels of stress in work groups, caused by MEI's deregulation, restructuring, and job changes – in essence, the change in the nature of work-induced, high levels of stress in most work groups.
- Stress had led to a deterioration in several performance measures, including medical costs, short-term disability, withdrawals (absenteeism, turnover), and job satisfaction.
- Employees were often not fully aware of stress factors and the effect stress had on them and their work.
- Employees had inadequate skills for coping with stress and adjusting to, managing, and eliminating highly stressful situations.

- Managers had more insight into the causes of stress but did not have the skills or mechanisms to deal with most stressful situations.

PROGRAM PLANNING AND DESIGN

Several inherent factors about work groups and data at MEI influenced the program and its subsequent evaluation. MEI was organized around teams, and groups were not usually identical. However, many teams had similar performance measures. The HR database was rich with a variety of measures and with data about employees and work unit factors. Because of the team environment and the important role of the team leader/manager, the program to reduce stress needed to involve the management group in a proactive way. Any efforts to reduce stress needed to shift much of the responsibility to participants and therefore reduce the amount of time off the job. Job pressures in the deregulated environment provided fewer off-the-job opportunities for meeting and development activities.

Program Design

Although several approaches could have feasibly satisfied this need, four issues surfaced that influenced program design:

- A skills and knowledge deficiency existed, and some type of learning event was necessary.
- Several stress management programs were commercially available, which could prevent developing a new program from scratch.
- Managers needed to be involved in the process to the greatest extent possible.
- Because of the concerns about time away from the job, the actual classroom/formal meeting activities needed to be limited to one or two days.

With this in mind, the program outlined in Figure 3-1 was designed to meet this important need.

Why ROI?

HR programs usually targeted for a Level 5 ROI evaluation are those perceived to be adding significant value to the company, and closely linked to the organizational goals and strategic objectives. The evaluation is then pursued to confirm the added value. Based on the results of the analysis,

Figure 3-1. Stress Management for Intact Work Teams

Departments or work groups of 10 or more people who are committed to improving the satisfaction and effectiveness of their teams will benefit by this more comprehensive approach to stress. The process uses the StressMap® tool as the starting point.

Managers and representative employees will participate in focus groups to identify work satisfiers and distressors and then will collaborate on alleviating systemic sources of stress.

What Group Members Will Learn
- How to identify sources of stress and their personal response to them.
- That individuals have the ability to make a difference in their lives.
- How to take the first steps to enhance personal health and overall performance.
- How to access resources, internally and externally, to help teach personal goals.

What the Group/Manager Will Learn
- Group profile of sources of stress and response patterns.
- Additional information about sources of both work distress and work satisfaction obtained through focus groups and themes identified when possible.
- New stress reduction skills specific to the needs of the group.
- Development of recommendations for next steps to improve work satisfaction and productivity.

Highlights
- Through completion of a comprehensive self-assessment tool called StressMap®, individuals will be able to immediately score themselves on 21 stress scales dealing with work and home life, as well as learn about their preferred coping styles and the thinking and feeling patterns that impact their ability to manage stress. Anonymous copies of each member's StressMap® will be compiled to create a group score.
- A 3–4 hour StressMap® debriefing session designed to help individuals better interpret their scores will be followed by a four-hour module suited to the needs of the group (such as situation mastery, changing habits, creating climate for agreement). Total of one day.

Pre-course Requirements
- Management commitment to the process is essential. Employees will complete the StressMap® tool and submit a confidential copy.

Length and Format
- Lead time of three to four weeks minimum for preparation and communication.
- Consultant on-site 1-1/2 days.
- Initial follow-up one to two weeks later on-site or by phone to senior management (Subsequent follow-up on impact of the initiative to occur as negotiated with three to four hours of telephone follow-up included).

Cost
- Approximately $XXXX (plus taxes) US per group of 8 to 25; $XX US per set of materials. Travel and living expenses for consultant are additional.

these programs may be enhanced, redesigned, or eliminated if the results are insufficient. Stress management can be different. If the results are inadequate, the program may not be discontinued but may be altered for future sessions, particularly if behavior changes are not identified in the Level 3 evaluation.

At MEI, the stress management program was chosen for an ROI evaluation for two reasons. First, the HR department was interested in the accountability of all programs, including stress management. Second, positive results would clearly show management that these types of programs, which are preventive in nature, could significantly contribute to the bottom line when implemented and supported by management.

Because the program could have been expensive if applied to the entire company, it was decided to try it on a limited basis to determine its success and then to either adjust the program, discontinue the program, or expand the program to other areas in MEI. The evaluation methodology provided the best information to make that decision.

Data Collection Plan

Figure 3-2 shows the data collection plan for the stress management program. Broad objectives were established for Levels 1, 2, 3, and 4 data collection. The data collection plan was comprehensive but necessary to meet all of requirements at each of the four levels of data collection. The timing and responsibilities were detailed. For measuring learning, three tools were used. The StressMap® was one measure of learning in the awareness category. Completion of the StressMap® provided insight into stress factors and stress signals. In addition, built into the one-day program was an end-of-course self-assessment to measure learning. Finally, the facilitator had a brief checklist to indicate the extent of learning for the group.

At Level 3 data collection, the completion of the 21-day plan provided some evidence that the participants had changed behavior to reduce stress. A conference call was planned with the facilitator, team manager, and the team 21 days after the course. This provided a review of issues and addressed any concerns or barriers to further implementation. A follow-up session was planned with the team, co-facilitated by the manager and facilitator, approximately one to two weeks after the one-day program, to discuss changes in behavior and to address barriers. To determine the extent to which the participants were using internal or external resources to address stress related problems, records of those requests were scheduled

Figure 3-2. Data Collection Plan

Program: <u>Stress Management for Intact Groups</u>   Responsibility: _____   Date: _____

Level	Broad Program Objective(s)	Data Collection Method	Timing of Data Collection	Responsibilities for Data Collection
I — Reaction, Satisfaction, and Planned Actions	• Positive Reaction • Suggestions for Improvements • Planned Action	• Standard Questionnaire • 21-Day Action Plan	• End of 1-Day Course • End of Course	• Facilitator • Facilitator
II — Learning	• Personal Stress Awareness • Coping Strategies • Stress Reduction Skills	• StressMap® • Self-Assessment • Facilitator Assessment	• Prior to Course • End of Course • End of Course	• Facilitator • Facilitator • Facilitator
III — Application	• Change Behavior to Reduce Stress • Develop Group Action Plan and Communicate to Group • Access Internal/External Resources • Application of Skills/ Knowledge	• Completion of 21-Day Plan • Conference Call • Follow-Up Session • Review Records • Follow-Up Questionnaire	• 21 Days After Course • 21 Days After Course • 1-2 Weeks After 1-Day Course • 6 Months After Course • 6 Months After Course	• No Report • Facilitator • Facilitator/Manager • Program Coordinator • External Consultant
IV — Business Impact	• Reduce Medical Care Costs • Reduce Absenteeism • Reduce Turnover • Increase Productivity • Increase Job Satisfaction	• Group Records • Group Records • Group Records • Group Records • Follow-Up Questionnaire	• 6 Months After Course • 6 Months After Course • 6 Months After Course • 6 Months After Course • 6 Months After Course	• Program Coordinator • Program Coordinator • Program Coordinator • Program Coordinator • External Consultant

to be reviewed for approximately six months. Finally, a detailed follow-up questionnaire was planned for six months after the program to collect both Levels 3 and 4 data. This questionnaire was intended to capture sustained behavior changes, indicate barriers to improvement, and identify impact measures for both groups and individuals. Group records were expected to reveal changes in medical costs, absenteeism, turnover, and productivity six months after the program. In addition, increased job satisfaction was to be determined from the follow-up questionnaire, which would be administered six months after the program (the same questionnaire described earlier).

ROI Analysis Plan

Figure 3-3 shows the ROI analysis plan. For most data items, the method to isolate the effects of the program would be obtained in a control group arrangement in which the performance of the group involved in the program would be compared with the performance of a carefully matched companion control group. In addition, for most of the data items, trendline analysis was scheduled for use. Historical data were projected in a trend and compared with the actual data to determine the impact of the program.

The methods of converting data involved a variety of approaches, including tabulating direct costs, using standard values, using external data, and securing estimates from a variety of target audiences. The cost categories represented fully loaded costs for the program. Expected intangible benefits from the program were based on the experience of other organizations and other stress reduction programs. The communication target audience consisted of six key groups ranging from corporate and business unit managers to participants and their immediate supervisors.

Management Involvement

Management involvement was a key issue from the beginning and was integrated throughout the design of the program. The manager served as the team leader for the program, although a facilitator provided assistance and conducted a one-day workshop.

Figure 3-4 illustrates the tool used for identifying initial problems as the work group began using the stress management program. With this brief questionnaire, the manager identified specific problem areas and provided appropriate comments and details. This exercise allowed program planning to focus on the problems and provided guidance to the facilitator and the team.

Figure 3-3. Evaluation Strategy: ROI Analysis

Program: Stress Management for Intact Groups **Responsibility:** _____ **Date:** _____

Data Items (Usually Level 4)	Methods of Isolating the Effects of the Program	Methods of Converting Data	Cost Categories	Intangible Benefits	Other Influences/ Issues	Communication Targets
Medical Health Care Costs— Preventable Claims	• Control Group Arrangement	• Direct Costs	• Needs Assessment • ProgramDevelopment • Program Materials • Participant Salaries/ Benefits • Participant Travel (if applicable) • Facilitator • Meeting Facilities (Room, Food, Beverages) • Program Coordinator • Training and Education Overhead • Evaluation Costs	• Improved Communication Time Savings • Fewer Conflicts • Teamwork • Improvement in Problem Solving	• Match Groups Appropriately • Limit Communications with Control Group • Check for Team- Building Initiatives During Program • Monitor Restructuring Activities During Program • 6 Groups Will Be Monitored	• Program Participants • Intact Team/ Manager • Senior Manager/ Management in Business Units • Training and Education Staff • Safety and Health Staff • Senior Corporate Management • Prospective Team Leaders
Absenteeism	• Control Group Arrangement • Trend line Analysis	• Standard Value • Supervisor Estimation				
Employee Turnover	• Control Group • Trend line Analysis	• External Study— Cost of Turnover in High Tech Industry • Management Review				
Employee Job Satisfaction	• Control Group Arrangement • Management Estimation	• Management Estimation				
Employee/Group Productivity	• Control Group Arrangement • Trend line Analysis	• Standard Values • Management Estimation				

Figure 3-4. Manager Input: Potential Area for Improvement Stress Reduction for Intact Work Teams

Before you begin the stress reduction program for your team, it is important to capture specific concerns that you have about your work group. Some of these concerns may be stress related and therefore may be used to help structure specific goals and objectives for your team.

For each of the following potential areas of improvement, please check all that apply to your group. Add others if appropriate. Next to the item, provide specific comments to detail your concerns and indicate if you think this concern may be related to excessive stress.

- Employee Turnover. Comments: _____
  _____
  _____

- Employee Absenteeism. Comments: _____
  _____
  _____

- Employee Complaints. Comments: _____
  _____
  _____

- Morale/Job Satisfaction. Comments: _____
  _____
  _____

- Conflicts with the Team. Comments: _____
  _____
  _____

- Productivity. Comments: _____
  _____
  _____

- Quality. Comments: _____
  _____
  _____

- Customer Satisfaction. Comments: _____
  _____
  _____

- Customer Service. Comments: _____
  _____
  _____

- Work Backlog. Comments: _____
  _____
  _____

- Delays. Comments: _____
  _____
  _____

- Other Areas. List and Provide Comments: _____
  _____
  _____

Figure 3-5 illustrates manager responsibility and involvement for the process. This handout, provided directly to the managers, details 12 specific areas of responsibility and involvement for the managers. Collectively, initial planning, program design, and detailing of responsibilities pushed the manager into a higher-profile position in the program.

Figure 3-5. Manager Responsibility and Involvement Stress Management for Intact Work Teams

With the team approach, the team manager should:

1. Have a discussion with the facilitator to share reasons for interest in stress reduction and the desired outcome of the program. Gain a greater understanding of the StressMap® and the OD approach. Discuss recent changes in the work group and identify any known stressors. This meeting could be held with the senior manager or the senior management team.
2. Identify any additional work group members for the consultant to call to gather preliminary information.
3. Appoint a project coordinator, preferably an individual with good organizing and influencing skills, who is respected by the work group.
4. Send out a letter with a personal endorsement and signature, inviting the group to participate in the program.
5. Allocate eight hours of work time per employee for completion of StressMap® and attendance at a StressMap® debriefing and customized course.
6. Schedule a focus group after discussing desired group composition with the facilitator. Ideal size is 10 to 22 participants. The manager should not attend.
7. Attend the workshop and ensure that direct reports attend.
8. Participate in the follow-up meeting held after the last workshop, either in per- son or by conference call. Other participants to include are the HR representative for your area, the Safety and Health representative for your area, and your management team. The facilitator will provide feedback about the group issues and make recommendations of actions to take to reduce work stress or increase work satisfaction.
9. Commit to an action plan to reduce workplace distress and/or increase work- place satisfaction after thoughtfully considering feedback.
10. Communicate the action plan to your work group.
11. Schedule and participate in a 21-day follow-up call with the consultant and your work group.
12. Work with your team (managers, HR, safety and health, facilitator) to evaluate the success of the action plan and determine the next steps.

Control Group Arrangement

The appropriateness of control groups was reviewed in this setting. If a stress reduction program was needed, it would be appropriate and ethical to withhold the program for certain groups while the experiment was being conducted. It was concluded that this approach was appropriate because the impact of the planned program was in question. Although it was clear that stress-induced problems existed at MEI, there was no guarantee that this program would correct them. Six control groups were planned. The control group arrangement was diligently pursued because it represented the best approach to isolating the effects of the program, if the groups could be matched.

Several criteria were available for group selection. Figure 3-6 shows the data collection instrument used to identify groups for a control group arrangement. At the first cut, only those groups that had the same measures were considered (that is, at least 75 percent of the measures were common in the group). This action provided an opportunity to compare performance in the six months preceding the program.

Next, only groups in the same function code were used. At MEI, all groups were assigned a code depending on the type of work, such as finance and accounting or engineering. Therefore, each experimental group had to be in the same code as the matched control group. It was also required that all six groups span at least three different codes.

Two other variables were used in the matching process: group size and tenure. The number of employees in the groups had to be within a 20 percent spread, and the average tenure had to be within a two-year range. At MEI, as with many other utilities, there was a high-average tenure rate.

Although other variables could have been used to make the match, these five were considered the most influential in the outcome. In summary, the following criteria were used to select the two sets of groups:

- Same measures of performance
- Similar performance in the previous six months
- Same function code
- Similar size
- Similar tenure

Figure 3-6. Manager Input: Group Measures and Characteristics Stress Management for Intact Work Teams.

To measure the progress of your team, a brief profile of performance measures for employees and your work group is needed. This information will be helpful to determine the feasibility of using your group in a pilot study to measure the impact of the stress management program. Changes in performance measures will be monitored for six months after the program.

Listed below are several categories of measures for your work group. Check the appropriate category and please indicate the specific measure under the description. In addition, indicate if it is a group measure or an individual measure. If other measures are available in other categories, please include them under "Other."

Key Performance Measures _____ Dept _____

Performance Category	Measure	Description of Measure	Group Measure	Individual Measure
Productivity	1. 2.		☐ ☐	☐ ☐
Efficiency	3. 4.		☐ ☐	☐ ☐
Quality	5. 6.		☐ ☐	☐ ☐
Response Time	7. 8.		☐ ☐	☐ ☐
Cost Control/ Budgets	9. 10.		☐ ☐	☐ ☐
Customer Satisfaction	11. 12.		☐ ☐	☐ ☐
Absenteeism	13.		☐	☐
Turnover	14.		☐	☐
Morale/ Job Satisfaction	15. 16.		☐ ☐	☐ ☐
Other (please specify)	17. 18. 19. 20.		☐ ☐ ☐ ☐	☐ ☐ ☐ ☐

Group Characteristics

Average tenure for group:_____years

Average job grade for group: _____

Number in group: _____

Group function code: _____

Average age: _____

Average educational level: _____

The six pairs of groups represented a total level of employment of 138 team members and six managers for the experimental groups, and 132 team members and six managers for the control groups.

PROGRAM RESULTS

Questionnaire Response

A follow-up questionnaire, Figure 3-7, served as the primary data collection instrument for participants. A similar, slightly modified instrument was used with the managers. In all, 73 percent of the participants returned the questionnaire. This excellent response rate was caused, in part, by a variety of actions taken to ensure an appropriate response rate. Some of the most important actions were:

- The team manager distributed the questionnaire and encouraged participants to return it to the external consulting firm. The manager also provided a follow-up reminder.
- A full explanation of how the evaluation data would be used was provided to participants.
- The questionnaire was reviewed during the follow-up session.
- Two types of incentives were used.
- Participants were promised a copy of the questionnaire results.

Application Data

The application of the program was considered an outstanding success with 92 percent of the participants completing their 21-day action plan. A conference call at the end of the 21 days showed positive feedback and much enthusiasm for the progress made. The follow-up session also demonstrated success because most of the participants had indicated changes in behavior.

The most comprehensive application data came from the six-month questionnaire administered to participants and managers. The following skills and behaviors were reported as achieving significant success:

- Taking full responsibility for one's actions.
- Identifying or removing barriers to change behavior.
- Applying coping strategies to manage stressful situations.
- Responding effectively to conflict.
- Creating a positive climate.
- Acknowledging a complaint properly.

Figure 3-7. Stress Management for Intact Work Teams Impact Questionnaire

Check one: ☐ Team Member   ☐ Team Leader/Manager

1. Listed below are the objectives of the stress management program. After reflecting on this program, please indicate the degree of success in meeting the objectives.

OBJECTIVES	Failed	Limited Success	Generally Successful	Completely Successful
PERSONAL				
• Identify sources of stress in work, personal, and family worlds				
• Apply coping strategies to manage stressful situations				
• Understand to what degree stress is hampering your health and performance				
• Take steps to enhance personal health and overall performance				
• Access internal and external resources to help reach personal goals				
GROUP				
• Identify sources of stress for group				
• Identify sources of distress and satisfaction				
• Apply skills to manage and reduce stress in work group				
• Develop action plan to improve work group effectiveness				
• Improve effectiveness and efficiency measures for work group				

2. Did you develop and implement a 21-day action plan?

☐ Yes   ☐ No

If yes, please describe the success of the plan. If not, explain why. _____

Figure 3-7. *(continued)*

3. Please rate, on a scale of 1–5, the relevance of each of the program elements to your job, with (1) indicating no relevance, and (5) indicating very relevant.

_____ StressMap® Instrument   _____ Action Planning

_____ Group Discussion   _____ Program Content

4. Please indicate the degree of success in applying the following skills and behaviors as a result of your participation in the stress management program.

	1	2	3	4	5	No Opportunity To Use Skills
	No	Little	Some	Significant	Very Much	
a) Selecting containable behavior for change						
b) Identifying measures of behavior						
c) Taking full responsibility for your actions						
d) Selecting a buddy to help you change behavior						
e) Identifying and removing barriers to changing behavior						
f) Identifying and using enablers to help change behavior						
g) Staying on track with the 21-day action plan						
h) Applying coping strategies to manage stressful situations						
i) Using control effectively						
j) Knowing when to let go						
k) Responding effectively to conflict						

l) Creating a positive climate					
m) Acknowledging a complaint properly					
n) Reframing problems					
o) Using stress talk strategies					

5. List (3) behaviors or skills you have used most as a result of the stress management program.

_____

_____

_____

6. When did you first use one of the skills from the program?

_____ During the program

_____ Day(s) after the program (indicate number)

_____ Week(s) after the program (indicate number)

7. Indicate the types of relationships in which you have used the skills.

☐ Coworkers

☐ Manager or supervisor

☐ MEI employee in another function

☐ Spouse

☐ Child

☐ Friend

☐ Other (list):

PERSONAL CHANGES

8. What has changed about your on-the-job behavior as a result of this program? (positive attitude, fewer conflicts, better organized, fewer outbursts of anger, etc.)

_____

_____

_____

Figure 3-7. (continued)

9. Recognizing the changes in your own behavior and perceptions, please identify any specific personal accomplishments/improvements that you can link to this program. (time savings, project completion, fewer mistakes, etc.) _____

_____

10. What specific value in U.S. dollars can be attributed to the above accomplishments/improvements? Although this is a difficult question, try to think of specific ways in which the above improvements can be converted to monetary units. Use one year of data. Along with the monetary value, please indicate the basis of your calculation.

$ _____

Basis _____

_____

11. What level of confidence do you place in the above estimations? (0% = No Confidence, 100% = Certainty) _____ %

12. Other factors often influence improvements in performance. Please indicate the percent of the above improvement that is related directly to this program. _____ %

Please explain. _____

_____

GROUP CHANGES

13. What has changed about your work group as a result of your group's participation in this program? (interactions, cooperation, commitment, problem solving, creativity, etc.)

_____

_____

14. Please identify any specific group accomplishments/improvements that you can link to the program. (project completion, response times, innovative approaches)

_____

_____

_____

15. What specific value in U.S. dollars can be attributed to the above accomplishments/improvements? Although this is a difficult question, try to think of specific ways in which the above improvements can be converted to monetary units. Use one year of values. Along with the monetary value, please indicate the basis of your calculation.

$ _____

Basis _____

_____

_____

16. What level of confidence do you place in the above estimations? (0% = No Confidence, 100% = Certainty) _____ %

17. Other factors often influence improvements in performance. Please indicate the percent of the above improvement that is related directly to this program. _____ %

_____

_____

18. Do you think this program represented a good investment for MEI?

☐ Yes   ☐ No

Please explain. _____

_____

_____

Figure 3-7. (continued)

19. What barriers, if any, have you encountered that have prevented you from using skills or knowledge gained in this program? Check all that apply. Please explain, if possible.

- ☐ Not enough time
- ☐ Work environment does not support it
- ☐ Management does not support it
- ☐ Information is not useful (comments)
- ☐ Other _____

20. Which of the following best describes the actions of your manager during the stress management program?

- ☐ Very little discussion or reference to the program
- ☐ Casual mention of program with few specifics
- ☐ Discussed details of program in terms of content, issues, concerns, etc.
- ☐ Discussed how the program could be applied to work group
- ☐ Set goals for changes/improvements
- ☐ Provided ongoing feedback about the action plan
- ☐ Provided encouragement and support to help change behavior
- ☐ Other (comments): _____

21. For each of the areas below, indicate the extent to which you think this program has influenced these measures in your work group.

	No Influence	Some Influence	Moderate Influence	Significant Influence	Very Much Influence
a) Productivity					
b) Efficiency					
c) Quality					
d) Response Time					
e) Cost Control					
f) Customer Service					
g) Customer Satisfaction					

h) Employee Turnover			
i) Absenteeism			
j) Employee Satisfaction			
k) Healthcare Costs			
l) Safety and Health Costs			

Please cite specific examples or provide more details.

_____

_____

_____

22. What specific suggestions do you have for improving the stress management program? Please specify.

☐ Content

☐ Duration

☐ Presentation

☐ Other

23. Other comments:

_____

_____

Coworkers were the most frequently cited group in which relationships had improved through use of the skills, with 95 percent indicating application improvement with this group.

Barriers

Information collected throughout the process, including the two follow-up questionnaires, indicated few barriers to implementing the process. The two most frequently listed barriers were:

- There is not enough time.
- The work environment does not support the process.

Management Support

Manager support seemed quite effective. The most frequently listed behaviors of managers were:

- Managers set goals for change and improvement.
- Managers discussed how the program could apply to the work group.

Impact Data

The program had significant impact with regard to both perceptions and actual values. On Figure 3-7, the follow-up questionnaire, 90 percent of the participants perceived this program as a good investment for MEI. In addition, participants perceived that this program had a significantly influenced:

- Employee satisfaction
- Absenteeism
- Turnover
- Healthcare cost
- Safety and health cost

This assessment appears to support the actual improvement data, outlined below. For each measure below, only the team data were collected and presented. Because managers were not the target of the program, manager performance data were not included. An average of months five and six, instead of the sixth month, was used consistently for the post-program data analysis to eliminate the spike effect.

Healthcare Costs. Healthcare costs for employees were categorized by diagnostic code. It was a simple process to track the cost of stress-induced illnesses. Although few differences were shown in the first three months after the program began, by months five and six, an average difference of $120 per employee per month was identified. This was apparently caused by the lack of stress-related incidents and the subsequent medical costs resulting from the stress. It was believed that this amount would be an appropriate improvement to use. The trend line projection of healthcare costs was inconclusive because of the variability of the medical care costs prior to the program. A consistent trend could not be identified.

Absenteeism. There was significant difference of absenteeism in the two groups. The average absenteeism for the control group for months five and six was 4.65 percent. The absenteeism rate for the groups involved in the program was 3.2 percent. Employees worked an average of 220 days. The trend line analysis appeared to support the absenteeism reduction. Because no other issues were identified that could have influenced absenteeism during this time period, the trend-line analysis provided an accurate estimate of the impact.

Turnover. Although turnover at MEI was traditionally low, in the past two years it had increased because of significant changes in the workplace. A turnover reduction was identified using the differences in the control group and experimental group. The control group had an average annual turnover rate of 19.2 percent for months five and six. The experimental group had an average of 14.1 percent for the same two months. As with absenteeism, the trend line analysis supported the turnover reduction.

Productivity. Control group differences showed no significant improvement in productivity. Of all the measures collected, the productivity measure was the most difficult to match between the two groups, which may account for the inconclusive results. Also, the trend line differences showed some slight improvement, but not enough to develop an actual value for productivity changes.

Job Satisfaction. Because of the timing difference in collecting attitude survey data, complete job satisfaction data were not available. Participants did provide input about the extent to which they felt the program actually influenced job satisfaction. The results were positive, with a significant influence rating for that variable. Because of the subjective nature of job satisfaction and the difficulties with measurement, a value was not assigned to job satisfaction.

Monetary Values

The determination of monetary benefits for the program was developed using the methods outlined in the ROI analysis plan. The medical costs were converted directly. A $120 per month savings yielded a $198,720 annual benefit. A standard value had routinely been used at MEI to reflect the cost of an absence. This value was 1.25 times the average daily wage rate. For the experimental group, the average wage rate was $123 per day. This yielded an annual improvement value of $67,684. For employee turnover, several turnover cost studies were available, which revealed a value of 85 percent of annual base pay. As expected, senior managers felt this cost of turnover was slightly overstated and preferred to use a value of 70 percent, yielding an annual benefit of $157,553. No values were used for productivity or job satisfaction. The total annual benefit of the stress management program was $423,957. Table 3-1 reflects the total economic benefits of the program.

The medical costs were converted directly. A $120 per month savings yielded a $198,720 annual benefit. Other values are as follows:

Unit Value for an Absence
$123 x 1.25 = $153.75

Unit Value for Turnover
$31,980 x 70% = $22,386

Improvement for Absenteeism
138 employees x 220 workdays x 1.45% x $153.75 = $67,684

Improvement for Turnover
138 employees x 5.1% x $22,386 = $157,553

Table 3-1. Annual Monetary Benefits for 138 Participants

	Monthly Difference	Unit Value	Annual Improvement Value
Medical Costs	$120	-	$198,720
Absenteeism	1.45%	$153.75	$ 67,684
Turnover	5.1% (annualized)	$22,386	$157,553
TOTAL			**$423,957**

No values were used for productivity or job satisfaction.

Intangible Benefits

Several intangible benefits were identified in the study and confirmed by actual input from participants and questionnaires. The following benefits were pinpointed:

- Employee satisfaction
- Teamwork
- Improved relationships with family and friends
- Time savings
- Improved image in the company
- Fewer conflicts

No attempt was made to place monetary values on any of the intangibles.

Program Costs

Calculating the costs of the stress management program also followed the categories outlined in the evaluation plan. For needs assessment, all the costs were fully allocated to the six groups. Although the needs assessment was necessary, the total cost of needs assessment, $16,500, was included. All program development costs were estimated at $95 per participant, or $4,800. The program could have possibly been spread through other parts of the organization, and then the cost would ultimately have been prorated across all the sessions. However, the costs were low because the materials were readily available for most of the effort, and the total development cost was used.

The salaries for the team members averaged $31,980, while the six team managers had average salaries of $49,140. The benefits factor for MEI was 37 percent for both groups. Although the program took a little more than one day of staff time, one day of program was considered sufficient for the cost. The total salary cost was $24,108. The participants' travel cost ($38 per participant) was low because the programs were conducted in the area. The facilitator cost, program coordination cost, and training and development overhead costs were estimated to be $10,800. The meeting room facilities, food, and refreshments averaged $22 per participant, for a total of $3,968. Evaluation costs were $22,320. It was decided that all the evaluation costs would be allocated to these six groups. This determination was extremely conservative because the evaluation costs could be prorated if the program was implemented over other areas.

Table 3-2 details the stress management program costs. These costs were considered fully loaded with no proration, except for needs assessment. Additional time could have been used for participants' off-the-job activities. However, it was concluded one day should be sufficient (for the one-day program).

Table 3-2. Program Costs

Cost Category	Total Cost
Needs Assessment	$16,500
Program Development	$4,800
Program Materials (144 x $95)	$13,680
Participant Salaries/Benefits Based on 1 day 138 x $123 x 1.37 and 6 x 189 x 1.37	$24,108
Travel and Lodging 144 x 38	$5,472
Facilitation, Coordination, T&D Overhead	$10,800
Meeting Room, Food, and Refresments 144 x 22	$3,168
Evaluation Costs	$22,320
TOTAL	**$100,848**

Results: ROI

Based on the given monetary benefits and costs, the return on investment and the benefits/costs ratio are shown below.

$$BCR = \frac{\$423,957}{\$100,848} = 4.20$$

$$ROI = \frac{\$423,957 \; \$100,848}{\$100,848} = 320\%$$

Although this number is considered quite large, it is still conservative because of the following assumptions and adjustments:

- Only first-year values were used. The program should actually have second and third-year benefits.
- Control group differences were used in analysis, which is often the most effective way to isolate the effects of the program. These differences were also confirmed with the trend line analysis.
- The participants provided additional monetary benefits, detailed on the questionnaires. Although these benefits could have been added to the total numbers, they were not included because only 23 participants of the 144 supplied values for those questions.
- The costs are fully loaded.

When considering these adjustments, the value should represent a realistic value calculation for the actual return on investment.

Communication Strategies

Because of the importance of sharing the analysis results, a communication strategy was developed. Table 3-3 outlines this strategy. Three separate documents were developed to communicate with the different target groups in a variety of ways.

Table 3-3. Communication Strategies

Communication Document	Communication Target	Distribution
Complete report with appendices (75 pages)	• Training and Education Staff • Safety and Health Staff • Intact Team Manager	Distributed and discussed in a special meeting
Executive Summary (8 pages)	• Senior Management in the Business Units • Senior Corporate Management	Distributed and discussed in routine meeting
General interest overview and summary without the actual ROI calculation (10 pages)	• Program Participants	Mailed with letter
Brochure highlighting program, objectives, and specific results	• Prospective Team Leaders	Included with other program descriptions

Policy and Practice Implications

Because of the significance of the study and the information, two issues became policy. Whenever programs are considered that involve large groups of employees or a significant investment of funds, a detailed needs assessment should be conducted to ensure the proper program is developed. Also, an ROI study should be conducted for a small group of programs to measure the impact before complete implementation. In essence, this influenced the policy and practice on needs assessment, pilot program evaluation, and the number of impact studies developed.

Questions for Discussion

1. What is the purpose of the needs assessment?
2. What specific sources of data should be used?
3. Critique the data collection plan.
4. What other methods could be used to isolate the effects of the program?
5. Critique the methods to convert data to monetary values.
6. Are the costs fully loaded? Explain.
7. Is the ROI value realistic? Explain.
8. Critique the communication strategy.

Chapter 4

Measuring ROI in a Safety Incentive Program

National Steel

by Al Pulliam

This case addresses measuring the effectiveness of an incentive program designed to influence employee behavior and to reduce accidents in a manufacturing environment. Although top executives were concerned about the safety and well-being of employees, they also wanted to reduce the cost of accidents. The cost of accidents was reaching the point that it was an obstacle to the company becoming a low-cost provider of products in a competitive industry. This case demonstrates that an evaluation of an HR program can be implemented with minimal resources. It also demonstrates that although some programs may achieve a return on investment, it is sometimes best to communicate the ROI results to a limited audience.

BACKGROUND

National Steel is a large manufacturing operation with divisions in the southeastern, southwestern, and midwestern United States. Each division has multiple plants. The company also has several foreign plants in operation and two others in the construction phase. The plants produce steel products such as bar stock and plate steel. They also fabricate specialized fasteners used in the commercial building industry. The nature of National's manufacturing business requires that safety always receive a top priority with management and the work force. The concern for employee safety is a significant issue.

This case was prepared to serve as a basis for discussion rather than to illustrate either effective or ineffective administrative and management practices. The authors, dates, places, names and organizations may have been disguised at the request of the author or organization.

Additionally, domestic and foreign competition is a major factor in National's strategy to become a low-cost producer.

The company had always been concerned about the human element of a safe work environment, but economic issues were now a significant concern being driven by the cost of accidents. The company had long had a group, the Central Safety Committee, in place to continually review safety issues, direct accident investigations, and establish policy and best practices. The committee was made up of a senior line officer (who served as the sponsor), one line manager, two foremen, six members of the work force, the corporate manager of safety, and the VP of HR.

A Performance Problem

The committee had recently informed the senior management of National Steel that the midwestern division of the company was experiencing unacceptable accident frequency rates, accident severity rates, and total accident costs. For a two-year period, these costs had been in the $400,000 to $500,000 range, annually—much too high for the Central Safety Committee and management to accept.

The Needs Assessment

The safety manager was directed to meet with managers and employees in the three plants of the midwestern division to seek causes of the problem and to work with the division manager to implement the appropriate solutions. A team of HR specialists completed the assignment. The team also analyzed the cost and types of accidents. The team of specialists concluded:

- Employees' safety habits were inconsistent, and they were not focusing enough attention on safety.
- Employees knew and understood safety guidelines and practices; therefore, training was not an issue.
- A significant number of accidents and accident-related costs involved injuries of a questionable nature.
- Some type of monetary incentive would likely influence employee behavior.
- Peer pressure could possibly be used to help employees focus on safety practices and on the need to avoid the costs of seeing a physician when it was unnecessary.

The Solution

As a result of the assessment, the team recommended that the division implement a group-based safety incentive plan at the three plants. A monetary incentive had been successful in another division during previous years. The division manager reviewed the details of the plan and even helped craft some of the components. He accepted the recommendations and agreed to sponsor the implementation. The two objectives of the recommended plan were:

1. Reduce the annual accident frequency rate from a level of 60 to a much lower level of approximately 20, or less.
2. Reduce the annual disabling accident frequency rate from a level of 18 to 0.

PLANNING

The HR team expressed the need to track certain measures on a continual basis. Once the incentive plan's objectives were established, the team identified the specific data needed to analyze safety performance. The measures identified were:

*   Number of medical treatment cases
*   Number of lost-time accidents
*   Number of lost-time days
*   Accident costs
*   Hours worked
*   Incentive costs

The team decided that data should be collected monthly. Because the data collection system had been in place before the implementation of the safety incentive plan, no additional data collection procedures were needed. The HR specialists also used the same system when the Central Safety Committee asked them to review the problem and make recommendations. Management was also interested in a payback for the incentive program. Although accident reduction and severity were major concerns, there was also a need to achieve low-cost provider goals. Management requested to see figures that demonstrated that the benefits from the plan exceeded the costs of implementation. The team members concluded that they could use the same tracking system to determine the return on investment.

The Incentive Plan

The incentive plan consisted of a cash award of $75, after taxes, to each employee in the plant for every six months the plant worked without a medical treatment case. A medical treatment case was defined as an accident that could not be treated by plant first-aid and, therefore, needed the attention of a physician. Each plant had a workforce of about 120 employees. A team effort at each plant was important because the actions of one employee could impact the safety of another. Peer pressure was necessary to keep employees focused and to remind them to avoid unnecessary physician costs. Therefore, the award was paid at each of the three plants independently. An award was not paid unless the entire plant completed a six-month period without a medical treatment case. When a medical treatment case occurred, a new six-month period began.

Implementation of the Incentive Plan

The plant managers implemented the plan at the beginning of the year so results could easily be monitored and compared with performance in previous years. Each plant manager announced the plan to employees and distributed the guidelines for payout. The managers communicated the details of the plan and answered questions during the regular monthly safety meeting at each plant. Thorough communication ensured that each employee clearly understood how the plan functioned and what the group had to accomplish to receive an award.

Cost Monitoring

Two groups of costs were monitored: the total accident costs, and the incentive compensation costs. Total accident costs were monitored prior to the safety incentive plan as part of collecting routine safety performance data. The additional costs related directly to incentive compensation were also tabulated. Because the $75 cash was provided after taxes, the cost to the division was approximately $97.50 per employee for each six-month period completed without a medical treatment case. Additional administration costs were minimal because the data used in analysis were already collected prior to the new plan and because the time required to administer the plan and calculate the award was almost negligible. No additional staff was needed, and no overtime for existing staff could be directly attributed to the plan. However, a conservative estimate of $1,600 per year of plan administration costs was used in the tabulation of incentive costs.

RESULTS

In addition to the two-year data history, data were collected during a two-year period after the plan implementation to provide an adequate before-and-after comparison. Medical treatment injuries, lost-time injuries, accident frequency rates, and accident costs were all monitored to show the contribution of the safety incentive plan. The data shown in Table 4-1 document the accident costs for the four-year period. The data reveal significant reductions in accident costs for the two-year period after the implementation of the plan.

When comparing the average of Years 3 and 4 (after the incentive plan) with the Years 1 and 2 average (before the incentive plan), the accident frequency was reduced by 68 percent, while the disabling accident frequency was reduced by 74 percent. The annual cost of accidents (averaging the two years before and the two years after the incentive plan) dropped from $523,244 to $18,701, producing a significant savings of $504,543.

Table 4-1. Accident Costs and Frequency for All 3 Plants

	Year 1 Before Plan	Year 2 Before Plan	Year 3 After Plan	Year 4 After Plan
Accident Frequency	61.2	58.8	19.6	18.4
Disabling Frequency	17.4	18.9	5.7	3.8
Medical Treatment Injuries	121	111	19	17
Lost-Time Injuries	23	21	6.8	5.2
Actual Cost of Accidents	$468,360	$578,128	$18,058	$19,343

The objective of the plan to reduce the annual accident frequency rate to less than 20 was met with a post-plan average of 19. The objective of reducing the annual disabling accident frequency rate from 18 to 0 was not achieved. Although the average after two years dropped significantly from 18.15 annually to 4.75 annually, this was still short of the target. Both calculations are shown below.

BEFORE INCENTIVE PLAN
Accident Frequency 61.2 + 58.8 = 120
Annual Average (÷ 2) = 60 ANNUALLY

AFTER INCENTIVE PLAN
19.6 + 18.4 = 38
= 19 ANNUALLY

Annual Improvement 60 – 19 = 41
% Accident Improvement 41 ÷ 60 = 68%

BEFORE INCENTIVE PLAN
Disabling Frequency 17.4 + 18.9 = 36.3
Annual Average (÷ 2) = 18.15 ANNUALLY

AFTER INCENTIVE PLAN
5.7 + 3.8 = 9.5
= 4.75 ANNUALLY

Annual Improvement 18.15 – 4.75 = 13.4
% Disabling Improvement 13.4 ÷ 18.15 = 74%

These impressive results demonstrated a positive business impact. The incentive plan resulted in a safer work environment, fewer accidents, and fewer disabling accidents. Although these results improved the overall safety program considerably, the issue of cost savings remained unanswered. Did the incentive plan bring greater monetary benefits than the cost incurred to implement and administer it? Table 4-2 details the additional cost issues. There was also the issue of how much the incentive plan influenced improvement in the measures when compared with other actions that may have influenced improvements.

Table 4-2. The Contribution of the Safety Incentive Plan for All 3 Plants

	Year 1 Before Plan	Year 2 Before Plan	Year 3 After Plan	Year 4 After Plan
Needs Assessment Costs (spread)	—	—	$1,200	$1,200
Plan's Annual Administration and Evaluation Costs	—	—	$1,600	$1,600
Safety Incentive Plan Payout Costs	—	—	$58,013	$80,730
Actual Cost of Accidents	$468,360	$578,128	$18,058	$19,343
Total Cost of Accidents and Prevention	$468,360	$578,128	$78,871	$102,873

*Plan implemented beginning in Year 3

The needs assessment cost of $2,400 consisted of capturing the time and travel expenses for the HR team to conduct 20 interviews with plant operations and management staff and to develop recommendations. The cost to administer the incentive plan was $1,600 annually. The cost of the incentive plan payout must be captured and included in the total cost of accident prevention. Payout is determined by calculating the amount of incentive awards paid to employees in Years 3 and 4. Table 4-3 provides a breakdown of the payout.

Table 4-3. The Safety Incentive Plan Payout

Plant 1 Payout, Year 3:	115 employees x $97.50 x 1 PAYOUT = $11,213
Plant 2 Payout, Year 3:	122 employees x $97.50 x 2 PAYOUTS = $23,790
Plant 3 Payout, Year 3:	118 employees x $97.50 x 2 PAYOUTS = $23,010
	Total Payout, Year 3 $58,013
Plant 1 Payout, Year 4:	115 employees x $97.50 x 2 PAYOUTS = $22,425
Plant 2 Payout, Year 4:	122 employees x $97.50 x 2 PAYOUTS = $23,790
Plant 3 Payout, Year 4:	118 employees x $97.50 x 3 PAYOUTS = $34,515
	Total Payout, Year 4 $80,730
	Total Payout, Years 3 and 4 $138,743

Data Interpretation and Conclusion

The contribution of the safety incentive plan was determined by adding the accident and administrative costs for Years 3 and 4 to the safety incentive plan payout costs and then comparing this total with the accident costs of Years 1 and 2. As Table 4-2 shows, the total costs were reduced significantly. Accident costs from Years 1 and 2 (see Table 4-2) totaled $1,046,488, for an average of $523,244 annually. Accident and prevention costs for Years 3 and 4 totaled $181,744, for an average of $90,872 annually. This was an annual improvement of $432,372.

The Central Safety Committee discussed the issue of isolating the effects of the safety incentive plan. As a group, committee members decided the incentive plan should be credited for most of the improvement. They felt that it was the incentive plan that influenced a new safety awareness and caused peer pressure to work. After much debate, they accepted an estimate from the in-house expert, the safety manager, using data from an industry trade group that presented convincing evidence that management's attention to safe work habits had been shown to reduce the cost of accidents by 20 percent. Before these data were presented, the improvement was going to be attributed entirely to the incentive plan because no other factors that could have influenced safety performance during this period had been identified. Also, the safety record at the other two divisions showed no improvement during the same time period.

Calculating the Return on Investment

To determine the return on investment, the costs and monetary benefits of the incentive plan were needed. The annual cost of incentive payouts (two-year average of $69,372) added to annual administration costs ($1,200 plus $1,600) provided a total incentive plan cost of $72,172. The benefits were calculated starting with the annual monetary benefits of $432,372. Because the Central Safety Committee accepted the suggestion of the safety manager—that management attention played a role in influencing the improvement (20 percent)—then an adjustment had to be made. Therefore, 80 percent of $432,372 resulted in an estimated impact of $345,898. The ROI became:

$$\text{ROI} = \frac{\text{Net Benefits}}{\text{Costs}} = \frac{\$345,898 - \$72,172}{\$72,172} = 3.79 \times 100 = 379\%$$

Communication of Results

The results of the safety incentive plan were communicated to a variety of target audiences to show the contribution of the plan. First, the division president summarized the results in a monthly report to the chief executive officer of the corporation. The focal point was on the reduction in accident frequency and severity, the reduction in costs, the improvement in safety awareness, and the return on investment for the incentive plan.

The HR department presented the results in its monthly report to all middle and upper division management with the same focus that was presented to the CEO. Return on investment information was reserved for the eyes of management because it was felt that employees might misunderstand this as being the focus of plant safety.

The results were presented to all plant employees through the monthly Safety Newsletter. This communication focused on the reduction in medical treatment injuries, as well as improvements in lost-time accidents, disabling accidents, and accident frequency. It also recognized employees for their accomplishments, as did all the communication.

Finally, the results were communicated to all division employees through the division newsletter. This communication focused on the same issues presented to plant employees. Communications were positive and increased the awareness of the need for the continuation of the incentive plan.

Questions for Discussion

1. What questions would you have asked during the needs assessment?
2. Should reaction, learning, and application data be collected and presented?
3. What are your thoughts about the way the Central Safety Committee decided to isolate the effects of the safety incentive plan?
4. What other alternatives could have been explored to isolate the effects?
5. Would you have sought approval to collect additional data from employees during the follow-up evaluation regarding what caused the improvements? Why would you want additional data? How would you have justified the cost of this additional work?
6. Were there additional costs that should have been included? Should the cost of communication be included?
7. How would you have communicated the results differently?
8. How credible is this study?

Chapter 5

Measuring ROI in an eLearning Sales Program

United Petroleum International

by Patrick Whalen

This case addresses measuring the effectiveness and return on investment of an e-learning solution in an international sales environment. This can be especially challenging when management wants the program to pay for itself in the first year. This case demonstrates that, with a proper needs assessment and support from the organization, a well-designed e-learning program can influence business measures significantly. The program contribution to sales and other business measures determined by using one or more methods to isolate the effects of the program. The $500,000 projected price tag of the training was a key factor in management's decision to support an impact study to determine the return on investment.

BACKGROUND

United Petroleum International (UPI) is an international organization headquartered in the southwestern United States. UPI operates several refineries and engages in the sales and service of petroleum products worldwide. UPI has approximately 17,500 employees. International sales of petroleum products have plummeted during the last three quarters, and the outlook shows this trend will continue.

Increased competition abroad and a diminishing quality of sales relationships with customers/prospects were determined to be the major reasons for the lack of performance. The results from quarterly customer satisfaction surveys revealed specific areas of low performance. The executive vice president (EVP) of international sales asked for an assessment of the performance improvement needs of the UPI International Sales Organization (ISO). International Sales has 117 sales engineers and eight sales managers. They are supported by 50 administrative employees who maintain the customer/prospect database, develop sales quotes for the sales engineers, maintain pricing and inventory lists, and provide HR services.

A senior representative from corporate HR and two of UPI's internal consultants teamed with an external consultant to implement the Performance Assessment and Analysis Process to identify problems, opportunities, and solutions in ISO. The report provided to the EVP identified overall findings, performance gaps, and recommended solutions. At the end of the presentation, the EVP agreed to fund an intense improvement effort, including sales training and restructuring of the ISO incentive pay plan, which was no longer competitive in the changing markets. Funding was also made available for the consultant to design and implement a comprehensive evaluation system to determine business impact and return on investment. The EVP was particularly interested in knowing the ROI for the program. A business objective was established to improve three business measures. Measures to be tracked were identified as sales, monthly closing ratios, and customer satisfaction. Because measurement is an inherent component of the process, the methods and timing were designed and put into place. Baseline data were collected from UPI's performance records.

Designing and Implementing the Solutions

The HR department worked with the design team to design and implement a more appropriate and competitive incentive plan. This new incentive plan was designed after a review of several models and an analysis of application to UPI's markets. The plan was approved and scheduled for implementation in June.

The second solution, addressing the skill and knowledge needs within the sales force, was more difficult to design and implement. Client workload, time constraints, and the scattered locations of the sales engineers were impediments to implementing traditional instructor-led learning. Electronic learning methods were considered a viable alternative. A plus for this delivery method at ISO was that all sales engineers had online capabilities on their laptop computers. Another plus was that the flexibility of the electronic delivery method allowed it to be available at any time of the day. This flexibility is attractive to participants who are compensated principally through incentive pay and who desire to spend their available time making customer contacts. The decision was made that the 117 sales engineers and eight sales managers would receive an electronically delivered interactive program to improve their skills and effectively achieve the business objectives. During the performance analysis, it was discovered that the corporate HR group had identified sales competencies from a previous project and had already begun developing a curriculum. Much of this in-work product served as an important input for the new initiative and greatly assisted the on-time completion of the project.

The design called for a more focused e-learning effort, paying specific attention to the sales relationships engaged by sales engineers and allowing for significant practice of the required skills. The program had to present numerous job scenarios and challenges currently being encountered in the marketplace. The EVP of International Sales assigned the project to the manager of sales training, who subsequently established a project team to provide the coordination, design, and development of this project.

Several modules were developed with the support of corporate professionals, including technical writers, learning technology specialists, graphic designers, information technology specialists, and consultants. The team consisted of five full-time employees and four external consultants. Given the short timeframe for completion (management allowed a few months to design and implement the program), work began immediately to develop focused e-learning programs based on the desired business impact (the business objectives), job performance competencies, and field sales encounters. Several members of the design team were concerned that traditional face-to-face learning methods could not be replaced by an interactive e-learning program. The learning technology specialists addressed these concerns, and field testing established the design as a success in achieving learning goals. The e-learning program that was developed for the sales engineers became known affectionately as the TLC program, the Technology Learning Competency program. After design completion, it was implemented in June and July, shortly after the new incentive plan was implemented.

The Technology Learning Competency (TLC) Program

The TLC program was an interactive, self-paced learning process designed to assess current skill level and needs of the sales engineer. Each module was designed to build on a specific set of UPI sales skills (that is, client partnerships, product pricing and contracting, selling more profitable products, uncovering objections, handling objections, defining product features as unique benefits for the customer, expanding existing contracts, handling dissatisfied customers, building community awareness of UPI, and UPI product awareness/knowledge).

The TLC program was designed to allow the participant to respond to various sales relationship scenarios and to determine the appropriate decision to move closer to a sale. Each decision made by the engineer activated another scenario, which allowed additional choices or decisions to be made. The program continued on a predetermined path initiated by the engineer until a string of choices confirmed the responses as appropriate or until the decision was redirected. Video of a subject matter expert provided analysis of decision choices and helpful suggestions. This took maximum advantage of learning opportunities presented when a participant worked through the program. The engineer experienced real-world issues and situations, had the help of an expert, and was able to learn from mistakes in a nonthreatening manner.

A pretest at the beginning of each module was used to determine the skill areas that needed improvement and to load the appropriate learning modules. All the 117 sales engineers were pretested to establish a baseline. The program then linked participants to recommended modules that addressed their skill gaps. Each engineer was allowed a two-month window to complete the required e-learning, either during or after hours as his schedule allowed. So that they could be more effective coaches, the eight managers completed all modules plus a coaching module.

The TLC program contained a programmed mechanism that captured the results from the various decision paths chosen by the participant. After each learning module, an individual report was generated, which highlighted the learning achievement and the decisions made by the engineer. This report was provided to each participant and his manager for discussion in the follow-up coaching session. This provided additional learning opportunities and a means for recognition and feedback. Sales engineers were asked to schedule the follow-up planning and coaching meeting with their managers to occur within two weeks of their TLC program implementation.

MEASUREMENT METHODS AND DATA ANALYSIS

Measures to evaluate the effectiveness of a program can be designed and tracked through five distinct levels, as shown in Table 5-1. In addition to the five levels of data illustrated in this table, intangible benefits are reported for important outcomes that cannot be converted to monetary values.

The executive vice president of international sales requested that the return on investment (Level 5) be calculated for this program because of the high cost and potential business impact of the TLC program. Therefore, it became necessary to analyze data at the five levels, plus any intangible benefits.

Table 5-1. Five Levels of Data

Level and Type of Measure	Measurement Focus
Level 1. Reaction/Planned Action	Measures participant satisfaction and captures planned actions
Level 2. Learning	Measures changes in knowledge, skills, and attitudes
Level 3. Application	Measures changes in on-the-job behavior
Level 4. Business Impact	Measures changes in business impact variables
Level 5. Return on Investment	Compares program benefits with the costs

ROI Model and Process

Executive management expressed concern that the process used to evaluate TLC was a credible process. Figure 5-1 explains the process used to address this concern. This process has been applied in virtually every industry and in numerous international settings to evaluate training programs, HR programs, technology initiatives, and performance improvement programs. The process flows sequentially from step to step until the ROI is developed. The impact study captures both Level 3 (application) and Level 4 (business impact) data. The ROI (Level 5) is developed from Level 4 data. Improvements that cannot be converted to monetary values are reported as intangible benefits. A conservative approach is used to ensure that only benefits that can be legitimately attributed to the program are captured.

Figure 5-1. ROI Methodology ™ Process Model

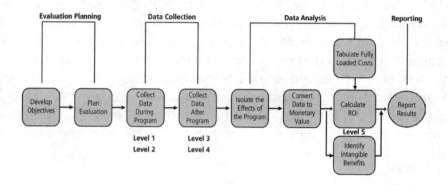

The Data Collection Plan and ROI Analysis Plan

After the business measures were determined and the framework for the TLC training program was known, the data collection plan focusing on Level 3 (application) and Level 4 (business impact) measures was developed. The Level 3 measures were behavior changes and frequency of application linked to the TLC program objectives. After exploring performance data availability in the ISO unit, the quality of the specific data, and the perceived linkage to the TLC program, the Level 4 measures were targeted and included in the data collection plan, which is presented in Figure 5-2.

The Level 4 data items were then transferred to the ROI analysis plan so that the planning process could be completed. The methods for isolation, data conversion, cost categories, and other items were determined and documented on the ROI analysis plan, which is presented in Figure 5-3.

RESULTS

Reaction and Learning Data

Level 1 data were captured through an online feedback questionnaire that assessed course content, usefulness of the TLC program, and job applicability. Participants rated questions on a Likert-type scale from 1 to 7. Participant average for the overall course content was 6.6, and overall usefulness of the system was 6.5. Applicability of the course to the job was rated 6.8. Level 1 data are consolidated in the first three columns of Table 5-2.

Figure 5-2. Data Collection Plan United Petroleum International

Program: Technology Learning Competency Program (TLC)   **Responsibility:** _____   **Date:** _____

Level	Objective(s)	Measures/Data	Data Collection Method	Data Sources	Timing	Responsibilities
Level I Reaction and Satisfaction	Employee positive reaction to: • Appropriateness of the technology delivery program • Usefulness of the TLC • TLC application to the job	• Participants perception and attitude	• Online questionnaire	• Participant	• End of each segment (3-5 modules) • End of program	• Program coordinator
Level II Learning	Module learning assignments-based on knowledge/skill gaps: • Client partnerships • Product pricing & contracting • Identification & handling objections	1. Skill gaps identified 2. Learning occurs as gaps closed through each module implemented	1. Online pre-test questionnaire on all modules 2. Online post-test by module	• Participant	1. Prior to training to establish baseline 1. Prior to each module as required 2. At end of each module	• Program coordinator
Level III Application & Implementation	1. Review post-course report and participate in follow-up planning meeting with manager 2. Application of skills to achieve business posts	1. Goals set and achieved 2. Skills applied in sales planning and sales situations	1. And 2. follow-up questionnaire	1. And 2. Participants 1. And 2. Managers	1. Coaching and planning session within two weeks of TLC 1. And 2. Follow-up questionnaire four months after TLC	• Program coordinator initiates follow-up • Manager and participant initiate planning and coaching
Level IV Business Impact	1. Improved closing ratio 2. Increased revenue 3. Customer satisfaction	1. Increase in monthly closes 2. Increase in profit margin 3. Customer satisfaction index	1. Performance monitoring 2. Performance monitoring 3. Customer survey (existing)	1. Sales record—marketing 2. Sales record—marketing 3. Customer quarterly survey	1. Monthly 2. Monthly 3. Monthly	• Program coordinator
Level V ROI	*Because of the strict requirement for development costs (see comments) an ROI at 20% will be acceptable.*					

Comments: *Because training will be completed for all current engineers within first year of roll-out, management desires to achieve a return on investment during the first year. Therefore, development costs will not be prorated over the life of the program as is customary.*

Figure 5-3. ROI Analysis Plan United Petroleum International

Program: Technology Learning Competency Program (TLC)   Responsibility: _____   Date: _____

Data Items (Usually Level 4)	Methods for Isolating the Effects of the TLC Program	Methods of Converting Data to Monetary Values	Cost Categories	Intangible Benefits	Communication Targets for Final Report	Other Influences/ Issues During Application	Comments
Closes per month	•Participant estimates •Manager estimates	N/A; captured in monthly revenue below	•Development costs •Materials and software •Equipment •Time of subject matter experts •Salaries and benefits during training (while on company time) •Analysis and evaluation costs	•Recruiting tool •Increase in employee satisfaction •Improved partnership and communication between manager and sales engineer	•Sales engineers •Leadership of sales organization •UPI executive management	•Customers may not be able to identify if or how "engineer skills" impact their satisfaction •Influence of other factors on the three measures •Quality of coaching/ expectations session •Short time frame inhibited ability to field test the TLC modules	•Must capture % of time that training occurs on company time
Monthly revenue	•Participant estimates •Customer estimates	Profit margin of revenue					
Customer satisfaction index		Executive management estimate					

Level 2 data were assessed using pre- and post-testing. The pre- and post-testing for TLC was designed based on job performance expectations. Subject matter experts (SMEs) determined the testing components, which were then validated by sales managers.

The SMEs, working with the program designers, validated program content based on competency requirements and skill gaps of the sales organization. They also provided input to design pre- and post-tests. Pretests were administered electronically at the beginning of each learning module to determine individual knowledge and skill gaps. The results showed that participants averaged a 50 percent knowledge level on the pretest and averaged a 91 percent knowledge level on the post-test. These Level 2 data are consolidated in the last two columns of Table 5-2.

Application Data

Level 3 (application) included three components to evaluate results: 1) follow-up planning and coaching sessions between sales engineers and sales managers, (2) self-assessment of skill application using a follow-up questionnaire, and (3) managers' assessment of skill application using a follow-up questionnaire.

Engineers completed follow-up planning and discussion meetings with their respective managers within two weeks of completing the TLC program. A plan including goals and expectations was created as a result of each discussion. To allow appropriate time for evaluation and application of skills, it was imperative for managers to have these planning and coaching sessions as close to the end of the training as possible. The sessions occurred during July and August and averaged two hours in length. Because of the dispersed locations of the engineers and managers, some of these meetings were conducted face-to-face and some by telephone or video conferencing.

Table 5-2. Reaction and Learning Results—1 to 7 Scale

Reaction: Overall Course	Reaction: Overall Usefulness of TLC	Reaction: Job Applicability	Learning: Pre-test Overall Score	Learning: Post-test Overall Score
6.6	6.5	6.8	50%	91%

The follow-up questionnaire was developed during the program design phase and field-tested with a random sample of sales engineers and sales managers. By advice of the sales managers, the questionnaire was administered four months after the completion of the TLC program. Four months was deemed an appropriate timeframe to determine the successful application of skills. A series of questions on the follow-up questionnaire also focused on engineers' progress with the improvement goals established in the follow-up discussions between managers and sales engineers. In addition, sales managers each received a follow-up questionnaire focusing on the performance of sales engineers and isolating the effects of the TLC program. These performance data were consolidated and documented in the final evaluation report. Figure 5-4 presents a summary of the follow-up questions from the sales engineers' questionnaire.

Business Impact Data

Business impact data (Level 4) were monitored by reviewing the quarterly customer satisfaction index scores, the monthly sales closing averages, and the profit margin of monthly sales revenue. These data were readily available within the organization, and all but customer satisfaction were used in the determination of business impact and the return on investment of the TLC program. Customer satisfaction data were reviewed for progress, but a standard monetary value did not exist for improvements; therefore, there was no conversion to a monetary value.

Figure 5-4. Summary of Follow-Up Questions

1. Did you have a follow-up coaching session with your sales manager?

2. Did you complete a follow-up plan and set related goals?

3. How do you rate the quality of the planning and discussion session with your manager?

4. Based on the discussion and planning session you had with your manager, what specific improvement goals have you completed? What improvement goals still need to be completed?

5. How have you and your job changed as a result of participating in TLC?

6. How are you specifically applying what you learned as a result of participating in TLC?

Figure 5-4. Summary of Follow-Up Questions (*continued*)

7. What is the impact of these changes for the customer and the ISO organization?

8. Rank (estimate the percentage) the effect each of the following had on any improvement in your sales performance. Allocate from 0 to 100% to the appropriate factors (the total percentage of all items selected must equal 100%):

   TLC Training Program Influence _____%

   Market Influences _____%

   Manager Coaching Incentives _____%

   Other (specify) _____%

9. What barriers (if any) were a deterrent as you applied what you learned?

10. List any skills you did not have an opportunity to apply during the evaluation time-frame?

11. Estimate the total hours you were involved in accessing/completing TLC training during regular company work hours:_____hours.

Isolating the Effects of the Program

To assess the Level 4 and 5 data accurately, it was imperative that the various influences on any improvement in sales performance be isolated. To isolate the effects of how each factor influenced sales (that is, TLC training, the new incentive plan, market changes, management influence, and so on), each had to be assessed by a credible source. The influence of each factor was determined by using participant and manager estimates regarding each factor. Because the managers work closely with the sales engineers (participants), it was felt that managers could respond credibly to these issues. The data were gathered from the participants in the Level 3 and 4 follow-up questionnaires and from the managers in a separate follow-up questionnaire. Table 5-3 reports the consolidated data.

Design and Implementation Costs

The development costs of $354,500 for this project included the salaries for development time of one project manager, five full-time employees, and four contract consultants. The costs associated with time spent in meetings and interviews with executive management, senior sales staff, and SMEs were also included. This included the time of the interviewer, as well as the people being interviewed. The cost of travel, meals, and lodging during development was also included.

Table 5-3. Consolidated Estimates—Isolating the Effects

Influencing Factor	Sales Engineers Average from 104 Respondents	Sales Managers Average from 8 Respondents	Combined Average
New Incentive Plan	35%	37%	36%
TLC Training Program	38%	36%	37%
Executive Management Influence	8%	6%	7%
Coaching by Sales Manager	16%	18%	17%
Other (market changes, new products, product improvements, etc.)	3%	3%	3%

The material costs of $68,500 included a comprehensive workbook for participants, distribution of tutorial CDs, and some additional networking software.

The equipment cost of $91,000 included upgrades (systems, processors, and video/graphics capability) to the specified hardware setup. This cost category also included the purchase of several new laptops for the sales engineers, digital editing equipment for editing the video and graphics in each module, and two platform servers capable of handling the multi-operational usage.

Eight SMEs were assigned to the project. These eight lead sales engineers were paid their sales average ($150 per day) for the 18 days each spent on the module designs, video shoots, and other project duties.

The analysis and evaluation costs of $71,000 included all costs associated with the initial performance analysis and evaluation process (for example, employee time during interviews and questionnaires). This cost category also included the use of an outside consulting firm to plan and implement the performance analysis and evaluation methodology for this project.

All the 117 sales engineers reported completing all modules during their personal time. Because they were compensated mostly by commissions, they usually spent their work hours conducting sales planning and call activities. Table 5-4 summarizes the fully loaded costs for the TLC program.

Because no sales were occurring for SMEs during the 18 project days, the commission payments may represent a cost to the sales bottom line. The management team felt the lead sales engineers would be able to maintain their average sales throughout the year even with their involvement in this project. Therefore, they did not feel that lost sales should be included as an opportunity cost. Salaries and benefits and opportunity costs for the "actual training time" are not included in the calculations because none of the 104 sales engineers reported implementing the TLC training during normal company work hours.

Table 5-4. Fully Loaded Costs

Development Costs	$354,500
Materials/Software	$68,500
Equipment	$91,000
SME Time (commission paid to expert sales engineers for lost opportunity) eight people @ $150/day X 18 days	$21,600
Analysis and Evaluation Costs	$71,000
TOTAL	**$606,600**

Analysis

The results of the initiative were encouraging. Prior year sales records revealed that sales engineers' overall performance showed an average of 14 closes per month at $980 profit margin per close. Six months after the implementation of TLC, the engineers averaged 16.65 closes per month at $1,350 profit margin per close. From the previous year, this was an average increase of 2.65 closes per month and an additional $370 profit margin on revenue.

The design team decided to use the ROI Methodology's conservative process when calculating the ROI based on revenue generated from new or increased closes. This decision helped to enhance the credibility of the data because participant and manager estimates were the only methods used to isolate the impact of training. The profit margin portion of the revenue increase attributable to the training (TLC) was used as a basis for the ROI calculation.

The Level 5 data were calculated by comparing the cost with the net benefits attributable to the TLC implementation. The benefit attributed to the use of TLC for improvement was considered to be 37 percent, based on the lowest value of the two estimates (manager estimates) from Table 5-3.

The benefits, except for improved customer satisfaction, were then converted to a monetary value, and a return on investment was calculated. Customer satisfaction improvements and other data that could not be converted to monetary values were captured as intangible benefits. Level 3 and 4 performance data and intangible benefits were documented in the final evaluation report.

ROI Results

Monitoring the performance records revealed the total increase in sales attributable to all influencing factors was $5,022,810. There was an average of 2.65 additional closes per month (16.65 − 14.0). However, based on the lowest estimates, only 37 percent of this increase in sales was influenced by the TLC program.

The conservative adjustment of benefits resulting from the TLC program was a factor of 0.98 additional closes per month (2.65 × 0.37). This resulted in an average of $1,323 profit margin per close ($1,350 × 0.98). Multiplied by 12 months and 117 engineers to annualize, this produced $1,857,492 in monetary benefits attributable to TLC.

- 2.65 closes × 0.37 = 0.98 factor for additional closes attributable to TLC program
- 0.98 × $1,350 per close = $1,323
- $1,323 × 12 months = $15,876 × 117 sales engineers = $1,857,492

The total cost of the TLC training program was $606,600. After rounding the benefits from the program, the ROI for the TLC program was calculated as follows:

$$\text{ROI (\%)} = \frac{\$1,857,000 - \$606,000}{\$606,600} \times 100 = 206\%$$

In addition to the impact of the TLC training, participants and managers reported the new incentive plan implemented in June had influenced an increase in sales by 36 percent, or $1,808,000.

Intangible Benefits

The results from quarterly customer satisfaction surveys were used to compare the previous year with the current year. Positive improvements and trends were identified. These data were not converted to a monetary value because management had no standard monetary value for an increase in customer satisfaction. It was also difficult to determine how much the skills and behavior from the training actually influenced the improvement in customer satisfaction. Data to isolate and substantiate this would need to come directly from customers because many factors could influence their satisfaction level. When using estimates, only customers are likely to know the extent of such influences. However, executive management felt the customer satisfaction scores were a good indicator of how the organization was responding to the market.

The customer satisfaction scores showed an average improvement of 23 percent since the previous year. Sales engineers and sales managers reported additional intangible benefits, such as increased job satisfaction, better understanding of expectations, reduced turnover, and increased recruiting effectiveness of future sales engineers.

Lessons Learned

This program demonstrated favorable results. The results can be attributed to several things: a comprehensive front-end analysis process that accurately identified the appropriate gaps and solutions, the support of corporate HR, the support of executive management, and the sales organization providing the resources and clarification of expected outcomes prior to designing this initiative.

A major learning issue involved meeting management's requirement for a short lead time to design and implement the program. Executive management expected the program to be implemented within a few months because the competitive environment and need for improved skills were having a negative impact on sales. This created little time to conduct a pilot program. Also, there was not enough time to create all the modules needed for the full range of competency and skill needs of the sales organization. The most salient competencies were targeted and given development priority.

The need to more accurately isolate the effects of this initiative was another learning issue. Several factors influenced the results. Although participant estimates can be effective (participants know what influences their performance), additional methods, like a control group arrangement or trend-line analysis, can often isolate the impact more convincingly.

REPORTING TO STAKEHOLDER GROUPS

The target population for this initiative included four groups: the sales engineers, the leaders of the sales organization, the SMEs, and the executive management team of UPI. All played a critical role in the success of the TLC program. All were provided a final report showing the results from the impact study.

The primary group was the 117 sales engineers who actually participated in the TLC program. They were the most instrumental of the groups in creating the success enjoyed by TLC. They dedicated the time to the system and took full advantage of the opportunity to improve performance based on what they learned from the technology-supported training. They also provided tremendous constructive feedback to enhance the system for future engineers.

The second group consisted of the leaders of the sales organization, who were responsible and accountable for the success of sales at UPI. Ten people—including one executive vice president, one director, and eight sales managers—were key factors in the success. They supported the up-front analysis and the validation of the job skills and gaps that were to be measured. By conducting planning and coaching sessions with sales engineers and by discussing expectations, the leaders of the sales organization were essential factors in the transfer and application of skills on the job.

The third group was the SMEs, who provided timely and accurate feedback about each module being developed, and the corporate professionals and consultants, who demonstrated diligence and expertise. On frequent occasions, they worked beyond normal work hours to keep the project on track.

The fourth group was the members of the executive management team of UPI, who funded the project and showed interest in the entire training process. The executive management team supported the project by allocating the necessary resources and setting the expectations for outcomes.

Questions for Discussion

1. Identify the influencing factors that contributed to the success of the TLC program.
2. How would you convince management that a control group arrangement would be beneficial to the study?
3. What recommendations would you make to management to convert customer satisfaction improvements to a monetary value?
4. How credible are the estimates in this evaluation?
5. How credible is this study?

Chapter

Measuring ROI in Performance Management Training

Cracker Box, Inc.

by Jack J. Phillips and Patti P. Phillips

This case study describes how one organization—a restaurant chain—built evaluation into the learning process and positioned it as an application tool. This approach is a powerful one that uses action plans, which participants develop during the training program to drive application, impact, and return-on-investment (ROI) data. This training program adds significant value to the restaurant store chain in this case study and shows how the evaluation process can be accomplished with minimum resources. The keys to success are planning for the evaluation, building it into the learning process, and using the data to help future participants.

BACKGROUND

Cracker Box, Inc. is a large, fast-growing restaurant chain located along major interstates and thoroughfares. In the past 10 years, Cracker Box has grown steadily and now has over 400 stores with plans for continued growth. Each store has a restaurant and a gift shop. A store manager is responsible for both profit units. The turnover of store managers is approximately 25 percent, lower than the industry average of 35 percent, but still excessive. Because of the store's growth and manager turnover, the organization needs to develop almost 150 new store managers per year.

Store managers operate autonomously and are held accountable for store performance. Working with the members of the store team, managers control expenses, monitor operating results, and take actions as needed to improve store performance. Each store has dozens of performance measures reported in a monthly operating report and other measures weekly.

Stores recruit managers both internally and externally and require that they have restaurant experience. Many of them have college degrees. The training program for new managers usually lasts nine months. When selected, the store manager trainee reports directly to a store manager who serves as a mentor to the trainee. Trainees are usually assigned to a specific store location for the duration of manager training. During the training period, the entire store team reports to the store manager trainee as the store manager coaches the trainee. As part of the formal training and development, each store manager trainee attends at least three, one-week programs at the company's corporate university, including the Performance Management Program.

Performance Management Program

The Performance Management Program teaches new store managers how to improve store performance. Program participants learn how to establish measurable goals for employees, provide performance feedback, measure progress toward goals, and take action to ensure that goals are met. The program focuses on using the store team to solve problems and improve performance. Problem analysis and counseling skills are also covered. The one-week program is residential and evening assignments are often part of the process. Skill practice sessions are integrated throughout the sessions during the week. The program is taught by both the corporate university staff and operation managers. Program sessions take place at the location of the corporate university near the company's headquarters.

Needs Assessment

The overall needs assessment for this process was in two parts. First, there was a macro-level needs assessment for the store manager position. The corporate university's performance consultants identified specific training needs for new managers, particularly with issues involving policy, practice, performance, and leadership. This needs assessment was the basis for developing the three programs for each new manager trainee. The second part of the assessment was built in to this program as the individual manager trainees provided input for a micro-level or store-level needs assessment.

The program facilitator asked participants to provide limited needs assessment data prior to the program. Each participant was asked to meet with the store manager (his or her mentor) and identify at least three operating measures that, if improved, should enhance store performance. Each measure was to focus on changes that both the store manager and manager trainee thought should be made. These business impact measures could be productivity, absenteeism, turnover, customer complaints, revenues, inventory control, accidents, or any other measure that could improve performance. It would be possible for each participant in a specific manager trainee group to have different measures.

To ensure that the job performance needs are met, each participant was asked to review the detailed objectives of the program and select only measures that can be improved by the efforts of the team and skills taught in the program. The important point in this step is to avoid selecting measures that cannot be enhanced through the use of the input of the team and the skills covered in the program.

As participants register for the program, they are reminded of the requirement to complete an action plan as part of the application process. This requirement is presented as an integral part of the program and not as an "add on" data collection tool. Action planning is necessary for participants to see the improvements generated from the entire group of program participants. Credit is not granted until the action planning process is completed.

MEASUREMENT REQUIREMENTS

Why Evaluate This Program?

The decision to conduct an ROI analysis for this program was reached through a very methodical and planned approach. A corporate university team decided at the outset that data would be collected from this program. Therefore, the team built the evaluation into the program. This decision was based on the following three reasons.

- This program is designed to add value at the store level and the outcome is expressed in store-level measures that are well-known and respected by the management team. The evaluation should show the actual value of improvement.

- This evaluation positions the data collection process from an evaluation perspective to an application process. The manager trainees did not necessarily perceive that the information they provided was for the purpose of evaluation, but saw it as more of an application tool to show the impact of their training.
- The application data enables the team to make improvements and adjustments. The data also helps the team gain respect for the program from the operating executives as well as the store managers.

The ROI Process

The Corporate University staff used a comprehensive evaluation process in many of its programs. This approach, called the ROI process, generates the following six types of data.

- Reaction and satisfaction
- Learning
- Application and implementation
- Business impact
- ROI
- Intangible measures

To determine the contribution the training program makes to the changes in business impact measures, a technique to isolate the effects of the program is included in the process.

Figure 6-1 shows the ROI process model. It begins with detailed objectives for learning, application, and impact. It shows development of data collection plans and ROI analysis plans before data collection actually begins. Four different levels of data are collected, namely, the first four types of data listed above. The process includes a method to isolate the effects of a program and techniques to convert data to monetary value. The ROI is calculated when comparing the monetary benefits to the cost of the program. The intangible measures, the sixth type of data, are those measures not converted to monetary value. This comprehensive model allows the organization to follow a consistent standardized approach each time it is applied to evaluate training and development programs.

Figure 6-1. ROI Methodology ™ Process Model

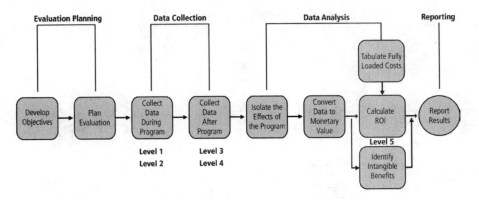

PLANNING FOR EVALUATION

Planning for the evaluation is critical to saving costs and improving the quality and quantity of data collection. It also provides an opportunity to clarify expectations and responsibilities and shows the client group—in this case, the senior operating team—exactly how this program is evaluated. Two documents are created: The data collection plan and the ROI analysis plan.

Data Collection Plan

Figure 6-2 shows the data collection plan for this program. Broad objectives are detailed along the five levels of evaluation, which represent the first five types of data collected for programs. As the figure illustrates, the typical reaction and satisfaction data is collected at the end of the program by the facilitator. Learning objectives focus on the five major areas of the program: establishing employee goals, providing feedback and motivating employees, measuring employee performance, solving problems, and counseling employees. Learning measures are obtained through observations from the facilitator as participants practice the various skills.

Through application and implementation, participants focused on two primary broad areas. The first was to apply the skills in appropriate situations, and the second was to complete all steps in their action plan. In terms of skill application, the evaluation team developed a follow-up questionnaire to measure the use of the skills along with certain other related issues. This was planned for three months after the program. Six months after the program, the action plan data is provided to show the actual improvement in the measures planned.

Figure 6-2. Data Collection Plan

Program: <u>Performance Management Program</u> **Responsibility:** _____ **Date:** _____

Level	Objective(s)	Measures/Data	Data Collection Method	Data Sources	Timing	Responsibilities
1	**Reaction/Satisfaction** • Obtain positive reaction to program and materials • Identify planned actions	• Average rating of 4 out of 5 on quality, quantity, and usefulness of material • 100% submit planned actions	• Standard feedback questionnaire	• Participant	• End of program	• Facilitator
2	**Learning** • Establishing employee goals • Providing feedback and motivating employees • Measuring employee performance • Solving problems • Counseling employees	• Be able to identify 100% of steps necessary to establish, monitor, and achieve goals • Demonstrate ability to provide employee feedback, solve problems	• Skill practice • Facilitator assessment • Participant assessment	• Participant	• During program	• Facilitator

3	**Application/ Implementation** • Apply skills in appropriate situations • Complete all steps of action plan	• Ratings on questions • The number of steps completed on action plan	• Follow-up questionnaire • Action plan	• Participant • Participant	• 3 months after program • 6 months after program	• Corporate University staff
4	**Business Impact** • Identify 3 measures that need improvement	• Varies	• Action plan	• Participant	• 6 months after program	• Corporate University staff
5	**ROI** • 25%					

Comments: _____

_____

_____

Business impact objectives vary with the individual because each store manager trainee identifies at least three measures needing improvement. These measures appear on the action plan and serve as the basic documents for the corporate university staff to tabulate the overall improvement.

The overall ROI objective is 25 percent, which was the standard established for internal programs of Cracker Box. This was slightly above the internal rate of return expected from other investments such as the construction of a new restaurant and gift shop.

ROI Analysis

The ROI analysis plan, which appears in Figure 6-3, shows how the organization processes and reports data. Business impact data is listed and forms the basis for the rest of the analysis. The method for isolating the effects of the program at Cracker Box was participant estimation. The method to convert data to monetary values relied on three techniques: standard values (when they were available), expert input, or participant's estimate. Cost categories represent a fully loaded profile of costs, anticipated intangibles are detailed, and the communication targets are outlined. The ROI analysis plan basically represents the approach to process business impact data to develop the ROI analysis and to capture the intangible data. Collectively, these two planning documents outline the approach for evaluating this program.

Action Planning: A Key to ROI Analysis

Figure 6-4 shows the sequence of activities from introduction of the action planning process through reinforcement during the program. The requirements for the action plan were communicated prior to the program along with the request for needs assessment information. On the first day of training, Monday, the program facilitator described the action planning process in a 15-minute discussion. At Cracker Box, participants received specially prepared notepads on which to capture specific action items throughout the program. They were instructed to make notes when they learned a technique or skill that could be useful in improving one of the measures on their list of three. In essence, this notepad became a rough draft of the action plan.

Figure 6-3. ROI Analysis Plan

Program: Performance Management Program Responsibility: _____ Date: _____

Data Items (Usually Level 4)	Methods for Isolating the Effects of the Program/Process	Methods of Converting Data to Monetary Values	Cost Categories	Intangible Benefits	Communication Targets for Final Report	Other Influences/Issues During Application	Comments
• 3 measures identified by manager trainee and manager	• Participant estimation	• Standard values • Expert input • Participant estimation	• Needs assessment • Program development • Program material • Travel & lodging • Facilitation & coordination • Participant salaries plus benefits • Training overhead • Evaluation	• Achievement • Confidence • Job satisfaction • Permanent store assignment	• Store managers • Participants • Corporate University staff • Regional operating executives • VP store operations • Senior VP Human Resources		

Figure 6-4. Sequence of Activities for Action Planning

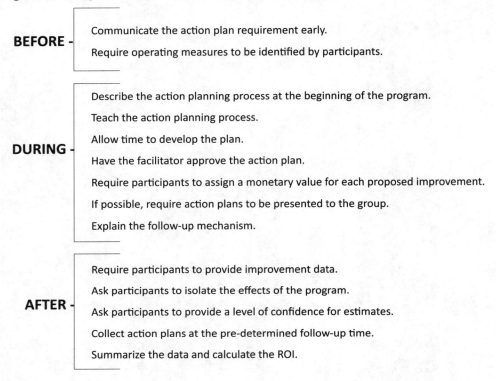

BEFORE -
Communicate the action plan requirement early.
Require operating measures to be identified by participants.

DURING -
Describe the action planning process at the beginning of the program.
Teach the action planning process.
Allow time to develop the plan.
Have the facilitator approve the action plan.
Require participants to assign a monetary value for each proposed improvement.
If possible, require action plans to be presented to the group.
Explain the follow-up mechanism.

AFTER -
Require participants to provide improvement data.
Ask participants to isolate the effects of the program.
Ask participants to provide a level of confidence for estimates.
Collect action plans at the pre-determined follow-up time.
Summarize the data and calculate the ROI.

The action planning process was discussed in greater detail in a one-hour session on Thursday afternoon. This discussion included three parts:

- Actual forms
- Guidelines for developing action plans and SMART (Specific, Measurable, Achievable, Realistic, and Time based) requirements
- Examples to illustrate what a complete action plan should look like

The program facilitator distributed the action planning forms in a booklet containing instructions, five blank action plans (only three are required, one for each measure), and the examples of completed action plans. On Thursday evening, participants completed the booklets in a facilitated session that lasted approximately one and a half hours. Participants worked in teams to complete all three action plans. Each plan took about 20 to 30 minutes to complete. Figure 6-5 shows a blank action plan. During the session, participants completed the top portion, the left column on which they list the action steps, and parts A, B, and C in the right column. They completed the remainder of the form—parts D, E, and F as well as intangible benefits, and comments—in a six-month follow-up. The senior facilitator monitored most of these sessions and sometimes an operations executive was also present. The involvement of the operations executive provided an additional benefit of keeping the participants focused on the task. Also, this involvement usually impressed operating executives with the focus of the program and the quality of the action planning documents.

The action plan could focus on any specific steps as long as they were consistent with the skills required in the program and were related to the business improvement measures. The most difficult part of developing the plan was to convert the measure to a monetary value. Three approaches were offered to the participants. First, standard values are available for most of the operating measures. Operations managers had previously assigned a cost (or value) to a particular measure for use in controlling costs and to develop an appreciation for the impact of different measures. Second, when a standard value was not available, the participants were encouraged to use expert input. This option involved contacting someone in the organization who might know the value of a particular item. The program facilitator encouraged participants to call the expert on Friday morning and include the value in the action plan. Third, when a standard value or expert input was not available, participants were asked to estimate the cost or value using all of the knowledge and resources available to them. Fortunately, the measure was a concern to the trainee and the store manager so there was some appreciation for the actual value. An estimation was possible in every case when standard values and expert input were not available. It was important to require that this value be developed during the program or at least soon after completion of the program.

The next day, Friday, the participants briefly reviewed the action planning process with the group. Each action plan took about five minutes. To save time, each group chose one action plan to present to the entire group to underscore the quality of the action planning process. The program facilitator explained the follow-up steps to the group. Staff of the corporate university and operation managers recommended that the manager trainee and the store manager discuss the document before they send a copy to the university staff. They should include contact information in case a staff member has a question about the data.

Figure 6-5. Action Plan Form

Name: _____ Instructor Signature: _____ Follow-Up Date: _____

Objective: _____ Evaluation Period: _____ to _____

Improvement Measure: _____ Current Performance: _____ Target Performance: _____

Action Steps	Analysis
1. _____	A. What is the unit of measure? _____
2. _____	B. What is the value (cost) of one unit? $ _____
3. _____	C. How did you arrive at this value?
4. _____	_____
5. _____	_____
6. _____	D. How much did the measure change during the evaluation period? (monthly value) _____
7. _____	E. What percent of this change was actually caused by this program? _____ %
Intangible Benefits:	F. What level of confidence do you place on the above information? (100% = Certainty and 0% - No Confidence) _____ %

Comments: _____

RESULTS

Staff of the corporate university and operation managers reported the results in all six categories developed by the ROI process, beginning with reaction and moving through ROI and the intangibles. Following are the results in each category together with additional explanation about how some of the data was processed.

Reaction and Learning

Reaction data is collected at the end of the program using a standard questionnaire, which focuses on issues such as relevance of the material, the amount of new information, and intention to use the skills. The content, delivery, and facilitation are also evaluated. Table 6-1 shows a summary of the reaction data on a rating scale in which one is unsatisfactory and five is exceptional.

Learning improvement is measured at the end of the program using a self-assessment and a facilitator assessment. Although these measures are subjective, they provide an indication of improvements in learning. Typical programs usually report significant improvements in both the self-assessments and facilitator-assessments. In this study, the facilitator-assessment data reported that all participants had acquired the skills at a satisfactory level.

Table 6-1. Reaction of Program Participants

Topic	Rating
Relevance of material	4.3
Amount of new information	3.8
Intention to use skills	4.6
Content of the program	3.7
Delivery of the program	4.1
Facilitation of the program	4.2

Application and Implementation

To determine the extent to which the skills are being used and to check progress of the action plan, participants received a questionnaire three months after the program. This two-page, user-friendly questionnaire covered the following areas:

- Skill usage
- Skill frequencies
- Linkage to store measures
- Barriers to implementation
- Enablers for implementation
- Progress with the action plan
- Quality of the support from the manager
- Additional intangible benefits
- Recommendations for program improvements

Participants reported progress in each of the areas and indicated that they had significant use of the skills even beyond the projects involving action plans. Also, the store manager trainees indicated linkage of this program with many store measures beyond the three measures selected for action planning. Typical barriers of implementation that they reported included lack of time, understaffing, changing culture, and lack of input from the staff. Typical enablers were the support from the store manager and early success with the application of the action plan. This follow-up questionnaire allowed manager trainees an opportunity to summarize the progress with the action plan. In essence, this served as a reminder to continue with the plan as well as a process check to see if there were issues that should be explored. The manager trainees also gave the store managers high marks in terms of support provided to the program. Participants suggested several improvements, all minor, and store managers implemented those that added value. Explanations of some intangible benefits that participants identified appear later.

Business Impact

Participants collected business impact data that were specific to the manager trainees. Although the action plan contains some Level 3 application data (the left side of the form), the primary value of the action plan was business impact data obtained from the planning documents.

In the six-month follow-up the participants were required to furnish the following five items:

1. The actual change in the measure on a monthly basis as included in part D of the action plan. This value is used to develop an annual (first year) improvement.

2. The only feasible way to isolate the effects of the program is to obtain an estimate directly from the participants. As they monitor the business measures and observe their improvement, the participants probably know the actual influences driving a particular measure, at least the portion of the improvement related to their actions, which are detailed on the action plan. Realizing that other factors could have influenced the improvement, the manager trainees were asked to estimate the percent of improvement resulting from the application of the skills required in the training program (the action steps on the action plan). Each manager trainee was asked to be conservative with the estimate and express it as a percentage (part E on the action plan).

3. Recognizing that the above value is an estimate, the manager trainees were asked to indicate the level of confidence in their allocation of the contribution to this program. This is included in part F on the action plan, using 100 percent for certainty and 0 percent for no confidence. This number reflects the degree of uncertainty in the value and actually frames an error range for the estimate.

4. The participants were asked to provide input on intangible measures observed or monitored during the six months that were directly linked to this program.

5. Participants were asked to provide additional comments including explanations.

Figure 6-6 shows the completed action plan. The example focuses directly on absenteeism from participant number three. This participant has a weekly absenteeism rate of 8 percent and a goal to reduce it to 5 percent. Specific action steps appear on the left side of the form. The actual value is $41 per absence, an amount that represents a standard value. The actual change on a monthly basis is 2.5 percent, slightly below the target. The participant estimated that 65 percent of the change is directly attributable to this program, and that he is 80 percent confident in this estimate. The confidence estimate frames a range of error for the 65 percent allocation, allowing for a possible 20 percent plus or minus adjustment in the estimate. The estimate is conservative, adjusted to the low side, bringing the contribution rate of this program to absenteeism reduction to 52 percent:

$$65\% \times 80\% = 52\%$$

This particular location, which is known because of the identity of the store manager trainee, has 40 employees. Also, employees work an average 220 days. The actual improvement value for this example can be calculated as follows:

40 employees x 220 days x 2.5% x $41 = $9,020

This is a total first-year improvement before the adjustments. Table 6-2 shows the annual improvement values on the first measure only for the 14 participants in this group. (Note that participant number five did not return the action plan so that person's data was omitted from the analysis.) A similar table is generated for the second and third measures. The values are adjusted by the contribution estimate and the confidence estimate. In the absenteeism example, the $9,020 is adjusted by 65 percent and 80 percent to yield $4,690. This same adjustment is made for each of the values, with a total first-year adjusted value for the first measure of $68,240. The same process is followed for the second and third measures for the group, yielding totals of $61,525 and $58,713, respectively. The total first-year monetary benefit for this group is the sum of these three values.

Table 6-2. Business Impact Data

Participant	Improvement ($ Values)	Measure	Contribution Estimate from Manager Trainees	Confidence Estimate	Adjusted $ Value
1	5,500	Labor Savings	60%	80%	2,640
2	15,000	Turnover	50%	80%	6,000
3	9,020	Absenteeism	65%	80%	4,690
4	2,100	Shortages	90%	90%	1,701
5	0	-------	-------	-------	-------
6	29,000	Turnover	40%	75%	8,700
7	2,241	Inventory	70%	95%	1,490
8	3,621	Procedures	100%	80%	2,897
9	21,000	Turnover	75%	80%	12,600
10	1,500	Food Spoilage	100%	100%	1,500
11	15,000	Labor Savings	80%	85%	10,200
12	6,310	Accidents	70%	100%	4,417
13	14,500	Absenteeism	80%	70%	8,120
14	3,650	Productivity	100%	90%	3,285

Total Annual Benefit for First Measure is $68,240
Total Annual Benefit for Second Measure is $61,525
Total Annual Benefit for Third Measure is $58,713

Program Cost

Table 6-3 details the program costs for a fully loaded cost profile. The cost of the needs assessment is prorated over the life of the program, which is estimated to be three years with 10 sessions per year. The program development cost is prorated over the life of the program as well. The program materials and lodging costs are direct costs. Facilitation and coordination costs were estimated. Time away from work represents lost opportunity and is calculated by multiplying five days times daily salary costs adjusted for 30 percent employee benefits factor (that is, the costs for employee benefits). Training and education overhead costs were estimated. Actual direct costs for the evaluation are included. These total costs of $47,242 represent a conservative approach to cost accumulation.

Table 6-3. Program Cost Summary

Items	Cost ($)
Needs Assessment (Prorated over 30 sessions)	$1,500
Program Development (Prorated over 30 sessions)	1,700
Program Materials – 14 @ $40	560
Travel & Lodging – 14 @ $900	12,600
Facilitation & Coordination	8,000
Facilities & Refreshments – 5 days @ $350	1,750
Participants Salaries Plus Benefits – 14 @ 521 x 1.3	9,482
Training & Education Overhead (Allocated)	900
ROI Evaluation	10,750
	$47,242

ROI Analysis

The total monetary benefits are calculated by adding the values of the three measures, totaling $188,478. This leaves a benefits-to-cost ratio (BCR) and ROI as follows:

$$\text{BCR} = \frac{\$188,478}{\$47,242} = 3.98\%$$

$$\text{ROI} = \frac{\$188,478-\$47,242}{\$47,242} = 298\%$$

This ROI value of almost 300 percent greatly exceeds the 25 percent target value. The target audience considered the ROI value credible, although it is

Figure 6-6. Action Plan

Name: _John Mathews_   Instructor Signature: _____   Follow-Up Date: _1 September_

Objective: _Reduce Weekly Absenteeism Rate for Team_   Evaluation Period: _March to April_

Improvement Measure: _Absenteeism Rate_   Current Performance: _8%_   Target Performance: _5%_

Action Steps		Analysis
1. Meet with team to discuss reasons for absenteeism – using problem solving skills	_10 March_	A. What is the unit of measure? _One Absence_
2. Review absenteeism records for each employee – look for trends and patterns	_20 March_	B. What is the value (cost) of one unit? _$ 41.00_
3. Counsel with "problem employees" to correct habits and explore opportunities for improvement.		C. How did you arrive at this value? _Standard Value_
4. Conduct a brief "performance discussion" with an employee returning to work after an unplanned absence.		D. How much did the measure change during the evaluation period? (monthly value) _2.5%_
5. Provide recognition to employees who have perfect attendance.		E. What other factors could have influenced these results?
6. Follow-up with each discussion and discuss improvement or lack of improvement and plan other action.	_31 March_	F. What percent of this change was actually caused by this program? _65%_
7. Monitor improvement and provide recognition when appropriate.		G. What level of confidence do you place on the above information? (100% = Certainty and 0% - No Confidence) _80%_

Intangible Benefits: _Less Stress, Greater Job Satisfaction_

Comments: _Great Program – it kept me on track with this problem_ extremely high. Its credibility rests on the following principles on which the study was based:

1. The data comes directly from the participants in concert with their store manager.
2. Most of the data could be audited to see if the changes were actually taking place.
3. To be conservative, the data includes only the first year of improvements. With the changes reported in the action plans, there should be some second and third-year value that has been omitted from the calculation.
4. The monetary improvement has been discounted for the effect of other influences. In essence, the participants take credit only for the part of the improvement related to the program.
5. This estimate of contribution to the program is adjusted for the error of the estimate, adding to the conservative approach.
6. The costs are fully loaded to include both direct and indirect costs.
7. The data is for only those individuals who completed and returned the action plans. No data appeared for participant five in Table 7-2 because that person did not return an action plan.
8. The business impact does not include value obtained from using the skills to address other problems or to influence other measures. Only the values from three measures taken from the action planning projects were used in the analysis.

The ROI process develops convincing data connected directly to store operations. From the viewpoint of the chief financial officer, the data can be audited and monitored. It should be reflected as actual improvement in the stores. Overall, the senior management team considered the results credible and fully supported them.

Intangible Benefits

As a final part of the complete profile of data, the intangible benefits were itemized. The participants provided input on intangible measures at two time frames. The follow-up questionnaire provided an opportunity for trainees to indicate intangible measures they perceived to represent a benefit directly linked to this program. Also, the action plan had an opportunity for trainees to add additional intangible benefits. Collectively, each of the following benefits were listed by at least two individuals:

- A sense of achievement
- Increased confidence
- Improved job satisfaction
- Promotion to store manager
- Stress reduction
- Improved teamwork

To some executives these intangible measures are just as important as the monetary payoff.

The Payoff: Balanced Data
This program drives six types of data items: satisfaction, learning, application, business impact, ROI, and intangible benefits. Collectively these six types of data provide a balanced, credible viewpoint of the success of the program.

Communication Strategy
Table 6-4 shows the communication strategy for communicating results from the study. All key stakeholders received the information. The communications were routine and convincing. The information to store managers and regional managers helped to build confidence in the program. The data provided to future participants was motivating and helped them to select measures for action plans.

Table 6-4. Communication Strategy

Timing	Communication Medium	Target Audience
Within one month of follow-up	Detailed impact study (125 pages)	Program participants; Corporate University staff • Responsible for this program in some way • Involved in evaluation
Within one month of follow-up	Executive summary • Including business impact data	Corporate and regional operation executives
Within one month of follow-up	Report of results (1 page) • In-store manager magazine	Store managers
After registration	Report of results (1 page) • In prework material	Future participants

Lessons Learned

It was critical to build evaluation into the program, positioning the action plan as an application tool instead of a data collection tool. This approach helped secure commitment and ownership for the process. It also shifted much of the responsibility for evaluation to the participants as they collected data, isolated the effects of the program, and converted the data to monetary values, the three most critical steps in the ROI process. The costs were easy to capture, and the report was easily generated and sent to the various target audiences.

This approach has the additional advantage of evaluating programs where a variety of measures are influenced. This situation is typical of leadership, team building, and communication programs. The application can vary considerably, and the actual business measure driven can vary with each participant. The improvements are integrated after they are converted to monetary value. Thus, the common value among measures is the monetary value representing the value of the improvement.

Questions for Discussion

1. Is this approach credible? Explain.
2. Is the ROI value realistic?
3. How should the results be presented to the senior team?
4. What can be done to ease the challenge of converting data to monetary values?
5. How can the action planning process be positioned as an application tool?
6. What types of programs would be appropriate for this approach?

Chapter 7

Measuring ROI in Interactive Selling Skills

Retail Merchandise Company

by Patti P. Phillips

The case study represents a classic application of the return on investment (ROI) process. An interactive selling skills program drives sales increases at a pilot group of retail stores. A control group arrangement isolates the effects of the program. The organization uses the results to make critical decisions.

BACKGROUND

Retail Merchandise Company (RMC) is a large national chain of 420 stores, located in most major US markets. RMC sells small household items, gifts of all types, electronics, and jewelry, as well as personal accessories. It does not sell clothes or major appliances. The executives at RMC have been concerned about the slow sales growth and were experimenting with several programs to boost sales. One of the concerns focused on the interaction with customers. Sales associates were not actively involved in the sales process, usually waiting for a customer to make a purchasing decision and then proceed with processing the sale. Several store managers had analyzed the situation to determine if more communication with the customer would boost sales. The analysis revealed that the use of very simple techniques to probe and guide the customer to a purchase should boost sales in each store.

The senior executives asked the training and development function to consider a very simple customer interactive skills program for a small group of sales associates. The training staff would prefer a program produced by an external supplier to avoid the cost of development, particularly if the program is not effective. The specific charge from the management team was to implement the program in three stores, monitor the results, and make recommendations.

The sales associates are typical of the retail stores employee profile. They are usually not college graduates, and most have a few months or even years, of retail store experience. Turnover was usually quite high, and formal training has not been a major part of previous sales development efforts

The Solution

The training and development staff conducted a brief initial needs assessment and identified five simple skills that would need to be covered in the program. From the staff's analysis, it appeared that the sales associates did not have these skills or were very uncomfortable with the use of these skills. The training and development staff selected the "Interactive Selling Skills" program that makes significant use of skill practices. The program, an existing product from an external training supplier includes two days of training, in which participants have an opportunity to practice each of the skills with a fellow classmate, followed by three weeks of on-the-job application. Then, in a final day of training there is discussion of problems, issues, barriers, and concerns about using the skills. Additional practice and fine-tuning of skills takes place in that final one-day session. At RMC, this program was tried in the electronics area of three stores with 16 people trained in each store. The staff of the training supplier facilitated the program for a predetermined facilitation fee.

The Measurement Challenge

The direction from senior management was very clear: these executives wanted to boost sales and at the same time determine if this program represented a financial payoff, realizing that many of the strategies could be implemented to boost sales. Business impact and ROI were the measurement mandates from the senior team.

In seeking a process to show ROI, the training and development staff turned to a process that Jack Phillips developed. The ROI process generates six types of measures:

- Reaction and Planned Action
- Learning
- Application and Implementation
- Business Impact
- ROI
- Intangible measures

It also includes a technique to isolate the effects of the program or solution.

This process involves extensive data collection and analysis. As Figure 7-1 shows, the process includes steps to develop the ROI, beginning with evaluation planning. Four types of data are collected, representing the four levels of evaluation. The analysis develops a fifth level of data as well as the intangible benefits. The process includes a method to isolate the effects of the program and a method to convert data to monetary value. The fully loaded costs are used to develop the actual ROI. This process was already in place at RMC, and training and development selected it as the method to measure the success of this program.

Figure 7-1. ROI Methodology ™ Process Model

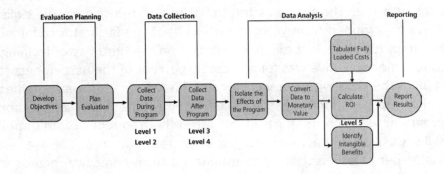

PLANNING FOR THE ROI

An important part of the success of the ROI evaluation is to properly plan for the impact study early in the training and development cycle. Appropriate up-front attention saves time later when data are actually collected and analyzed, thus improving the accuracy and reducing the cost of the evaluation. This approach also avoids any confusion surrounding what will be accomplished, by whom, and at what time. Two planning documents are key to the up-front planning, and the training staff completed them before the program was implemented.

Following are descriptions of each document.

Data Collection Plan

Figure 7-2 shows the completed data collection plan for this program. The document provides a space for major elements and issues regarding collecting data for the different levels of evaluation. Broad program objectives are appropriate for planning, as the figure shows.

The objective at Level 1 for this program was a positive reaction to the potential use of the skills on the job. The gauge for this level was a reaction questionnaire that participants completed at the end of the program and facilitators collected. The goal was to achieve four out of five on a composite rating. Also, the questionnaire asked participants to indicate how often and in which situations they would actually use the skills.

The measurement of learning focused on learning how to use five simple skills. The measure of success was a pass or fail on the skill practice that the facilitator observed and for which the observer collected data on the second day of the program.

For application and implementation evaluation, the objectives focused on two major areas. The first was the initial use of the five simple skills. Success was determined from verbal feedback that the facilitator obtained directly from participants in a follow-up session on the third day of training. The second major objective was for at least 50 percent of the participants to be using all of the skills with every customer. This information was obtained on the follow-up questionnaire, scheduled three months after completion of the program, at which the participants rated the frequency of utilization of the skills. Business impact focused just on increase in sales. The average weekly sales per sales associate was monitored from company records in a three-month follow-up. Finally, a 50 percent ROI target was set, which was much higher than the standard for many other ROI evaluations. Senior executives wanted a significant improvement over the cost of the program to make a decision to move forward with a wide scale implementation.

The data collection plan was an important part of the evaluation strategy. It provided clear direction on the type of data that would be collected, how it would be collected, when it would be collected, and who would collect it.

Figure 7-2. Data Collection Plan

Program: _____   Responsibility: _____   Date: _____

Level	Broad Program Objective(s)	Measures	Data Collection Method/Instruments	Data Sources	Timing	Responsibilities
1	**REACTION/SATISFACTION And PLANNED ACTIONS** • Positive reaction – 4 out of 5 • Action items	• Rating on a composite of five measures • Yes/No	• Questionnaire	• Participant	• End of program (3rd day)	• Facilitator
2	**LEARNING** • Learn to use five simple skills	• Pass/Fail on skill practice	• Observation of skill practice by facilitator	• Facilitator	• 2nd day of program	• Facilitator
3	**APPLICATION/ IMPLEMENTATION** • Initial use of five simple skills • At least 50% of participants use all skills with every customer	• Verbal Feedback • 5th item checked on a 1 to 5 scale	• Follow-up session • Follow-up questionnaire	• Participant • Participant	• 3 weeks after 2nd day • 3 months after program	• Facilitator • Store Training Coordinator
4	**BUSINESS IMPACT** • Increase in Sales	• Weekly average sales per sales associate	• Business performance monitoring	• Company records	• 3 months after program	• Store Training Coordinator
5	**ROI** • 50%					

Comments: _____

Isolating the Effects of the Program

One of the most important parts of this evaluation is isolating the effects of the training program. This is a critical issue in the planning stage. The key question is, "When sales data is collected three months after the program is implemented, how much of the increase in sales, if any, is directly related to the program?" While the improvement in sales may be linked to the training program, other non-training factors contribute to improvement. The cause-and-effect relationship between training and performance improvement can be very confusing and difficult to prove, but it can be accomplished with an acceptable degree of accuracy. In the planning process the challenge is to develop one or more specific strategies to isolate the effects of training and include it on the ROI analysis plan.

In this case study, the issue was relatively easy to address. Senior executives gave the training and development staff the freedom to select any stores for implementation of the pilot program. The performance of the three stores selected for the program was compared with the performance of three other stores that are identical in every way possible. This approach, control group analysis, represents the most accurate way to isolate the effects of a program. Fortunately, other strategies from the list of 10 approaches in the ROI process, such as trend line analysis and estimation, would also be feasible. Control group analysis, the best method, was selected given that the situation was appropriate.

The challenge in the control group arrangement is to appropriately select both sets of stores. The control group of three stores does not have the training, whereas the pilot group does. It was important for those stores to be as identical as possible, so the training and development staff developed several criteria that could influence sales. This list became quite extensive and included market data, store level data, management and leadership data, and individual differences. In a conference call with regional managers, this list was pared down to the four most likely influences. The executives selected those influences that would count for at least 80 percent of the differences in weekly store sales per associate. These criteria were as follows:

- *Store size,* with the larger stores commanding a higher performance level
- *Store location,* using a market variable of median household income in the area where customers live
- *Customer traffic levels,* which measures the flow of traffic through the store; this measure, originally developed for security purposes,

provides an excellent indication of customer flow through the store

- *Previous store performance,* a good predictor of future performance; the training and development staff collected six months of data for weekly sales per associate to identify the two groups.

These four measures were used to select three stores for the pilot program and match them with three other stores. As a fallback position, in case the control group arrangement did not work, participant estimates were planned. In this approach, the individuals would be provided with their performance data and would be asked to indicate the extent to which the training program influenced their contribution. This data, which is an estimate, would be adjusted for the error of the estimate and used in the analysis.

ROI Analysis Plan

Table 7-3 shows the completed ROI analysis plan, which captures information on several key items necessary to develop the actual ROI calculation. The first column lists the business impact measure. This is in connection with the previous planning document, the data collection plan. The ROI analysis builds from the business impact data by addressing several issues involved in processing the data. The first issue is the method of isolating the effects of the program on that particular business impact measure. The third column focuses on the methods to convert data to monetary value. In this case, sales data would have to be converted to value-added data by adjusting it to the actual profit margin at the store level.

The next column focuses on the key cost categories that would be included in the fully loaded cost profile. Next are the potential intangible benefits, followed by the communication targets. It is important for several groups to receive the information from the impact study. Finally, the last column lists any particular influences or issues that might have an effect on the implementation. The training staff identified three issues, with two being very critical to the evaluation. No communication was planned with the control group so there would not be potential for contamination from the pilot group. Also, because the seasonal fluctuation could affect the control group arrangement, this evaluation was positioned between Father's Day and the winter holiday season, thus taking away huge surges in volume. The data collection plan together with the ROI analysis plan provided detailed information on calculating the ROI and illustrating how the process will develop and be analyzed. When completed, these two planning documents provide the direction necessary for the ROI evaluation.

Figure 7-3. ROI Analysis Plan

Program: _____   Responsibility: _____   Date: _____

Data Items	Methods of Isolating the Effects of the Program	Methods of Converting Data	Cost Categories	Intangible Benefits	Communication Targets	Other Influences/Issues
• Weekly Sales Per Associate	• Control Group Analysis • Participant Estimate	• Direct Conversion Using Profit Contribution	• Facilitation Fees • Program Materials • Meals/Refreshments • Facilities • Participant Salaries/Benefits • Cost of Coordination/Evaluation	• Customer Satisfaction • Employee Satisfaction	• Program Participants • Electronics Dept. Managers – Target Stores • Store Managers – Target Stores • Senior Store Executives District, Region, Headquarters • Training Staff: Instructors, Coordinators, Designers, and Managers	• Must Have Job Coverage During Training • No Communication with Control Group • Seasonal Fluctuations Should be Avoided

RESULTS

Reaction and Learning Data

The first two levels of evaluation, reaction and learning, were simple and straightforward. The training staff collected five measures of reaction to determine if the objectives had been met. The overall objective was to obtain at least four out of five on a composite of these five measures. As Table 7-1 illustrates, the overall objective was met. Of the specific measures, the relevance of the material and the usefulness of the program were considered to be the two most important measures. In addition, 90 percent of the participants had action items indicating when and how often they would use these skills. Collectively, this Level 1 data gave assurance that sales associates had a very favorable reaction to the program.

The measurement of learning was accomplished with simple skill practice sessions observed by the facilitator. Each associate practiced each of the five skills, and the facilitator inserted a check mark on the questionnaire when the associate successfully practiced. While subjective, it was felt that this approach provided enough evidence that the participants had actually learned these basic skills.

Table 7-1. Level 1 Reaction Data on Selected Data

Success with Objectives	4.3
Relevance of Material	4.4
Usefulness of Program	4.5
Exercises and Skill Practices	3.9
Overall Instructor Rating	4.1
Composite	4.2

Application and Implementation

To measure application and implementation, the training and development staff administered a follow-up questionnaire three months after the end of the program. The questionnaire was comprehensive, spanning 20 questions on three pages, and was collected anonymously to reduce the potential for bias from participants. The questionnaire covered the following topics:

- Action plan implementation
- Relevance of the program

- Use of skills
- Changes in work routine
- Linkage with department measures
- Other benefits
- Barriers
- Enablers
- Management support
- Suggestions for improvement
- Other comments

While all of the information was helpful, the information on the use of skills was most critical. Table 7-2 shows the results from two of the 20 questions on the questionnaire. The first one provides some assurance that the participants are using the skills, as 78 percent strongly agree that they utilize the skills of the program. More important, the next question focused directly on one of the goals of the program. Fifty-two percent indicated that they use the skills with each customer, slightly exceeding the goal of 50 percent.

Because these are simple skills, with the opportunity to use them every day, this three-month follow-up provides some assurance that the associates have internalized the skills. The follow-up session three weeks after the first two days of training provided the first, early indication of skill transfer to the job. If the skills are still being used three months after training, it is safe to conclude that the majority of the participants have internalized them.

Table 7-2. Selected Application Data on Two of 20 Questions

	Strongly Agree	Agree	Neither Agree nor Disagree	Disagree	Strongly Disagree
I utilize the skills taught in the program.	52%	26%	19%	4%	0%
	With Each Customer	Every Third Customer	Several Times Each Day	At Least Once Daily	At Least Once Weekly
Frequency of use of skills.	52%	26%	19%	4%	0%

While many other data collection methods could have been used, it is important to understand the rationale for using the questionnaire. The most accurate, and expensive, method would be observation of the participants on the job by a third party. In that scenario, the "mystery shoppers" must learn the skills and be allowed to rate each of the 48 participants. This approach would provide concrete evidence that the participants had transferred the skills. This approach would be expensive, and it is not necessary under the circumstances. Because the management team is more interested in business impact and ROI, it has less interest in the lower levels of evaluation. Although some data should be collected to have assurance that the skills have transferred, the process does not have to be so comprehensive. This is a resource-saving issue and is consistent with the following guiding principles for the ROI process:

1. When a higher level evaluation is conducted, data must be collected at lower levels.
2. When an evaluation is planned for a higher level, the previous level of evaluation does not have to be comprehensive.
3. When collecting and analyzing data, use only the most credible sources.
4. When analyzing data, choose the most conservative among alternatives.
5. At least one method must be used to isolate the effects of the project or initiative.
6. If no improvement data are available for a population or from a specific source, it is assumed that little or no improvement has occurred.
7. Estimates of improvement should be adjusted for the potential error of the estimate.
8. Extreme data items and unsupported claims should not be used in ROI calculations.
9. Only the first year of benefits (annual) should be used in the ROI analysis of short-term projects or initiatives.
10. Project or program costs should be fully loaded for ROI analysis.

These are macro-level principles with a conservative approach for collecting and processing data. Guiding principle number two comes into play with this issue. When an evaluation is underway at a higher level than the previous level of evaluation, the earlier evaluation did not have to be comprehensive. This does not mean that Level 3 data cannot be collected or that it should not be collected. With limited resources, shortcuts must be developed and this principle allows us to use a less expensive approach. If the management team had asked for more evidence of customer interaction or wanted to know the quality and thoroughness of the actual exchange of information, then a more comprehensive Level 3 evaluation would be required and perhaps the evaluation would have even stopped at Level 3.

Business Impact

Weekly sales data were collected for three months after the program for both groups. Table 7-3 shows the data for the first three weeks after training, along with the last three weeks during the evaluation periods. An average for the last three weeks is more appropriate than data for a single week because that could have a spike effect that could affect the results. As the data shows, there is a significant difference between the two groups, indicating that the training program is improving sales. The percent increase, directly attributable to the sales training, is approximately 15 percent. If only a business impact evaluation is needed, this data would provide the information needed to show that the program has improved sales. However, if the ROI is needed, two more steps are necessary.

Table 7-3. Level 4 Data on Average Weekly Sales

Weeks After Training	Trained Groups ($)	Control Groups ($)
1	$9,723	$9,698
2	9,978	9,720
3	10,424	9,812
13	13,690	11,572
14	11,491	9,683
15	11,044	10,092
Average for Weeks 12, 14, 15	$12,075	$10,449

Converting Data to a Monetary Value

To convert the business data to a monetary value, the training and development staff had to address several issues. First, it is necessary to convert the actual sales differences to a value-added data—in this case, profits. The store level profit margin of 2 percent is multiplied by the difference or increase in sales. Table 7-4 shows the calculation, as the weekly sales per associate of $1,626 become a value-added amount of $32.50. Because 46 participants were still on the job in three months, the value-added amount gets multiplied by 46, for a weekly total of $1,495.

Mention of 46 participants brings another guiding principle—number six—into focus. That principle says, "If no improvement data are available for a population or from a specific source, it is assumed that little or no improvement has occurred." This is a conservative approach because the missing data is assumed to have no value. Two of the participants are no longer on the job and instead of tracking what happened to them, this rule is used to exclude any contribution from that group of two. However, the cost to train them would be included, although their values are not included for contribution.

Table 7-4. Annualized Program Benefits for 46 Participants

Average weekly sales per employee trained group	$12,075
Average weekly sales per employee untrained groups	10,449
Increase	1,626
Profit contribution (2% of stores sales)	32.50
Total weekly improvement (x 46)	1,495
Total Annual Benefits (x 48 weeks)	**$71,760**

Finally, annual benefits are used to develop a total benefit for the program. The ROI concept is an annual value, and only the first year benefits are used for short-term training programs. This is guiding principle number nine. Although this approach may slightly overstate the benefits for the first year, it is considered conservative because it does not capture any improvements or benefits in the second, third, or future years. This operating standard is also conservative and thus is a guiding principle. In summary, the total annualized program benefit of $71,760 is developed in a very conservative way using the guiding principles.

Program Cost

The program costs, shown in Table 7-5, are fully loaded and represent all the major categories outlined earlier. This is a conservative approach as described in guiding principle number 10. In this case, the costs for the development are included in the facilitation fee since the external supplier produced the program. The cost of the participants; time away from the job is the largest of the cost items and can be included, or the lost opportunity can be included, but not both. To be consistent, this is usually developed as the total time away from work (three days) is multiplied by the daily compensation rate including a 35 percent benefits factor. Finally, the estimated cost for the evaluation and the coordination of data collection is included. Since the company had an internal evaluation staff certified in the ROI process, the overall cost for this project was quite low and represents direct time involved in developing the impact study. The total fully loaded cost for the program was $32,984.

Table 7-5. Cost Summary for 48 Participants in Three Courses

Item	Cost ($)
Facilitation fees, three courses @$3,750	11,250
Program materials, 48 @ $35 per participant	1,680
Meals and refreshments, three days @ $28 per participant	4,032
Facilities, nine days @ $120	1080
Participants' salaries plus benefits (35% factor)	12,442
Coordination and evaluation	2,500
Total Costs	**$32,984**

ROI Calculation

Two ROI calculations are possible with use of the total monetary benefits and total cost of the program. The first is the benefit-cost ratio (BCR), which is the ratio of the monetary benefits divided by the costs:

$$\text{BCR} = \frac{\$71,760}{\$32,984} = 2.18$$

In essence, this suggests that for every dollar invested, 2.18 dollars are returned. When using the actual ROI formula, this value becomes:

$$\text{ROI (\%)} = \frac{\$71,760 - \$32,984}{\$32,984} = 118\%$$

This ROI calculation is interpreted as follows: For every dollar invested, a dollar is returned and another $1.18 is generated. The ROI formula is consistent with ROI for other types of investment. It is, essentially, earnings divided by investment. In this case, the ROI exceeds the 50 percent target.

Intangibles

This program generated significant intangible benefits:

- Increased job satisfaction
- Improved teamwork
- Increased confidence
- Improved customer service
- Improved image with customers
- Greater involvement

CONCLUSIONS AND ACTIONS

Communication of Results

It was important to communicate the results of this evaluation to the senior executives who requested a program, to the sales associates who were part of it, and to other personnel who were affected by it. First, the senior executives need the information to make a decision. In a face-to-face meeting, lasting approximately one hour, the training and development staff presented all six types of data with the recommendation that the program be implemented throughout the store chain. An executive summary and PowerPoint slides were distributed.

The participants received a two-page summary of the data, showing the results of the questionnaire and the business impact and ROI achieved from the process. There was some debate about whether to include the ROI in the summary, but eventually it was included in an attempt to share more information with the participants.

The electronics department managers, the participants' managers, received the executive summary of the information and participated in a conference call with the training and development staff. This group needed to see the benefits of training since they had to alter and rearrange schedules to cover the jobs while the participants were in training.

Finally, the training staff received a detailed impact study (approximately 100 pages), which was used as a learning document to help them understand more about this type of evaluation. This document became the historical record about the data collection instruments and ROI analysis.

Action

As a result of the communication of the impact study, senior executives decided to implement the program throughout the store chain. For all six types of data, the results were very positive with a very high ROI, significantly exceeding the target. The implementation proceeded with the senior executives' request that the sales data for the three target stores be captured for the remainder of the year to see the actual one-year impact of the program. While the issue of taking one year of data, based on a three-month snapshot, appears to be conservative since the second and third-year data are not used, this provided some assurance that the data does indeed hold up for the year. At the end of the year, the data actually exceeded the snapshot of performance in three months.

Lessons Learned

This evaluation provides some important insights into the ROI process. In the past, the store chain evaluated pilot programs primarily on Level 1 data (reactions from both the participants and their managers), coupled with the sales presentation from the vendor. The ROI approach provides much more data to indicate the success of training. In essence, companies can use Level 4 and 5 data for making a funding decision instead of making a funding decision on the basis of reaction data, Level 1.

From a statistical significance viewpoint, the small sample size does not allow for making an inference about the other stores at a 95 percent confidence. In essence, due to the small sample size it is impossible to say that the other stores would have the same results as the three in question. A sample size of 200 stores would be needed for statistical soundness. However, the economics of the evaluation and the practicality of the pilot implementation drove the sample size in this case, and in most other cases. No group of senior executives would suggest a sample size of 200 stores to see if the program should be implemented in the other 220 stores. It is important to note in the results that statistical inference cannot be made, but it is also important to remember two points:

- The six types of data represent much more data than previously used to evaluate these types of programs.
- Second, most managers do not take other funding decisions based on data that has been collected, analyzed, and reported at a 95 percent confidence level.

Finally, another lesson was learned about this application of the ROI process. This is a very simple case allowing for a control group arrangement. Many other situations are not this simple, and other methods of isolation have to be undertaken. Other studies, while feasible, are more complex and will require more resources.

Questions for Discussion

1. Are the data and results credible? Explain.
2. How should the results be communicated?
3. With such a small sample, how can the issue of statistical significance be addressed?
4. The use of a control group arrangement is not possible in many situations. How can other potential approaches be utilized? Explain.
5. Would you implement this program in the other 417 stores? Explain.

Chapter 8

Measuring ROI in Engagement
Linked to Retention Improvement

Southeast Corridor Bank

by Jack J. Phillips and Patti P. Phillips

This case study demonstrates how a retention improvement program at a regional bank generated an extremely high impact, including an impressive return on investment, using a strategic accountability approach to managing retention. By analyzing the turnover problem in branch bank operations, this case focuses on how the specific causes of turnover were determined, how the solutions were matched to the special causes, and how the calculation of the actual impact of the turnover reduction was developed. The strength of the case lies in the techniques used to ensure that the solutions were appropriate and that the turnover reduction represented a high-payoff solution.

BACKGROUND

Southeast Corridor Bank (SCB), a regional bank operating in four states with 60 branches, grew from a one-state operation to a multistate network through a progressive strategic campaign of acquisitions. As a result of its growth, the bank faced merger and integration problems, including excessive employee turnover: SCB's annual turnover was 57 percent, compared with an industry average of 26 percent. When he joined SCB, the new senior vice president for human resources (SVPHR) was faced with several important challenges, among them the need to reduce turnover. Although management was not aware of the full impact of turnover, it knew turnover was causing operational problems, taking up staff and supervisor time, and creating disruptive situations for customers.

A STRATEGIC ACCOUNTABILITY APPROACH

Retention was a strategic issue for SCB because it makes the difference between mediocre and excellent profits. Thus, accountability was built into the process, allowing management to fully understand the cost of the problem, the cost of the solutions, the potential impact of the solutions, and the actual impact of the solutions, all in monetary terms. To uncover the causes of turnover, the strategic accountability approach, outlined in Figure 8-1, became the basic model for this case study.

This approach moves logically through a series of eight steps necessary to manage the process. It's easy to stay on track because, for the most part, each step has to be completed before moving to the next. This approach brings structure, organization, and accountability to the process, and helps organizations avoid implementing solutions without analysis.

Figure 8-1. Strategic Accountability Approach to Managing Retention

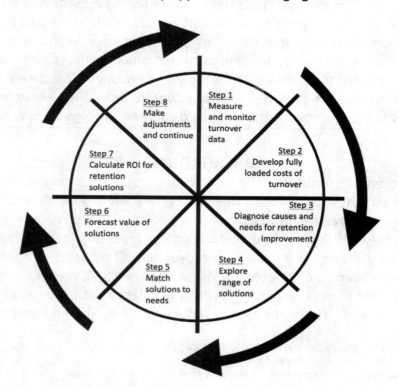

Step 1. Measure and Monitor Turnover Data

To properly monitor and measure turnover, there are several important steps:

- Define turnover consistently
- Report turnover rates by various demographics
- Report rates by critical job groups
- Include costs of turnover
- Compare turnover data with benchmarking targets
- Develop trigger points that stimulate action

Step 2. Calculate Fully Loaded Turnover Costs

The cost of turnover is one of the most underestimated and undervalued measures. It is often misunderstood because it is not fully loaded and does not reflect how much turnover actually costs a company. In addition, the impact of turnover is not regularly reported to the management team, keeping its members in the dark about the actual costs. However, when fully loaded costs of an organization's turnover are calculated for an entire year, the numbers can be extremely surprising.

When exploring turnover, the costs for recruiting, selecting, and training are typically considered because they are easily calculated. However, other costs are required to provide an accurate picture of the cost of turnover. A more comprehensive list includes 12 categories. The first seven are investments that are lost to some degree when an employee leaves:

- Exit expense
- Recruiting expense
- Employment expense
- Orientation expense
- Training expense
- Wage and salary expense while training
- Temporary replacement expense

The other five are related to the effect of turnover on conducting business:

- Lost productivity
- Quality problems

- Customer dissatisfaction
- Loss of expertise and knowledge
- Loss of management time because of turnover

Step 3. Diagnose Causes and Needs for Retention Improvement

Some causes of turnover may be obvious, but others can be extremely elusive. Collecting the appropriate data is often a challenge because of the potential for bias and the inaccuracies that can surface during data collection. Fortunately, a number of diagnostic processes are available, including:

- Demographic analysis
- Diagnostic instruments and mind mapping
- Focus groups and brainstorming
- Probing interviews
- Job satisfaction and organizational commitment surveys
- Exit interviews and surveys
- Nominal group technique
- Cause-and-effect diagrams and affinity diagrams
- Force field analysis

Step 4. Explore Possible Solutions

Many organizations are very creative in their approaches to retention problems, resulting in hundreds of excellent solutions. The critical point is to ensure that the solution is feasible for the organization. Most solutions fall into one of these categories:

- Offering a competitive total compensation package that includes salary, benefits, bonuses, incentives, awards, and recognition
- Building a great place to work, which champions teamwork, a healthy work environment, a supportive culture, and enabling systems
- Providing growth opportunities, such as work design, empowerment, career path development, training, and succession planning
- Creating a compelling future by creating a profitable organization with a competitive advantage, and developing a compelling mission, vision, and values

Step 5. Match Solutions to Needs

This step is related to Step 6, the need to forecast the value of the solutions. These two steps should be taken together because the solutions selected are assumed to meet specific needs, making the forecast of their anticipated value imperative. When attempting to match solutions to needs, consider these five key concerns:

- Avoid mismatches
- Only implement a minimum number of solutions
- Select a solution for a maximum return
- Verify the match early
- Check the progress of each solution

Step 6. Forecast the Value of the Solutions

Developing a forecast for a solution's value allows the team to establish priorities, work with a minimum number of solutions, and focus on solutions with the greatest return on investment (ROI). Difficult, challenging, and sometimes risky, forecasting is an expert estimation of what a solution should contribute. It is imperative to accumulate as much data as possible to back up the estimate and build credibility for the process. The payoff value can be developed if the percentage of expected turnover reduction can be related to it. For example, if the top cause of turnover is removed with a particular solution, what percentage of the turnover would actually be eliminated? Employees may be able to help with this when data are collected about the cause of turnover. This step may require several "what if" decisions that may result in various assumptions. This step may also involve building on previous experiences; in some cases, the experiences of other organizations can be helpful.

Step 7. Measure ROI for Retention Solutions

Another often-neglected step is calculating the actual financial impact of a turnover reduction strategy. This step is often omitted because it appears to be unnecessary. If accumulating a number of solutions is the only measure of success of turnover reduction or prevention, the impact of those solutions may be unimportant. But from a senior executive's point of view, accountability at least for major solutions is not complete until impact and ROI data have been collected. The ROI Methodology generates six types of data about the success of a turnover reduction strategy:

- Reaction to and satisfaction with the solution
- Skill and knowledge acquisition
- Application and implementation progress
- Business impact improvement
- Return on investment, expressed as an ROI formula
- Intangible measures not converted to monetary values

Step 8. Make Adjustments and Continue

The extensive set of data collected from the strategic accountability approach provides information for making adjustments and changes in turnover reduction strategies. It reveals the success of the turnover reduction solution at all levels, from reaction to ROI. It also examines barriers to success, specifically identifying what kept the solution from being effective or prevented it from becoming more effective. The approach also identifies the processes that enable or support a turnover reduction solution. This information helps determine whether the solution needs to be revised, discontinued, or amplified.

The next step in the process goes back to the beginning, monitoring the data to ensure that turnover levels continue to meet expectations . . . and the cycle continues.

MEASURING AND MONITORING TURNOVER

SCB monitored turnover in two categories, defining employee departures as either voluntary separations or terminations for performance. A voluntary termination occurred when an employee resigned at their own will. A termination for performance involved an important problem that might have been rectified if the performance deficiency had been recognized or prevented. Departures due to retirement or disability were not included in either definition.

The turnover rate was monitored by job group, region, and branch bank. Branches had the highest turnover, averaging 71 percent in the previous year, which far exceeded any expectations or industry averages acquired from other financial institutions and the American Bankers Association. Turnover was also considered excessive in a few entry-level clerical job classifications in regional and corporate offices.

Impact of Turnover

The impact of turnover was determined at the beginning of the study. External turnover studies in the banking industry showed fully loaded turnover costs for that year ranging from 75 percent to 125 percent of annual pay (Phillips and Edwards 2009). The fully loaded costs were developed using the 12 cost categories listed in Step 2. When reviewing the proposed program, the senior executive team suggested using the lower value for calculating the payoff (75 percent or 0.75 times an employee's annual pay) because it believed that turnover wasn't quite that expensive.

Determining the Cause of Turnover

Three basic techniques were used to pinpoint the actual cause of turnover. First, individual job groups and tenure within job groups were analyzed to give insight into where the turnover was occurring, the magnitude of the problem, and some indication of the cause. It was determined that much of the turnover occurred in the first six to 18 months of employment. Second, exit interviews with departing employees were examined to see if specific reasons for departure could be pinpointed. Accuracy was a concern with the exit data, as departing employees may give incomplete and inaccurate data when reporting their reasons for leaving in an effort to avoid burning bridges. Finally, the HR team used the nominal group technique to more precisely determine the actual causes of turnover.

Nominal Group Technique

The nominal group technique was selected because it allowed unbiased input to be collected efficiently and accurately across the organization. The team planned a focus group with 12 employees in each region, for a total of six groups representing all regions. In addition, two focus groups were planned for the clerical staff in corporate headquarters. This approach provided approximately a 10 percent sample, which was considered a sufficient number to pinpoint the problem.

Participants in the focus groups, who represented the areas in which turnover was highest, described why they believed their colleagues were leaving, not why they themselves would leave. Data was taken from individuals in a carefully structured format during two-hour meetings at each location, using third-party facilitators, and was integrated and weighted so the most important reasons were clearly identified. This process had the advantages of being low cost and highly reliable, as well as having a low degree of bias. Only two days of external facilitator time was needed to collect and summarize data for review.

The nominal group technique unfolded quickly in 10 steps:

1. The process steps were briefly described along with a statement of confidentiality. The importance of the participants' input was underscored so that they understood the consequences for the bank.

2. Participants were asked to list specific reasons why they believed their colleagues had left the bank or why others might leave. It was stressed that the question dealt with the actions or potential actions of employees other than themselves, although the bank realized that the participants' comments would probably reflect their own views (which were what was actually needed).

3. In a round-robin format, each person revealed one reason for turnover, which was then recorded on a flipchart. At this point, no attempt was made to integrate the issues, just to record the data. The list, containing as many as 50 or 60 items, was displayed on the walls.

4. The next step was to consolidate and integrate the list. Integration was easy when items contained the same words and meanings. However, it was important to ensure that the real reason behind the cause was the same before items were consolidated. (When this process was complete the list might have contained 30 or 40 different reasons for turnover.)

5. Participants were then asked to review all the items, carefully select those they considered to be the top 10 causes, and list them individually on index cards.

6. Next, participants ranked their top 10 items by importance, with the first item as the most important.

7. In a round-robin format, each individual revealed her number 1 item, and 10 points were recorded next to it on the flipchart. Then the next individual revealed his number 1 issue, and so on, until the entire group had offered a top reason. Next, the number 2 reason was identified, and nine points were recorded on the flipchart next to the

item. This process continued until all reasons had been revealed and points recorded.

8. After the numbers next to each item were totaled, it was determined that the item with the most points was the leading cause of turnover. The cause with the second-highest number of points was deemed the second most important cause of turnover, and so on, until the top 15 causes were captured from that group.

9. This process was completed for all six regional groups and the two clerical staff groups; trends began to emerge quickly from one group to the next.

10. The actual raw scores were then combined to integrate the results of the six regional focus groups and the two clerical groups.

The top 15 scores represented the top 15 reasons for turnover across all the branches and clerical groups.

Specific Needs

The following list shows the top 10 causes of turnover in the bank branches:

- Lack of opportunity for advancement
- Lack of opportunity to learn new skills and new product knowledge
- Pay level not adequate
- Not enough responsibility and empowerment
- Lack of recognition and appreciation of work
- Lack of teamwork in the branch
- Lack of preparation for customer service problems
- Unfair and unsupportive supervisor
- Too much stress at peak times
- Not enough flexibility in work schedules.

A similar list was developed for the clerical staff, but the remainder of this case study focuses directly on the efforts to reduce turnover in the branch network.

Branch turnover was the most critical issue because it involved the highest turnover rates and the largest number of employees, and the focus group results provided a clear pattern of specific needs. Recognizing that not all causes of turnover could be addressed immediately, the bank's management set out to work on the top eight reasons while it considered a variety of options to address stress and work flexibility. These top eight reasons are representative of classic engagement requirements for employees, as reported in the Gallup Twelve Questions and Surveys from the Great Place to Work Institute as well as many other surveys.

Increasing salaries in proportion to increased responsibilities links monetary rewards to employee engagement. Consequently, jobs were redesigned, the promotion and advancement system was radically changed, and the compensation system was adjusted to allow for pay increases to become more "engaged."

SOLUTION: ENGAGEMENT LINKED WITH A REWARD

An improved employee engagement system addressed the top eight reasons for turnover, particularly when a salary increase was attached. The program was designed to expand the scope of the employees' jobs and responsibilities, with increases in pay for acquiring skills, and to provide a clear path for advancement and improvement. Jobs were redesigned from narrowly focused teller duties to an expanded job with a new classification: banking representative I, II, or III. The job descriptions were revised to provide more empowerment, teamwork, and innovation in decision making. Table 8-1 shows the basic job duties for each level. Having employees perform multiple tasks was expected to broaden their responsibilities and empower them to provide excellent customer service. Pay increases were put in place to recognize skill acquisition, demonstrated accomplishment, and increased responsibility as the employees became more engaged.

Table 8-1. Proposed Job Levels

Banking Representative Level	Job Duties
I	Basic teller transactions (deposits, check cashing, etc.)
II	Same as above, plus opening and closing accounts and processing CDs, savings bonds, special transactions, etc.
III	Same as above, plus processing limited liability consumer loans, applications for all consumer loans, referrals for mortage loans, etc.

A branch employee would be a banking representative I if he could perform one or two simple tasks, such as processing deposits and cashing checks. As an employee at the banking representative I level took on additional responsibilities and performed different functions, she would be eligible for a promotion to banking representative II. If the representative could perform all the basic functions of the branch bank, including processing consumer loan applications, a promotion to banking representative III was appropriate. Training opportunities and self-study information was available to help employees develop the necessary job-related skills, and structured on-the-job training was also provided through the branch managers, assistant managers, and supervisors.

Although increased engagement had some definite benefits from the employee's perspective, there were also benefits for the bank. Not only was turnover expected to decrease, but actual staffing levels were expected to be reduced in larger branches. In theory, if a branch's employees could all perform every duty, then fewer employees would be needed. Prior to this time, minimum staffing levels were required in certain critical jobs, and those employees were not always available for other duties.

In addition, the bank hoped to provide an improved customer service experience, because the new approach would prevent customers from having to wait in long lines for specialized services. For example, it was not unusual to see long lines for such special functions as opening a checking account, closing out a CD, or taking a consumer loan application, whereas such activities as paying bills and receiving deposits often required little or no waiting. If each employee could perform all the tasks, shorter waiting lines would not only be feasible, but expected.

The marketing department even created a publicity campaign around this new arrangement by including a promotional piece with checking account statements introducing the concept "In our branches there are no tellers." This document described the new process and stated that because all branch employees could perform every branch function, it would provide faster service.

MEASURING SUCCESS

Measuring the success of the new solution required collecting data at four levels. At the first level, reaction and satisfaction were measured during regularly scheduled training sessions and meetings with the employees. This measurement provided input on how well employees were accepting the new arrangement and the different elements of the program. Using brief surveys, the team collected data on a five-point scale. As expected, the results were positive, averaging a 4.2 composite rating. Three important measures stood out: important to my success (4.3), I would recommend to others (4.1), and I intend to make this program successful (4.7).

At the second level, learning was measured in two different ways. Skill acquisition and knowledge increase were calculated for each training and learning opportunity, and informal self-assessments were taken for many of the programs. A few critical skills required actual demonstration to show that employees could perform them (for example, documentation, compliance, and customer services). When learning measurements revealed unacceptable performance, participants were given the opportunity to repeat training sessions or take more time to practice. In a limited number of cases, a third opportunity was provided. After one year of operation, only two employees were denied promotions based on their poor performance in training programs. The second area of learning measurements involved learning how the program works (4.2 out of 5) and how to become more engaged (4.1 out of 5).

At the third level, application and implementation were measured by collecting five types of data, as shown in Table 8-2. Actual participation in the program reflected the willingness of individuals to pursue skill acquisition and increased engagement through a variety of efforts. The results were impressive.

In all, 95 percent of the branch employees wanted to participate in the program. The remaining 5 percent were content with the banking representative I classification and were not interested in learning new skills. Actual requests for training and learning opportunities were a critical part of the formal process. Employees had to map out their own developmental efforts, which were then approved by the branch manager. In all, some 86 requests were logged per month, almost overtaxing the system's ability to provide training and learning opportunities.

Reviews of the status and progress—to be considered for the promotion for the next level—were significant, as this review was the formal way of demonstrating the skills required for promotion. The number of actual promotions increased quickly: As the table shows, there were 139 promotions during the year before the program; this number increased to 257 during the year after the program was initiated.

The company had not used a separate engagement survey before—only a few questions on the annual feedback survey. As part of the new program, however, an engagement survey with 10 items was sent to all branch staff involved in the program six months after it began. The survey included typical engagement issues. In all, the results of the survey revealed an average of 4.1 out of 5.

Table 8-2. Selected Application and Implementation Data

	1 Year Before	1 Year After
Participation in program	N/A	95%
Requests for training	45 per month	86 per month
Review Situations	N/A	138
Actual promotions	139	257
Engagement Survey	N/A	4.1

N/A = not applicable

The categories of business impact measures that were monitored are shown in Table 8-3, along with their definitions. In all, nine categories of data were expected to be influenced to some degree by this project, although four— monthly branch employee turnover, staffing levels, customer satisfaction, and job satisfaction—were considered to be the primary measures.

Reduction in turnover was the most important, as that was the major thrust of the project. The company also believed that with more highly skilled and engaged employees, fewer staff should be needed, at least for the larger branches. This would be reflected in staffing levels. Customer service was expected to increase because fewer customers would be waiting in line or moving from one line to another. Job satisfaction would be reflected in employees who were more satisfied with their work, their jobs, and career possibilities.

An increase in loan volume was also expected to be attributed to the project, thanks to the decrease in the number of customers waiting in line. Consequently, customers would visit more often or would not leave in frustration because of delays. This was expected to result in an increase in the number of deposits, consumer loans, new accounts, and transactions, as well as increases in successful cross-selling. However, these last five categories were measures of each branch and were expected to move very little because of this project.

Table 8-3. Business Measures Influenced by the Project

Business-Impact Measures	Definitions
1. Branch employee turnover (monthly)	Avoidable turnover (total number of employees leaving voluntarily and for performance reasons divided by the average number of employees in the branch for the month). This number was multiplied by 12 to develop the annual turnover rate.
2. Staffing level	The total number of employees in the branch, reported monthly.
3. Customer satisfaction	Customer reaction to the job changes (faster service, fewer lines) measured on a 1-to-5 scale.
4. Job satisfaction	Employee feedback on selected measures on the annual feedback survey process
5. Deposits	Savings, checking, and securities deposits by type and product
6. Loan volume	Consumer loan volume by loan type.
7. New accounts	New accounts opened for new customers.
8. Transaction volume	Number of face-to-face transactions, paying and receiving, by major category.
9. Cross-selling	New products sold to existing customers.

Isolating the Effects of the Project

In almost any situation, multiple influences will affect specific business measures, so it's important to isolate the actual impact of the engagement program from other influences. To add credibility and validity to the analysis, the team used estimates from branch managers and staff to isolate the effects of the project for each data item used in the ROI calculation (Table 8-5). In brief group meetings, the staff were told the actual results of the turnover reduction and asked to allocate what percentage of the reduction was linked directly to the engagement effort. Each branch provided this information.

Branch team members also discussed whether any other factors could have contributed to turnover reduction (only two were identified). Then, in a focus group format, they were asked to discuss the link between each factor and the actual turnover reduction. This improved the accuracy of the estimation. The team also added an error adjustment to the estimates: Individuals were asked to indicate the level of confidence in their estimate using a scale of 0 to 100 percent, with 0 percent meaning no confidence and

100 percent meaning absolute certainty. This number was used to discount that employee's allocation. For example, if an individual allocated 60 percent of the turnover reduction to this specific project and was 80 percent confident in that allocation, the adjusted value would be 48 percent (.6 ´ .8 = .48). This method of isolation provided a conservative estimate for the effect of the program on turnover reduction.

Branch managers were asked to calculate improvements in staffing levels. As before, branch managers indicated the degree to which the engagement program had resulted in actual staff reductions. However, staff reductions had only occurred in the larger branches, so this estimate only involved those branch managers. Because no other factors seemed to have contributed to the staff reduction, credit for the entire reduction was given to the program.

Table 8-4 shows the method for isolating each measure that was a part of the planning for the study. Increases in deposits, loan volume, new accounts, transactions, and cross-selling were minimal and influenced by many variables other than the new program, so no attempt was made to isolate the effect or to use them in the ROI analysis. However, they were reported as intangibles to provide evidence that they were, at least to some degree, affected by the turnover reduction program.

Customer reactions were provided by survey cards, which the customer

Table 8-4. Business Measures and Planned Analysis

Data Item	Method of Isolating the Effects	Method of Converting Data
Employee turnover	Branch manager and Staff Estimation estima- tion	External studies
Staffing levels	Branch manager estimation	Company payroll records
Customer service	Customer input	N/A
Job satisfaction	Staff input	N/A
Deposits, loan volume, new accounts	Branch manager estimation	Standard value (percent margin)
Transaction volume, cross-selling	Branch manager and Staff estimation	Standard value (average percent margin)

N/A = not applicable

could complete at the end of a transaction and deposit at the entrance to the branch.

The customers appreciated the new approach, liked the service delivered, and indicated that they would continue to use the branch. The annual employee job satisfaction survey showed that employees were pleased with the improvements in advancement opportunities, the chance to use skills, performance-based pay, and other related engagement issues. Because customer service and job satisfaction measures were not isolated or converted to monetary value, they were not used in the ROI calculation. However, these measures were very important and influential in the final evaluation and were listed as intangible benefits.

Converting Data to Money

Table 8-5 also shows the method used (or planned) to convert data to monetary value. Turnover was converted to monetary value starting with a value from external studies. The specific amount of one turnover was calculated using 0.9 multiplied by the annual salary. This value—developed and agreed to in a meeting with senior management during the planning phase of the project—was conservative; other studies used values ranging from .75 to 1.25 multiplied by annual earnings. Because the average annual salary of the branch bank staff was $28,200, an average savings of $21,150 was realized for each potential employee departure that was prevented ($28,200 x 0.75).

After one year of the engagement program, the company saw a turnover reduction of 109 (Table 8-6). That number was reduced to 75 prevented turnovers after adjusting for contribution factor and confidence error, which had been obtained in branch meetings, as described earlier. Then the average cost of a turnover ($21,150) was multiplied by 75 to yield an annual value of more than $1.5 million. At that point in data collection, the second-year value was unknown, so that amount was doubled to estimate the two-year savings.

Staffing levels were initially going to be converted to a monetary value using the actual salaries for the jobs that had been eliminated. However, as only a few branches were affected the actual number was multiplied by the average salary of the branch staff. The value was captured for one year using the same calculation process as for the turnover reduction, and then doubled to show a two-year benefit of nearly $1 million.

This program was not intended to be a short term solution and was

Table 8-5. Calculation of Actual Business Results

	Preceding Year	One Year After	Actual Difference	Contribution Factor	Confidence Estimate	Adjusted Amount	Unit Amount	First-Year Benefits	Two-Year Benefits
Turnover	271 (57%)	162 (35%)	109	84%	82%	75	$21,150	$1,586,250	$3,172,500
Staffing Levels	480 (average)	463 (end of year)	17	100%	100%	17	$28,200	$479,400	$958,800

expected to provide extended value. However, the team used a two-year timeframe because it is a conservative way to evaluate ROI (that is, one year of actual data and a forecast of one year), and additional benefits beyond the two years were excluded.

Analysis

The turnover reduction at the branches was significant, dropping from 71 percent to 35 percent in one year. Although some of the smaller branches did not see any changes in the staffing levels, the larger branches did have fewer staff members after a year. In all, 30 percent of the branches were able to reduce part-time or full-time staff levels by at least one member; 10 percent of the branches were able to reduce staff by two individuals.

As shown in Table 8-5 and outlined in the previous section, the total two-year benefits of the employee engagement program reached just over $3 million, with an addition savings of nearly $1 million in staffing levels.

Project Cost

Table 8-6 shows the fully loaded cost of the project. The initial analysis costs were included along with the time, direct costs, and travel expenses for the focus groups. The next two items were branch staff time, which represented an estimate of all the time employees and managers had to spend away from their normal work to understand the program and learn new skills, including a session on how to engage employees. Facilities cost and travel cost for meetings are also listed. Actual salary increases—the additional salaries in the branches as a result of promotions—were calculated. The total amount of staff salary increases or promotions during the first year ($977,600) was reduced by the rate of promotions that had occurred in the year before the program was implemented. This accounts for the change only.

The ongoing administration and operation costs involved the time required for the HR staff to administer the program. Finally, the evaluation costs represented the costs related to developing the study of the project's effect on the business. The total cost presented in this table includes several items that were involved only in the first year's actual cost one-year forecast; these costs are the totals for the project in those categories. Across all categories for two years, the total cost of the program is $941,596 + $433,200 = $1,374,796.

Table 8-6. Fully Loaded Project Costs

Project Costs	Year 1	Year 2
Initial analysis	$14,000	---
Program development	22,500	---
Participant time	345,600	195,000
Branch manager time	40,800	30,200
Facilities	35,000	
Travel	17,000	
Salary increases	446,696	203,900
Administration/operation	14,000	4,100
Evaluation	6,000	
	$941,596	$433,200

Calculating BCR and ROI

The two-year monetary benefits were combined with costs to develop the benefit-cost ratio (BCR) and the ROI. The solution benefit represents the total two-year benefits and is calculated by adding the total benefit from turnover to the total benefit from staffing levels ($3,172,500 + 958,800 = 4,131,300).

$$BCR = \frac{\text{Solution Benefits}}{\text{Solution Cost}} = \frac{\$4,131,300}{\$1,374,796} = 3.01$$

$$ROI = \frac{\text{Net Solution Benefits}}{\text{Solution Cost}} = \frac{\$4,131,300 - \$1,374,796}{\$1,374,796} \times 100 = 201\%$$

This BCR value indicates that for every $1 invested in the project, $3.01 is returned in monetary benefits. In terms of ROI, for every $1 invested, $2.01 is returned after the costs are captured. These results are excellent, since the ROI objective was 25%. The ROI was only one measure and should be considered in conjunction with other measures. However, because it was developed using a conservative approach, the ROI probably underestimated the actual return from this project.

Communicating Results

The results were communicated to the senior management team in an executive staff meeting, during which approximately 30 minutes were allocated to the project report. The discussion covered three points:

- The project was quickly reviewed, including the description of the solution.
- The methodology used for evaluating the project was described.
- The results were revealed one level at a time, presenting the:
  - Reaction of employees to the engagement program
  - Learning the system and how to use it
  - Application of the system
  - Business impact of engagement
  - ROI in engagement
  - Intangible measures linked to engagement.

This presentation provided a balanced profile of the project and was convincing to the senior management team. This was the first time an HR solution to a problem had been evaluated using a balanced measurement approach that included ROI. The intangible measures also were important, particularly the improvement in customer service. Overall, the senior management team was very pleased with the success of the project and impressed with the analysis.

Lessons Learned

Although this project arrived at the right solution, a few lessons were learned. First because forecasting is such an important step in the strategic accountability approach to managing retention, it may have been safer to forecast the ROI at the time the solution was developed. In particular, increasing the branch salaries to the extent planned for this solution was risky: It would have been difficult to retract this program had it not shown enough value to make it worthwhile. In addition, the branch and regional managers were not entirely convinced that improving employee engagement would add value, and additional effort was needed to capture their buy-in and help them understand the full cost of turnover. They needed to see how this system could alleviate many of their problems and add monetary value to the branches. A forecasted ROI could have provided more confidence before the program was put in place, but although this was considered, it was not pursued.

Finally, the team should have better estimated the time required of branch managers, who had to deal with numerous requests for training and juggle schedules to ensure the staff received the training they needed. The managers also had to provide additional training sessions and spend time assessing whether the bank representatives had obtained the skills necessary for promotion.

Questions for Discussion
1. This case study illustrates how the actual causes of turnover were determined. What is your reaction to this process?
2. Why do many organizations spend so little time determining the causes of turnover?
3. Calculating the ROI of an engagement program is rarely done, yet it can have tremendous benefits. Why is this step often omitted?
4. How can the data from this project be used in the future?
5. Critique the overall approach to this project, highlighting weaknesses and strengths.

References

Phillips, J.J., and L. Edwards. 2009. *Managing Talent Retention: An ROI Approach.* San Francisco: Pfeiffer.

Buckingham, M., and C. Coffman. 1999. *First Break All the Rules: What the World's Greatest Managers Do Differently.* New York: Simon & Schuster.

Phillips, P.P., and J.J. Phillips. 2015. *Real World Training Evaluation: Navigating Common Constraints for Exceptional Results.* Alexandria, VA: ATD Press.

Chapter 9

Measuring ROI in a
Masters Degree Program

Federal Information Agency

By Jack J. Phillips and Patti P. Phillips

This case study shows how a government agency tackled a serious problem with a creative solution to deliver a very positive ROI. The Federal Information Agency (FIA) was experiencing excessive turnover of critical talent, averaging about 38%, annually. Most of the exits occurred after one year of service, and usually for more salary. Because increasing salaries was not an option, this agency implemented a creative, but expensive, solution to meet two important needs, career enhancement and skill upgrading. The solution was to offer a Masters Degree in Information Science on agency time, at no cost to the employee. The agency head required a minimum 25% return on investment for the program.

PROBLEM AND SOLUTION

The Federal Information Agency (FIA) provides various types of information to other government agencies and businesses as well as state and local organizations, agencies, and interested groups. Operating through a network across the United States, the work is performed by several-hundred communication specialists with backgrounds in systems, computer science, electrical engineering, and information science. Almost all the specialists have bachelor's degrees in one of these fields. The headquarters and operation center is in the Washington, D.C. area, where 1,500 of these specialists are employed.

This case was prepared to serve as a basis for discussion rather than to illustrate either effective or ineffective administrative and management practices. The authors, dates, places, names and organizations may have been disguised at the request of the author or organization.

FIA has recently experienced two problems that have senior agency officials concerned. The first problem is an unacceptable rate of employee turnover for this group of specialists—averaging 38 percent in the past year alone. This has placed a strain on the agency to recruit and train replacements. An analysis of exit interviews indicated that employees leave primarily for higher salaries. Because FIA is somewhat constrained in providing competitive salaries, it has become extremely difficult to compete with the private sector for salaries and benefits. Although salary increases and adjustments in pay levels will be necessary to lower turnover, FIA is exploring other options in the interim.

The second problem concerns the need to continuously update the technical skills of the staff. While the vast majority of the 1,500 specialists have degrees in various fields, only a few have masters degrees in their specialty. In this field, formal education is quickly outdated. The annual feedback survey with employees reflected a strong interest in an internal masters degree program in information science. Consequently, FIA explored the implementation of an in-house masters degree in Information Science conducted by the School of Engineering and Science at Regional State University (RSU). The masters degree program would be implemented at no cost to the participating employee and conducted on the Agency's time during routine work hours. Designed to address both employee turnover and skill updates, the program would normally take three years for participants to complete.

Program Description

RSU was selected for the masters program because of its reputation and the match of their curriculum to FIA needs. The program allows participants to take one or two courses per semester. A two-course per semester schedule would take three years to complete. Both morning and afternoon classes were available, each representing three hours per week of class time. Participants were discouraged from taking more than two courses per term. Although a thesis option was normally available, FIA requested a graduate project be required for six hours of credit as a substitute for the thesis. A professor would supervise the project. Designed to add value to FIA, the project would be applied in the agency and would not be as rigorous as the thesis. Participants signed up for three hours for the project in both year two and three.

Classes were usually offered live with professors visiting the agency's center. Occasionally, classes were offered through videoconference or independent study. Participants were asked to prepare for classroom activities on their own time, but were allowed to attend classes on the agency's time. A typical three-year schedule is shown in Table 9-1.

Senior management approved the masters curriculum, which represented a mix of courses normally offered in the program and others specially selected for FIA staff. Two new courses were designed by university faculty to be included in the curriculum. These two represented a slight modification of existing courses and were tailored to the communication requirements of the agency. Elective courses were not allowed for two reasons. First, it would complicate the offering to a certain extent, requiring additional courses, facilities, and professors—essentially adding cost to the program. Second, FIA wanted a prescribed, customized curriculum that would add value to the agency while still meeting the requirements of the university.

Table 9-1. Typical Three-Year Schedule

M.S.—Information Science		
Year 1	**Year 2**	**Year 3**
Fall 2 Courses—6 hours	2 Courses—6 hours	2 Courses—6 hours
Spring 2 Courses—6 hours	2 Courses—6 hours	2 Courses—6 hours
Summer 1 Course—3 hours	1 Course—3 hours	Graduate Project –3 hours
	Graduate Project –3 hours	
Graduate Project—6 hours (Year 2 and 3)		
Total Semester Hours—48		

Selection Criteria

An important issue involved the selection of employees to attend the program. Most employees who voluntarily left the agency resigned within the first four years, and were often considered to have high potential. With this in mind, the following criteria were established for identifying and selecting the employees to enroll in the program:

1. A candidate should have at least one year of service prior to beginning classes.
2. A candidate must meet the normal requirements to be accepted into the graduate school at the university.

3. A candidate must be willing to sign a commitment to stay with the agency for two years beyond program completion.
4. A candidate's immediate manager must nominate the employee for consideration.
5. A candidate must be considered "high potential" as rated by the immediate manager.

The management team was provided initial information on the program, kept informed of its development and progress prior to actual launch and briefed as the program was described and selection criteria was finalized. It was emphasized that the selection should be based on objective criteria, following the guidelines offered. At the same time, managers were asked to provide feedback as to the level of interest and specific issues surrounding the nomination of candidates.

A limit of 100 participants entering the program each year was established. This limit was based on two key issues:

1. The capability of the university in terms of staffing for the program—RSU could not effectively teach more than 100 participants each semester.
2. This was an experiment that, if successful, could be modified or enhanced in the future.

Program Administration

Because of the magnitude of the anticipated enrollment, FIA appointed a full-time program administrator who was responsible for organizing and coordinating the program. The duties included registration of the participants, all correspondence and communication with the university and participants, facilities and logistics (including materials and books), and resolving problems as they occur. FIA absorbed the total cost of the coordinator. The university assigned an individual to serve as liaison with the agency. This individual was not additional staff; the university absorbed the cost as part of the tuition.

The Drivers for Evaluation

This program was selected for a comprehensive evaluation to show its impact on the agency using a four-year time frame. Four influences created the need for this detailed level of accountability:

1. Senior administrators had requested detailed evaluations for certain

programs considered to be strategic, highly visible, and designed to add value to the agency.

2. This program was perceived to be very expensive, demanding a higher level of accountability, including return on investment (ROI).

3. Because retention is such a critical issue for this agency, it was important to determine if this solution was the appropriate one. A detailed measurement and evaluation should reflect the success of the program.

4. The passage of federal legislation and other initiatives in the United States, aimed at bringing more accountability for taxpayers' funds, has created a shift in increased public sector accountability.

Consequently, the implementation team planned a detailed evaluation of this program beyond the traditional program evaluation processes. Along with tracking costs, the monetary payoff would be developed, including the ROI in the program. Because this is a very complex and comprehensive solution, other important measures would be monitored to present an overall, balanced approach to the measurement.

Recognizing the shift toward public sector accountability, the human resources staff had developed the necessary skills to implement the ROI process. A small group of HR staff members had been certified to implement the ROI process within the agency. The ROI process is a comprehensive measurement and evaluation process that develops six types of data and always includes a method to isolate the effects of the program (Phillips, Stone, and Phillips, 2001).

The evaluation of the masters program was conducted by several of these team members with the assistance of the original developer of the ROI process, Dr. Jack J. Phillips.

Program Costs

The costs of the program were estimated in advance and reflected a fully loaded cost profile, which included all direct and indirect costs. One of the major costs was the tuition for the participants. The university charged the customary tuition, plus $100 per semester course per participant to offset the additional travel, faculty expense, books, and handouts. The tuition per semester hour was $200 ($600 per three-hour course).

The full-time administrator was an FIA employee, receiving a base salary of $37,000/year, with a 45% employee benefits upload factor. The administrator had expenses of approximately $15,000 per year. Salaries for the participants represented another significant cost category. The average salary of the job categories of the employees involved in the program was $47,800, with a 45% employee benefits factor. Salaries usually increase approximately 4% per year. Participants attended class a total of 18 hours for each semester hour of credit. Thus, a three-hour course represented 54 hours of off-the-job time in the classroom. The total hours needed for one participant to complete the program for one participant was 756 hours (14 x 54).

Classroom facilities were another significant cost category. For the 100 participants, four different courses were offered each semester and each course was repeated at a different time slot. With a class size of 25, eight separate semester courses were presented each semester. Half the scheduled courses were offered in the summer. Although the classrooms used for this program were those normally used for other training and education programs offered at the agency, the cost for providing the facilities was included. (Because of the unusual demand, an additional conference room was built to provide ample meeting space.) The estimate for the average cost of all meeting rooms was $40 per hour of use.

The cost for the initial assessment was also included in the cost profile. This charge, estimated to be approximately $5,000, included the turnover analysis and was prorated for the first three years. FIA's development costs for the program were estimated to be approximately $10,000 and were prorated for three years. Management time involved in the program was minimal, but estimated to be approximately $9,000 over the three-year period. This consisted primarily of meetings and memos regarding the program. Finally, the evaluation costs, representing the cost to actually track the success of the program and report the results to management, was estimated to be $10,000.

Table 9.2 represents the total costs of the initial group in the program for three years using a fully loaded cost profile. All of the cost categories described above are included. This value is necessary for the ROI calculation.

ROI PLANNING

Data Collection Issues

To understand the success of the project from a balanced perspective, a variety of types of data had to be collected throughout program implementation. During the initial enrollment process, meetings were conducted with participants to obtain their commitment to provide data at different time frames. The program administrator had regular access to participants who were willing to provide data about their reaction to the program, and detail the extent of knowledge and skill enhancement, and the successes they achieved on the job. Measures were taken at four distinct levels:

1. Reaction to individual courses and the program, including the administrative and coordination issues
2. The knowledge and skills obtained from the individual courses and learning about the program
3. Application and implementation of the program as learning is applied on the job and the program is coordinated effectively
4. Changes in business measures in the agency directly related to the program

Table 9-2. Total Fully Loaded Costs of Masters Program for 100 Participants

	Year1	Year 2	Year 3	Total
Initial analysis (prorated)	$1,667	$1,667	$1,666	$5,000
Development (prorated)	3,333	3,333	3,334	10,000
Tuition-regular	300,000	342,000	273,000	915,000
Tuition-premium	50,000	57,000	45,500	152,500
Salaries/Benefits (participants)	899,697	888,900	708,426	2,497,023
Salaries/Benefits (program administrator)	53,650	55,796	58,028	167,474
Program coordination	15,000	15,000	15,000	45,000
Facilities	43,200	43,200	34,560	120,960
Management time	3,000	3,000	3,000	9,000
Evaluation	3,333	3,333	3,334	10,000
Total	**$1,372,880**	**$1,413,229**	**$1,145,848**	**$3,931,957**

In addition to these data items, program costs were monitored so that the return on investment could be calculated.

Collecting different types of data required measures to be taken at different time frames. It was agreed at the beginning of the program, that some data categories would be collected at the end of each semester. Reaction would be measured and learning would be monitored with individual grade point averages. At periodic intervals, follow-up data was collected to reflect the progress of the program and its application on the job. Finally, business impact data directly linked to the program was measured during the program as well as at the conclusion. While this program was perceived to have a long-term impact, data had to be collected throughout the process to reflect any early impact that developed.

Data Collection Plan

The program administrator was responsible for the initial data collection and semester feedback sections. Individual faculty members were asked to collect reaction and learning measures at the end of each course. While most of the data would come directly from the participants, the records from the agency were monitored for certain business measures, such as turnover. In addition, immediate managers of participants provided input concerning the actual use of the program on the job. Figure 9-1 shows the data collection plan for this program.

Reaction to the program was collected at specific time periods. A few issues involving reaction and satisfaction were collected from prospective participants at an information briefing when the program was announced. Perceived value, anticipated difficulty of the courses, and usefulness of the program on the job were captured in initial meetings. Next, reaction measures were collected for each individual course as the participants rated the course material, instructor, delivery style, and learning environment. Also, at the end of each semester, a brief reaction questionnaire was collected to provide constant feedback of perceptions and satisfaction with the program. Upon completion of the program, an overall reaction questionnaire was distributed.

The initial meeting with the participants provided an opportunity to collect information about their understanding of how the program works and their role in making the program successful. Most of the learning took place in individual courses. The faculty member assigned grades based on formal and informal testing and assessment. These grades reflected individual learning, skills, and knowledge. Professors used a variety of testing methodology such as special projects, demonstrations, discussion questions, case studies, simulations, and objective tests. The overall grade point average (GPA) provided an on-going assessment of the degree to which the participants were learning the content of the courses.

Application and implementation measures were assessed at several different time intervals. At the end of each year, a questionnaire was

Figure 9-1. Data Collection Plan

Program: <u>Federal Information Agency</u>   Responsibility: _____   Date: _____

Level	Broad Program Objective(s)	Measures	Data Collection Method/ Instruments	Data Sources	Timing	Responsibilities
1	**REACTION/ SATISFACTION** • Positive reaction to program, content, quality, and administration	• 4.0 on a scale from 1-5	• Reaction questionnaire	• Participants	• At the intro of the program • End of course • End of semester	• Program Administrator • Faculty • Program Administrator
2	**LEARNING** • Maintain above-average grades • Understand the purpose and the participant's role of the program	• 3.0 grade point average out of a possible 4.0 • 4.0 on a scale from 1-5	• Formal and informal testing in each course • Questionnaire at the end of initial meeting	• Participants • Participants	• End of each course • At the intro of the program	• Faculty • Faculty

Figure 9-1. Data Collection Plan (continued)

3	**APPLICATION/ IMPLEMENTATION** • Use of the knowledge and skills on the job • Develop and apply innovative projects to add operational value • Enjoy a very high completion rate	• Various measures on a scale of 1-5 • Completion of project • Completion rate of 80%	• Questionnaires • Action Plans • Monitoring Records	• Participants • Participants • Agency Records	• End of each year • One year follow-up • End of Program	• Program Administrator • Program Administrator • Program Administrator
4	**BUSINESS IMPACT** • Reduce avoidable turnover • Improve job satisfaction/commitment • Career Enhancement • Upgrade technology and agency capability • Improve operational results • Recruiting success	• Number of avoidable exits each month divided by the average number each month • 4.0 on a scale of 1-5 • Monetary values • Number of candidates	• Monitoring records • Questionnaires • Action Plans • Monitoring Records	• Agency Records • Participants • Managers • Participants • Agency Records	• Monthly • End of each year • End of Program • One year follow-up	• HR Staff • Program Administrator • Program Administrator • Program Administrator
5	**ROI** • Achieve a 25% Return on Investment					

Comments: _____

_____

_____

distributed where the participants indicated the success of the program in three areas:

1. The opportunities to use the skills and knowledge learned in the program
2. The extent to which the skills have actually been used on the job
3. The effectiveness in the use of the skills

In addition, several questions focused on the progress with (and barriers to) the implementation of the program. At this level of analysis, it was important to determine if the program material was actually being used on the job. Program statistics were collected, including dropout and completion rates of the participants.

Because the program was implemented to focus on retention of specialists, the primary business measure was turnover. Turnover rates for the participants in the program were compared directly with individuals not involved in the program to determine if the rates were significantly reduced. In addition to avoidable turnover, tenure of employees was tracked, which reflected the average length of service of the target job group. It was anticipated that the program would have an impact on a variety of other business measures as well, including the following:

1. Productivity (from projects)
2. Quality (from projects)
3. Enhanced agency capability
4. Technology upgrade
5. Job satisfaction
6. Employee commitment
7. Recruiting success
8. Career enhancement

In the planning process, it was decided that these measures would be explored to the extent feasible to identify improvements. If not, the perceived changes in these business measures would be collected directly from the participants.

Graduate Projects

An important part of the program was a graduate work-study project required to complete the master's degree. The project involved at least two semesters of work and provided six hours of credit. It was supervised by a faculty member and approved by the participants' immediate manager. The project had to add value to the agency in some way as well as improve agency capability, operations, or technology upgrade. At the same time, it should be rigorous enough to meet the requirements of the university. In a sense, it was a master's thesis although the participants were enrolled in a nonthesis option. Through this project, the participants were able to apply what they had learned. The project was identified during the first year, approved and implemented during the second year, and completed in the third year.

This project provided an excellent opportunity for participants to support the agency and add value to agency operations. As part of the project, participants developed an action plan detailing how their project would be used on the job. The action plan, built into the graduate project, provided the timetable and detail for application of the project. A part of the action plan is a detail of the monetary contribution to the agency (or forecast of the contribution). That was required as part of the project and, ultimately, became evidence of contribution of the project. Follow-up on the action plan provided the monetary amount of contribution from the graduate project.

Data Collection Summary

Table 9-3 shows a summary of the various instruments used to collect data, along with the level of evaluation data. As this table reveals, data collection was comprehensive, continuous, and necessary for a program with this much exposure and expense. Data collected at Levels 1, 2, and 3 were used to make adjustments in the program. Adjustments were made throughout the program as feedback was obtained. This action is particularly important for administrative and faculty-related issues.

ROI Analysis Plan

Figure 9-2 presents a completed planning document for the ROI analysis. This plan, which was completed prior to the beginning of the program, addresses key issues of isolating the influence of the program, converting the data to monetary values, and costing the program. As Figure 9-2 reveals, avoidable turnover, the key data item, is listed along with the technology and operations improvement expected from individual graduate projects. It was anticipated that the program would pay off on turnover and improvements from projects.

Recruiting success is also listed as a measure for potential isolation and conversion. An increase in the number of applicants interested in employment

Table 9-3. Data Summary by Evaluation Level

	Type of Instrument	Reaction/ Satisfaction	Learning	Application/ Implementation	Business Impact
1.	Questionnaire after intro to program	X	X		
2.	End-of-course instructor evaluation	X			
3.	End-of-semester evaluation questionnaire	X			
4	Individual course tests		X		
5.	Annual evaluation questionnaire			X	
6.	Action plans with follow up			X	X
7	One-year follow-up questionnaire			X	X
8.	Monitoring records				X

with FIA was anticipated as the communication and publicity surrounding the program became known in various recruiting channels. Other business impact measures were considered to be intangible and are listed in the intangible benefits column. Intangible benefits are defined as those measures purposely not converted to monetary values. During the planning stage, it was anticipated that measures such as improved job satisfaction, enhanced agency capability, and improved organizational commitment would not be converted to monetary value. Although very important, these measures would be listed as intangible benefits—only if they were linked to the program.

The cost categories discussed earlier were detailed in this planning document. Costs are fully loaded and include both direct and indirect categories. The communication targets were comprehensive. Seven groups were identified as needing specific information from this study.

The ROI analysis and data collection plans provide all the key decisions about the project prior to the actual data collection and analysis.

Isolating the Effects of the Program

Several methods were used to isolate the effects of the program, depending on the specific business impact measure. For avoidable turnover,

Figure 9-2. ROI analysis plan

Program: MS In Information Science   Responsibility: _____   Date: _____

Data Items (Usually Level 4)	Methods for Isolating the Effects of the Program/Process	Methods of Converting Data to Monetary Values	Cost Categories	Intangible Benefits	Communication Targets for Final Report	Other Influences/Issues During Application	Comments
Avoidable Turnover	• Comparison Group • Participants' Estimates • Manager Estimates	• External Studies	• Initial Analysis • Program Development • Tuition • Participant Salaries/Benefits • Program Coordination Costs • Facilities • Management Time • Evaluation	• Improved Job Satisfaction • Improved Operational Commitment • Career Enhancement • Enhanced Agency Capability • Technology Upgrade	• Participants • Immediate Managers of Participants • Program Sponsor • Senior Agency Administrators • Agency HR Staff • RSU Administrators • All Agency Employees	• Need to monitor external employment conditions • Need to identify other potential internal influences on turnover reductions	Payoff of program will probably rest on turnover reduction and improvements from projects
Technology and Operating Improvements	• Participants' Estimates	• Standard Values • Historical Costs • Expert Input • Participants' Estimates					
Recruiting Success	• Participants' Estimates	• Internal Expert Estimates					

three methods were initially planned. A comparison group was identified, which would serve as the control group in a traditional control group experiment. The individuals selected for the master's program would be matched with others not in the program, using the same tenure and job status characteristics. Recognizing the difficulty of success with a control group arrangement, both the participants and managers were asked to indicate the percent of the turnover reduction they believed to be directly related to this program. A questionnaire was provided to obtain this input.

For the technology and operations improvement data, participants' estimates were used as a method for isolating the effects of the program using data from action plans for the projects. The same approach was planned for isolating the effects of the program on recruiting success.

Converting Data to Monetary Values

The methods used to convert data to monetary values varied as well. For avoidable turnover, external studies were used to pinpoint the approximate value. From various databases, studies in similar job categories had revealed that the cost of turnover for these specialized job groups was somewhere between two and three times the average annual salary. This was considerably higher than the HR staff at FIA anticipated. As a compromise, a value of 1.75 times the annual salary was used. While this value is probably lower than the actual fully loaded cost of turnover, it is conservative to assign this value. It is much better to use a conservative estimate for this value than to calculate the fully loaded cost for turnover. Most retention specialists would agree that 175% of annual pay is a conservative, fully loaded cost of turnover for information specialists.

To obtain the monetary values of project improvements, participants were asked to use one of four specific methods to identify the value:

1. Standard values were available for many items throughout the agency, and their use was encouraged when placing monetary values on a specific improvement.
2. Historical costs could be used, capturing the various costs of a specific data item as it is improved, by the project. These cost savings values are taken directly from general ledger accounts and provide a very credible cost value.
3. If neither of the above methods is feasible, expert input, using internal sources was suggested.

4. Finally, if the other methods failed to produce a value, participants were instructed to place their own estimates for the value. In those cases, the confidence of the estimate would be obtained.

RESULTS

Reaction Measurements

Reaction measurements, taken during the initial program introductions, were informal and confirmed that the participants recognized the value of the program and its usefulness to them as well as the agency. Also, any concerns about the difficulty of the program were addressed during that meeting.

Two opportunities to collect reaction and satisfaction data occurred at the end of each semester. For each course, the instructor obtained direct feedback using standard instrumentation. Table 9-4 shows the faculty evaluation selected for this program. It was a slightly modified version of what RSU normally collects for its instructors. In addition to providing feedback to various RSU department heads, this information was provided to the program administrator as well as the major sponsor for this project. This constant data flow was an attempt to make adjustments if the faculty was perceived to be unresponsive and ineffective in delivering the desired courses. As Table 9-4 shows, on a scale from one to five, the responses were extremely effective. The only concerns expressed were with the presentation and ability to relate to agency needs. At several different times, adjustments were made in an attempt to improve these two areas. The ratings presented in Table 9-4 were the cumulative ratings over the three-year project for the 100 participants who initially began the program.

Table 9-4. Reaction to the Faculty

Issue	Average Rating*
Knowledge of Topic	4.35
Preparation for Classes	4.25
Delivery / Presentation	3.64
Level of Involvement	4.09
Learning Environment	4.21
Responsiveness to Participants	4.31
Ability to Relate to Agency Needs	3.77

*On a 1-5 scale, with 5 = exceptional

Table 9-5. Measures of Reaction to the Program

Issue	Average Rating*
Value of Program	4.7
Difficulty of Program	4.1
Usefulness of Program	4.5
Quality of Faculty	3.8
Quality of Program Administration	4.4
Appropriateness of Course Material	3.9
Intent to Use Course Material	4.2
Amount of New Information	3.7
Recommendation to Others	4.6

*On a 1-5 scale, with 5 = exceptional

At the end of each semester, a brief scanable questionnaire was collected to measure satisfaction with and reaction to the program. Table 9-5 shows the various items rated on this questionnaire. The goal was to have a composite of at least four out of five for this program, and it was achieved. The only areas of concern were the quality of the faculty, the amount of new information, and the appropriateness of the course material. Adjustments were made to improve these areas.

Learning Measurements

Learning was primarily measured through formal testing processes used by individual faculty members. As stated earlier, a variety of methods were used ranging from objective testing to simulations. The tests yielded an individual grade that translated into a grade point average. The grade objective for the overall program was to maintain a 3.0 grade point average out of a possible 4.0. Table 9-6 shows the cumulative grade point average through the three-year period ending with an average of 3.18, exceeding the target for the overall program.

Application and Implementation Measures

Application and implementation were measured with three instruments: the annual questionnaire at the end of each program year, the follow-up on the action plans, and a one-year follow-up questionnaire. The two questionnaires (annual and follow-up) provided information about overall application and use of the program and course material. Table 9-7 shows the categories of data for the annual questionnaire, which, for the most part, was duplicated in the follow-up questionnaire. As this table reveals, nine topical areas were explored with the focus on the extent to which the participants were using the program and the skills and knowledge learned. It also explored improvements and accomplishments over and above the individual project improvement. Barriers and enablers to implementation were detailed, in addition to input on the management support for the program, along with recommendations for improvement.

Table 9-6. Cumulative Grade Point Averages

Learning Measures	
Year	Cumulative Grade Point Average
Year 1	3.31
Year 2	3.25
Year 3	3.18

*Out of a possible 4.0

Several questions were devoted to each of these categories. For example, Table 9-8 presents application data for knowledge and skills, showing four specific areas and the ratings obtained for each. While these ratings reveal success, there was some concern about the frequency of use and opportunity to use skills. The input scale for these items was adjusted to job context. For example, in the frequency of skills, the range of potential responses was adjusted to reflect anticipated responses and, consequently, in some cases it may have missed the mark. Some skills should be infrequently used because of the skills and the opportunity to use them. Thus, low marks on these two categories were not particularly disturbing considering the varied nature of program application.

Business Impact

Although business data was monitored in several ways, the annual and follow-up questionnaire obtained input on the perceived linkage with impact measures. As shown in Table 9-7, the third category of data provided the opportunity for participants to determine the extent to which this program influenced several impact measures. As far as actual business improvement value, two data items were converted to monetary values: turnover and project application.

Table 9-7. Categories of Data for Annual Questionnaire

- Course Sequencing / Availability
- Use of Skills / Knowledge
- Linkage with Impact Measures
- Improvements / Accomplishments
- Project Selection and Application

- Barriers to Implementation
- Enablers to Implementation
- Management Support for Program
- Recommendations for Improvement

Table 9-8. Application Data: Use of Knowledge and Skills

Issue	Average Rating*
Opportunity to use skills / knowledge	3.9
Appropriateness of skills / knowledge	4.1
Frequency of use of skills / knowledge	3.2
Effectiveness of use of skills / knowledge	4.3

*On a 1-5 scale, with 5 = exceptional

Turnover Reduction. The primary value of the program would stem from annual turnover reduction of the target group. Table 9-9 shows the annualized, avoidable turnover rates for three different groups. The first is the total group of 1,500 specialists in this job category. The next group is the program participants, indicating that of the 100 initial participants, 12 left during the program (5 percent, 4 percent, 3 percent), and three left in the first year following completion, for a total of 15 in the four-year timespan. For the similar comparison group, 100 individuals were identified and the numbers were replenished as turnover occurred. As the numbers revealed, essentially the entire comparison group had left the agency by the end of the third year. This comparison underscores the cumulative effect of an excessive turnover rate. Using the comparison group as the expected turnover rate yields a total expected turnover of 138 in the four-year period (34 percent, 35 percent, 33 percent, and 36 percent). The actual, however, was 15 for the same period. Thus, the difference in the two groups (138 - 15) equals 123 turnover statistics prevented with this program, using the control group arrangement to isolate the results of the program.

The participants and managers provided insight into the percent of the turnover reduction attributed to the program. For their estimate, the process starts with the difference measured in the total group compared to the actual. Using a base of 100, the total group was expected to have 144

Table 9-9. Turnover data

Annualized Avoidable Turnover	1 Year Prior to Program	1st Year Sept to Aug	2nd Year Sept to Aug	3rd Year Sept to Aug	1 Year Post Program
Total Group 1,500	38%	39%	36%	35%	34%
Program participants Group	N/A	5% (5 participants)	4% (4 participants)	3% (3 participants)	3% (3 participants)
Similar Group	N/A	34%	35%	33%	36%

Four-Year Expected Turnover Statistics = 138
Four-Year Actual Turnover Statistics = 15
Four-Year Total Group Turnover Statistics = 144 (with a base of 100)

turnover statistics (39 percent, 36 percent, 35 percent, and 34 percent). The difference between the total group and the actual turnover statistic is 129 (144 - 15 = 129). Because there were other contributing factors, participants were asked to indicate what percentage of this reduction they attributed to the program. The participants' and managers' estimates were combined (using a simple average to reflect equal weight) to yield a 93 percent allocation to this program. The confidence estimate for this value is 83 percent (the average of the two).

Obviously, both groups realized that this program was accomplishing its major goal of reducing turnover. Thus, if 129 are adjusted by 93 percent and 83 percent, the yield is 100 turnover statistics. Given the choice of using 123 or 100, the lower number is used, although it might not be as credible as the actual control group comparisons. It is conservative to indicate that at least 100 turnover statistics were prevented in the four-year time frame for this analysis.

The value for the turnover reduction is rather straightforward, with 1.75 times the annual earnings used as a compromised value. The total value of the turnover improvement is 100 X $47,800 X 1.75 = $8,365,000. This is a significant, yet conservative, value for the turnover reduction.

Project Values. The participants developed projects that were designed to add value to the agency by improving capability and operations. Table 9-10 shows the summary of the data from the projects. Eighty-eight individuals graduated from the program, and all had approved and implemented projects. Of that number, 74 actually provided data on their project completion in the one-year follow-up on their action plan. Of that number, 53 were able to convert the project to a monetary value. The participants were asked to estimate the amount of improvement that was directly related to the project (percent), recognizing that other factors could have influenced the results. The values are reported as adjusted values in Table 9-10. Only 46 of those were useable values, as unsupported claims and unrealistic values were omitted from the analysis. For example, the highest value ($1,429,000) was eliminated because of the shock value of this number and the possibility of error or exaggeration. The average confidence estimate was 62 percent. When each project value is multiplied by the individual confidence estimate, the total adjusted usable value is $1,580,000.

Table 9-10. Monetary Values from Project

Number of Projects Approved and Implemented	88
Number of Projects Reporting Completion	74
Number of Projects Reporting Monetary Values	53
Number of Projects with Usable Monetary Values	46
Average Value of Project - Adjusted	$ 55,480
Highest Value of Project - Adjusted	$ 1,429,000*
Lowest Value of Project - Adjusted	$ 1,235
Average Confidence Estimate	62%
Total Value (Adjusted twice)	**$ 1,580,000**

*Discarded in the analysis

Intangibles

The intangible benefits were impressive with this program. Recruiting success was not converted to monetary value, but included instead as a subjective intangible value. All of the intangible measures listed in the initial data collection plan were linked to the program, according to participants or managers. A measure was listed as an intangible if at least 25 percent of either group perceived it as linked to the program. Thus, the intangibles were not included in the monetary analysis but were considered to be important and included in the final report.

BCR and ROI Calculations for Turnover Reduction

The benefits-cost ratio (BCR) is the total monetary benefits divided by the total program costs. For turnover reduction, the BCR calculation becomes:

$$BCR = \frac{\text{Monetary Benefits}}{\text{Total Program Costs}} = \frac{\$8,365,000}{\$3,931,957} = 2.13$$

The ROI calculation for the turnover reduction is the net program benefit divided by the cost. In formula form it becomes:

$$ROI = \frac{\text{Monetary Benefits - Total Program Costs}}{\text{Total Program Costs}} = \frac{\$4,433,043}{\$3,931,957} \text{ X } 100 = 113\%$$

BCR and ROI Calculations for Total Improvement

The BCR for the value obtained on turnover reduction and project completion yields the following:

$$BCR = \frac{\$8,365,000 + \$1,580,000}{\$3,931,957} = \frac{\$9,945,000}{\$3,931,957} = 2.53$$

The ROI—Usable program benefits for the two improvements—is as follows:

$$ROI = \frac{\$9,945,000 - \$3,931,957}{\$3,931,957} = \text{ X } 100 = 153\%$$

Communicating Results

Because these are large values, it was a challenge to communicate them convincingly to the senior team. The conservative nature of this approach helps defend the analysis and make the results more credible and believable.

The step-by-step results were presented to the senior team using the following sequence:

1. A brief review of the project and its objectives
2. Overview of the methodology
3. Assumptions used in the analysis
4. Reaction and satisfaction measures
5. Learning measures
6. Application and implementation measures
7. Business impact measures
8. ROI
9. Intangibles
10. Barriers and enablers
11. Interpretation and conclusions
12. Recommendations

This information was presented to the senior team in a one-hour meeting and provided an opportunity to present the methodology and results. This meeting had a three-fold purpose:

1. Present the methodology and assumptions for capturing the ROI, building credibility with the process and analysis
2. Using a balanced approach, show the impact of a major initiative and how it provides a payoff for the agency and taxpayers
3. Show how the same type of solution can be implemented and evaluated in the future
   The project was considered a success.

Questions for Discussion

1. Can the value of this program be forecasted? If so, how?
2. Most of these costs are estimated or rounded off. Is this appropriate? Explain.
3. What issues surface when developing cost data? How can they be addressed?
4. Are the ROI values realistic? Explain.
5. Is this study credible? Explain.
6. How can this type of process be used to build support for programs in the future? Explain.

Chapter 10

Measuring ROI in an Absenteeism Reduction Program

Metro Transit Authority

by Jack J. Phillips

This case illustrates how changes in human resource policies and selection processes can reduce absenteeism and prevent major problems in business operations. Because of unscheduled absences, the unavailability of bus drivers caused route schedule delays and bottlenecks, which resulted in dissatisfied customers, a loss of revenue, and increased operating costs. New guidelines and disciplinary policies for unscheduled absences, as well as a change in hiring practices, were initiated to correct the situation. The ability to demonstrate the costs associated with the absenteeism problem led to the two solutions being implemented. The evaluation team was able to isolate the effects of each of the two HR initiatives and calculate the operational savings to demonstrate an impressive return on investment.

BACKGROUND

The Metro Transit Authority (MTA) operates a comprehensive transportation system in a large metropolitan area. Over 1,000 buses operate regularly, providing essential transportation to citizens in the metro area. Many passengers depend on the bus system for their commute to and from work, as well as other essential travel. MTA employs over 2,900 drivers to operate the bus system around the clock.

This case was prepared to serve as a basis for discussion rather than to illustrate either effective or ineffective administrative and management practices. The authors, dates, places, names and organizations may have been disguised at the request of the author or organization.

As with many transit systems, Metro has been experiencing excessive absenteeism with drivers and the problem continues to grow. Just three years ago, absenteeism was 7 percent compared to the most recent 3-month period of 8.7 percent - too excessive to keep the transit system operating in a consistent manner.

To ensure that buses run on time, a pool of substitute drivers are employed to fill in for unexpected absences. The number of drivers in the pool is a function of the absenteeism rate. At present, the pool consists of 231 substitute drivers. When the drivers in the pool are not utilized in a substitute assignment, they perform almost no essential work for the Transit Authority although they are required to report to work. When a substitute driver is used, there is usually a delay in the bus schedule, as the bus is late for subsequent stops.

Causes of Problems and Solutions

To determine the cause of absenteeism, an analysis was conducted using focus groups, interviews, and an analysis of human resources records. Focus groups included drivers and their supervisors. Interviews were conducted with supervisors and managers. HR records were examined for trends and patterns in absenteeism. The conclusions from the analysis were as follows:

- Individuals who are frequently absent have a pattern of absenteeism that dates back to the beginning of their employment and in most cases, was present in other employment situations.
- Many of the absences could be avoided. The problem is primarily a motivation and discipline issue.
- The prevailing attitude among employees is to take advantage of the system whenever possible, up to the threshold of being terminated.

As a result of these findings, Metro initiated two processes:

1. **A no-fault disciplinary system was implemented.** With this policy, an employee who experiences more than six unexpected (unplanned) incidences in a six-month period was terminated— no questions asked. A sickness that extends more than one day was considered

on incidence. Thus, the policy would not unfairly penalize those who are absent for legitimate sickness or for scheduled surgery and other medical attention. The no-fault system was implemented after extensive negotiations with the union. When union officials realized the impact of excessive absenteeism, they agreed with the new policy.

2. **The selection process for new drivers was modified.** During the initial screening, a list of questions was developed and used to screen out applicants who had a history of absenteeism dating back to their high school days. The questions, with scoring and interpretation, were added to the current selection process and required approximately 30 minutes of additional time during the initial employment interview.

To bring appropriate attention to the absenteeism issue and to generate results as soon as possible, both solutions were implemented at the same time.

Objectives of the Solutions

The expected outcomes were established early in the form of implementation and impact objectives. The objectives of the two initiatives were to:

- Communicate the no-fault policy, including how the policy would be applied and the rationale for it
- Experience little or no adverse reaction from current employees as the no-fault absenteeism policy was implemented
- Maintain present level of job satisfaction as the absenteeism solutions were implemented and applied
- Use the new screening process for each selection decision so that a systematic and consistent selection process would be in place
- Implement and enforce the no-fault policy consistently throughout all operating units
- Reduce driver absenteeism at least 2 percent during the first year of implementation of the two solutions
- Improve customer service and satisfaction with a reduction in schedule delays caused by absenteeism

Supervisors were required to conduct meetings with their employees to explain the need for the policy and how it would be applied. Supervisors completed a meeting report form after the meeting and returned it to HR department.

The no-fault policy has the potential of influencing employment termination, essentially increasing employee turnover, which could create problems for some supervisors. Because of this, it was important to demonstrate to the management team that these programs are effective when they are administered properly. Also, senior management was interested in knowing the payoff for these types of initiatives; they need to be convinced that there is an adequate return on investment.

ROI PLANNING

Data Collection Plan

Figure 10-1 shows the Data Collection Plan for the absenteeism reduction initiatives at Metro Transit Authority. The objectives are defined and the data collection methods selected are typical for those types of programs. For Level 4 data, absenteeism is monitored on a post-program basis and compared to pre-program data. Table 10-1 shows the absenteeism for the year prior to and after implementing both the no-fault policy and the new selection process. A complete year of data was collected to show the full impact of both initiatives to capture the delayed effect in influencing the absenteeism measure. In addition, schedule delays of more than 5 minutes caused by unexpected absenteeism was monitored and is reported in Table 10-1.

Also, for implementation and business measures, a questionnaire was developed and administered to a sample of supervisors to determine the extent to which the programs have been implemented and are perceived to be operating effectively. Input was sought on problems and issues as well as success stories and changes in job satisfaction.

Learning measures were taken with a simple ten-item, true/false test. To ensure that employees understood the policy, the test was developed to be administered by supervisors in their meetings with employees. Scores were attached with the record of the meeting along with the time, place, and agenda and a list of the attendees. A sample of the test scores revealed an average value above the minimum acceptable level of 70.

Reaction measures were taken with a simple questionnaire using an objective format. The questionnaire was distributed at the meetings to obtain reaction to the no-fault policy.

Figure 10-1. Data Collection Plan

Level	Broad Program Objective(s)	Measures	Data Collection Method/Instruments	Data Sources	Timing	Responsibilities
1	**REACTION & SATISFACTION** • Positive Employee Reaction to the No Fault Policy	• Positive reaction from employees	• Feedback Questionnaire	• Employees	• At the end of employee meetings	• Supervisors
2	**LEARNING** • Employee understanding of the policy	• Score on post test, at least 70	• True/False test	• Employees	• At the end of the employee meetings	• Supervisors
3	**APPLICATION/ IMPLEMENTATION** 1. Effective and consistent implementation and enforcement of the programs 2. Little or no adverse reaction from current employees regarding No Fault policy 3. Use the new screening process	1. Supervisors' response on program's influence 2. Employee complaints and union cooperation	1. & 2. Follow-up questionnaire to supervisors (2 sample groups) 3. Sample review of interview and selection records	1. Supervisors 2. Company records	1. Following emp. meetings, sample 1 group at 3 months and another group at 6 months 2. Three mos. and six mos. after implementation	• HR Program Coordinator

Figure 10-1. Data Collection Plan *(continued)*

4	**BUSINESS IMPACT**			
	1. Reduce driver absenteeism at least 2% during first year 2. Maintain present level of job satisfaction as new policy is implemented 3. Improved customer service and satisfaction with reduction in schedule delays	1. Absenteeism 2. Employee Satisfaction 3. Delays impact on customer service	1. Monitor absenteeism 2. Follow-up questionnaire to supervisors 3. Monitor bus schedule delays	1. Company records 2. Supervisors 3. Dispatch records	1. Monitor monthly analyze 1 year pre and 1 year post imp 2. Three months and six months after employee meetings 3. Monthly	• HR Program Coordinator
5	**ROI** Target ROI ≥ 25%	**Comments:**				

Table 10-1. Absenteeism and Bus Delays Before and After Implementation

	Unscheduled Absenteeism Percent of Scheduled Days Worked		Absenteeism Related Bus Delays Percent of All Delays	
	PRE	POST	PRE	POST
July	7.2	6.3	23.3	18.3
August	7.4	5.6	24.7	18.0
September	7.1	5.0	24.9	17.5
October	7.8	5.9	26.1	18.2
November	8.1	5.3	25.4	16.7
December	8.4	5.2	26.3	15.9
January	8.7	5.4	27.1	15.4
February	8.5	4.8	26.9	14.9
March	8.6	4.9	26.8	14.7
April	8.5	4.9	27.8	14.4
May	8.8	4.0	27.0	13.6
June	8.8	4.9	26.4	13.7
Three-Month Average	8.7%	4.8%	27.1%	13.9%

Figure 10-2 shows the ROI analysis plan for evaluation of the absenteeism reduction initiatives. Major elements of the plan are discussed below.

Isolating the Effects of the Solutions

Several approaches were considered for the purpose of isolating the effects of the two solutions. Initially, a control group arrangement was considered, but was quickly discarded for three important reasons:

1. To purposefully withhold the policy change for a group of employees could create contractual and morale problems for the individuals in the control group.
2. Because the new policy would be known to all employees, contamination would occur in the control group, at least temporarily, as employees learned about the "crackdown' on absenteeism. The policy would have the short-term effect of reducing absenteeism in those areas where it is not implemented.
3. Because of the operational problems and customer service issues associated with absenteeism, it was not desirable to withhold a needed solution just for experimental purposes.

Trend line analysis was initially feasible since only a small amount of variance was noticeable in the pre-program trend data that had

Figure 10-2. ROI Analysis Plan

Program: Absenteeism Reduction   Responsibility: Date:

Data Items (Usually Level 4)	Methods for Isolating the Effects of the Program/Process	Methods of Converting Data to Monetary Values	Cost Categories	Intangible Benefits	Communication Targets for Final Report	Other Influences/Issues During Application	Comments
1. Absenteeism	1. Trend line analysis and Supervisor Estimates	1. Wages & benefits and standard values	<u>Screening Process</u> • Development • Interviewer preparation • Administration • Materials <u>No Fault Policy</u> • Development • Implementation • Materials	• Sustain employee satisfaction • Improve employee morale • Improve customer satisfaction • Fewer disruptive bottlenecks in transportation grid • Ease of implementation by supervisors	• Senior management • Managers and supervisors • Union representatives • HR staff	• Concern about supervisors consistent administration • Partner with Union reps on how to communicate results of study to employees	
2. Employee Job Satisfaction	2. Supervisor estimates	N/A					
3. Bus Schedule Delays (Influence on Customer Satisfaction)	3. Management estimates	N/A					

developed. Because of the possibility of this option, in the planning stage, trend line analysis was considered as a method to estimate the impact of both absenteeism initiatives. However, because multiple influences on absenteeism later developed, such as a change in economic conditions, the trend line analysis was aborted.

Finally, as a backup strategy, estimations were taken directly from supervisors as they completed the follow-up questionnaire. Supervisors were asked to identify various factors, which had influenced the absenteeism rate and allocate percentages to each of the factors, including the new screening process and no fault policy.

Converting Data to Monetary Values

Since the primary business measure is absenteeism, a monetary value had to be developed for the cost of an unexpected absence. The value could subsequently be used to calculate the total cost of the absenteeism improvement. While there are several approaches to determine the cost of absenteeism, the analysis at Metro was based on the cost of replacement driver staffing.

Substitute drivers, as well as the regular drivers, are expected to work an average of 240 days per year, leaving 20 days for vacation, holidays, and sick days. The average wages for the substitute drivers is $33,500 per year and the employee benefits factor is 38% of payroll. When a regular driver is unexpectedly absent, he or she may charge the absence either to sick leave or vacation, thus substituting a planned paid day (vacation) for the unexpected absence.

The number of substitute drivers planned was a function of expected absenteeism. Consequently, the substitute driver staffing level did not always meet the exact level needed for a specific day's unscheduled absences. Because of the service problems that could develop as a result of understaffing, the company planned for an excessive number of substitute drivers for most days.

To minimize potential delays, all substitute drivers are required to report to work each day. Substitute drivers not utilized in driver seats essentially perform no productive work that could be counted as added value. During the previous year, over staffing occurred about 75 percent of the time for weekdays and non-holidays. This overstaffing represented 4,230 days of wasted time. During the weekends and holidays, which represent 114 days, overstaffing occurred almost half of the time, representing a total of 570 wasted days.

On some days, there was actually a shortage of substitute drivers, which causes the buses to run late and overtime must be used to make the adjustment. During the last year there had been 65 instances where a driver was not available, and it was estimated that in 45 of those situations, a regular driver was paid double time to fill in the schedule. In the other 15 situations, the bus route was cancelled.

Average daily cost of wages and benefits for a substitute driver:

$$\$33,500 \times 1.38 \div 240 = \$192.63$$

Approximate cost of overstaffing, weekdays:

$$192.63 \times 4,230 = \$814,800$$

Approximate cost of overstaffing, weekends and holidays:

$$192.63 \times 570 = \$109,800$$

Approximate cost of understaffing, overtime (only one salary is used for double-time pay):

$$192.63 \times 45 = \$8,670$$

Approximate cost of recruiting, training, maintaining, and supervising pool of drivers:

$$33,500 \times 231 \times 0.25 = \$1,934,600$$

Costs for Solutions

The cost for the new screening process contains four components: development, interviewer preparation, administrative time, and materials.

The total development cost, including pilot testing, was $20,000. An additional $5,000 was charged for preparing the interviewers to administer the test. The materials and time were variable costs, depending on the number of drivers employed. About 400 drivers were hired each year. For each new driver hired, an average of three candidates are interviewed. Thus, 1,200 interviews are conducted each year, with an average time of 30 minutes each. The average hourly wage for the interviewers is $14.50 per hour. The materials are $2 per test. Table 10-2 shows the cost of the screening process.

Table 10-2. Cost of Screening Process

Development cost	$20,000
Interviewer preparation	$5,000
Administrative time (1,200 x ½ x $14.50)	$8,700
Materials (1,200 @ $2.00)	$2,400
Total	$36,100

The cost for the no-fault policy included development and implementation. The development cost was incurred internally and was estimated to be $11,000, representing the time of internal specialists. The material distributed to employees accounted for another $3,800. The costs of meetings with all supervisors and with employees were estimated at $16,500. The cost for routine administration was not included because the alternative to continue to administer the no-fault policy is to administer a progressive discipline process, and the two should take about the same amount of time. Table 10-3 shows the cost of the no-fault policy.

Table 10-3. Cost of No-Fault Policy

Development cost	$11,000
Materials	$3,800
Meeting time	$16,500
Total	$31,300

RESULTS
Reaction, Learning, and Application Data
Employees expressed some concern about the new policy, but the overall reaction to the change was favorable. They perceived the new policy to be

fair and equitable. In addition, employees scored an average of 78 on the true /false test about the no-fault policy. A score of 70 on the end-of-meeting test was considered acceptable.

A follow-up questionnaire, administered anonymously to a sample of supervisors, indicated that the policy had been implemented in each area and had been applied consistently. Although supervisors reported some initial resistance from the habitual absenteeism violators, the majority of employees perceived the policy to be effective and fair. The supervisors also reported that the new policy took less time to administer than the previously used progressive discipline approach.

A review of HR records indicated that 95 percent of the supervisors conducted the meeting with employees and completed a meeting report form. In addition, a review of a sample of interviews and selection records indicated that the new screening process was used in every case.

Business Impact

Absenteeism dramatically declined after implementing both processes, yielding an average absenteeism rate of 4.6 percent for the last 3 months of the evaluation period compared to the pre-program rate of 8.7 percent for the same period one year earlier. In the MTA situation, a reduction in absenteeism generates a cost savings only if the substitute driver pool is reduced. Because the pool staffing was directly linked to absenteeism, a significant reduction was realized. Table 10-4 shows the cost savings realized, using the approach to develop calculations described earlier in Table 10-3.

Table 10-4. Cost of Absenteeism Comparisons

Cost Item	One Year Prior to Initiatives	One Year After Initiatives
Cost of overstaffing, weekdays	$814,000	$602,400
Cost of overstaffing, weekends and holidays	$109,800	$51,500
Cost of understaffing	$8,670	$4,340
Cost of recruiting, training, and maintaining driver pool	$1,934,600	$1,287,750
Total cost of absenteeism	**$2,867,070**	**$1,945,990**

In addition, on the questionnaires, supervisors estimated and allocated percentages for the contribution of each factor to absenteeism reduction. The results are presented in Table 10-5.

The bus schedule delays caused by absenteeism declined from an average of 27.1 percent for the three months prior to the initiatives to 13.9 percent for the last three months of the evaluation period.

In addition, several intangible measures were identified, including increased moral, improved customer service, and fewer bottlenecks in the entire system.

Table 10-5. Supervisor Estimates to Isolate the Effects of the Solutions

Factor	Contribution Percentage	Confidence Percentage
No-fault policy	67%	84%
Screening	22%	71%
Economic Conditions	11%	65%
Other	1%	90%

Monetary Benefits

Because the total cost of absenteeism for drivers is known on a before-and-after basis (as shown in Table 10-4) the total savings can be developed as follows:

Pre-Program	$ 2,867,070
Post-Program	$ 1,945,990
Savings	$ 921,080

The contribution of the no fault policy:

$$\$ 921,080 \times 67\% \times 84\% = \$ 518,383 = \$ 518,000$$

The contribution of the new screening process:

$$\$ 921,080 \times 22\% \times 71\% = \$ 143,873 = \$ 144,000$$

Total First Year Benefit = $ 518,000 + $ 144,000 = $ 662,000

Costs

The total costs for both initiatives (shown in Tables 2 and 3) are as follows:

$$\text{Total Costs} = \$\,36,100 + \$\,31,300 = \$\,67,400$$

ROI Calculation

The benefits-cost ratio (BCR) and ROI are calculated as follows:

$$BCR = \frac{\$662,000}{\$67,400} = 9.82$$

$$ROI\ (\%) = \frac{\$662,000 - \$67,400}{\$67,400} \times 100 = 882\%$$

Questions for Discussion

1. What are feasible ways to isolate the effects of the solutions?
2. Can the cost of absenteeism be developed for MTA? Explain.
3. Are the costs of the solutions adequate? Explain.
4. Critique the actual monetary benefits of the reduction in absenteeism.
5. Is this study methodology credible? Explain.
6. Is the ROI value realistic? Explain.
7. How should the results be communicated to various groups?

Chapter

Measuring ROI in
Leadership Development

Global Car Rental

by Patti P. Phillips

This case describes how one organization—a leading car rental corporation—implemented a program to improve profitability and efficiency by developing leadership competencies for first-level managers. The learning and development team was asked to identify measures influenced by this program and link these competencies to job performance and business impact. However, the team was faced with a difficul challenge because it was not given the time, resources, or encouragement to conduct a comprehensive analysis to link the need for leadership development to business needs. Could the participants themselves help with this task?

BACKGROUND

Global Car Rental (GCR) operates in 27 countries with 27,000 employees. The U.S. division has 13,000 employees and operates in most major cities in the United States. The auto rental business is very competitive, and several major firms have been forced into bankruptcy in the last few years. The industry is price sensitive, and customer service is critical. Operating costs must be managed carefully to remain profitable. Senior executives were exploring a variety of ways to improve GCR, and they perceived that developing leadership competencies for first-level managers would be an excellent way to achieve profitable growth and efficiency.

The Need

A recent needs assessment for all functional areas conducted by the learning and development (L&D) staff determined that several leadership competencies were needed for first-level managers. The needs included typical competencies such as problem solving, counseling, motivation, communication, goal setting, and feedback. In addition to developing these competencies, the L&D staff attempted to link the competencies to job performance needs and business needs.

The senior management team, however, did not want the L&D staff to visit all locations to discuss business needs and job performance issues. The senior executives were convinced that leadership skills are needed and that these skills should drive a variety of business measures when applied in the work units. The L&D team was challenged to identify the measures influenced by this particular program. Additionally, top executives were interested in knowing the impact and maybe even ROI for a group of U.S. participants in this program.

This challenge created a dilemma. The L&D staff members realized that for a positive ROI study to be generated, the program should be linked to business needs. They knew, though, that they did not have the time, resources, or the encouragement to conduct a comprehensive analysis linking the need for the leadership development to business needs. The team was faced with the challenge of connecting this program to business impact. They thought that perhaps the participants themselves could help with this task.

Attempting to address the needs, the L&D staff developed a new program, the Leadership Challenge, designed for team leaders, supervisors, and managers who are responsible for those who actually do the work (the first level of management). Program participants were located in rental offices, service centers, call centers, regional offices, and headquarters. Most functional areas were represented, including operations, customer service, service and support, sales, administration, finance and accounting, and information technology. Essentially, this was to be a cross-functional program in the organization.

The Leadership Challenge involved four days of off-site learning with input from the immediate manager who served as a coach for some of the learning processes. Before attending, the program participants had to complete an online pre-training instrument and read a short book. Because few senior executives at GCR had challenged the L&D staff to show the business impact of a program, two groups were evaluated with 36 participants total (i.e., 18 in one group and 18 in the other).

Business Alignment

To link the program to business and job performance needs, prior to attending the program, each manager was asked to identify at least two business measures in the work unit that represent an opportunity for improvement. The measures were available in operating reports, cost statements, or scorecards. The selected measures had to meet an additional two-part test:

1. They had to be under the control of the team when improvements were to be considered.
2. They had to have the potential to be influenced by team members with the manager using the competencies in the program. A description of the program was provided in advance, including a list of objectives and skill sets.

A needs assessment appeared appropriate for the situation, even though there was some concern about whether it could be thorough. The initial needs assessment on competencies uncovered a variety of deficiencies across all the functional units and provided the information necessary for job descriptions, assignments, and key responsibility areas. Although basic, the additional steps taken to connect the program to business impact were appropriate for a business needs analysis and a job performance needs analysis.

Identifying two measures in need of improvement was a simple business needs analysis for the work unit. Restricting the selected measures to only those that could be influenced by the team with the leader using the skills from the program essentially defines a job performance need. (In essence, the individual leader is identifying something that is not currently being done in the work unit that could be done to enhance the business need.) Although more refinement and detail would be preferred, the results of this assessment process should have sufficed for this project.

Objectives

The L&D staff developed the following objectives for the program:

1. Participants will rate the program as relevant to their jobs.
2. Participants will rate the program as important to their job success.
3. Participants must demonstrate acceptable performance on each major competency.
4. Participants will use the competencies with team members on a routine basis.
5. Participants and team members will drive improvements in at least two business measures.

ROI Appropriateness

With the business and job performance needs analyses complete, this program became a good candidate for the ROI. Without these two steps, it would have been difficult to conduct a successful ROI study. A consideration for conducting the ROI study was identifying the drivers for ROI analyses. In this case, the senior team was challenging the value of leadership development. An ROI study should provide convincing evidence about a major program. Also, this was a highly visible program that merited evaluation at this level because it was strategic and expensive. Consequently, the L&D staff pursued the ROI study, and an ROI objective of 20 percent was established.

ROI PLANNING

Data Collection Plan

Figure 11-1 shows the completed data collection plan. Although several data collection methods were possible, the team decided to use a detailed follow-up questionnaire to reflect the progress made with the program. Focus groups, interviews, and observations were considered too expensive or inappropriate. The L&D team explored the possibility of using the 360-degree feedback process to obtain input from team members but elected to wait until the 360-degree program was fully implemented in all units in the organization. Therefore, the questionnaire was deemed the least expensive and least disruptive method.

The questionnaire was sent directly to the participant 3 months after program completion. At the same time, a shorter questionnaire was sent

Figure 11-1. Data Collection Plan for the Leadership Challenge Program

Purpose of This Evaluation _____

Program: _____   Responsibility: _____   Date: _____

Level	Objective(s)	Measures/Data	Data Collection Method	Data Sources	Timing	Responsibilities
1	**Reaction/Satisfaction** • Participants rate the program as relevant to their jobs. • Participants rate the program as important to their job success	• 4 out of 5 on a 5-point rating scale	• Questionnaire	• Participants	• End of Program	• Facilitator
2	**Learning** • Participants demonstrate acceptable performance on each major competency	• 2 out of 3 on a 3-point scale	• Observation of skill practices • Self-assessment via questionnaire	• Facilitator • Participants	• End of Program • End of Program	• Facilitator • Facilitator
3	**Application/Implementation** • Participants utilize the competencies with team members routinely	• Various measures (ratings, open-ended items, and so forth)	• Questionnaire • Questionnaire	• Participants • Participants' managers	• 3 months	• L&D staff
4	**Business Impact** • Participants and team members drive improvements in at least two business measures	• Various work unit measures	• Questionnaire	• Participants	• 3 months	• L&D staff
5	**ROI** • Achieve a 20 percent ROI					

Comments: _____

to the participants' immediate manager. Initially, a 6-month follow-up was considered instead of the 3-month follow-up shown on the data collection plan. However, the L&D staff thought that 6 months was too long to wait for results and too long for managers to make the connection between the program and the results.

Questionnaire Topics

Figure 11-2 shows the email questionnaire used with this group. Important areas explored included application of skills, impact analysis, barriers to application, and enablers. A similar questionnaire that explored the role of the manager in the coaching process was sent to the next level managers without the questions on the impact data.

To achieve a response rate of 81 percent, the L&D team used 12 different techniques:

1. Provide advance communication about the questionnaire.
2. Clearly communicate the reason for the questionnaire.
3. Indicate who will see the results of the questionnaire.
4. Show how the data will be integrated with other data.
5. Communicate the time limit for submitting responses.
6. Review the questionnaire at the end of the formal session.
7. Allow for responses to be anonymous or at least confidential.
8. Provide two follow-up reminders, using a different medium each time.
9. Have the introduction letter signed by a top executive.
10. Enclose a giveaway item with the questionnaire (pen).
11. Send a summary of results to the target audience.
12. Have a third party collect and analyze the data.

Another important techniques was to review the questionnaire with participants—question by question—at the end of the four-day workshop to clarify issues, create expectations, and gain commitment to provide data. Third-party collection was achieved by using automated external data collection. Essentially, the data was sent by email to the data collector's server.

Figure 11-2. Questionnaire for Leaders

Follow-Up Questionnaire	
Program Name	**End Date of Program**

Our records indicate that you participated in the above program. Your participation in this follow-up survey is important to the continuous improvement of the program. Completion of this survey may take 45 to 60 minutes. Thank you in advance for your input.

CURRENCY

1. This survey requires some information to be completed in monetary value. Please indicate the currency you will use to complete the questions requiring monetary value. _____

PROGRAM COMPLETION

2. Did you ☐ complete ☐ partially complete ☐ not complete the program? If you did not complete, go to the final question.

REACTION	Strongly Disagree				Strongly Agree	Not Applicable
	1	2	3	4	5	
3. I recommended the program to others.	☐	☐	☐	☐	☐	☐
4. The program was a worthwhile investment for my organization.	☐	☐	☐	☐	☐	☐
5. The program was a good use of my time.	☐	☐	☐	☐	☐	☐
6. The program was relevant to my work.	☐	☐	☐	☐	☐	☐
7. The program was important to my work.	☐	☐	☐	☐	☐	☐
8. The program provided me with new information.	☐	☐	☐	☐	☐	☐

LEARNING	Strongly Disagree				Strongly Agree	Not Applicable
	1	2	3	4	5	
9. I learned new knowledge/skills from this program.	☐	☐	☐	☐	☐	☐
10. I am confident in my ability to apply the knowledge/skills learned from this program.	☐	☐	☐	☐	☐	☐

Figure 11-2. Questionnaire for Leaders *(continued)*

11. Rate your level of improvement in skill or knowledge derived from the program content. A 0% is no improvement and a 100% is significant improvement. Check only one.

0%	10%	20%	30%	40%	50%	60%	70%	80%	90%	100%
☐	☐	☐	☐	☐	☐	☐	☐	☐	☐	☐

APPLICATION	None				Very Much	Not Applicable
	1	2	3	4	5	
12. To what extent did you apply the knowledge/skills learned during the program?	☐	☐	☐	☐	☐	☐

	Infrequently (unacceptable)				Frequently (acceptable)	Not Applicable
	1	2	3	4	5	
13. How frequently did you apply the knowledge/skills learned during the program?	☐	☐	☐	☐	☐	☐

	Low				High	Not Applicable
	1	2	3	4	5	
14. What is your level of effectiveness with the knowledge/skills learned during the program?	☐	☐	☐	☐	☐	☐
15. Rate the effectiveness of the coach.	☐	☐	☐	☐	☐	☐

	Not Critical				Very Critical	Not Applicable
	1	2	3	4	5	
16. How critical is applying the content of this program to your job success?	☐	☐	☐	☐	☐	☐

	Not Well				Very Well	Not Applicable
	1	2	3	4	5	
17. To what extent did you stay on schedule with your planned actions?	☐	☐	☐	☐	☐	☐

18. What percent of your total work time did you spend on tasks that require the knowledge/skills presented in this program. Check only one.

0%	10%	20%	30%	40%	50%	60%	70%	80%	90%	100%
☐	☐	☐	☐	☐	☐	☐	☐	☐	☐	☐

BARRIERS/ENABLERS TO APPLICATION

19. Which of the following deterred or prevented you from applying the knowledge/skills learned in the program? (check all that apply.)

No opportunity to use the skills	☐
Lack of management support	☐
Lack of support from colleagues and peers	☐
Insufficient knowledge and understanding	☐
Lack of confidence to apply knowledge/skills	☐
Systems and processes within organization will not	☐
support application of knowledge/skills	☐
Other	☐

20. If you selected "other" above, please describe here. _____

_____

21. Which of the following supported you in applying knowledge/skills learned in the program? (check all that apply.)

Opportunity to use the skills	☐
Management support	☐
Support from colleagues and peers	☐
Sufficient knowledge and understanding	☐
Confidence to apply knowledge/skills	☐
Systems and processes within organization will	☐
support application of knowledge/skills	☐
Other	☐

22. If you selected "other" above, please describe here. _____

_____

RESULTS – 1st Measure

23. Please define the first measure you selected and its unit for measurement. For example, if you selected "sales," your unit of measure may be "1 closed sale." _____

_____

24. For this measure, what is the monetary value of improvement for one unit of this measure? For example, the value of a closed sale is sales value times the profit margin ($10,000 x 20%=$2,000). Although this step is difficult, please make every effort to estimate the value of a unit. Put the value in the currency you selected, round to the nearest whole value, enter numbers only. (e.g. $2,000.50 should be input as $2,000.)

_____

25. Please state your basis for the value of the unit of improvement you indicated above. In the closed sale example, a standard value, profit margin, is used, so "standard value" is entered here.

_____

26. For the measure listed as most directly linked to the program, how much has this measure improved in performance? If not readily available, please estimate. If you selected "sales," show the actual increase in sales (e.g., 4 closed sales per month, input the number 4 here). You can input a number with up to 1 decimal point. Indicate the frequency base for the measure. _____

☐ daily   ☐ weekly   ☐ monthly   ☐ quarterly

Figure 11-2. Questionnaire for Leaders *(continued)*

RETURN ON INVESTMENT – 1st Measure

27. What is the annual value of improvement in the measure you selected above? Multiply the increase (question 26) by the frequency (question 26) times the unit of value (question 24). For example, if you selected "sales," multiply the sales increase by the frequency to arrive at the annum value (e.g. 4 sales per month x 12 x 2,000=$96,000). Although this step is difficult, please make every effort to estimate the value. Put the value in the currency you selected, round to nearest whole value, enter numbers only. (E.g. $96,000.50 should be input as 96,000.)

_____

28. List the other factors that could have influenced these results. _____
_____

29. Recognizing that the other factors could have influenced this annual value of improvement, please estimate the percent of improvement that is attributable (i.e. isolated) to the program. Express as a percentage out of 100%. For example, if only 60% of the sales increase is attributable to the program, enter 60 here.
_____%

30. What confidence do you place in the estimates you have provided in the questions above? A 0% is no confidence, a 100% is certainty. Round to nearest whole value, and enter a number only (e.g. 37.5% should be entered as 38).
_____%

RESULTS – 2nd Measure

31. Please define the second measure you selected and its unit for measurement. For example, if you selected "sales," your unit of measure may be "1 closed sale."

_____

32. For this measure, what is the monetary value of improvement for one unit of this measure? For example, the value of a closed sale is sales value times the profit margin ($10,000 x 20%=$2,000). Although this step is difficult, please make every effort to estimate the value of a unit. Put the value in the currency you selected, round to nearest whole value, and enter numbers only (e.g. $2,000.50 should be input as $2,000).

_____

33. Please state your basis for the value of the unit of improvement you indicated above. In the closed sale example, a standard value, profit margin, is used, so "standard value" is entered here.

_____

34. For the measure listed as most directly linked to the program, how much has this measure improved in performance? If not readily available, please estimate. If you selected "sales," show the actual increase in sales (e.g., 4 closed sales per month, input the number 4 here). You can input a number with up to 1 decimal point. Indicate the frequency base for the measure. _____

    ☐ daily   ☐ weekly   ☐ monthly   ☐ quarterly

RETURN ON INVESTMENT – 2nd Measure

35. What is the annual value of improvement in the measure you selected above? Multiply the increase (question 34) by the frequency (question 34) times the unit of value (question 32). For example, if you selected "sales," multiply the sales increase by the frequency to arrive at the annum value (e.g. 4 sales per month x 12 x 2,000=$96,000). Although this step is difficult, please make every effort to estimate the value. Put the value in the currency you selected, round to nearest whole value, and enter numbers only (e.g. $96,000.50 should be input as 96,000).

36. List the other factors that could have influenced these results. _____

_____

37. Recognizing that the other factors could have influenced this annual value of improvement, please estimate the percent of improvement that is attributable (i.e. isolated) to the program. Express as a percentage out of 100%. For example, if only 60% of the sales increase is attributable to the program, enter 60 here.

_____%

38. What confidence do you place in the estimates you have provided in the questions above? A 0% is no confidence; a 100% is certainty. Round to nearest whole value, and enter a number only (e.g. 37.5% should be entered as 38).

_____%

39. What other benefits have been realized from this program? _____

_____

40. Please estimate your direct costs of travel and lodging for your participation in this program. Put the value in the currency you selected, round to nearest whole value, and enter numbers only (e.g. $10,000.49 should be input as $10,000).

_____

41. Please state your basis for the travel and lodging cost estimate above. _____

_____

FEEDBACK

42. How can we improve the training to make it more relevant to your job?

_____

_____

_____

_____

Thank you for taking the time to complete this survey!

ROI Analysis Plan

The completed ROI analysis plan is shown in Figure 11-3. This plan details the specific issues that must be addressed and the particular techniques selected to complete the ROI analysis.

Method of Isolation. The method the L&D team used to isolate the effects of the program proved to be a challenge. Because the managers represented different functional areas, there was no finite set of measures that could be linked to the program for each participant. Essentially, each manager could have a different set of measures as he or she focused on specific business needs in the work unit. Consequently, the use of a control group was not feasible. In addition, the trend line analysis and forecasting methods proved to be inappropriate for the same reason.

Therefore, the evaluation team had to collect estimations directly from participants on the questionnaire. Question 29 isolated the effects of this program using an estimate. Question 30 adjusted for the error of the estimate. The challenge was ensuring that participants understood this issue and were committed to provide data for the isolation.

Converting Data to Monetary Value. The participants provided estimates for converting their selected measures to monetary values. In the planning, the L&D team assumed that there were only a few feasible approaches for participants to place monetary value on measures. Because there was little agenda time to discuss this issue, the L&D staff had to rely on easy-to-obtain data using three options. The good news was that in GCR, as with many other organizations, standard values have been developed for the measures that matter and they were the first option. If a measure is something that the company wants to increase, such as productivity or sales, someone already will have placed a value on that measure to show the contribution of the improvement. If it is a measure the company wants to reduce, such as turnover, accidents, or absenteeism, someone has more than likely placed a monetary value to show the impact of these critical measures. Consequently, the participants were asked to use standard values if they were available.

If these were not available, as a second option participants could call on an internal expert who knew more about that particular measure. In many cases, this person was an individual from the department furnishing a

Figure 11-3. The ROI Analysis Plan

Program: _____ Responsibility: _____ Date: _____

Data Items (Usually Level 4)	Methods for Isolating the Effects of the Program/Process	Methods of Converting Data to Monetary Values	Cost Categories	Intangible Benefits	Communication Targets for Final Report	Other Influences/Issues During Application	Comments
• Varies, depending on measures selected	• Participant estimate	• Standard value • Expert value • Participant estimate	• Needs assessment (prorated) • Program development (prorated) • Facilitation fees • Promotional materials • Facilitation and coordination • Meals and refreshments • Facilities • Participants' salaries and benefits for time away from work • Managers' salaries and benefits for time involved in program • Cost of overhead • Evaluation costs	• Job satisfaction for first-level managers • Job satisfaction for team members • Improved teamwork • Improved communication	• Participants (first-level managers) • Participants' managers • Senior executives • L&D staff • Prospective participants • L&D council members	• Several process improvement initiatives are going on during this program implementation	• Must gain commitment to provide data • A high response rate is needed

particular report because the data came directly from the operating reports. Essentially this was expert input. If no standard was available or experts identified, the last option was for the participants to estimate the value. Because this was a measure that mattered to the participant, he or she should have some perception about the value of improving it.

The actual amount was entered on Question 24. Then, Question 25 provided the basis for showing the details for how that value was developed. Question 25 is critical. If omitted, the business impact measure was removed from the analysis under the guiding principle of not using an unsupported claim in the analysis. Incidentally, the participants were informed about this principle as the questionnaire was reviewed with them at the end of the workshop.

Costs

The costs for the program were typical—analysis, design, development, and delivery components—and represented the fully loaded costs containing both direct and indirect categories.

Other Issues

The L&D team anticipated some intangible benefits and, consequently, added a question to identify improvements in these intangible benefits (Question 39). To ensure that all the key stakeholders were identified, the evaluation team decided which groups should receive the information in the impact study. Six specific groups were targeted for communication. The remainder of the ROI analysis plan listed other issues about the study.

RESULTS

Twenty-nine questionnaires were returned for an 81 percent response rate. Participants provided a rich database indicating success at each level of evaluation.

Reaction Data

Table 11-1 shows the reaction data obtained from the follow-up questionnaire. Although some initial reaction was collected at the end of the workshop using a standard reaction questionnaire, the team decided to collect and present to the senior team the reaction obtained in the follow-up. Each of the reaction measures exceeded the goal of a 4.0 rating, except for the issue about the amount of new information, which was slightly less than the desired level.

Table 11-1. Reaction Data from Participants

Issue	Rating*
Recommended to others	4.2
Worthwhile investment	4.1
Good use of time	4.6
Relevant to my work	4.3
Important to my work	4.1
Provided me with new information	3.9

*Rating scale: 1 = Strongly disagree; 5 = Strongly agree

Learning Data Although several skill practices and self-assessments were taken during the workshop to measure learning, the team decided to present the learning data directly from the follow-up questionnaire. As shown in Table 11-2, the learning measures met or exceeded expectations in terms of the amount of new skills and knowledge and confidence in using them. Also, the average skill or knowledge improvement was 48 percent (Question 11).

Table 11-2. Learning Data from Participants

Issue	Rating*
Learned new knowledge/skills	4.3
Confident in my ability to apply new knowledge/skills	4.1

*Rating: 1 = Strongly Disagree; 5 = Strongly Agree

Application Data

Table 11-3 shows application data obtained in the follow-up questionnaire. The applications exceeded expectations, and the effectiveness of the coach rating was a particular highlight. The percentage of time spent on tasks requiring the use of the acquired knowledge/skills averaged 43 percent

(Question 18). The participants' managers received the questionnaire primarily about the coaching component, and they reported success. They routinely coached the participants when requested and frequently reinforced the use of the skills.

Table 11-3. Application Data from Participants

Issue	Rating*
Extent of use of knowledge/skills	4.3
Frequency of application of knowledge/skills	3.8
Effectiveness with using knowledge/skills	4.3
Effectiveness of coach	4.7
Criticalness to job	4.2
Stay on Schedule	4.1

*Rating: 1=Lowest; 5=Highest

Barriers and Enablers

Much to the surprise of the staff, the barriers were minimal and the enablers were strong. The program enjoyed good management support and was tailored to the job environment. Therefore, few barriers prevented the transfer of learning, and the enablers were built into the program. Table 11-4 shows the barriers and enablers.

Business Impact Data

Business impact data (Level 4) is shown in Table 11-5. This table shows specific improvements identified directly from the questionnaire, by participant number, for the first 15 participants. To save space, the remaining 14 participants are included as a total. Usually, each participant provided improvements on two measures. The total for the second measure is shown at the bottom of Table 11-5.

The top row of Table 11-5 reveals the linkage between the questions on the questionnaire and the columns in this table. The total annual improvement for each measure is reported first. Incidentally, the specific measure was identified and could be reported as well, but to reduce confusion only the measure categories were reported. The heading "Converting Data to

Monetary Value" shows the extent to which the three options were used to convert data to monetary value. Most participants selected "Standard" because standard values were readily available. The column of "Other Factors" indicates the number of other factors that contributed to the results. In most cases several factors were present. No more than four other factors were identified in any section. In a few cases, there were no other factors. In summary, the standard values were used 71 percent of the time, and other factors were identified 85 percent of the time.

Table 11-4. Top Five Barriers and Enablers Identified by Participants

Barrier	Frequency
No Opportunity to Use Skills	14%
Lack of Support from Colleagues and Peers	14%
Insufficient Knowledge and Understanding	10%
Lack of Management Support	7%
Lack of Confidence to Apply Learning	3%

Enablers	Frequency
Management Support	55%
Opportunity to Use Skills	52%
Confidence to Apply Learning	38%
Support from Colleagues and Peers	34%
Sufficient Knowledge and Understanding	34%

ROI Analysis

The total cost of the program, using a fully loaded analysis, is shown in Table 11-6. The needs assessment was prorated over 4 years, based upon the anticipated life cycle of the project. A thousand managers in the United States would attend this program in the four-year time period before another needs assessment was conducted. Program development was prorated over three years assuming that the delivery could change significantly in that timeframe.

Table 11-5. Business Impact Calculations

Participant Number	Annual Improvement (Q27)*	Measure (Q23)*	Converting Data to Monetary Value (Q25)*	Contribution from Program (Q29)*	Other Factors (Q28)*	Confidence Estimate (Q30)*	Adjusted Value†
1	$ 13,100	Sales	Standard	60%	3	80%	$ 6,288
3	41,200	Productivity	Expert	75%	1	95%	29,355
4	5,300	Sales	Standard	80%	1	90%	3,816
6	7,210	Cost	N/A	70%	2	70%	3,533
9	4,215	Efficiency	Standard	40%	3	75%	1,265
10	17,500	Quality	Expert	35%	4	60%	3,675
12	11,500	Time	Standard	60%	2	80%	5,520
14	3,948	Time	Standard	70%	1	80%	2,212
15	14,725	Sales	Standard	40%	3	70%	4,123
17	6,673	Efficiency	Estimate	50%	3	60%	2,002
18	12,140	Costs	N/A	100%	0	100%	12,140
19	17,850	Sales	Standard	60%	2	70%	7,497
21	13,920	Sales	Standard	50%	3	80%	5,568
22	15,362	Cost	N/A	40%	4	90%	5,530
23	18,923	Sales	Standard	60%	1	75%	8,515
				Total for the items above			$ 101,039
				Total for the next 14 items			$ 84,398
				Total for 2nd measure			$ 143,764
				Total Benefits			$ 329,201

* Question numbers in Figure 2 Questionnaire.

† Total Monetary Benefits = Q27 x Q29 x Q30.

The remainder of the costs were directly charged and included the delivery expenses, the salaries for the participants (the first level managers), as well as their managers (second level). The training and education overhead was allocated using a figure of $312 per day of training.

Table 11-6. Summary of Fully Loaded Costs

Cost of Item	Cost
Needs assessment (prorated over 4 years)	$ 900
Program development (prorated over 3 years)	2,000
Program materials ($120/participant)	4,320
Travel, meals, and Lodging ($1,600/participant)	57,600
Facilitation and coordination ($4,000/day)	32,000
Facilities and refreshments ($890/day)	7,120
Participants salaries (plus benefits) for time and program	37,218
Manager salaries (plus benefits) for time involved in program	12,096
Training and education overhead (allocated)	2,500
ROI evaluation costs	5,000
Total for 36 participants	**$ 160,754**

The BCR was calculated as follows:

$$BCR = \frac{\text{Total Benefits}}{\text{Total Costs}} = \frac{\$329,201}{\$160,754} = 2.05$$

The ROI was calculated as follows:

$$ROI = \frac{\text{Net Total Benefits}}{\text{Total Costs}} = \frac{\$329,201 - \$160,754}{\$160,754} \times 100 = 105\%$$

Credibility of Results

The data were perceived to be credible by both the L&D staff and senior management group. Credibility rests on seven major issues:

1. The information for the analysis was provided directly from the new managers. The managers had no reason to be biased in their input.
2. The data was provided anonymously because no one had to provide his or her name on the questionnaire. Anonymity helped eliminate the possibility of bias.

3. The data collection process was conservative under the assumption that an unresponsive individual has realized no improvement. This concept—no data, no improvement—is an ultraconservative approach to data collection.
4. The L&D staff did not assign complete credit to this program. The participants isolated a portion of the data that should be credited directly to this program.
5. The data was adjusted for the potential error of the estimate. Estimates were used to isolate the effects of the program.
6. Only the first year of benefits were used in the analysis. Most of the improvement should result in second and third-year benefits.
7. The costs of the program were fully loaded. All direct and indirect costs were included, including the time away from work for the participants and managers.

The data represents a balanced profile of success. Very favorable reaction, learning, and application data was presented along with business impact, ROI, and intangibles. Collectively, these issues made a convincing case for the program.

Communication Strategy

To communicate appropriately with the target audiences outlined in the ROI analysis plan, the L&D team produced three specific documents. The first report was a detailed impact study showing the approach, assumptions, methodology, and results using all six data categories. In addition, barriers and enablers were included in the study, along with conclusions and recommendations. The second report was an eight-page executive summary of the key points, including a one-page overview of the methodology. The third report was a brief, five-page summary of the process and results. These documents were presented to the different groups according to the plan presented in Table 11-7.

Because this was the first ROI study conducted in this organization, face-to-face meetings were conducted with the executives. The purpose was to ensure that executives understood the methodology, the conservative assumptions, and each level of data. The barriers, enablers, conclusions, and recommendations were an important part of the meeting. In the future, after two or three studies have been conducted, this group will receive only a one-page summary of key data items. A similar meeting was conducted with the L&D council. The council members were advisors to the L&D department who are usually middle and upper-level executives and managers. Finally, a face-to-face meeting was held with the learning and development staff where the complete impact study was described and used as a learning tool.

Table 11-7. Distribution Plan for Leadership Challenge Evaluation Reports

Audience	Document
Participants	Brief summary
Managers of participants	Brief summary
Senior executives	Complete study, executive summary
L&D staff	Complete study
L&D Council	Complete study, executive summary
Prospective participants	Brief summary

Lessons Learned

This case study shows how the evaluation process can be accomplished with minimal resources. The approach shifted much of the responsibility for evaluation to the participants as they collected data, isolated the effects of the program, and converted the data to monetary values—the three most critical steps in the ROI process. The results were easily communicated to various target groups through three specific documents. L&D staff and senior management perceived the data to be credible. The ROI was positive, and the program showed important connections with business results.

Questions for Discussion

1. Is this approach credible? Explain.
2. Is the ROI value realistic?
3. What types of programs would be appropriate for this approach?
4. What additions or revisions could be made to the evaluation strategies provided?
5. What evaluation strategies other than the questionnaire could be used in this situation?

Chapter 12

Measuring ROI in
Effective Meeting Skills

TechnoTel Corporation

by Patti P. Phillips

Long, meaningless meetings can seriously impair workplace productivity. This case study presents the benefits that can be achieved by reducing the length of meetings, the number of meetings, and the number of meeting participants. The program evaluated is a two-day workshop intended to teach managers, supervisors, and project leaders skills in planning, managing, and facilitating the meeting process. A needs assessment, which included dialogue between the Chief Learning Officer and the President of Manufacturing led to the identification of application and business impact measures. Pre-program data were collected using a meeting profile worksheet, and post-program data were collected using a comprehensive questionnaire. Participant estimates were used to isolate the effects of the workshop on the time savings resulting from less time in meetings, fewer meetings, and fewer people attending meetings. Standard values of time (salary and benefits) were used to convert data to monetary values. Fully-loaded program costs were developed.

BACKGROUND

TechnoTel Corporation is a maker of telecommunications equipment. Although the firm has twenty-two locations, this case study takes place in Frankfurt, Germany. A comprehensive needs assessment targeting managerial and supervisory competencies revealed a lack of effective meeting skills, including the ability to prepare, conduct, facilitate, and follow up on meetings. This needs assessment was initiated by a conversation between the Chief Learning Officer (CLO) and the President of Manufacturing in Frankfurt.

The President of Manufacturing explained to the CLO his concerns that the learning function placed too much emphasis on activity. An example of his observation was presented in a meeting with the CEO during which the CLO reminded executives how many programs the learning function was developing. He explained to her in manufacturing the focus is on efficiencies – building more with less while improving quality.

> **President:** In the manufacturing division we focus on efficiencies—building more with less as well as ensuring quality. We recognize that, while the organization is doing well economically, there has to be some way to manage our resources. We want to make sure that we are getting the most for the investments we make, even when we make them in our people.
>
> But, I look around and I see waste—time being one of the biggest waste factors. Meetings and training appear to be unproductive.
>
> For example, my managers and supervisors, as good as they are technically, cannot run an effective meeting. They invite everyone they can think of, with half of the participants sitting around looking at their watches, checking BlackBerries, or configuring process design models. When the meeting is underway, there is no structure and no agenda. The meetings invariably run over the time allotted. On top of this, there is a meeting on everything. My team spends more time meeting than any other group, only to leave the meetings and do nothing as a result of them.

His concern was the time wasted in meetings. According to the president, there were:

- Too many meetings
- Too many people attending the meetings
- Meetings were too long

He explained his concern that time in meetings meant money wasted and productivity lacking. While no definitive dollar amount was known, it was estimated that the cost of lost productivity due to time wasted was in the hundreds of thousands in U.S. dollars per year.

The conversation set the stage for further investigation as to why so many meetings were being held, why too many people were attending the meetings, and why the meetings were too long. With clear instructions not to disrupt productivity any more than necessary, the president agreed to allow the CLO to delve deeper into the cause of the meeting problem by asking some of his staff. Three focus groups, each including eight managers, supervisors, project leaders, and/or employees who participate in meetings on a routine basis, would be conducted to find the cause of the business problems identified by the president.

Focus Groups

Prior to the focus group selection, the president initiated a communiqué explaining that the learning function was in the process of helping him identify the cause of so many meetings in the division. It was also communicated that if a cause was identified, consideration would be given to a variety of solutions. The decision as to which solution would be made based on cost and convenience, as well as potential effectiveness.

Each focus group was scheduled at the plant for a maximum of two hours. Participants were randomly selected from 150 managers, supervisors, and project leaders, along with the employees at large, to participate in the focus group, then randomly assigned to the focus group in which they would participate. In some cases a person identified to participate in the focus group process would have a conflict and could not participate at the designated time. When this occurred, they would swap their time with someone scheduled for a more convenient time slot. In those few cases when a selected participant was unwilling, a new participate was selected.

The focus group was structured, focusing specifically on the cause of each of the business problems identified by the president. Each business problem was written on separate pages on a flip chart. Each focus group participant was given a stack of large Post-it® Notes.

The facilitator explained the purpose of the focus group, then flipped the page on the flip chart to the first business problem:

- There are too many meetings

Each participant was given approximately two minutes to comment on this issue. Then the facilitator wrote a question on a second flip chart:

- What is happening or not happening on the job that is causing there to be too many meetings?

Focus group participants were asked to write down their observations on the Post-it Notes, one per note. Then the facilitator would asked to post their observation on the flip chart. The facilitator, along with participants, organized the responses into meaningful categories and discussed them to ensure clarity in the meaning of the observations.

The facilitator then wrote another question on the flip chart:

- What knowledge, skills, or information are needed in order to change what is happening or not happening on the job that is causing there to be too many meetings?

Again, the focus group participants wrote their answers on the Post-it Notes and placed them on the flip chart. The responses were again categorized.

A final question was written on the flip chart:

- How best can the knowledge, skills, and information identified be presented so that they will change what is happening or not happening on the job that is causing there to be too many meetings.

Once again, participants provided their responses, and the responses were posted and grouped into meaningful categories. This process of identifying job performance needs, learning needs, and preferences for acquiring knowledge was repeated for each of the other two business needs: 1) too many people attending meetings and 2) meetings are too long.

The facilitator, along with the help of the CLO, reviewed the findings and developed a summary table that was presented to the president along with the proposed solution. Table 12-1 presents the summary of the focus group results.

Table 12-1. Summary of Needs Assessment

Level of Need Needs	
Economic Need	**What is the economic opportunity or problem?** Specific dollar amount unknown. Estimate hundreds of thousands in U.S. dollars due to time wasted in meetings.
Business Need	**What are the specific business needs?** · Too many meetings · Too many people attending meetings · Meetings are too long
Job Performance Need	**What is happening or not happening on the job that is causing the business need?** · Meetings are not planned · Agendas for meetings are not developed prior to the meeting · Agendas for meetings are not being followed · Consideration of time and cost of unnecessary meetings is lacking · Poor facilitation of meetings · Follow-up on actions resulting from the meeting is not taking place · Conflict that occurs during meetings is not being appropriately managed · Proper selection of meeting participants is not occurring · Good meeting management practices are not implemented · Consideration of cost of meetings is not taking place
Learning Need	**What knowledge, skill, or information is needed in order to change what is happening or not happening on the job?** · Ability to identify the extent and cost of meetings · Ability to identify positives, negatives, and implications of basic meeting issues and dynamics · Effective meeting behaviors
Preferences	**How best can this knowledge, skill, or information be communicated so that change on the job occurs?** · Facilitator-led workshop · Job aids and tools provided · Relevant and useful information a requirement

Solution

The summary of needs and a proposed two-day workshop were presented to the president. Program objectives suggest that upon completion of the workshop, participants would have:

- The tools and techniques to prepare, conduct, and follow up on meetings
- An understanding of the human dynamics of meetings
- Strategies for participating in or leading meetings more effectively

In addition to these program outputs, participation in the program was expected to lead to shorter meetings, fewer meetings, and a fewer number of participants attending meetings.

Program Design

To meet the identified objectives, the two-day Effective Meeting Skills workshop included a variety of knowledge-based exercises as well as skill-based practices and tasks. Table 12-2 presents the complete outline for the program.

To assist the transfer of skills to the job, a brief action plan was required so that participants could identify specific new and enhanced behaviors and track their progress as they conduct future meetings. Although an important part of the program, the action plan was used primarily to assist participants in their tracking actual use of knowledge and skills.

Along with the action plan, a meeting profile was designed into the program to capture the current level and cost of meetings. It also provided baseline data for comparing improvements resulting from the program. Table 12-3 presents the meeting profile.

Target Audience

While the target audience would include all managers, supervisors, and project leaders throughout TechnoTel, the more immediate need was in the Manufacturing Division. The president was interested in conducting the program for 150 of his managers. However, due to the concern about productivity interruption and the president's skepticism toward another training program, he wanted to ensure that the investment was achieving some return. He committed to allow three groups of twenty-four participants to be targeted for the comprehensive evaluation. Understanding that the benefits of the program would be reported for only the seventy-two participants and that the program costs would reflect only the costs of the seventy-two participants, the president saw value in the process and wanted confidence that training was more than an activity. He also made it clear that the value returned should exceed the investment being made in the program.

Table 12-2. Outline for the Effective Meetings Program

1. Meeting activity profile completed by participants
2. Definition for an effective meeting
3. Criteria for effective meetings
4. Causes behind ineffective meetings
5. Tips for conducting effective meetings
   a. Determine purpose
   b. Recognize the type of meeting
   c. Arrange seating appropriately
   d. Set the agenda
   e. Assemble a set of all appropriate attendees
   f. Establish ground rules
   g. Bring closure and plan follow-up
6. Skill practices
7. Key roles in meetings
8. Meeting tasks
9. The human function in meetings
10. Debriefing model
11. Brainstorming
12. Decision making
13. Encouraging participation
14. Handling group dynamics
15. Dealing with difficult participants
16. Providing feedback
17. Handling conflict
18. Meeting simulations/exercises
19. Action plan requirements

Table 12-3. Meeting Profile

Current Meeting Activity (Month Before Program)	
• Number of meetings chaired each month	_____ A
• Average number of individuals attending each meeting each month	_____ B
• Average length of time for each meeting (in hours)	_____ C
Total Time Consumed in Meetings (A × B × C)	_____ D
• Average hourly compensation of attendees (salary plus benefits)	_____ E
Total Meeting Costs (D × E)	_____ F

Evaluation Need

The nature of the business and the president's interest in accountability led the president to request a comprehensive evaluation of the program. Not only was he interested in whether or not the program resulted in reduced meetings and fewer participants, but expressed interested in whether the benefits of his putting his people through the program exceeded the costs.

The president's desire to ensure a positive return on his investment, as well as the corporate learning department's desire to gather data to improve the program overall, led the learning staff's plan of a comprehensive evaluation. Therefore, the learning staff implemented the ROI Methodology in its entirety.

EVALUATION METHODOLOGY

The ROI Methodology had been integrated into TechnoTel's corporate learning function two years prior to the launch of the Effective Meeting Skills program. TechnoTel has successfully sustained the use of this process because it:

- Reports a balanced set of measures
- Follows a methodical step-by-step process
- Adheres to standards and philosophy of maintaining a conservative approach and credible outcomes

The ROI Methodology categorizes evaluation data into five levels as shown in Table 12-4. These five levels tell the complete story of program success. The five levels balance economic impact with measures that address individuals' perspectives of the program and success with the transfer of learning.

Table 12-4. The Evaluation Framework

Level	Measurement Focus
1. Reaction, Satisfaction and Planned Action	Measures participant satisfaction with the program and captures planned action
2. Learning	Measures changes in knowledge, skills, and attitudes
3. Application and Implementation	Measures changes in on-the-job behavior
4. Impact	Measures changes in critical business measures
5. Return on Investment (ROI)	Compares the monetary benefits to the costs

Level 1: Reaction and Planned Action

This initial level of evaluation is the most commonly used within the TechnoTel learning environment. Reaction and satisfaction data are collected using a standard end-of-course questionnaire. Planned actions are often collected using action plans, however, a question asking the participants' intent to use what they learned is included on the end-of-course questionnaire and suffices for the planned action measure when action plans are not used.

The TechnoTel learning environment is interested in a variety of measures at Level 1, some of which are relevant only to the learning staff and their efforts to improve the learning process. These measures address course design and delivery as well as participant perception of the learning environment. Because management is interested in potential use of all programs, TechnoTel's Level 1 evaluation also answers five important questions:

1. Is the program relevant to participants' jobs?
2. Is the program important to participants' jobs?
3. Do participants intend to use what they learned in the program?
4. Did the program provide participants with new information?
5. Would participants recommend the programs to others?

An acceptable rating, using a 1 to 5 rating scale (1 = Worst Case; 5 = Best Case), for all TechnoTel courses is 4.0 or above. Any measures that fall below these ratings are flagged and actions are taken to improve them in future courses.

Level 2: Learning

Participant understanding of the knowledge and skills taught in a program is imperative to their ability to change behavior. Learning measurement at TechnoTel takes place during the program through a variety of techniques such as tests, facilitator assessment, peer assessment, self-assessment, observation, and reflective thinking with documentation. The questions that TechnoTel strives to answer when measuring learning are:

1. Do participants understand what they are supposed to do and how to do it?
2. Are participants confident to apply their newly acquired knowledge and skills when they leave the classroom?

Level 3: Application and Implementation

For many programs, TechnoTel's supervisors and managers are interested in what participants do with what they learn. When this is the case, programs are evaluated at Level 3 using a variety of techniques including self-administered questionnaires, 360-degree feedback, observations, focus groups, and interviews. Because there is more to learning transfer than just attending the program or course, it is important to TechnoTel to gather data related to how the organizational system (management, technology, and so forth) supports the transfer of training. With these considerations, three basic questions are answered at Level 3 for some TechnoTel learning initiatives:

1. How much have participants changed their approach, behavior, or performance?
2. If they are applying their knowledge and skills, what is supporting their effort?
3. If they are not applying their knowledge and skills, why not?

Level 4: Impact

For many programs TechnoTel is interested in impact on output, quality, cost, and time-measures. For these programs, the organization may also want to know how programs influence customer satisfaction and employee satisfaction—measures that are critical to organizational success but not monetized, only tracked using corporate metrics. The ultimate question answered at Level 4 is, "So what?" By answering this basic question, stakeholders gain an understanding of the consequences of participant application of newly acquired knowledge and/or skill.

Level 5: ROI

This final measure of success answers the question: "Do the monetary benefits of the program exceed the costs?"

For some programs, the organization is not interested in calculating ROI. But for programs that are costly or high profile, that drive business impact, or that are of particular interest to management, ROI is important. A standard ROI target of 25 percent is set for programs being evaluated to this level. This represents a slightly higher ROI than the ROI being achieved by other investments made by TechnoTel.

The balanced set of measures that is yielded by answering the key questions posed at each level of evaluation provides TechnoTel's corporate learning department a complete story of program success. Through this story, the department not only improves the immediate learning process, but also enhances how the system as a whole works to ensure successful transfer of learning and the achievement of desired outcomes. TechnoTel uses all of this information in combination with the ROI metric to determine if a program is a wise investment—either alone or in comparison to alternative programs that may yield similar outcomes.

Step-By-Step Process

The ten steps in the ROI Methodology constitute a methodical process to evaluation. As shown in Figure 12-1, the evaluation process begins with identifying program objectives and evaluation planning. From there, execution requires that data be collected and analyzed before developing a final report.

Figure 12-1. ROI Methodology™

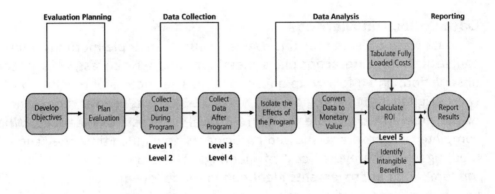

DATA COLLECTION PROCEDURES

A pragmatic approach to data collection was taken for the evaluation of the Effective Meeting Skills program. Because the cost of the program (as will be described in a later section) was not excessive, the corporate learning department staff determined that the prudent approach for this particular evaluation would be to keep the cost low while ensuring credible results. The data collection process began with a review of the objectives and measures of success, identification of the appropriate data collection methods and the most credible sources of data, and a determination of the timing of data collection.

Program Objectives and Measures

The needs assessment identified the knowledge and skill deficiencies that kept managers from conducting effective meetings. Through the needs assessment process and the design of the Effective Meeting Skills program, specific outputs were defined, as well as specific impact measures that would result if participants applied their newly acquired knowledge and skills. Measures of success at Level 1 are standard (4.0 out of 5.0), as is the measure of success at Level 5 (25 percent); measures of success for the other levels of evaluation were dependent on the program or the client expectations. In this case, the president of the division implementing the workshop was interested in improvement in the impact measures; even though he did not specify what improvement he was looking for, he did indicate by his request that the benefits should exceed the cost of the program. Therefore, the improvement must be such that when converted to monetary value a positive ROI was achieved. Table 12-5 summarizes the program's objectives and the measures used to determine success.

Data Collection Methods

Data were collected for this evaluation using multiple methods: end-of-course questionnaire, action plans, meeting profile, written test, skills practice observation, and a follow-up questionnaire. The successful meeting profile was designed into the program (see Table 12-3). It was used at the beginning of the program to capture the current level and costs of meetings. When completed, this exercise showed participants how much time they spent in meetings and the overall cost of meetings. These data served as baseline for comparing improvements identified in the follow-up questionnaire. The written test measured the improvements in knowledge of basic issues and meeting dynamics, and skill practices measured success in using effective meeting skills.

The action plan was an important part of understanding how participants applied what they learned when they returned to the job; however, the follow-up questionnaire was the primary data collection method for Level 3 and Level 4 follow-up data. Table 12-6 presents the complete follow-up questionnaire.

Table 12-5. Objectives and Measures of Success for the Effective Meeting Skills Program

	Broad Objectives	Measures
Reaction Objectives	Positive reaction and planned action with the knowledge and skills presented in the course	Ranking of 4 out of 5 on: • Relevance • Importance • Intent to use • New information • Recommendation to others
	Planned action	Three different actions to be taken when returning to the job from each participant
Learning Objectives	Ability to identify the extent and cost of meetings	Given cost guidelines, determine the cost of last three meetings
	Ability to identify positives, negatives, and implications of basic meeting issues and dynamics	From a list of 30 positive and negative meeting behaviors, correctly identify the implications of each behavior
	Acquisition of effective meeting behaviors	Demonstrate appropriate responses to eight of ten active role play scenarios
Application Objectives	Use of effective meeting behaviors	Reported changes in behavior toward planning and conducting meetings
	Barriers to application	Number and variety of barriers identified
	Enablers to application	Number and variety of enablers identified
Impact Objectives	Shorter meetings	Reported time savings
	Fewer meetings	Reported time savings
	Fewer meeting participants	Reported time savings
	Other benefits related to improvement in productivity	Reported times savings, cost savings, output improvement, quality improvement, project turnaround, etc.
ROI	25%	

Because of their desire to limit the cost of the evaluation, the corporate learning department staff decided on the most feasible methods for data collection. Cost data were developed using company records, and Table 12-7 summarizes the other data collection methods.

Table 12-6. Effective Meeting Skills Follow-up Impact Questionnaire

Are you currently in a people management role/capacity?　　Yes ☐　　　　No ☐

1. Listed below are the objectives of the Effective Meetings program. After reflecting on this program, please indicate the degree of success in meeting the objectives:

As a result of this program, participants will have:	Failed	Limited Success	Generally Successful	Completely Successful
a. The tools and techniques to prepare for, conduct, and follow up on meetings.	☐	☐	☐	☐
b. An understanding of the human dynamics of meetings	☐	☐	☐	☐
c. Strategies to participate in, and lead or chair meetings more effectively	☐	☐	☐	☐

2. Did you develop and implement an on-the-job action plan for Effective Meetings?

    Yes ☐　　　　No ☐

    If yes, please describe the nature and outcome of the plan. If not, explain why. _____
    _____
    _____
    _____

3. Please rate, on a scale of 1-5, the relevance of each of the program elements to your job, with (1) indicating no relevance, and (5) indicating very relevant.

	1	2	3	4	5
Interactive Activities	☐	☐	☐	☐	☐
Groups Discussions	☐	☐	☐	☐	☐
Networking Opportunities	☐	☐	☐	☐	☐
Reading Materials/Video	☐	☐	☐	☐	☐
Program Content	☐	☐	☐	☐	☐

4. Have you used the written materials since you participated in the program?

    Yes ☐　　　　No ☐

    Please explain. _____
    _____

5. Please indicate the degree to which you have changed the use of the following items/actions/behaviors enhanced as a result of your participation in *Effective Meetings*:

		No Change	Little Change	Some Change	Significant Change	Very Much Change	No Opportunity To Use Skill
a.	Participating Effectively in Meetings	☐	☐	☐	☐	☐	☐
b.	Avoiding Meetings Unless they are Necessary	☐	☐	☐	☐	☐	☐
c.	Minimizing the Number of Participants Attending Meetings	☐	☐	☐	☐	☐	☐
d.	Setting Objectives for Meetings	☐	☐	☐	☐	☐	☐
e.	Developing an Agenda for Each Meeting	☐	☐	☐	☐	☐	☐
f.	Controlling Time of Meetings	☐	☐	☐	☐	☐	☐
g.	Enhancing Participant Satisfaction in Meetings	☐	☐	☐	☐	☐	☐
h.	Arranging the Meeting Site for Maximum Effectiveness	☐	☐	☐	☐	☐	☐
i.	Scheduling the Optimum Time for Meetings	☐	☐	☐	☐	☐	☐
j.	Communicating the Ground Rules for Meetings	☐	☐	☐	☐	☐	☐
k.	Assigning Appropriate Roles for Meeting Participants	☐	☐	☐	☐	☐	☐
l.	Reaching Consensus in Meetings When Appropriate	☐	☐	☐	☐	☐	☐
m.	Listening Actively to Meeting Participants	☐	☐	☐	☐	☐	☐
n.	Encouraging Participation in Meetings	☐	☐	☐	☐	☐	☐
o.	Using Brainstorming in Meetings When Appropriate	☐	☐	☐	☐	☐	☐
p.	Dealing with Difficult Meeting Participants	☐	☐	☐	☐	☐	☐

Table 12-6. Effective Meeting Skills Follow-up Impact Questionnaire *(continued)*

q.	Providing Feedback to Meeting Participants	☐	☐	☐	☐	☐	☐
f.	Handling Conflict in Meeting	☐	☐	☐	☐	☐	☐
g.	Keeping the Meeting on Focus	☐	☐	☐	☐	☐	☐
h.	Accomplishing Meeting Objectives	☐	☐	☐	☐	☐	☐
u.	Evaluating the Meeting Process	☐	☐	☐	☐	☐	☐
v.	Implementing Action Plans	☐	☐	☐	☐	☐	☐
w.	Planning a Follow-up Activity	☐	☐	☐	☐	☐	☐

6. List the five (5) *Effective Meeting* behaviors or skills you have used most frequently as a result of the program.

_____

_____

_____

7. What has changed about your meeting activity profile as a result of this program? (Fewer meetings, fewer participants, shorter meetings, etc.)

_____

_____

_____

8. Please estimate the following monthly time saving measures. Use the most recent month compared to the month before attending this program. Provide only improvements directly related to this program and only when the time saved is used productively.

☐ Number of meetings avoided each month with improved planning and analysis _____

☐ Average time saved per meeting per month (in hours) _____

☐ Average number of participants reduced per meeting per month _____

9. What level of confidence do you place on the above estimations? (0% - No Confidence, 100% = Certainty) _____ %

10. Please identify any specific accomplishments/improvements that you can link to this program (on time schedules, project completion, response times, better decisions, more ideas from group, etc.)

    _____

    _____

    _____

11. What specific value in US Dollars can be attributed to the above accomplishments/ improvements? Use first year values only. While this is a difficult question, try to think of specific ways in which the above improvements can be converted to monetary units. Along with the monetary value, please indicate the basis of your calculation.
    $_____
    Basis _____

    _____

12. What level of confidence do you place on the above estimations?

    (0% - No Confidence, 100% = Certainty) _____ %

13. Other factors often influence improvements in performance. Please indicate the percent of the above improvement that is related directly to this program. _____%

    Please explain. _____

    _____

14. Do you think the *Effective Meetings* program represented a good investment for Techno Tel?

    Yes ☐   No ☐

    Please explain. _____

    _____

    Was it a good investment of your time?

    Yes ☐   No ☐

    Please explain. _____

    _____

Table 12-6. Effective Meeting Skills Follow-up Impact Questionnaire *(continued)*

15. Indicate the extent to which you think the *Effective Meetings* program has influenced each of these measures in your work unit, department, or business unit:

	No Influence	Some Influence	Moderate Influence	Significant Influence	Very Much Influence
a. Productivity	☐	☐	☐	☐	☐
b. Customer Response Time	☐	☐	☐	☐	☐
c. Cost Control	☐	☐	☐	☐	☐
d. Employee Satisfaction	☐	☐	☐	☐	☐
e. Customer Satisfaction	☐	☐	☐	☐	☐
f. Quality	☐	☐	☐	☐	☐
g. Other _____	☐	☐	☐	☐	☐

16. What barriers, if any, have you encountered that have prevented you from using skills or knowledge gained in this program. Please explain, if possible.

_____

_____

_____

17. What enablers, if any, are present to help you use the skills or knowledge gained from this program? Please explain.

_____

_____

_____

18. What additional benefits have been derived from this program?

_____

_____

_____

19. What specific suggestions do you have for improving this program?

_____

_____

20. Other Comments:

_____

_____

_____

Table 12-7. Data Collection Methods

	Level 1	Level 2	Level 3	Barriers / Enablers	Level 4	Costs
End-of-Course Questionnaire	X					
Meeting Profile		X				
Written Test		X				
Skill Practice Observation		X				
Action Plan	X		X			
Questionnaire			X	X	X	
Company Records						X

Data Sources

Data source selection is a critical step in data collection in that the source drives the credibility and validity of the study. Who knows best about the measures being taken? The primary source of data for the effective meeting skills evaluation was the participants. The managers and project leaders participating in the workshop know the extent to which they apply their knowledge and skills; they are the people who plan and lead the meetings; they are the people who recognize the cost of too many unproductive meetings (they are the ones calling the meetings). Although it may have been valuable to administer surveys to the professional staff participating in the meetings, this step would have added additional cost to the data collection process. The information they would have provided would have been valuable, but the perceived value of their input did not appear to outweigh the time and cost involved in collecting and analyzing the additional data. It was decided that the participants would serve as the source of data for this evaluation.

While the program was implemented to all 150 managers and supervisors, the president agreed to allow 72 people (three groups) to participate initially in the evaluation. This limitation would save cost and time of evaluation and would provide the president the data he needed to make a fair assessment of the success of the program.

Data Collection Timing

When conducting a comprehensive evaluation such as that completed for the Effective Meeting Skills workshop, data is collected at two different timeframes: Levels 1 and 2 data are collected during the program, and Levels 3 and 4 data are collected after participants have had time to apply knowledge and skills on a routine basis. It was determined that, given the type of skills being developed in the Effective Meeting Skills program and the numerous opportunities managers have to apply the skills, three months would be ample time for the acquired skills to be internalized and produce results. Therefore, three months after completing the program, participants would receive the follow-up questionnaire.

Table 12-8 presents the complete data collection plan. The corporate learning staff presented the data collection plan and the ROI analysis plan (described in the next section) to the division president for concurrence prior to execution.

Success with Data Collection

A data collection administration strategy is important for ensuring that the appropriate amount of data is provided. In the case of the Effective Meeting Skills workshop, the administrative strategy consisted of four primary actions:

1. The evaluation strategy was presented at the beginning of the program.
2. The facilitators reinforced the need for participants to respond to the follow-up questionnaire at the end of the program.
3. The division president signed a letter that was distributed three days prior to the questionnaires being mailed.
4. The questionnaire did not require that participants include their name or other demographic information; therefore, respondents remained anonymous.

All participants responded to the Level 1 and 2 evaluations; the follow-up for Levels 3 and 4 proved to be challenging, however. The overall response rate was 67 percent (48 respondents), which was satisfactory to the evaluation team and the division president. Unfortunately, only 43 percent (31 respondents) of the participants provided useable data on questions 8, and 9 (see Table 12-6). These two questions were directly related to follow-up on the impact measures. With the understanding that the results would reflect only that which occurred for those responding, the division president was satisfied with the response rate.

DATA ANALYSIS PROCEDURES

Data analysis comprises five key steps, each of which was carefully considered during the evaluation of this workshop:

1. Isolating the effects of the program
2. Converting data to monetary value
3. Tabulating fully loaded costs
4. Identifying intangible benefits
5. Comparing the monetary benefits to the costs.

Isolating the Effects of the Program

This step of the ROI Methodology answers the question, "How do you know it was your program that influenced the measures?" Isolating the effects of the program considers all other variables that may have influenced improvement in specific measures of success for a program. Four of the 10 potential techniques were considered for the Effective Meeting Skills workshop: control group, trendline analysis, forecasting, and participant estimations.

Because only 72 of the 150 were being evaluated, it was first suggested that a control group arrangement could be used to isolate the effects of the program. The thought was that the groups not participating in the evaluation process could serve as the control group. After much deliberation, however, it was agreed that it would be difficult to maintain the integrity of the experiment and it would be disruptive.

Participants completed a meeting profile during the program to determine the time, frequency, and participation of meetings along with the costs. To collect similar data from the control group, its members would have to complete meeting profiles, as well. This would not only contribute the contamination of the experiment, but would require additional work for the control group members. It was important to the division president to keep the evaluation low key by not requiring too much additional work and by not disrupting the organization. For these reasons, the control group arrangement was eliminated as an option.

Table 12-8. Data Collection Plan

Program: <u>Effective Meetings</u> Responsibility: _____ Date: _____

Level	Broad Program Objective(s)	Measures	Data Collection Method/Instruments	Data Sources	Timing	Responsibilities
1	**REACTION/ SATISFACTION & PLANNED ACTIONS** • Positive Reaction • Planned Actions	• Average rating of at least 4.0 on 5.0 scale on quality, usefulness and achievement of program objectives. • 100% submit planned actions	• End of Course Questionnaire • Completed Action Plans	• Participants	• End of Course	• Facilitator
2	**LEARNING** • Identify the extent and cost of meetings • Identify positives, negatives and implications of basic meeting issues and dynamics • Acquisition of Effective Meeting Behaviors	• Given cost guidelines, identify the cost of last three meetings • From a list of 30 positive and negative meeting behaviors, correctly identify the implications of each behavior • Demonstrate appropriate response to 8 of 10 active role play scenarios	• Meeting Profile • Written Test • Skill Practice Observation	• Participants	• At the Beginning of Program • At the Beginning of the Program (Pre) • At the End of the Program (Post) • During Program	• Facilitator
3	**APPLICATION/ IMPLEMENTATION** • Use of Effective Meeting behaviors • Examine the need for a meeting and scrutinize the list of participants invited	• Reported actions to influence more effective meetings • Reported use of effective meeting planning and meeting conduct behaviors	• Action Plan • Questionnaire (For 3 Groups)	• Participants	• 3 Months	• Program Owner

4	**BUSINESS IMPACT** • Time savings from fewer meetings, shorter meetings, and fewer participants (Hours Savings Per Month) • Variety of Business Impact Measures from more successful meetings	• Time savings • Time savings, cost savings, out- put improvement, quality improvement, project turn- around, etc. as reported	• Questionnaire (For 3 Groups)	• Participants	• 3 Months	• Program Owner
5	**ROI** Target ROI at least 25 percent	Comments: _____ _____ _____				

Historical data were not available for the primary measure (time savings), so trend line analysis and forecasting were inappropriate as well. The only remaining option was the use of participant estimations for isolating the effects of the workshop on the three impact measures: shorter meetings, reduced number of meetings, and fewer participants attending meetings.

Converting Data to Monetary Value

When moving from Level 4 to Level 5 evaluation, this step is the most critical because it determines the numerator (top number) in the ROI equation. Ten techniques to convert data to monetary value are possible. For this evaluation, however, the technique was apparent. As the outcome measures were all time related, the standard value of hourly compensation (salary plus benefits) for the participant chairing the meeting as well as those attending the meeting was used. If other business measures improved due to the programs, they would be converted to money using participant estimates unless standard values were available.

Tabulating Fully Loaded Costs

To calculate ROI, it is imperative to use the fully loaded costs of the program. Costs categories for the Effective Meeting Skills workshop were:

- Needs Assessment (facilitator time, participant time, materials, refreshments)
- Program fee (facilitator costs, materials, program design and development)
- Travel, lodging, meals
- Facilities
- Participants' salaries and benefits for their time in the classroom
- Evaluation costs

Identifying Intangible Benefits

Intangible benefits are any unplanned benefits derived from the program or any benefits not converted to monetary value. There were many intangible benefits of the Effective Meeting Skills workshop, which will be listed in the Evaluation Results section that follows.

Calculating ROI

The ROI equation compares net benefits (earnings) to the program costs (investment). It can be reported as a BCR by comparing the benefits to the program costs. ROI is well-used within the TechnoTel organization. Managers and professionals alike recognize the acronym for what it is; therefore, to ensure that the corporate learning department speaks the same language as the business, the following equation is used to report ROI:

$$BCR = \frac{Benefits}{Costs}$$

$$ROI = \frac{Net\ Program\ Benefits}{Costs} \times 100$$

A 25 percent ROI target is standard for most programs being evaluated at this level. Because of the nature of the program, the evaluation team and the division president believed this to be a conservative target.

Table 12-9 presents the completed ROI analysis plan. As in the case of the data collection plan, the ROI analysis plan was presented to the division president prior to implementing the evaluation. The division president concurred with the plan.

The ROI Methodology used for evaluating the Effective Meeting Skills program adhered to a set of operating standards or guiding principles as presented in Table 12-10. These Twelve Guiding Principles keep the process consistent and conservative.

EVALUATING RESULTS

The results of the study indicated that the program was successful. Participants enjoyed the workshop, but, even more important, they saw it as relevant and useful. Participants quickly grasped the ability to define meeting costs and began implementing the new knowledge and skills. Although there were some barriers to application, they were minimal. From the perspective of the division president, however, the impact on time spent in meetings was significant; the investment returned positive results.

Table 12-10. Twelve Guiding Principles of ROI

1. When conducting a higher-level evaluation, collect data at lower levels.
2. When planning a higher level evaluation, the previous level of evaluation is not required to be comprehensive.
3. When collecting and analyzing data, use only the most credible sources.
4. When analyzing data, select the most conservative alternatives for calculations.
5. Use at least one method to isolate the effects of the program or project.
6. If no improvement data are available for a population or from a specific source, assume that little or no improvement has occurred.
7. Adjust estimates of improvements for the potential error of the estimates.
8. Avoid use of extreme data items and unsupported claims when calculating ROI calculations.
9. Use only the first year of annual benefits in the ROI analysis of short-term solutions.
10. Fully load all costs of the solution, project, or program when analyzing ROI.
11. Intangible measures are defined as measures that are purposely not converted to monetary values.
12. Communicate the results of the ROI Methodology to all key stakeholders.

Reaction Data

Level 1 objectives included reaction and satisfaction measures important to improving facilitation, content, and materials. The key measures of interest, however, addressed issues indicating intent to use, including three defined actions to be taken upon return to the job. The measure of success was a minimum score of 4.0 out of 5.0. Results were successful in regard to relevance, importance, intent to use, and willingness to recommend the workshop to others. Only one measure (new information) fell below the 4.0 target. This was anticipated in that most of the concepts were familiar, but the packaging and tools provided a new perspective on the familiar topics.

The participants listed three defined actions they planned to take when returning to the job. The most noted action was implementing the meeting activity profile as a routine tool when reflecting on meetings each month. Also participants indicated they would follow the seven steps to conducting an effective meeting as listed in the program outline (see Table 12-2).

Table 12-9. ROI Analysis Plan

Program: Effective Meetings   Responsibility: ___   Date: ___

Data Items (Usually Level 4)	Methods for Isolating the Effects of the Program/Process	Methods of Converting Data to Monetary Values	Cost Categories	Intangible Benefits	Communication Targets for Final Report	Other Influences/Issues During Application	Comments
• Time Savings	• Participant's Estimate	• Hourly Wage and Benefits	• Needs Assessment • Program Fee Per Participant	• Improvement in individual productivity not captured elsewhere	• Business Unit President • Senior Managers	• Participants must see need for providing measurement	• Participants will identify specific improvements as a result of meetings being conducted more effectively
• Miscellaneous Business Measures	• Participant's Estimate	• Participant's Estimate - (using standard values when available)	• Travel / Lodging Meals • Facilities	• Stress reduction • Improved planning and scheduling	• Managers of Participants • Participants • Training and Development Staff	• Follow-up process will be explained to participants during program	
			• Participant Salaries Plus Benefits • Evaluation Costs	• Greater participation in meetings		• Three groups will be measured	

Learning Data

Level 2 objectives suggested that participants should be able to:

- identify the extent and cost of meetings
- identify positives, negatives, and implications of basic meeting issues and dynamics
- acquire effective meeting behaviors

The meeting profile identifying costs of meetings was successfully completed by participants. They felt comfortable with the tool and indicated the ability to complete similar items during the follow-up. A simple multiple-choice test was administered to ensure that participants understood the basic issue of meetings. The average score on the test was a 92 out of a possible 100.

Exercises and skill practice indicated that participants were equipped with the knowledge and skills to successfully conduct meetings while reducing the cost of meetings by conducting shorter meetings, fewer meetings, and including fewer meeting participants.

Application and Implementation Data

The follow-up evaluation (see Table 12-6) took place three months after the workshop. Questions 4, 5, 6, 16, and 17 related to application of knowledge and skills. The fundamental question with regard to application was Question 5, which assessed how much participants had changed their approach to planning and conducting meetings using the knowledge and skills they learned from the workshop. Table 12-11 summarizes the degree of change in behavior that occurred. For the most part, participants did change their meeting practices; some measures, however, indicated that little change occurred in some areas. Providing feedback to meeting participants (item Q), evaluating the meeting process (item U), and planning follow-up activity (item W), and planning follow-up activity appeared to be the least used skills.

Examining the barriers (Question 16) to the use of the knowledge and skills learned in the workshop shed some light on the reasons why there was less change in some areas than in others. The most often cited barrier was time. Some participants indicated they did not have the time to evaluate the success of the meeting or follow-up with meeting participants; however, others indicated that both of these actions were a valuable part of the meeting process.

Enabling factors (Question 17) supported the use of meeting skills learned in the workshop. The most often cited enabling factors were the job aids and materials participants took with them from the course. The workbook was cited as being the most valuable tool. Some participants indicated that senior management's interest in the tools and the workshop encouraged them to take the application of what they learned seriously.

Impact Data

The intended outcomes of the Effective Meeting Skills workshop were shorter meetings, fewer meetings, and fewer meeting participants. Other measures of improvement were of interest, but the president was specifically interested in the payoff of the program with respect to these measures. By applying the knowledge and skills learned in the workshop, improvement in these three time-related measures occurred. Table 12-12 presents a comparison of the original meeting profile data obtained from participants during the program to the average post-program data. The average amounts taken from Question 8 are subtracted from the average pre-program data to get the average post-program data. Only 31 participants (43 percent) responded to Questions 8 and 9; the average confidence in the estimates for the group responding was 81 percent. The figure shows that the intended outcomes (reduction in the number of meetings, less time spent in meetings, and fewer participants attending meetings) were achieved as a result of the program.

Other measures improved as a result of the program as well. Respondents indicated improvement in overall productivity and quality of the meetings, and six managers placed monetary values on these measures. However, the monetary payoff of the program is based on the time savings from the above measures. The other measures were reported as "other benefits" because they were not as credible as the time savings.

ROI Analysis

The ROI for the Effective Meeting Skills workshop was calculated based on time savings. To calculate the ROI, improvement in time savings due to shorter meetings, fewer meetings, and fewer meeting participants were converted to monetary value and then compared to the costs of the program.

Table 12-11. Level 3 Evaluation Responses

	No Change	Little Change	Some Change	Significant Change	Very Much Change	No Opportunity To Use Skill
A. Participating Effectively in Meetings	0	0	25%	44%	31%	0
B. Avoiding Meetings Unless they are Necessary	0	0	19%	46%	35%	0
C. Minimizing the Number of Participants Attending Meetings	0	0	19%	50%	31%	0
D. Setting Objectives for Meetings	0	0	25%	42%	33%	0
E. Developing an Agenda for Each Meeting	0	4%	27%	44%	25%	0
F. Controlling Time of Meetings	0	0	6%	44%	50%	0
G. Enhancing Participant Satisfaction in Meetings	0	10%	31%	44%	15%	0
H. Arranging the Meeting Site for Maximum Effectiveness	0	0	4%	65%	31%	0
I. Scheduling the Optimum Time for Meetings	0	0	25%	42%	33%	0
J. Communicating the Ground Rules for Meetings	0	4%	27%	44%	25%	0
K. Assigning Appropriate Roles for Meeting Participants	0	0	6%	44%	50%	0
L. Reaching Consensus in Meetings When Appropriate	0	0	13%	52%	35%	0
M. Listening Actively to Meeting Participants	0	0	4%	65%	31%	0

N. Encouraging Participation in Meetings	0	0	25%	42%	33%	0
O. Using Brainstorming in Meetings When Appropriate	0	4%	27%	44%	25%	0
P. Dealing with Difficult Meeting Participants	0	0	6%	44%	50%	0
Q. Providing Feedback to Meeting Participants	0	19%	56%	25%	0	0
R. Handling Conflict in Meeting	0	4%	31%	50%	15%	0
S. Keeping the Meeting on Focus	0	0	25%	42%	33%	0
T. Accomplishing Meeting Objectives	0	4%	27%	44%	25%	0
U. Evaluating the Meeting Process	0	10%	38%	38%	15%	0
V. Implementing Action Plans	0	2%	33%	46%	19%	0
W. Planning a Follow-up Activity	0	6%	42%	35%	17%	0

Table 12-12. Improvement in Time Spent on Meetings Here

Current Meeting Activity (Month Before Program)		Average Pre-Program Data	Average Post-Program Data
Number of meetings chaired each month	A	6.5	5.2
Average number of individuals attending each meeting each month	B	7.2	5.1
Average length of time for each meeting (in hours)	C	2.6	1.7
Total Time Consumed in Meetings (A x B x C)	D	121.68	45.1

Averaged Responses to Question 8 (Follow-up Questionnaire)	
Meetings Avoided Estimate of number of meetings avoided each month	1.3
Shorter Meetings Estimate of average time saved per meeting (in hours)	0.9
Reduced Number of Participants in Meetings Estimate of number of participants reduced for each meeting	2.1

Number completing programs	72 (three groups)
Number of questionnaires returned	48 (67 percent)
Number of questionnaires with usable data for questions 8 and 9	31 (43 percent)
Average value of confidence level from Question 9	81 percent

Monetary Benefits

The data conversion technique used was a standard value of time, which equates to average hourly compensation of attendees plus the benefits factor of 32 percent. The average hourly cost of an attendee was calculated to be $31. As shown in Table 12-13, an average monthly savings in meeting costs based on the three measures was $2,373.98.

Table 12-13. Monetary Benefits of Time Savings

Current Meeting Activity (Month Before Program)		Average Pre-Program Data	Average Post-Program Data	
Number of meetings chaired each month	A	6.5	5.2	
Average number of individuals attending each meeting each month	B	7.2	5.1	
Average length of time for each meeting (in hours)	C	2.6	1.7	
Total Time Consumed in Meetings (A x B x C)	D	121.68	45.1	
Average hourly compensation of attendees (salary plus benefits)	E	$31.00	$31.00	
Total Meeting Costs (D x E)	F	$3,772.08	$1,398.10	
Meetings Avoided Estimate of number of meetings avoided each month			1.3	G
Shorter Meetings Estimate of average time saved per meeting (in hours)			0.9	H
Reduced Participants in Meetings Estimate of number of participants reduced for each meeting			2.1	I
Total Savings **Monthly Meeting Savings (Pre – Post Costs)**			$2,373.98	J
Annual Savings (J x 12)			$28,487.76	K

This amount represents the difference in pre-program costs ($3,772.08) and post-program costs ($1,398.10). The ROI is an annual value, and the division president wanted to see a payoff within one year. The savings were annualized using this monthly average, yielding a monetary benefit of $28,487.76 for one participant.

To calculate the full benefits of the program, the monthly value was multiplied by the number of participants who provided useable data (31); the error adjustment was also considered (81 percent). The full value of the Effective Meeting Skills workshop was:

$$(\$28,487.76 \times 31) \times 0.81 = \$715,327.65$$

Fully Loaded Costs

Program costs included the program fee, which incorporated materials and facilitator costs; travel, lodging, and meals for participants; facilities; participants' time in the workshop (salaries and benefits); and evaluation costs. The needs assessment of $5,000 was also included. However, since the program was intended to go out to the entire 150 managers and supervisors, these costs were prorated over the number of people attending the program, and calculated only for the 72 in the evaluation. Even though the benefits were calculated only for those responding, program costs accounted for all participants costs. The fully loaded costs of the Effective Meeting Skills workshop are shown in Table 12-14.

Table 12-14. Costs Used in the ROI Calculation for the Effective Meeting Skills Workshop

Item	Calculation	Cost
Needs Assessment	$5,000 prorated over 150 participants	$2,400
Program Fee	$800 per participant **x** 72	$57,600
Travel, Lodging, Meals	$245 **x** 72	$17,640
Facilities	$190 **x** 6	$1,140
Participant Time	$219 per day **x** 1.32 **x** 2 **x** 72	$41,628
Evaluation Costs		$5,000
	Total Costs	**$125,408**

The return on investing in the Effective Meeting Skills workshop was 470 percent, as shown by the calculation below.

$$\text{BCR} = \frac{\$715,327.65}{\$125,408} = 5.7\!:\!1$$

$$\text{ROI} = \frac{\$715,327.65 - \$125,408}{\$125,408} \times 100 = 470\%$$

The ROI told the division president that for every dollar spent on the workshop, TechnoTel received $4.70 after costs. On the surface, the ROI seemed high in comparison to other investments. But because the division president knew the value of time and knew how much time had been wasted in meetings in the past, the ROI calculation was believable. The evaluation team had been diligent in advising the division president of the evaluation process and keeping him abreast of the findings, thereby enhancing the credibility of the ROI process.

Intangible Benefits

The financial impact to TechnoTel was an important outcome of the evaluation. However, other important outcomes occurred as well. Along with improvement in overall productivity and quality of meetings, employees and their supervisors in TechnoTel were becoming happier in the work setting due to the reduction in wasteful meetings. The groups who had attended the Effective Meeting Skills workshop took the process seriously and had a keen desire to improve their meeting process; therefore, tools were being implemented. This also helped improve customer satisfaction—both external and internal customers. Respondents to the evaluation reported being more accessible and more focused on customer concerns.

An interesting unexpected benefit of the program was that the division president began using the meeting profile worksheet as a tool to manage the cost of his own meetings. He asked that his senior leaders do the same. The tool has become a time management tool throughout this division of TechnoTel.

Communication Strategy

The success of the ROI study at TechnoTel can be attributed to the continuous communication throughout the process. From the outset, the division president was kept informed of the progress with the study. He was involved in the planning stage and data collection. As results at Levels 3 and 4 began rolling in, the evaluation team kept him informed. Once the study was completed and the division president was aware of the results, the senior management team participated in a one-hour briefing. Because there were several new senior managers who were unfamiliar with the evaluation practice at TechnoTel, a full presentation was conducted. The presentation topics included:

- Need for effective meetings
- Program design
- Need for evaluation
- Evaluation methodology
- Evaluation results

At the end of the presentation, each person received a copy of the complete report, as well as a summary copy.

Based on the questions and the response to the presentation, the senior management saw the evaluation process as credible. Even more important, they saw the value of the Effective Meeting Skills workshop and asked that the program be implemented in other areas of TechnoTel.

Lessons Learned

Regardless of the number of evaluation studies conducted, there are always lessons to learn. Because the evaluation team thought there was an understanding of the evaluation process, they did not spend time explaining Questions 8 and 9. Had they done a better job covering those questions on the questionnaire, they might have achieved a greater response rate.

Because evaluation is routine at TechnoTel, the questionnaire administration strategy seemed appropriate. However, with only a 67 percent response rate, there was room for improvement.

Questions for Discussion

1. Was the president justified in asking for a comprehensive evaluation of an effective meetings skills workshop?
2. How could the needs assessment have been improved?
3. What steps could have been taken to ensure a higher response rate, especially for Questions 7, 8, and 9 on the questionnaire?
4. How credible are the time savings data?
5. How would you have approached the evaluation strategy for the Effective Meeting Skills workshop?

Chapter 13

Measuring ROI in Business Coaching

Nations Hotel

by Jack J. Phillips

The learning and development team at the Nations Hotel Corporation was challenged to identify learning needs to help executives find ways to improve efficiency, customer satisfaction, and revenue growth in the company. A key component of the program was the development of a formal, structured coaching program, Coaching for Business Impact. The corporate executives were interested in seeing the actual ROI for the coaching project. This case study provides critical insights into how coaching creates value in an organization including ROI.

BACKGROUND

Nations Hotel Corporation (NHC) is a large U.S.-based hotel firm with operations in 15 countries. The firm has maintained steady growth to include more than 300 hotels in cities all over the world. NHC enjoys one of the most recognized names in the global lodging industry, with 98 percent brand awareness worldwide and 72 percent overall guest satisfaction.

The hospitality industry is competitive, cyclical, and subject to swings with the economy. Room rentals are price sensitive, and customer satisfaction is extremely important for NHC. Profits are squeezed if operating costs get out of hand. NHC top executives constantly seek ways to improve operational efficiency, customer satisfaction, revenue growth, and retention of high-

---

performing employees. Executives—particularly those in charge of individual properties—are under constant pressure to show improvement in these key measures.

The learning and development function, the Nations Hotel Learning Organization (NHLO), conducted a brief survey of executives to identify learning needs to help them meet some of their particular goals. NHLO was interested in developing customized learning processes including, the possibility of individual coaching sessions. Most of the executives surveyed indicated that they would like to work with a qualified coach to assist them through a variety of challenges and issues. The executives believed that this would be an efficient way to learn, apply, and achieve results. Consequently, NHLO developed a formal, structured coaching program— Coaching for Business Impact (CBI)—and offered it to the executives at the vice president level and above.

As the project was conceived, the senior executive team became interested in showing the value of the coaching project. Although they supported coaching as a method to improve executive performance, they wanted to see the actual ROI. The goal was to evaluate 25 executives, randomly selected (if possible) from the participants in CBI.

The Program

Figure 13-1 shows the steps in the new coaching program from the beginning to the ultimate outcomes. This program involves 14 discrete elements and processes.

1. *Voluntary participation:* Executives had to volunteer to be part of this project. Voluntary commitment translates into a willing participant who is not only open to changing, improving, and applying what is being learned, but also is also willing to provide the necessary data for evaluating the coaching process. The voluntary nature of the coaching program, however, meant that not all executives who needed coaching would be involved. When compared to mandatory involvement, however, the volunteer effort appeared to be an important ingredient for success. It was envisioned that, as improvements were realized and executives reflected on the positive perceptions of coaching, other executives would follow suit.

Figure 13-1. Coaching for Business Impact Steps

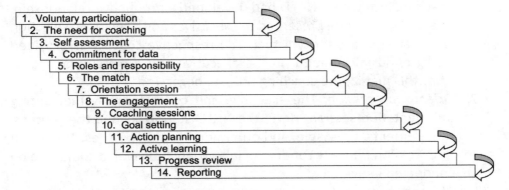

1. Voluntary participation
2. The need for coaching
3. Self assessment
4. Commitment for data
5. Roles and responsibility
6. The match
7. Orientation session
8. The engagement
9. Coaching sessions
10. Goal setting
11. Action planning
12. Active learning
13. Progress review
14. Reporting

2. *The need for coaching:* An important part of the process was a dialog with the executive to determine if coaching was actually needed. In this step, NHLO staff used a checklist to review the issues, needs, and concerns about the coaching agreement. Along with establishing a need, the checklist revealed key areas where coaching could help. This step ensured that the assistance desired by the executive could actually be provided by the coach.

3. *Self-assessment:* As part of the process, a self-assessment was taken from the individual being coached, his or her immediate manager, and direct reports. This was a typical 360-degree assessment instrument that focused on areas of feedback, communication, openness, trust, and other competencies necessary for success in the competitive hospitality environment.

4. *Commitment for data:* As a precondition, executives had to agree to provide data during coaching and at appropriate times following the engagement. This up-front commitment ensured that data of sufficient quality and quantity could be obtained. The data made evaluation easier and helped executives see their progress and realize the value of coaching.

5. *Roles and responsibility:* For both the coach and the executive, roles and responsibilities were clearly defined. It was important for the executive to understand that the coach was there to listen, provide feedback, and evaluate. The coach was not there to make decisions for the executive. This clear distinction was important for productive coaching sessions.

6. *The match:* Coaches were provided from a reputable business coaching firm where NHLO had developed a productive relationship. Coach profiles were presented to executives and a tentative selection was made on a priority listing. The respective coach was provided background information on the executive and a match was made. After this match, the coaching process began.

7. *Orientation session:* The executive and coach formally met during an orientation session. Here, the NHLO staff explained the process, requirements, timetable, and other administrative issues. This was a brief session typically conducted in a group; however, it could also be conducted individually.

8. *The engagement:* One of the most important aspects of the process involved making sure that the engagement was connected to a business need. Typical coaching engagements focused on behavioral issues (e.g., an executive's inability to listen to employees). To connect to the business impact, the behavior change must link to a business consequence. In the initial engagement, the coach uncovered the business need by asking a series of questions to examine the consequences of behavior change. This process involved asking "so what?" and "what if?" as the desired behavior changes were described. As the business needs were identified, the measures must be in the categories of productivity, sales, efficiency, direct cost savings, employee retention, and customer satisfaction. The engagement should be connected to corresponding changes in at least three of those measures. Without elevating the engagement to a business need, it would have been difficult to evaluate coaching with this level of analysis.

9. *Coaching sessions:* Individual sessions were conducted at least once a month (usually more often) lasting a minimum of 1 hour (sometimes more), depending on the need and issues at hand. The coach and executive met face-to-face, if possible. If not, coaching was conducted in a telephone conversation. Routine meetings were necessary to keep the process on track.

10. *Goal setting:* Although individuals could set goals in any area needing improvements, the senior executives chose five priority areas for targeting: sales growth, productivity/operational efficiency, direct

cost reduction, retention of key staff members, and customer satisfaction. The executives selected one measure in at least three of these areas. Essentially, they would have three specific goals that would require three action plans, described next.

11. *Action planning:* To drive the desired improvement, the action planning process was utilized. Common in coaching engagements, this process provided an opportunity for the executive to detail specific action steps planned with the team. These steps were designed to drive a particular consequence that was a business impact measure. Figure 13-2 shows a typical action-planning document used in this process. The executive was to complete the action plan during the first two to three coaching sessions, detailing step-by-step what he or she would accomplish to drive a particular improvement. Under the analysis section, Part A, B, and C are completed in the initial development of the plan. The coaches distributed action plan packages that included instructions, blank forms, and completed examples. The coach explained the process in the second coaching session. The action plans could be revised as needed. At least three improvement measures were required out of the five areas targeted with the program. Consequently, at least three action plans had to be developed and implemented.

12. *Active learning:* After the executive developed the specific measures in question and the action plans, several development strategies were discussed and implemented with the help of the coach. The coach actually facilitated the efforts, utilizing any number of typical learning processes, such as reading assignments, self-assessment tools, skill practices, video feedback, journaling, and other techniques. Coaching is considered to be an active learning process where the executive experiments, applies, and reflects on the experience. The coach provides input, reaction, assessment, and evaluation.

13. *Progress review:* At monthly sessions, the coach and executive reviewed progress and revised the action plan, if necessary. The important issue was to continue to make adjustments to sustain the process.

14. *Reporting:* After six months in the coaching engagement, the executive reported improvement by completing other parts of the

Figure 13-2. Action Plan Form

Name: _____ Instructor Signature: _____ Follow-Up Date: _____

Objective: _____ Evaluation Period: _____ to _____

Improvement Measure: _____ Current Performance _____ Target Performance _____

Action Steps	Analysis
1. _____	A. What is the unit of measure? _____
2. _____	B. What is the value (cost) of one unit? $ _____
3. _____	C. How did you arrive at this value? _____
4. _____	
5. _____	D. How much did the measure change during the evaluation period? (monthly value) _____
6. _____	E. What percent of this change was actually caused by this program? _____ %
7. _____	F. What level of confidence do you place on the above information? (100% = Certainty and 0% - No Confidence) _____ %

Intangible Benefits:

Comments:

action plan. This includes Part D, E, F, and G and intangible benefits and comments. If the development efforts were quite involved and the measures driven were unlikely to change in the interim, a longer period of time was utilized. For most executives, six months was appropriate.

These elements reflected a results-based project appropriate called "Coaching for Business Impact."

EVALUATION METHODOLOGY

Objectives

An effective ROI study flows from the objectives of the particular project being evaluated. For coaching, it is important to clearly indicate the objectives at different levels. Figure 13-3 shows the detailed objectives associated with this project. The objectives reflect the four classic levels of evaluation plus a fifth level for ROI. Some of the levels, however, have been adjusted for the coaching environment. With these objectives in mind, it becomes a relatively easy task to measure progress on these objectives.

Planning for Evaluation

Figure 13-4 shows the shows how the various types of data are collected and integrated to provide an overall evaluation of the program. Figure 13-5 shows the completed data collection plan for this project:

- *Objectives:* The objectives are listed as defined in Figure 13-3 and are repeated only in general terms.
- *Measures:* Additional definition is sometimes needed beyond the specific objectives. The measures used to gauge progress on the objective are defined.
- *Methods:* This column indicates the specific method used for collecting data at different levels. In this case, action plans and questionnaires are the primary methods.
- *Sources:* For each data group, sources are identified. For coaches, sources are usually limited to the executive, coach, or manager of the executive, and the individual/team reporting to the executive. Although the actual data provided by executives will usually come from the records of the organization, the executive will include the

data in the action plan document. Thus, the executive becomes a source of the data to NHLO.

- *Timing:* The timing refers to the time for collecting specific data items from the beginning of the coaching engagement.
- *Responsibility:* The responsibility refers to the individual(s) who will actually collect the data.

Figure 13-3. Objectives of Business Impact Coaching

Level 1. Reaction Objectives

After participating in this coaching program, the executive will:

1. Perceive coaching to be relevant to the job
2. Perceive coaching to be important to job performance at the present time
3. Perceive coaching to be value added in terms of time and funds invested
4. Rate the coach as effective
5. Recommend this program to other executives

Level 2. Learning Objectives

After completing this coaching pro- gram, the executives should improve their understanding of or skills for each of the following:

1. Uncovering individual strengths and weaknesses
2. Translating feedback into action plans
3. Involving team members in projects and goals
4. Communicating effectively
5. Collaborating with colleagues
6. Improving personal effectiveness
7. Enhancing leadership skills

Level 3. Application Objectives Six

months after completing this coaching program, executives should:

1. Complete the action plan
2. Adjust the plan accordingly as need- ed for changes in the environment

Level 3. Application Objectives (continued)

1. Show improvements on the following items:
   a. uncovering individual strengths and weaknesses
   b. translating feedback into action plans
   c. involving team members in projects and goals
   d. communicating effectively
   e. collaborating with colleagues
   f. improving person- al effectiveness
   g. enhancing leadership skills.
2. Identify barriers and enablers

Level 4. Impact Objectives

After completing this coaching program, executives should improve at least three specific measures in the following areas:

1. Sales growth
2. Productivity/operation- al efficiency
3. Direct cost reduction
4. Retention of key staff members
5. Customer satisfaction

Level 5. ROI Objective

The ROI value should be 25 percent.

Figure 13-4. Data Integration Plan for Evaluating the Program

Data Category	Executive Questionnaire	Senior Executive Questionnaire	Action Plan	Company Records
Reaction	X			
Learning	X	X		
Application	X	X	X	
Impact			X	X
Costs				X

Figure 13-6 shows the completed plan for data analysis. This document addresses the key issues needed for a credible analysis of the data and includes the following:

1. *Data items:* The plan shows when business measures will be collected from the one of the five priority areas.
2. *Isolating the effects of coaching:* The method of isolating the effects of coaching on the data is estimation, where the executives actually allocate the proportion of the improvement to the coaching process (more on the consequences of this later). Although there are more credible methods, such as control groups and trend-line analysis, they are not appropriate for this situation. Although the estimates are subjective, they are developed by those individuals who should know them best (the executives), and the results are adjusted for the error of the estimate.
3. *Converting data to monetary values:* Data is converted using a variety of methods. For most data items, standard values are available. When standard values are not available, the input of an in-house expert is pursued. This expert is typically an individual who collects, assimilates, and reports the data. If neither of these approaches is feasible, the executive estimates the value.
4. *Cost categories:* The standard cost categories included are the typical costs for a coaching assignment.
5. *Communication targets:* Several audiences are included for coaching results, representing the key stakeholder groups: the executive, the executive's immediate manager, the sponsor of the program, and the

Figure 13-5. Completed Data Collection Plan

Program: Coaching for Business Impact   **Responsibility:** _____   **Date:** _____

Level	Objective(s)	Measures/Data	Data Collection Method	Data Sources	Timing	Responsibilities
1	**Reaction/Satisfaction** • Relevance to job • Importance to job success • Value add • Coach's effectiveness • Recommendation to others	• 4 out of 5 on a 1 to 5 rating scale	• Questionnaire	• Executives	• Six months after engagement	• NHLO Staff
2	**Learning** • Uncovering strengths/ weaknesses • Translating feedback into action • Involving team members • Communicating effectively • Collaborating with colleagues • Improving personal effectiveness • Enhancing leadership skills	• 4 out of 5 on a 1 to 5 rating scale	• Questionnaire	• Executives • Coach	• Six months after engagement	• NHLO Staff
3	**Application/Implementation** • Complete and adjust action plan • Identify barriers and enablers • Show improvements in skills	• Checklist for action plan • 4 out of 5 on a 1 to 5 rating scale	• Action Plan • Questionnaire	• Executives • Coach	• Six months after engagement	• NHLO Staff
4	**Business Impact (3 of 5)** • Sales growth • Productivity/efficiency • Direct cost reduction • Retention of key staff members • Customer satisfaction	• Monthly revenue • Varies with location • Direct monetary savings • Voluntary turnover • Customer satisfaction index	• Action Plan	• Executives	• Six months after engagement	• NHLO Staff
5	**ROI** • 25 percent					

Comments: *Executives are committed to providing data. They fully understand all the data collection issues prior to engaging into the coaching assignment.*

Figure 13-6. The ROI Analysis Plan for Coaching for Business Impact

Data Items (Usually Level 4)	Methods for Isolating the Effects of the Program	Methods of Converting Data to Monetary Values	Cost Categories	Intangible Benefits	Communication Targets for Final Report	Other Influences/Issues During Application	Comments
• Sales growth	Estimates from executive (Method is the same for all data items)	• Standard Value • Expert input • Executive estimate (Method is the same for all data items)	• Needs assessment • Coaching fees • Travel costs • Executive time • Administrative support • Administrative overhead • Communication expenses • Facilities • Evaluation	• Increased commitment • Reduced stress • Increased job satisfaction • Improved customer service • Enhanced recruiting image • Improved teamwork • Improved communication	• Executives • Senior executives • Sponsors • NHLO staff • Learning & Development Council • Prospective participants for CBI	A variety of other initiatives will influence the impact measure including our Six Sigma process, service excellence program, and our efforts to become a great place to work.	It is extremely important to secure commitment from executives to provide accurate data in a timely manner.
• Productivity/operational efficiency							
• Direct cost reduction							
• Retention of key staff members							
• Customer satisfaction							

EVALUATION RESULTS

The careful data collection planning allowed the coaching program to be evaluated at all five levels.

Reaction Data

Reaction to the coaching program exceeded expectations of the NHLO staff. Comments received for Level 1 evaluation included these:

- "This program was very timely and practical."
- "My coach was very professional."

On a scale of 1 to 5 (1 = unacceptable and 5 = exceptional), the average rating of five items was 4.1, exceeding the objective of 4.0. Table 13-1 shows the items listed.

Learning Data

As with any process, the executives indicated enhancement of skills and knowledge in certain areas:

- "I gained much insight into my problems with my team."
- "This is exactly what I needed to get on track. My coach pointed out things I hadn't thought of and we came up with some terrific actions."

Table 13-1. Executive Reaction to Coaching

Level 1 Evaluation	Rating*
Relevance of Coaching	4.6
Importance of Coaching	4.1
Value of Coaching	3.9
Effectiveness of Coach	3.9
Recommendation to Others	4.2

*Scale 1-5, where: 1 = Unacceptable 5 = Exceptional

Table 13-2 shows seven items with inputs from both the executives and their coaches. For this level, it was considered appropriate to collect the data from both groups, indicating the degree of improvement. The most accurate, and probably most credible, is the input directly from the executive. The coach may not be fully aware of the extent of learning.

Table 13-2. Learning from Coaching

Measures	Executive Rating*	Coach Rating*
Understanding strengths and weaknesses	3.9	4.2
Translating feedback into action plans	3.7	3.9
Involving team members in projects and goals	4.2	3.7
Communicating effectively	4.1	4.2
Collaborating with colleagues	4.0	4.1
Improving personal effectiveness	4.1	4.4
Enhancing leadership skills	4.2	4.3

*Program value scale 1 to 5.

Application Data

For coaching to be successful, the executive had to implement the items on the action plans. The most important measure of application was the completion of the action plan steps. Eighty-three percent of the executives reported completion of all three plans. Another 11 percent completed one or two action plans.

Also, executives and the coach provided input on questions about changes in behavior from the use of skills. Here are some comments they offered on the questionnaires:

- "It was so helpful to get a fresh, unique point of view of my action plan. The coaching experience opened my eyes to significant things I was missing."
- "After spending a great deal of time trying to get my coach to understand my dilemma, I felt that more effort went into to this than I expected."
- "We got stuck in a rut on one issue and I couldn't get out. My coach was somewhat distracted and I never felt we were on the same page."

The response rates for questionnaires were 92 percent and 80 percent for executives and coaches, respectively. Table 13-3 shows a listing of the skills and the rating, using a scale of 1 to 5 where 1 was "no change in the skill" and 5 was "exceptional increase."

Table 13-3. Application of Coaching

Measures	Executive Rating*	Coach Rating*
Translating feedback into action plans	4.2	3.9
Involving team members in projects and goals	4.1	4.2
Communicating more effectively with the team	4.3	4.1
Collaborating more with the group and others	4.2	4.2
Applying effective leadership skills	4.1	3.9

*Program value scale 1 to 5, where: 1 = No change in skills 5 = Exceptional increase

Barriers and Enablers

With any process, there are barriers and enablers to success. The executives were asked to indicate the specific barriers (obstacles) to the use of what was learned in the coaching sessions. Overall the barriers were weak, almost nonexistent. Also, they were asked to indicate what supported (enablers) the process. The enablers were very strong. Table 13-4 shows a list of the barriers and enablers.

Table 13-4. Barriers and Enablers of the Coaching Process

Barriers	Enablers
• Not enough time	• Coach
• Not relevant	• Action plan
• Not effective when using the skill	• Structure of CBI
• Manager didn't support it	• Support of management

Impact Data

Specific business impact measures varied with the individual but, for the most part, were in the categories representing the five priority areas. Table 13-5 shows the listing of the actual data reported in the action plans for the first measure only. The table identifies the executive and the area of improvement, the monetary value, the basis of the improvement, the method of converting the monetary value, the contribution from coaching,

Table 13-5. Business Impact from Coaching

Exec Number	Measurement Area	Total Annual Value	Basis	Method for Converting Data	Contribution Factor	Confidence Estimate	Adjusted Value
1	Revenue growth	$ 11,500	Profit margin	Standard value	33%	70%	$ 2,656
2	Retention	175,000	3 turnovers	Standard value	40%	70%	49,000
3	Retention	190,000	2 turnovers	Standard value	60%	80%	91,200
4	Direct cost savings	75,000	From cost statements	Participant estimate	100%	100%	75,000
5	Direct cost savings	21,000	Contract services	Standard value	75%	70%	11,025
6	Direct cost savings	65,000	Staffing costs	Standard value	70%	60%	27,300
7	Retention	150,000	2 turnovers	Standard value	50%	50%	37,500
8	Cost savings	70,000	Security	Standard value	60%	90%	37,800
9	Direct cost savings	9,443	Supply costs	N/A	70%	90%	5,949
10	Efficiency	39,000	Information technology costs	Participant estimate	70%	80%	21,840
11	Retention	215,000	4 turnovers	Standard value	75%	90%	145,125
12	Productivity	13,590	Overtime	Standard value	75%	80%	8,154
13	Retention	73,000	1 turnover	Standard value	50%	80%	29,200
14	Retention	120,000	2 annual turnovers	Standard value	60%	75%	54,000
15	Retention	182,000	4 turnovers	Standard value	40%	85%	61,880
16	Cost savings	25,900	Travel	Standard value	30%	90%	6,993
17	Cost savings	12,320	Administrative support	Standard value	75%	90%	8,316
18	Direct cost savings	18,950	Labor savings	Participant estimate	55%	60%	6,253
19	Revenue growth	103,100	Profit margin	Participant estimate	75%	90%	69,592
20	Revenue	19,500	Profit	Standard value	85%	75%	12,431
21	Revenue	21,230	Profit %	Standard value	80%	70%	18,889
22	Revenue growth	105,780	Profit margin	Standard value	70%	50%	37,023
	TOTAL	$1,716,313					

TOTAL		$817,126
2nd Measure Total		$649,320
3rd Measure Total		$394,712
TOTAL Benefits		$1,861,158

the confidence estimate of the contribution, and the adjusted value. Since there are three measures, a total of all three tables are developed. The total for the three is $1,861,158.

Figure 13-7 shows a completed action plan from one participant, Caroline Dobson (executive number 11). In this example, Caroline reduced annual turnover to 17 percent from 28 percent – an improvement of 11 percent. This represented four turnovers on an annual basis. Using a standard value of 1.3 times base salaries for the cost of one turnover and adding the total base salaries yields a total cost savings of $215,000.

As mentioned earlier, the estimates were used to isolate the benefits of coaching. After the estimates were obtained, the value was adjusted for the confidence of the estimate. Essentially, the executives were asked to list other factors that could have contributed to the improvement and allocate the amount (on a percentage basis) that was directly attributable to coaching. Then, using a scale of 0 percent (no confidence) to 100 percent (total certainty), executives provided the confidence levels for their estimates.

ROI

The costs were fully loaded and included both the direct and indirect costs of coaching. Estimates were used in some cases. Table 13-6 shows the costs of coaching for all 25 executives in the study.

Table 13-6. Costs of Coaching Twenty-five Executives

Item	Cost
Needs Assessment/Development	$ 10,000
Coaching Fees	480,000
Travel Costs	53,000
Executive Time	9,200
Administrative Support	14,000
Administrative Overhead	2,000
Telecommunication Expenses	1,500
Facilities (Conference Room)	2,100
Evaluation	8,000
Total	**$ 579,800**

Only a small amount of initial assessment cost was involved, and the development cost was minor, as well, because the coaching firm had developed a similar coaching arrangement previously. The costs for sessions conducted on the phone were estimated, and sometimes a conference room was used instead of the executive offices.

Figure 13-7. An Example of an Executive's Completed Action Plan

Name: Caroline Dobson   Coach: Pamela Mills   Follow-Up Date: 1 September

Objective: Improve retention for staff   Evaluation Period: January to July

Improvement Measure: Voluntary turnover   Current Performance: 28% Annual   Target Performance: 15% Annual

Action Steps		Analysis
1. Meet with team to discuss reasons for turnover – using problem-solving skills.	31 Jan	A. What is the unit of measure? One voluntary turnover
2. Review exit interview data with HR – look for trends and patterns.	15 Feb	B. What is the value (cost) of one unit? Salary x 1.3
3. Counsel with "at-risk" employees to correct problems and explore opportunities for improvement.	1 Mar	C. How did you arrive at this value? Standard Value
4. Develop individual development plan for high-potential employees.	5 Mar	D. How much did the measure change during the evaluation period? 11% (annual %) (4 turnovers annually)
5. Provide recognition to employees with long tenure.	Routinely	E. What other factors could have contributed to this improvement? Growth opportunities, changes in job market
6. Schedule appreciation dinner for entire team.	31 May	
7. Encourage team leaders to delegate more responsibilities.	31 May	F. What percent of this change was actually caused by this program? 75%
8. Follow-up with each discussion and discuss improvement		
9. or lack of improvement and plan other action.	Routinely	G. What level of confidence do you place on the above information? (100% = Certainty and 0% = No Confidence) 90%
10. Monitor improvement and provide recognition when appropriate.	11 May	

Intangible Benefits: Less stress on team, greater job satisfaction

Comments: Great Coach – He kept me on track with this issue

Using the total monetary benefits and total cost of the program, two ROI calculations can be developed. The first is the benefit-cost ratio (BCR), which is the ratio of the monetary benefits divided by the costs:

$$BCR = \frac{\$1,861,158}{\$579,800} = 3.21:1$$

This value suggests that for every dollar invested, $3.21 was generated in benefits. The ROI formula for investments in training, coaching, or any human performance intervention is calculated in the same way as for other types of investments: earnings divided by investment. For this coaching solution, the ROI was calculated thus:

$$ROI\ (\%) = \frac{\$1,861,158 - \$579,800}{\$579,800} \times 100 = 221\%$$

In other words, for every dollar invested in the coaching program, the invested dollar was returned and another $2.21 was generated. In this case, the ROI exceeded the 25 percent target.

Intangibles

As with any project, there were many intangibles revealed by this analysis. Intangibles were collected on both the follow-up questionnaire and the action plan. Two questions were included on the questionnaire; one involved other benefits from this process and the other asked for comments about the program. Some individuals indicated intangibles when they listed the comments. Also, the action plan contained a place for comments and intangibles. The intangible benefits identified through these data sources included:

- Increased commitment
- Improved teamwork
- Increased job satisfaction
- Improved customer service
- Improved communication

Note that this list includes only measures that were identified as being an intangible benefit by at least four of the 25 executives. In keeping with the conservative nature of the ROI Methodology, it was decided that intangibles identified by only a couple of executives would be considered extreme data items and not credible enough to list as an actual benefit of the program.

Credibility of the ROI Analysis

The critical issue in this study is the credibility of the data. The data were perceived to be very credible by the executives, their immediate managers, and the coaches. Credibility rests on eight major issues:

1. The information for the analysis was provided directly by the executives. They had no reason to be biased in their input.
2. The data was taken directly from the records and could be audited.
3. The data collection process was conservative, with the assumption that an unresponsive individual had realized no improvement. This concept—no data, no improvement—is ultraconservative in regard to data collection. Three executives did not return the completed action plans.
4. The executives did not assign complete credit to this program. Executives isolated only a portion of the data that should be credited directly to this program.
5. The data was adjusted for the potential error of the above estimate.
6. Only the first year's benefits were used in the analysis. Most of the improvements should result in second and third-year benefits.
7. The costs of the program were fully loaded. All direct and indirect costs were included, including the time away from work for the executives.
8. The data revealed a balanced profile of success. Very favorable reaction, learning, and application data were presented along with business impact, ROI, and intangibles.

Collectively, these issues made a convincing case for the CBI program.

Communication Strategy

To communicate appropriately with the target audiences outlined in the ROI analysis plan, three specific documents were produced. The first report was a detailed impact study showing the approach, assumptions, methodology, and results using all the data categories. In addition, barriers and enablers were included, along with conclusions and recommendations. The second report was an eight-page executive summary of the key points, including a one-page overview of the methodology. The third report was a brief, five-page summary of the process and results. These documents were presented to the different groups according to the plan in Figure 13-8.

Figure 13-8. NHLO's Plan for Communicating Evaluation Results

Audience	Document
Executives	Brief summary
Managers of executive (senior executives)	Brief summary
Sponsor	Complete study, executive summary
NHLO staff	Complete study
Learning and development council	Complete study, executive summary
Prospective participants	Brief summary

Because this was the first ROI study conducted in this organization, face-to-face meetings were conducted with the sponsor and other interested senior executives. The purpose was to ensure that executive sponsors had a clear understanding of the methodology, the conservative assumptions, and each level of data. The barriers, enablers, conclusions, and recommendations were an important part of the meeting. In the future, after two or three studies have been conducted, this group will receive only a one-page summary of key data items.

A similar meeting was conducted with the learning and development council. The council consisted of advisors to NHLO—usually middle-level executives and managers. Finally, a face-to-face meeting was held with the NHLO staff at which the complete impact study was described and used as a learning tool.

As a result of this communication, the senior executive decided to make only a few minor adjustments in the program and continued to offer CBI to others on a volunteer basis. They were very pleased with the progress and were delighted to have data connecting coaching to the business impact.

Questions for Discussion

1. How did the decision to conduct an ROI study influence the design of the coaching program?
2. Critique the evaluation design and method of data collection.
3. Discuss the importance of getting participants committed to provide quality data.
4. What other strategies for isolating the impact of the coaching program could have been employed here?
5. Discuss the importance of credibility of data in an ROI study.
6. How can the outcomes of coaching be linked to your organization's business objectives?

Chapter 14

Measuring ROI in
Organization Culture Change

Agua Manufacturing Company

by Lizette Zuniga

This organizational culture change case study explores the details of the transition of a large manufacturing company (AMC) from a traditional organization to one that is marked by strong and empowering leadership, and an execution-friendly environment with clear strategy, goals, and priorities.

BACKGROUND

AMC is a large manufacturing company that serves an international customer base. Even in a slow economy, AMC has continued to increase revenues in the past several years, increasing its employee base by 25 percent. Although the company's revenue has grown, expenses incurred in the organization have been extraordinarily high and instead of enjoying a positive profit margin, the company has been in the red for the past three years. The leadership team met and discussed bringing in an external consultant to help understand underlying causes for these problems and look for course- correcting solutions.

ORGANIZATION ANALYSIS AND DIAGNOSTICS—
ALIGNMENT AND DECISION TO CHANGE

The main purpose for conducting organization diagnostics was to understand the reasons for the problems the organization was having. It was during the initial consulting meeting that several methods were selected to collect data and more fully understand the concerns.

Capstone Organization Culture Assessment

The first method selected to understand the organization culture and potential area for change was the Capstone Organization Culture Assessment (Beard and Zuniga, 2006). This assessment was administered to gather data in the areas of leadership, decision making, values, planning, and structure. Approximately 700 were invited to participate and with 653 responding, the response rate was 93 percent. Some of the scores clustered near the mean, indicating a traditional organizational climate. AMC presents itself as an established organization, relying on the same products, services, and processes it has always used to remain successful. Given the changes in the marketplace and global economy, AMC cannot rely on business-as-usual practices. Currently, AMC does not appear to be a company poised for transformational growth. This kind of profile indicates status quo. The key findings were threefold:

1. **Leadership:** Scoring lowest in the leadership domain shows that this group of leaders is deficient in the areas of delegating and communicating with direct reports. The main leadership style is one with tendencies toward autocratic and tight management.
2. **Planning:** The planning domain scores also show gaps, specifically in unclear priorities, unclear goals, and no clear strategy.
3. **Decision Making:** The decision-making process is rather sluggish in getting decisions made, relying on a process to make decisions that involves getting buy-in from multiple parties and multiple layers.

Interviews with Key Individuals

While the assessment provided comprehensive information on major aspects of the company, it was not enough to draw conclusions about some of the primary concerns as well as underlying factors. To expedite the process, the assessment findings were used to generate a set of interview questions. This way, the questions were more targeted and specific to the company. Interviews were conducted with four executives, four members of the middle management team, and four non-supervisory team members to delve deeper and help specify gaps in performance and impact.

Five concerns were expressed:

- In the area of quality, they noted an increase in the number of errors made.
- In turnaround time to fulfill customer orders, orders were taking longer to complete; and therefore, more factories were reporting problems filling orders on time.
- With the increase in new employees, they needed more leaders prepared and poised for promotion.
- Given the change of the business and the fact that more change was needed, it was apparent that the existing leadership model was inadequate.
- They had experienced unusually high turnover.
- The most recent customer satisfaction survey indicated a marked decrease in customer satisfaction.

Johari Window

Figure 14-1 shows the Johari window created by Luft and Ingam (1955). In the Johari window, there are four aspects that describe an individual. When applied to organizations, the first domain is open for both insiders and outsiders to see. The second domain is hidden from outsiders but known to those on the inside. The third domain is one that the company doesn't see whereas an outsider could more readily see, otherwise known as blind spots. The fourth domain is one that neither the company nor an outsider readily sees, otherwise described as unknown. When using the concept of the Johari window in this case, the organizational features were plugged into the four quadrants to illustrate key aspects for this organization. Data from the initial meeting, organization culture assessment, and interview findings were used to populate what is seen in Figure 14-2.

Open. Several characteristics are apparent to insiders as well as outsiders. The company has been in business for several decades, and has an annual report that is made available internally as well as externally. The communication that exists is formal and written. This company has a reputation for being hardworking, possessing a strong work ethic, and as willing to do what it takes to fulfill the customer's request.

Figure 14-1. The Johari Window

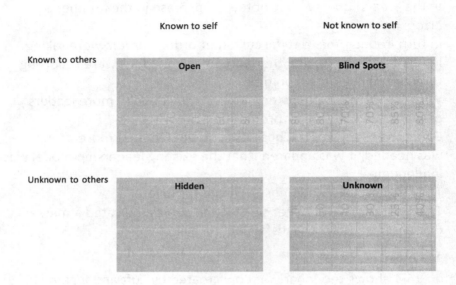

	Known to self	Not known to self
Known to others	Open	Blind Spots
Unknown to others	Hidden	Unknown

Figure 14-2. The Johari Window Applied to Case

	Known to self	Not known to self
Known to others	**Open** • Public history • Formal communication • Strong work ethic • Customer driven	**Blind Spots** • Rigid thinking, keeping status quo • Cautious • Lack top-down communication
Unknown to others	**Hidden** • Productivity • Dependent on CEO • No strong successor • Lack clear direction • Micro-manage	**Unknown** • Lack of trust from leadership toward workforce • Workforce viewed as lazy, not pulling own weight

Hidden. Those who work for AMC are forthright about their reliance on their CEO and that there is no clear successor. They also are acutely aware that the CEO is nearing retirement age and there is heightened anxiety about this fact. Like the CEO, the executive team members also have no succession plan in place. In addition to there being no succession plan in place, there is no strategic plan that is communicated or known in the organization. Interviewees identified patterns of micro-management, tightly held supervision, and that employees felt a general sense of frustration.

Blind Spots. The Capstone Organization Culture Assessment and the interviews revealed several areas that we categorized as blind spots. Culturally speaking, the unwritten rules that were operational in AMC formed expectations around acceptable risk, innovation, limited internal communication, and maintaining status quo. While AMC may not have been cognizant of these patterns, the collected data were confirming of these points.

Unknown. During the interviews, two underlying themes were noted. What the executive interviewees conveyed was confirmed by middle managers and non-supervisory team members. The two themes were:

- Leadership did not trust workforce.
- Leadership viewed workforce as lazy and not pulling their own weight.

These are categorized as unknown since they are not overtly expressed in the workplace. The unknown, in this case, is similar to Schein's description of underlying assumptions that are difficult to discern because they exist on an unconscious level (2010).

FEEDBACK GIVEN AND SOLUTION SELECTED

A report was generated that illustrated the findings from the interviews and the Capstone Organization Culture Assessment. While the report had conclusions and recommendations, a meeting was arranged between the consultant and the leadership team. It was during this meeting that findings were discussed and together, several key decisions were made. The decision was made to form a Guiding Coalition Group in the organization to assume responsibility for the changes that needed to be made. Realizing that resistance to change was likely, organizational readiness for change and flexibility were key, focusing on employees who were accountable to achieve results.

The Guiding Coalition was headed up by an executive champion and comprised of cross-functional employees with a mix of leaders and non-leaders. Under this group's direction, the organization took on the challenge of recreating itself by taking two significant steps:

1. **Master Action Planning Sessions:** The Guiding Coalition Group participated in strategic planning sessions, defining long-term and strategic plans and communicating those plans in the organization. Not only did the organization's scores on the assessment indicate that planning was a deficit, but they also could see consequences of operating their business in a "shoot-from-the-hip" modality. Three sub-groups emerged from this exercise, and each group was tasked with developing an action plan that would ultimately roll up to a Master Action Plan. The first group focused on initiatives to address the business needs at hand, including reducing error, reducing time for order completion, and increasing customer satisfaction. The second group dedicated themselves to succession planning for the CEO and the executive team, reducing turnover, increasing the internal fill rate and promotable leadership positions. The third group worked on devising a communication plan to support the change initiative. It was important to define and communicate the challenge, defining where the company was headed.

2. **Leadership Development:** This was going to be one of the toughest areas to tackle. Going from an autocratic style of management to one characterized as democratic or empowering was no easy feat. This fact led the OD team to create an innovative way to transform their leadership team. In addition to designing an eight-module leadership program, each leader was asked to create an action plan to implement new behaviors, which supported the Master Action Plan. Leaders were asked to work with their team of direct reports and identify solutions to one of four existing problems: 1) error rates, 2) turnaround time for order completion, 3) customer satisfaction, 4) turnover. The leaders were asked to lead these teams, not in an

autocratic way, but in a democratic way—challenging the team to identify solutions to existing problems. Leaders were encouraged to use brainstorming, and in turn, they were to submit their team's findings to the Guiding Coalition Group. This helped foster an empowering type of leadership and atmosphere, while generating potential solutions for the Guiding Coalition Group.

DATA COLLECTION PLAN

Table 14-1 shows the data collection plan for the change management project. Multilevel objectives were created for Levels 1 through 5. The data collection plan shows targets for each level, along with timing of the data collection and who is responsible for collecting data at each level.

For Levels 1 and 2, two brief questionnaires were administered at the conclusion of the intervention and were used to collect reaction and learning data. The main items of concern for Level 1 are relevance and importance of the interventions, as well as action items identified through strategic planning and leadership development. For Level 2, the focus was on increasing knowledge and skills in leadership and planning.

Since the organization scored lower than average on leadership and planning, the main target for Level 3 was increasing organization planning behavior, changing the work effort to be aligned with the initiatives identified on the Master Action Plan, and improving leadership behaviors. Several sources of data were used to measure change in behavior. The main source of data, to examine whether the work effort was changing, was through the company's monthly progress reports. Additionally, action plans were used to gauge the degree that planning behaviors were being used in day-to-day jobs. The 360-degree feedback assessments were also used to measure leadership behaviors and progress made.

Internal HR and business databases were used to collect Level 4 data at six months and one year after the intervention. Specifically, job satisfaction and turnover were collected from HR. Factories reporting problems with time to complete, error rates, and customer satisfaction were collected from the operations department through its business database.

Table 14-1. Data Collection Plan

Level	Objective(s)	Measures/Data	Data Collection Method	Data Sources	Timing	Responsibilities
1	**SATISFACTION/PLANNED ACTION** • Relevance to organization • Importance to organization success • Action items identified on Master Action Plan • Action items identified by leaders participating in leadership development	• Average of 4 on 5-point scale	• Questionnaire	• Guiding Coalition Group • Leaders participating in leadership development	• Immediately following: 1. strategic planning sessions 2. leadership development	• OD team
2	**LEARNING** • Enhancing leadership skills • Improving planning skills	• Average of 4 on 5-point scale	• Questionnaire	• Guiding Coalition Group • Leaders participating in leadership development	• Immediately following: 1. strategic planning sessions 2. leadership development	• OD team
3	**BEHAVIOR CHANGE** • Increase organization planning behavior • Improve leadership behaviors • Change work effort according to Master Action Plan	• Improvement made on Master Action Plan • Improved leadership behavior	• Master Action Plan update report • Action plan • 360 feedback report	• Guiding Coalition Group • Leaders participating in leadership development	• Six months after strategic planning and leadership development	• OD team

Table 14-1. Data Collection Plan *(continued)*

4	BUSINESS IMPACT			
	• Increase customer satisfaction • Reduce number of factories reporting problems with time to fulfill customer orders • Reduce turnover • Reduce errors • Increase in promotions	• Reduce time to fulfill customer orders • Decrease turnover • Increase in promotion • Increase customer satisfaction • Reduce errors	• HR database • Quality database • Brief questionnaire	• Guiding Coalition Group • Leaders participating in leadership development	• Six months and one year after strategic planning and leadership development	• OD team
5	ROI 25%					
	Comments: Action plans are provided and explained during leadership development program.					

ROI ANALYSIS PLAN

Table 14-2 shows the ROI Analysis Plan. For the Level 4 data items, two methods were used to isolate the effects of the intervention: 1) trendline analysis and 2) estimates from the Guiding Coalition. In this case, historical data were projected in a trend and compared with the actual data to determine the impact. For error rates and turnover, estimates were also collected through a brief questionnaire from the Guiding Coalition to further corroborate the isolation factor.

Methods of converting data to money involved the use of standard values that had already been identified. The HR department already had identified standard values for turnover and the operations department had previously assigned standard values for error rates.

The project's fully loaded cost profile included the following: costs associated with diagnostics, which included conducting the Capstone Organization Culture Survey; the expense and time of those involved in conducting interviews; the two-fold intervention; facilities expense; administrative overhead; communication and evaluation costs.

Expected intangible benefits included improved communication, improved problem solving, and increased job satisfaction. Targets for communication and reporting were threefold, including the executive team, leadership team, and OD team.

RESULTS

Level 1, Reaction and Planned Action Results

A questionnaire was used to capture reaction data. Overall, the results were positive, indicating that the planning sessions and leadership development were timely and important for the future of the organization. Master Action Plans were created as a result of the planning intervention, and leadership action plans were created as a result of the leadership development initiative.

Level 2, Learning Results

In addition to the Level 1 items, the same questionnaire was used to collect Level 2 data. Items were included on the questionnaire that measured organization learning of leadership and knowledge and skills of planning.

Table 14-2. ROI Analysis Plan for Organization Culture Change Project

ROI ANALYSIS PLAN

Intervention: Organization Culture Change Project　　　Responsibility: Lizette Zuniga　　　Date:

Data Items (Usually Level 4)	Methods for Isolating the Effects of the Intervention	Methods of Converting Data to Monetary Values	Cost Categories	Intangible Benefits	Communication Targets for Final Report	Other Influences/ Issues During Application	Comments
• Reduction in errors	• Trend Line • Guiding Coalition's Estimates	• Standard value	• Diagnostics • Time of those involved in process • Strategic planning sessions • Leadership development initiative • 360° feedback • Administrative overhead • Communication expenses • Facilities • Evaluation	• Improved communication • Improved problem solving • Increased job satisfaction	• Executives • Guiding Coalition Group • Those involved in leadership development • OD team	• N/A	• There was overlap between those involved in strategic planning and those involved in leadership development
• Reduction in turnover	• Trend Line • Guiding Coalition's Estimates	• Standard value					
• Reduce reporting problems with filling customer orders on time	• Trend Line	• N/A					
• Increase customer satisfaction	• Trend Line	• N/A					
• Increase promotions	• Trend Line	• N/A					

Level 3, Behavior Change Results

The Master Action Plan reflected the specific organization initiatives and behaviors the group felt were necessary to affect the desired change. Six months after the plan was created, the OD team reviewed the monthly progress reports for months one through six to discern the change. Updates on the action plans created by leadership were also collected at the same time (after six months). Finally, 360-degree feedback data were also used to measure changes in awareness and leadership behaviors.

Level 4, Impact Results

The Level 4, Impact results were broken down into five categories, detailed below. See Table 14-3 for an overview of Level 4 results.

Factories Reporting Problems with Time-to-Order Completion. This measure was significant as it also affected customer satisfaction. In the beginning of the project, there was discussion as to the best way to report this measure. Every attempt was made to collect an average time for order completion, but after viewing the data and identifying the multiple types of orders and variations, it was decided that a meaningful way to track this item would be to show whether the trend went downward on the number of factories who reported problems with completing customer orders on time. The baseline showed that 31 factories reported problems with completing customer orders on time. Six months later, the number of factories went down to 18; one year later, the number of factories reporting problems with completing customer orders on time was six.

Error Rates. Error rates were tallied using common work practices of counting the number of error rates per 100. The average number of error rates was 35 per 100 at the start of this project. Six months later, it had decreased to 24 per 100. One year later, the number of error rates significantly decreased to seven per 100.

Turnover Costs. Although turnover had been traditionally low, in the last three years it had increased, due to significant changes in the workplace. One year after the intervention, turnover was reduced from 655 to 275. The trend-line analysis supported the turnover reduction.

Promotions. Trending data showed moderate improvement in promotions. The baseline was 5 percent prior to the intervention. One year later, the percent of promotions had increased to 18 percent.

Customer Satisfaction. Customer satisfaction surveys were conducted routinely in this organization. Two key items used for this project were:

- AMC moving aggressively to meet customer needs
- Long-term commitment to AMC

On both items, customer satisfaction increased. In the beginning of the project, 60 percent indicated that AMC moved to aggressively meet customer needs; whereas one year later, this number reached 82 percent. As for long-term commitment to AMC, 45 percent stated they were committed to a long-term relationship; whereas one year later, this figure was up to 68 percent.

Several intangible benefits were identified in the study and confirmed by actual input from responses on the questionnaire administered to the Guiding Coalition Group. The following benefits were realized as a result of the intervention:

- Improved communication
- Improved problem solving
- Increased job satisfaction

No attempt was made to place monetary values on any of the intangibles.

Level 5, ROI Results

The ROI results, Level 5, were calculated for costs and benefits.

Costs. Table 14-4 outlines the costs of the intervention. Calculating the cost of the intervention follows the categories outlined in the evaluation plan. For diagnostics, the total cost was $12,000. The strategic planning sessions were $112,000. Development and instructor time in leadership development were estimated at $550,000, and the 360-degree assessment costs were $25,000. The materials were $22,000, while a percentage for overhead was

Table 14-3. Level 4 Measures

Level 4 Measure	Baseline (Before Intervention)	Six Months Later	One Year Later
Factories reporting problems with filling customer orders on time	31	18	6
Reduce error rates	35 errors per 100	24 errors per 100	7 errors per 100
Increase customer satisfaction	• 60% indicated they moved to aggressively meet customer needs; • 45% said they were committed to long term relationship	N/A	• 82% indicated they moved to aggressively meet customer needs; • 68% said they were committed to long term relationship
Reduce turnover	655	299	275
Increase promotions	5%	8%	18%

allocated to this intervention with an estimate of $1,500. Facilities, food, and refreshments came to $8,000; and since there were communication tasks and activities involved to help with change management, these costs were factored in, totaling $5,000.

The time involved for those in the Guiding Coalition and those participating in the leadership development program was also factored in. Salaries and benefits multiplied by the total time came to $95,000. The meeting room facilities, food, and refreshments were estimated at $8,000, while the evaluation costs were $18,500. Tallying all of these cost factors together brings the total to $849,000.

Benefits. The determination of monetary benefits for intervention was developed using the methods outlined in the ROI analysis plan. A standard value has routinely been used at AMC to reflect the cost of annual improvement value. As Table 14-5 illustrates, the error rates were converted

Table 14-4. Intervention Costs

Cost of Item	Cost
Diagnostics	$12,000
Strategic planning sessions	$112,000
Leadership development faculty/sessions	$550,000
360° assessment	$25,000
Program materials	$22,000
Overhead	$1,500
Facilities, food, and refreshments	$8,000
Communication	$5,000
Participant salaries (plus benefits) for time involved	$95,000
Evaluation costs	$18,500
Total	**$849,000**

based on a standard value of $750 per error. With 28 errors prevented each month, this yielded a $21,000 monthly improvement. When annualizing this improvement, the value is $252,000. After factoring in the average confidence percentage from the Guiding Coalition Group at 92 percent, the annual improvement is $231,840.

Value for Errors Rates
$750 per error x 28 (change) = $21,000 (monthly)

$21,000 x 12 (months) = $252,000 (annual)

$252,000 x 92% (confidence 5%) = $231,840

The turnover rates were converted based on a standard value of $3,200 per unit of turnover. The majority of those who vacated their positions were in non-supervisory positions. Out-of-pocket expenses were the main cost categories that this organization used for costing turnover for non-supervisors. These categories included sign-on bonuses, recruitment, relocation, and severance. With 380 prevented during the year, this yielded an improvement value of $1,216,000. After factoring in the average confidence percentage from the Guiding Coalition Group, at 85 percent, the annual improvement is $1,033,600. The ROI calculation is on the next page.

Table 14-5. Monetized Benefits

	Annual Change in Measure	Unit Value	Annual Improvement Value	Guiding Coalition Group Confidence %	Adjustments Based on Confidence %
Error rates	336	$750	$252,000	92%	$231,840
Turnover	380	$3,200	$1,216,000	85%	$1,033,600

$$\text{ROI} = \frac{\$1,265,440 - \$849,000}{\$849,000} = 49\%$$

CONCLUSIONS AND RECOMMENDTIONS

Several assumptions need to be mentioned in the discussion of conclusions and recommendations. One is that high turnover rates in a tight labor market can make the required hiring numbers an absolute barrier to growth plans. Another assumption made is that the main reason people leave their jobs is due to their relationship with their manager, and while this has been documented in research (Connaughton, 1999), it is not 100 percent certain that this is the primary reason for this organization. This assumption, nevertheless, is worth noting, due to the actions that were taken to develop the leadership pool. One final assumption to highlight is that the estimates collected by the Guiding Coalition Group were credible in isolating the effects of the solution. While a more objective method for isolating the effects was preferred (such as control group), the timing and rollout of the intervention did not allow for this approach in this case. When considering gathering estimates, out of all involved, this group appeared to be in the best position to assign estimates based on its depth of involvement in the project.

While this is a preliminary analysis of the impact of this culture change intervention, results from this study indicate that this intervention appears to be affecting turnover and error rates across the business in a significant way. Reports from the factories indicate a marked decrease among those reporting problems with filling customer orders in a timely manner. Customer satisfaction has also increased, noted on the two items that were particularly relevant for this study. From the action plans that were gathered from those participating in the leadership development initiative, improvement was made in communication and problem solving. Overall the intervention is contributing to behavioral changes among those participating in the Guiding Coalition Group and the sub-group planning sessions.

For purposes of this study, the cost of turnover was a particularly conservative estimate. Cost factors for contract labor, sign on bonuses, referral bonuses, temp help, overtime, and training were not included in the turnover calculations.

Promotion data suggest that there has been a moderate increase. Ongoing collection of promotion data is highly recommended. Data that shows cross-business unit transfers is another way to assess the impact of this intervention.

Improved job satisfaction was identified as an intangible benefit that was desired. At the time of this report, the annual employee satisfaction survey was being prepared for company-wide distribution; therefore, there are no data available to report on this measure at this time.

Recommendations include continuing to track the impact of the intervention, including the job satisfaction data when it will be available. As organization culture change projects are long-term solutions and can take three to five years to take root in an organization and yield desirable change, there would be value in reviewing data collected after year two and year three of this intervention. To see if there is a marked difference in the organizational behaviors that were identified during the culture assessment and diagnostics phase, it is recommended to administer the assessment again after ample time has passed to assess whether these behaviors have changed. Preliminary and informal (anecdotal data) data confirm that the key organizational behaviors of leadership and planning had changed, and the ROI analysis confirms that major business metrics were favorably affected. These findings support that the intervention was a worthwhile effort.

Questions for Discussion

1. For the remaining Level 4 improvement measures that were not converted to money, are there credible techniques to monetize these metrics? Which additional ones would you convert to money? Please explain.
2. Discuss alternatives for isolating the impact for this OD intervention.
3. Are there items of interest that warrant follow up or further understanding/ analysis? If yes, what are they, and what methods would you employ to follow up?

4. What is the best way to communicate these findings?
5. Would the methods used in this case study be relevant for a potential case in your organization? Why or why not?

Chapter

Measuring ROI in
Leadership for Performance

Fashion Stores Incorporated

by Jack J. Phillips

This large fashion retailer with popular brands is planning for growth and profitability. The store managers were identified as the most critical talent in the organization. The leadership development program was carefully designed for more than 4,000 store managers, with an upfront needs assessment and initial alignment. It is designed to drive key performance measures within the stores using a combination of learning portals, coaches, 360-degree feedback, and a two-day classroom session.

BACKGROUND

Fashion Stores, Inc. (FSI) is a large international retailer with four major brands. The retailer operates stores in more than 50 countries with more than 100,000 employees. Store managers, who are considered to be the critical talent in the organization, manage the stores. The retailer has plans for tremendous growth, with a goal to have stores in more than 100 countries and to be the most profitable retail store chain. While all employees are considered to be important talent, the store managers are considered critical for achieving these two goals. To make this growth and profitability a reality, FSI wants to invest in leadership development for store managers. Moving beyond the current manager-training program, sales training, and other types of learning and development opportunities offered to this group, this new program is aimed at developing leaders who can develop high-performance teams that will drive superior results for the stores.

The Analysis

Meeting the needs of the executives to develop this program required the leadership development team to focus on two important areas. The first is to determine the specific competencies necessary for high-performance teams and to ensure that those competencies are needed in the stores. The second important area of the process is to ensure that this program directly aligns with very specific business metrics.

The first part of the analysis included a review of the literature on leadership development for high-performance teams to determine some of the common threads between high-performance workplaces. Next, through interviews with the senior executives and regional store executives, the competencies were further tuned and customized to the company's situation and culture. In addition, a dozen store managers participated in a focus group to understand how these competencies fit into the structure and culture of the stores. The discussion also focused on the extent to which the current store managers currently possessed those competencies. This led to further adjustments, and 10 competencies and skills of high-performance teams were determined to be directly related to this culture and type of business:

1. Identifying opportunities for improvements
2. Addressing challenges and roadblocks
3. Building trust and confidence
4. Setting clear goals and expectations
5. Managing conflicts and differences
6. Recognizing and rewarding team members
7. Improving average performers
8. Fostering open and clear communications
9. Providing feedback and support
10. Action planning, reflecting, and adjusting

With these competencies identified, the next phase was to determine the best way to deliver the program and achieve business alignment.

Program Design

As with most retail organizations, taking managers away from their work for an extensive period of time was nearly impossible. Presently, the learning and development team and the leadership development team were using a variety of different types of technology-based learning methods. After reviewing the effectiveness of the different learning delivery methods, and considering the cost and convenience, a learning design was developed that would include e-learning modules, the use of a learning portal, classroom learning, coaching support, and the use of 360-degree feedback—all focused on achieving business impact. Figure 15-1 shows the program design.

Figure 15-1. Program Design: Leadership for Performance

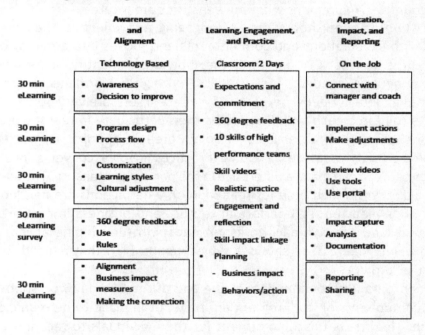

The program begins with five 30-minute e-learning modules that participants complete before attending the program. The first module focuses on the awareness of the process, the need to improve results, and how the program is designed to increase store performance, which usually attracts the interest of the store managers. The next module focuses on the program design and how it will flow through the different module segments and components. The third module indicates how the program is customized to their needs, designed around various learning styles, and adapted to cultural differences. This is connected to HR data using a process that matches the individual's learning style, as well as the culture of the store and country. The fourth e-learning module presents the 360-degree feedback process, which describes its purpose, use, and particular rules and conditions. Participants will take the survey shortly after this module is completed. Finally the last, and perhaps most critical, is the fifth e-learning module, which covers the alignment process. It starts with the business impact measures in the store by asking each store manager to select at least two measures that would need to improve using the competencies in the program. This begins with the end in mind, with the end defined as business performance improvement. With these modules complete, participants are scheduled to attend a two-day workshop near their store. These workshops are offered in major cities, or in countries and regions where fewer stores are located.

The two-day workshop is relevant, engaging, and reflective. The workshop starts with expectations and commitments and moves into a review of the 360-degree feedback. From that, the individuals identify actions where improvement is needed. The 10 skills for high-performance teams are explored in detail. Videos, developed for the skill sets, are very powerful and used to reinforce each skill. Individuals then participate in realistic practice sessions focusing on a particular problem area or opportunity as defined by the business measure. The skill practices involve conversations with employees who can make a difference in the particular measure. The learning is engaging with much time for reflection on what actions are needed. The linkage between the high-performance skills and business impact are also discussed, and the two-day workshop ends with developing at least two action plans. Figure 15-2 shows a typical action plan that is used for this particular project.

The program is not complete at the end of the two-day workshop—five more components of the program are now put in place to be managed on the job. The first is the appointment for the individuals to reconnect with their manager about the measures selected for improvement, give feedback on the program, and secure manager support going forward. There is also an appointment to connect with a coach that was selected by the store manager (the participant). The coach is prepared to assist them along the way, providing guidance and support as needed to make the process work. The second component is to implement actions and make adjustments when necessary. After discussing the issues with the manager and coach, there may be some adjustments in both the business measure and the specific actions necessary to improve the measures.

Figure 15-2. Action Plan Template

Participant: _____ Manager: _____ Program Manager: _____

Objective: Increase Sales with existing clients by 20%

Evaluation Period: Jan – March

Improvement Measure: Monthly Sales

Current Performance: $56,000/mo. Target Performance: $67,000

Action Steps		Analysis
Meet with key clients to discuss issues, concerns, opportunities.	Jan. 31	A. What is the unit of measure? Monthly sales, existing clients
Review customer feedback data—look for trends and patterns.	Feb. 1	B. What is the value (cost) of one unit? 25% profit margin
Counsel with "at risk" clients to correct problems and explore opportunities for improvement.	Feb. 2	C. How did you arrive at this value? Standard value
Develop business plan for high-potential clients.	Feb. 5	D. How much did the measure change during the evaluation period (monthly value)? $13,000
Provide recognition to clients with long tenure.	Routinely	E. What other factors could have contributed to this improvement? Changes in market, new promotion
Schedule appreciation dinner for key clients.	Feb.15	F. What percent of this change was actually caused by this program? 30%
Encourage marketing to delegate more responsibilities.	Feb.20	G. What level of confidence do you place on the above information? (100% = Certainty and 0% = No confidence) 60%
Follow up with each discussion and discuss improvement and plan other action.	Routinely	
Monitor improvement, provide support when appropriate.	March 15	

Intangible benefits: Client satisfaction, loyalty

Comments: Excellent, hard-hitting program

The third component of the project's application is using the videos and tools provided in the learning portal. This includes reviewing the videos, checklists, and job aids that might be helpful in working with the team using the competencies. A fourth component, which is a very important part of the process, is to record the impact improvement, conduct an analysis, isolate the effects of the program from other influences, and calculate the monetary value of each process. The information and tools for this were provided in the workshop and are available to them online and from store databases. The summary information was recorded on each action plan. Finally, the last component is to report results to the leadership development team. This information is then shared with the rest of the group.

The program components, shown in Table 15-1, represent a tremendous amount of variety, all designed to enhance learning, encourage engagement, facilitate application, and drive business impact. Technology use is significant, with much of the program operating virtually. E-learning is an important part of this program, with five modules serving as the prelude to the classroom. The classroom is supplemented with a coach, support, and tools that are available virtually. The learning portal provides a variety of tools, templates, process checklists, and the videos used in the workshop— all of which are aimed at reinforcing, explaining, and enhancing performance as the managers use the competencies and drive store performance. In addition, the program has the flexibility of being adapted to different learning styles and can be adjusted culturally to the different countries where the program is conducted.

Table 15-1. Program Components

1.	E-learning
2.	Learning portal
3.	360-degree assessment
4.	Classroom involvement and engagement
5.	Practice in real situations
6.	Learning, reflection, and action
7.	Cultural adjustment
8.	Learning styles
9.	Realistic videos
10.	Coaching support

The leadership development team was in charge of this project from the very beginning. They engaged with external vendors for needs assessment, the program design, and a separate production company for the videos. Finally, an external firm was involved in the evaluation.

THE EVALUATION APPROACH

Eventually, this program will be available to 4,000 managers. Although it is required, if managers are convinced that they have the necessary skill sets, they have the option to skip the classroom portion, but they still have to take on the part of the process that involves application and impact. It is anticipated that very few, if any, will opt out of this process because they will understand the need for the program and realize that it is aimed at improving store performance.

To understand how well the program is working and to see if adjustments are made, the organizers targeted about 100 people for the initial evaluation, with representatives from one workshop in each of the four largest markets in the company—the United States, South America, Asia, and Europe. An early workshop will be offered in those areas if possible, and it is anticipated that approximately 25 participants will attend each workshop. However, attendance numbers may be higher or lower depending on availability and the concentration of managers in the area.

Because of the cost of the program and its link to the success of the business and strategic objectives, the management team would like the evaluation to include both the impact and the ROI. The leadership development team engaged the services of the global leader in ROI evaluation to provide oversight, guidance, support, and advice for the evaluation. Its role was planning the evaluation, data collection and analysis, and presentation to the senior executives. In addition, the ROI expert worked hand-in-hand with the leadership development team to develop this level of evaluation capability internally for future projects.

Data Collection

Figure 15-3 shows the data collection plan for this program. The plan starts with the objectives and defines the measures, data collection method and source, timing, and responsibilities. This is a classic plan for ROI analysis.

ROI Analysis Plan

Figure 15-4 presents the ROI analysis plan for this project, and represents a very common approach to this type of analysis. It begins with the business impact measures that will be influenced by the program. Each participant selects at least two measures to improve, using the competencies and skills

Figure 15-3. Data Collection Plan

Program/Project: Leadership for Performance Responsibility: _____ Date: _____

Level	Broad Program Objective(s)	Measures	Data Collection Method/Instruments	Data Sources	Timing	Responsibilities
1	**SATISFACTION/PLANNED ACTION** Participants will rate the following reactions: • The program was important to my success • My coach was helpful • Content is relevant • The technology was effective • I will use the content with my team • The classroom session was valuable • I would recommend this program to others • The program is easy to follow • The action plan was valuable	• 4 out of 5 on a 5-point scale	• Questionnaire	• Participants	• 2 to 4 months from start of program (some items collected one month after end of workshop)	• Leadership development team
2	**LEARNING** Demonstrate successful use of the following skill sets: • Identifying opportunities for improvement • Addressing challenges and road blocks • Building trust and confidence • Setting clear goals and expectations • Managing conflicts and differences • Providing feedback and support • Recognizing and rewarding team members • Improving average performers • Fostering open and clear communication • Action planning, reflecting, and adjusting	• 3 out of 4 on a 4-point scale	• Observation	• Facilitator	• At the end of the workshop	• Facilitator

Figure 15-3. Data Collection Plan (continued)

Level	Broad Program Objective(s)	Measures	Data Collection Method/Instruments	Data Sources	Timing	Responsibilities
	Participants will know how to: • Increase effectiveness as a leader • Build high-performance teams • Build self-assessed learning change	4 out of 5 on a 5-point scale	Questionnaire	Facilitator	At the end of the workshop	Facilitator
3	APPLICATION/IMPLEMENTATION Participants will: • Complete the action plan within 4 months • Use the coach • Use the learning portal • Apply the 10 leadership skills • Use the 10 skills frequently • Will achieve success with the 10 skills	• Checklist • 4 out of 5 on a 5-point scale	Questionnaire Action Plan	Participants	2 months	Leadership development team
4	BUSINESS IMPACT Participants will make improvements in at least two of the following measures: • Increased sales with existing customers • New customers • Staff turnover • Store profit margin • Inventory shrinkage • Product returns • Store expenses • Customer complaints • Staff sick leave • Other:		Action plan	Participants	4 months after workshop	Leadership development team
5	ROI 20%	Comments:				

Figure 15-4. ROI Analysis Plan

Purpose of this evaluation: _____

Program/Project: Leadership for Performance _____ Responsibility: _____

Date: _____

Data Items (Usually Level 4)	Methods for Isolating the Effects of the Program/Process	Methods of Converting Data to Monetary Values	Cost Categories	Intangible Benefits	Communication Targets for Final Report	Other Influences/Issues During Application	Comments
At least two measures selected by participant	Participant's estimate	Standard values or expert input	• Initial analysis and assessment • Development of solutions • Implementation and application • Salaries and benefits for LD team • Salaries and benefits for participants' time • Salaries and benefits for coaches' time • Program materials • Hardware and software • Travel, lodging, and meals • Use of facilities • Administrative support and overhead • Evaluation and reporting	• Job engagement • Career satisfaction • Net promoter score • Image • Reputation • Brand	• Top executives • Regional store managers • HR team • Participants • Leadership development team • Prospective participants		

for high-performance teams. The method of isolation is the participant's estimate. A comparison group would be best; however, experimental versus control group comparison is not possible because participants may have selected different measures. With participant estimates, the data are collected in a nonthreatening, nonbiased way, and there are adjustments for error in their estimates. The method used to convert data to money is using standard items (presented later) provided to participants in the two-day workshop or through experts.

RESULTS

A total of 93 participants attended the workshop and applied the competencies. A variety of data collection methods were used, including questionnaires, action planning, and observation to provide the results organized by different levels.

Level 1 (Reaction) Results

Table 15-2 shows how participants reacted to the program. This was done one month after the workshop to give individuals an opportunity to clarify their reactions and provide responses. The group's average reaction was meeting or exceeding expectations (four out of five on a five-point scale). A total of 89 responded to this questionnaire, representing a 96 percent response rate. The technology effectiveness question (question four) had a lower than expected result. There were a few technology glitches that got in the way and some managers had difficulty following the program's different modules and processes. Otherwise, the reaction to the program was quite good, with "intent to use" being the star measure.

Table 15-2. Reaction Results

The program was important to my success.	4.2
My coach was helpful.	3.7
Content is relevant.	4.1
The technology was effective.	3.9
I will use the content with my team.	4.7
The classroom session was valuable.	4.4
I would recommend this program to others.	4.3
The program was easy to follow.	3.9
The action plan was valuable.	4.3

*Using a 5-point scale

Level 2 (Learning) Results

The first measure of learning was the observation of the skill practices. Because they had repeated practices if the skills were unsatisfactory, all participants scored satisfactory, as reported by the facilitators. Additional learning results were connected, as displayed in Figure 15-3, with the individuals rating the extent to which the program changed their knowledge and use of skills. This was completed during the one-month follow up after the workshop. In addition, they were asked two knowledge questions regarding being a more effective leader and knowing how to build high-performance teams. In both cases, the results exceeded expectations. A total of 89 responded.

Table 15-3. Learning Results

I know more about my effectiveness as a leader.	4.7
I know how to build a high-performance team.	4.5
10 skill self-assessment on learning change.	4.1

*Using a 5-point scale

Level 3 (Application) Results

Application results were collected two months after the workshop. It begins with the percent of individuals completing action plans (86 percent) which is a very high number considering the detail involved in the actual planning process. The percent using coaching was a little less than expected (72 percent), as well as those using the learning portal (54 percent). Although there were no objectives set for portal use or coach use, it was expected that almost all the participants would use both. Pre- and post-feedback showed gains, although the skill sets were already there for many participants. The pre-feedback score of 3.82 is close to where it needs to be for success (four out of five). On the post-assessment, the results moved to 4.6 for total skill assessment. For extent of use, on a five-point scale, this result just barely met the objective (4.2), and was lower for frequency and success with use (3.8 and 3.9, respectively). The most valuable skill was improving the average performer, the least valuable skill was managing conflicts and differences, and the most difficult skill was fostering open and clear communications. These results were what would be expected for this kind of process.

Barriers and Enablers

Table 15-4 shows the barriers and enablers to use. As expected, there were not many barriers. The greatest barrier was not enough time, and this was anticipated given the time constraints for the e-learning and virtual modules. The other noted barriers were minor, ranging from technology to lack of support, although lack of support was in the acceptable range. Overall, barriers were not a problem.

Also, as expected, the enablers were present with many of the participants. This is encouraging because there was high use of the skill and follow-through on the action plans. The greatest enabler was the content, which was relevant for the managers. Following this was regional manager support. It was anticipated that the coach would be rated higher, but the learning portal was rated a little higher than expected. The 360-degree feedback did not seem to be much of an enabler to manager success.

Table 15-4. Barriers and Enablers

Barriers to Use	Percent responding	Enablers to Success	Percent responding
1. Not enough time to do it properly	14%	1. Great content	72%
2. Technology problems	11%	2. Regional manager support	85%
3. Lack of support from regional manager	7%	3. Convenient to participate/use	58%
4. Program was too complicated	6%	4. Effective design	45%
5. Doesn't fit the culture	5%	5. Videos were helpful	32%
6. Too difficult to use the skills	3%	6. Coaching was effective	19%
7. Other	7%	7. Learning portal	18%
		8. Other	14%

Level 4 (Impact) Results

Table 15-5 shows the impact results in terms of the particular measures chosen by the participants. Each participant was asked to select at least two measures to improve using the competencies in the program. As expected, the number one measure was increasing sales in existing customers—taking extra effort to up-sell, cross-sell, and entice existing customers to come in the store more often and provide excellent service to make them buy more (38 percent of the managers selected this measure). The next most often selected measure was acquiring new customers. FSI provided mechanisms to reach out to individuals who are not current clients and that was important for the managers who selected that particular measure for improvement (27 percent). Not surprisingly, staff turnover came in third with 24 percent, although turnover at FSI is lower than typical retail stores.

Increasing the store profit margin was the next measure (20 percent), which was improved by controlling expenses, limiting waste, and avoiding price discounting or the need to give discounts to compensate problems. Inventory shrinkage was another important measure for consideration with 18 percent. Product returns were reduced and 15 percent selected this measure. Returns occur when customers aren't fully satisfied with the product they have purchased or the product has not lived up to expectations. Good customer service can reduce returns. Controlling costs and reducing customer complaints were the next two measures (15 percent and 12 percent, respectively). Cost control is related to store profit margin and was not that difficult to tackle. Recognizing that there are fewer complaints at the store—and the goal was to have zero complaints—a few of the managers took on complaints as an opportunity for reduction.

Finally, some managers addressed the sick leave measure (11 percent). The store pays employees when they are on sick leave unless it becomes excessive. However, some employees were taking too many sick days, which was a costly and disruptive process. There were several other miscellaneous measures that were either unique to a particular store or an unusual problem that was not one of the main measures. A few ambitious managers selected more than two measures and one manager selected four measures for improvement.

Table 15-5. Impact Results

Business Measures Selected	Percent Selecting
Increased sales with existing customers	38%
New customers	27%
Staff turnover	24%
Store profit margin	20%
Inventory shrinkage	18%
Product returns	15%
Store expenses	15%
Customer complaints	12%
Staff sick leave	11%
Other	28%
Each manager was required to select at least two measures. A total of 176 usable measures were selected. A few managers selected three measures. One participant selected four measures. n = 85	

Isolating the Effects of the Program

To have a credible analysis, initial steps had to be taken to isolate the effects of the program from other influences. Given the sales and marketing metrics that were used, there are many other factors that affect these measures, which often leaves a program like this with only a minor part of improvement. While several processes were considered, such as setting up a control group or using simple trend line analysis, the team settled on using estimates from the participants.

The estimates would be collected on the action-planning document with explanation in the classroom as to what was involved and how important the issue was to the final analysis. In addition, the estimate was adjusted for error using a confidence estimate. Research has shown that estimates from credible people are accurate and conservative.

Converting Data to Money

To determine the monetary benefits, each individual data item has to be converted to money for use. This has to be profit-added, costs reduced, or costs avoided. The measures that are driven in this program are shown in Table 15-6 with the monetary value. These monetary values were provided to the participants in the program, so it took almost no effort on their part to locate and use them in their action plan.

Table 15-6. Converting Data to Money

Data Item	Value
Sales with existing customers	23% margin
New account	$745
Staff turnover	50% of annual salary
Store profit margin	All is value add
Inventory shrinkage	All is value add
Product returns	5% of average sale
Store expenses	All is value add
Customer complaints	$550 per complaint
Sick leave	$150 per day

For the first measure, sales to existing customers, the store operating profit margin is the value add, which is averaging 23 percent. For new accounts the marketing analytics section calculated the value based on the profit from the customer over the lifetime of the customer. This number appears to be low, but is accepted by executives. In essence, if the customer stays active with the company for an average of five years, the company will make $745 in profit during that time.

The staff turnover figure comes from external studies in the cost of turnover for the retail industry—it totals 50 percent of annual pay and this number is accepted within the company as a credible, conservative number. This figure includes all recruiting, selection, and onboarding, as well as the disruption cost of the exit.

The store profit margin is already converted to money and any increases in value are benefits. The operations department used 5 percent of the average sale to calculate inventory shrinkage cost. The cost is based on the assumption that the items may be damaged and cannot be resold, the items always need to be restocked, and sometimes there is an alteration or adjustment made.

Store expenses are direct cost reductions, and are value added directly into the calculation. Customer complaints come from the customer relations division in marketing, where complaints are investigated locally, regionally, and globally if needed. The group uses a model that estimates it costs the company $550 per complaint. This assumes the time to deal with the complaint, the cost of making the customer happy (which sometimes includes waiving part or all of the charge), and the ill will caused by the complaint.

The human resources department provided a standard value of $150 lost for each day that a person uses a sick day. Although sick days are allowed, ideally, they only want them to be taken when a person is really sick. Some employees abuse this, and the company wants to prevent excessive sick leave days.

Monetary Benefits

When the changes in impact measures, identified in Table 15-5, are adjusted for the effect of the program and converted to monetary values using the data in Table 15-6, the monetary benefits are developed. The amount of improvement is different from one store manager to another—96 people completed the workshop and every manager's task was to improve at least two measures. Ideally, approximately 192 measures would be influenced by this program. Unfortunately, for a variety of reasons not fully known by the team, 11 out of the 96 store managers did not provide an action plan after completing the two-day workshop. Although it would be helpful to find out what happened to these individuals, in terms of the analysis, there is a very specific rule for addressing missing data. Guiding Principle 6 indicates that missing data get a zero in the process. Thus, the total benefits are adjusted based on the 85 individuals who provided data, but the cost will be based on all 96 store managers. Table 15-7 shows a one-page sample of 12 pages of data showing the improvements connected to this program. This table represents only 14 measures, illustrates the variety of data represented in the program, and shows how the adjustments are made.

Next, the first year value of this measure is developed using the data conversion numbers in Table 15-6. Although there could be some argument to suggest that this is a long-term program and that benefits should be considered for a longer period, only the first year of benefits are calculated. This means that after the impact has occurred, when the action plans were delivered, the amount is extrapolated for the entire year. Some may suggest that this is not credible because the data might not continue at that level for the entire first year. However, when considering that the vast majority of the store managers will still be in their jobs the second, third, and perhaps, even a fourth year, there should be some benefit from this program as long as they are in that job. Because it is possible to take the prework, attend the two-day workshop, and work the virtual process in the weeks after the live session, this could be considered a two-year solution. But, to be conservative, Guiding Principle 9 is applied and only one year of benefits are considered for a short-term solution. Table 15-7 shows the monetary value for one year.

The contribution factor is the allocation to this program, as the store manager gave a particular percent of the improvement directly to the Leadership for Performance program. The next column is the confidence, which reflects the error in the allocation. Following the process, particularly with Guiding Principle 7, the three values are multiplied to provide an adjusted value. When these are calculated for all 85 participants, including both measures, the total is 170 measures improved, at least by some amount, with a few minor exceptions, as some people suggested that the measure did not improve or could not properly estimate the improvement connected to this program. However, some managers provided three measures and one manager provided four measures. With all of these totaled, the improvement is based on 176 measures and valued to be $1,341,970.

Table 15-7. Business Impact Data

Participant	Annualized Improvement ($Values)	Measures	Other Factors	Contribution Estimate From Program	Confidence Estimate	Adjusted $ Value
1	39,000	Sales-Existing	3	30%	60%	7,020
2	17,880	New Accounts	2	50%	85%	7,599
3	90,000	Turnover	2	40%	70%	25,200
4	50,200	Sales-Existing	3	35%	70%	12,299
5	12,000	Product Returns	1	40%	60%	2,880
6	26,870	New Accounts	2	30%	80%	6,449
7	1,800	Sick Leave	0	100%	90%	1,620
8	28,000	Store Expense	0	100%	80%	22,400
9	18,300	Inventory	1	50%	80%	7,320
10	6,600	Customer Complaints	1	40%	70%	1,848
11	68,000	Turnover	2	30%	70%	14,280
12	55,600	Store Profit	4	25%	85%	11,815
13	46,250	Sales-Existing	2	40%	80%	14,800
14	43,550	Store Expenses	1	60%	80%	20,904

Total this group $156,439

The Costs

Table 15-8 shows the costs allocated to this program. Some costs were prorated just to this sample size. For example, the needs assessment cost was estimated to be approximately $15,000. That amount involves all of the upfront analysis necessary to decide on the specific need for this program. The most significant cost was the development. Some content was purchased from a major supplier for leadership development, an outside production company produced the videos, and other content was developed under contract with freelancers or by the L&D team. In total, the development and production costs for the workshops and videos totaled $478,000.

The content for the learning portal was developed for approximately $60,000. The learning portal was already operational, but its development costs ($45,000) were allocated entirely to this program. The development of each e-learning module represented about $12,000, totaling $60,000. These costs were prorated over the 4,000 managers to develop a cost per participant. The total costs allocated to this sample of 96 represent the cost per participant multiplied by 96. Table 15-8 shows the prorated costs for these items.

The coach's time was allocated at a half day per participant, because not all of the participants used their coach and others used the coach for more than half a day total. For the participants, the costs were calculated by their time for the two days, the time away from work for the e-learning modules, and the other virtual activities (this totaled three days of time). Most store managers also required a travel expense. And a very nominal amount was included for the use of their devices to access the virtual materials and the e-learning modules. Although some would question whether that should even be included, a very nominal amount (6 percent) was included for the workshops to be completely transparent in all costs.

In addition, there was an overhead cost for the total learning development team, including the L&D leadership not directly involved in the program. This was at $400 per day or $800 for the program, totaling $3,200 for the four programs. The cost of the evaluation, which included the planning, data instrument design, data collection, analysis report writing, and briefings, was $40,000. The total cost of the briefings with travel was $25,000. When all of the costs are included, the total as indicated in Table 15-8 is $576,865.

Table 15-8. Program Cost Summary

Needs assessment (prorated over all sessions) 15,000/4,000 = 3.75 x 96	360
Program development and production costs (prorated over all sessions) 478,000/4,000 = 119.50 x 96	11,472
Content development for learning (prorated over all sessions) 60,000/4,000 = 15 x 96	1,440
Learning portal (prorated over all sessions) 45,000/4,000 = 11.25 x 96	1,080
E-learning programs (prorated over all sessions) 60,000/4,000 = 15 x 96	1,440
Devices used by participants	670
Program materials 120 x 96	11,520
Travel and lodging (participants) 982 x 96	94,272
Facilitation and coordination 19,000 x 4	76,000
Facilities and refreshments 8 days at 250	2,000
Participants' salaries, plus benefits 2,674.62 x 96	256,763
Coaches' salaries, plus benefits 538 x 96	51,648
Overhead	3,200
ROI evaluation 40,000 + 25,000	65,000
Total	**$576,865**

ROI Calculation

When the total monetary benefits from Table 15-8 are compared with the total fully loaded costs from Table 15-8 the calculations are as follows:

$$BCR = \frac{\$1,341,970}{\$576,865} = 2.33$$

$$ROI = \frac{\$1,341,970 - \$576,865}{\$576,865} \times 100 = 133\%$$

This is a very impressive ROI that greatly exceeds the objective of 20 percent. For every dollar invested in this program, the dollar is returned plus another $1.33 in monetary benefits.

Intangible Benefits

The following intangibles were connected with this project:

- Job engagement
- Career satisfaction
- Net promoter score
- Image
- Reputation
- Brand

The participants were asked to indicate the extent to which these intangibles were influenced by this program. In order to be included on this list, at least 10 percent of participants had to identify the influence as at least three out of five on a five-point scale.

These intangibles represent an important data set for executives. If they were converted to monetary value, there would be even more value from this program and a higher ROI.

Credibility of the Data

When leadership development is connected to the business in a program like this, there are always questions about the credibility of data. Here is what makes these data credible:

1. The business impact, which drives the ROI, represented actual store measures. They can be identified directly to the store, tracked, and validated if necessary.
2. The participants selected the measures that were important to them with input from their immediate manager.
3. Store managers had a desire to improve the measure and took ownership in this program as they connected the skills of developing high-performance teams to those important measures.
4. For participants who did not provide data, (12 individuals in this case), there was an assumption that they received no value from the program. In reality, some of these individuals changed stores, either through promotion or transfer, and actually added value despite not completing the project. The conservative approach is to use zero for them.

5. Only one year of improvement was recognized in the calculation. In reality, the significant behavior change, which was validated with the data collection at Level 3, should provide some value for the second, third, and even fourth year. However, to be conservative, only the first year was used.

6. All of the costs were included, including time away from work. Some of these costs are debatable, but to be credible, every cost category was included.

7. Using participant estimates to isolate the effects of the program was not the most favored approach, but it is credible. The estimation was collected in a very nonthreatening, unbiased way, and was adjusted for error. This credible method is backed by much research as a conservative approach representing an understatement of the actual results.

8. A balanced profile of financial and nonfinancial, quantitative and qualitative data was presented. This provided executives with a great data set to make decisions about the future implementation.

Communication Of Results

With the results in hand, the data was communicated to the groups according to the communication plan. First, a live briefing was conducted with top executives and those responsible for the implementation of the program. Because of the dispersion of the groups in the study, this briefing was held at four locations in North America, Europe, South America, and Asia. In addition, briefings were conducted with regional executives during normal meetings and with the HR team. A three-page summary was sent to all store managers. The participants received a summary of the results shortly after they submitted them, as well as a summary of the changes made as a result of the program.

Based on the briefings with the executive team, the following adjustments were made:

- Improvements were made to the technology to make it easier and more reliable.
- The role of the participant's manager was strengthened to make sure that proper measures are selected and any needed support is provided.

- The role of the coach was diminished.
- Some efforts were taken to strengthen the link between the 360-degree feedback and the rest of the program. There was concern that the 360-degree feedback was not tightly integrated into the program.

Lessons Learned

In this program several important lessons were learned:

- The power of connecting this program directly to business was phenomenal. The store managers saw this as a way to improve store performance, which was something they wanted and needed to do.
- The concept of developing a high-performance work team was intriguing to these individuals and was partially responsible for the good results that followed.
- The program design, using a mix of learning approaches, delivery mechanisms, and customization options, made it a workable project across cultures and countries.

Questions For Discussion

1. Critique the credibility of this study.
2. Do you think these results are CEO and CFO friendly? Explain.
3. Could there be alternative ways to isolate the effects of the program? Explain.
4. Would it have been better if all store managers addressed the same measure? Explain.
5. Why are leadership development directors reluctant to connect leadership development to business, as illustrated in this case?

Chapter 16

Measuring ROI in Selection and Onboarding

Global Bank Inc.

by Patti P. Phillips

This case study measures the success of a project that is very common to large organizations. Each year companies hire new MBA graduates and integrate them into the organization in leadership roles. Some of the new prospects are successful and some are not. This is an example of a program that worked extremely well because it was designed to achieve the desired results. It involves changes in recruiting and selection of rotational assignments where the participants add value to the department to which they are assigned. This study shows the impact and financial ROI of this revised program.

BACKGROUND

Global Bank Inc. (GBI) is a large commercial and consumer banking organization with a strong presence in the United States and a significant presence outside the United States. Functionally, Global Bank operates through different divisions, including retail banking, electronic banking, international banking, consumer loans, commercial loans, home mortgages, wealth management, corporate services, and investments. The bank provides services to several regions in the United States as well as globally, with a strong presence in six countries. GBI is experiencing significant growth and is planning for future growth; however, the management team is concerned that the management talent is not deep enough in the organization.

The Situation

Each year, Global Bank recruits from major business schools, hiring more than 100 MBA graduates. Executives had two concerns about the program: there were not enough new MBAs and the turnover among newly hired MBAs seemed too high. The records show that up to 30 percent of new MBA hires left in the first two years, after GBI invested a significant amount of money in their development. GBI had experimented with rotational training programs in the past, but that did not seem to work out well, and the turnover rate was even higher. Management was convinced that the turnover had more to do with the way new hires transitioned into the bank. They concluded that three issues were contributing to the problem:

- The need for a distinct career path.
- A lack of meaningful assignments in rotational areas.
- Placements were not occurring as quickly as they should be.

These three challenges led the global talent management team to develop a new onboarding program for MBA candidates.

Needs Analysis

The talent management team decided to conduct additional analyses to understand what was causing the high turnover rates and to understand why the previous program was not more successful. They also wanted to understand how a new program could be implemented in a different way so that it would be successful. The ultimate goal is to retain these individuals, assign them to key positions, and have them perform exceptionally.

Although the team felt that these conclusions were correct, HR wanted to make sure they were approaching the right solution. With this in mind, the HR team reviewed exit interview data and made calls to previous MBA hires who had left the company to ask what would have been helpful to improve the program. They also explored what they could have done differently to keep the graduates at Global Bank. These proved to be very fruitful conversations.

Current MBA graduates who were still employed were invited to join focus groups to understand why some of their colleagues had left and to solicit specific actions to lower the turnover rate. This approach, using the nominal group technique, removed the pressure for current MBAs to explain why they might leave—no one wants to admit that leaving the company is something they plan to do. Some analysis was run on the MBA graduates employed by the company to uncover the cause of their success. This was conducted in an attempt to understand whether school, age, gender, marital status, or grades were linked to tenure and career progression. This analysis revealed that grades, age, gender, and marital status made very little difference. However, three schools had significantly higher tenure and career success, which seemed to be based on the MBA curriculum in those schools that was applied to and focused on leadership.

Finally, the selection process itself was reviewed to see whether some adjustments could be made to ensure that the right candidate was selected. This analysis revealed some insight and new assessment possibilities that could predict success. With these analyses complete, the program was developed and proposed.

PROGRAM DESCRIPTION

The new program involved three parts: The first part was recruiting and selection, which had three changes. The second part was the MBA rotational assignment, which had five changes. Finally, the third part was a comprehensive, two-week workshop.

Recruiting/Selection

In the first change, the recruiting team placed an emphasis on the three schools that seemed to generate more success. These particular schools had a higher number of graduates who had progressed in the organization. After interviewing these candidates it appeared that the philosophy of the business schools was to produce graduates who accelerate quickly and take more responsibility in a leadership position.

The second change represented an assessment tool that was customized to GBI and was focused on three important dimensions:

- Eagerness to lead a team
- Willingness to assume responsibility and accountability quickly
- The values of the candidate compared with the culture of GBI

This instrument, purchased from a reputable supplier and adjusted for GBI, was used to connect these issues with retention. Low scores on this assessment would normally mean that the candidate would not be employed.

However, there could be some overriding exceptions, so at this point it was merely used as an indicator, not an absolute cutoff. Only after more data analysis would it be used as a go or no-go decision maker.

The third change was to focus the interviews on three areas: the culture of the organization, a sense of responsibility and accountability, and the desire to lead teams to success.

Rotational Assignments

The rotational program had five changes. The first focused on the amount of time in the program. Previously, graduates completed the program in two years, with each assignment set for three or six months. Now, those times are negotiated between the participants, a career advisor, and the appropriate departments.

The second change involved the nature of the rotational assignment. With this change, the participant is assigned to fill a current job within a particular department and is expected to rise to the average performance level of that job within two months. For most of the departments, that should not be a difficult task.

The third change was that participants would have to recommend changes to improve the function within their assigned department. They were encouraged to take a fresh look at the process, examine the tasks, and review the systems. Any suggested improvements could be technology driven, procedure driven, or leadership driven, or involve human resources in terms of reward systems, job design, and so on. Recommendations are required in the new program, and showing the monetary value of the improvement using a conservative estimation process is even better.

A fourth change involved the rotational schedule. Participants must now complete at least six rotations, ideally seven or eight. This would be in part determined by the eagerness of the participants to assume the full-time responsibility, and their readiness for a full-time assignment. Thus, participants will not always be rotating through functions that have little need for them, saving the functions with the most growth opportunities near the end of their rotations. This way they can likely translate their assignments into full-time positions.

The final change in this process is that the new candidates must assume a leadership role in their permanent assignment, ideally within a year after employment. The objective of this program is to develop leaders who had business experience before they entered the graduate MBA program. These candidates should be able to rapidly move into leadership roles and up the career ladder.

Formal Training

An important part of this program is a comprehensive two-week workshop that provides the training necessary to succeed at Global Bank. The workshop is taught by external faculty and internal experts, covering 16 modules:

1. Introduction to the MBA Program
2. Company Mission, Vision, Values, and Strategic Objectives
3. Retail Banking
4. Electronic Banking
5. International Banking
6. Corporate Services
7. Consumer Lending
8. Commercial Lending
9. Home Mortgages
10. Wealth Management
11. Investment Services
12. Negotiations
13. Process Improvement
14. Managing Change
15. Performance Management
16. Leadership Development

Because only a few participants have banking experience, this aligns the new MBA recruits to the company and the banking business, while covering key soft-skills topics that are necessary to succeed in the bank.

THE EVALUATION APPROACH

Rationale for ROI

Some conversations with the senior team revealed a desire to see the impact of this program and maybe the financial ROI. The most important measure to track is retention, as these high-potential candidates need to remain with the bank. Second, and just as important, is that they should be successful when they are placed in permanent jobs. Third, they need to meet the performance levels with their rotating assignments. Finally, the participants need to drive improvements throughout the system as they rotate through the program. It was decided to measure this program using the ROI Methodology process, which captures reaction, learning, application, impact, and ROI. This is the most comprehensive evaluation system and is ideally suited for this type of analysis.

The Objectives

The objectives of this program were comprehensive and follow the levels of evaluation. All objectives were developed with input from executives and other stakeholders.

For Level 1 (Reaction), the program should be perceived by participants as relevant to their individual needs, important to their own career success, and something they would recommend to others. The managers in the departments where the participants work need to see the program as necessary and important to the company's success.

For Level 2 (Learning), before participants can begin their rotational assignments they must learn the basics of banking and the organization during the two-week classroom program. This program includes a variety of exercises and the learning is measured using a combination of self-assessments, quizzes, role plays, and simulations. The objective is to have a minimum of 90 percent of participants successfully complete this program. If participants do not complete the program successfully, they could be removed from the program. This would be examined on a case-by-case basis with the decision based on objective criteria.

As participants proceed through the assignments they must complete a simple quiz about the work in that function. They are briefed ahead of time about the topics, which are all focused on the work of that particular department. This quiz is designed to ensure that participants know the key elements of activity for that department. Those who fail to score at least 80 percent would have an opportunity to try again with verbal questions. If the results are unsatisfactory, the participant will usually have to work in the department for a longer period. Additionally, during every assignment participants complete a self-assessment on how well the program is meeting their learning needs.

For Level 3 (Application), the application part of the process focuses on job assignments and individual projects. As participants learn a particular job, they must perform it. Job performance is measured with very specific criteria and success is defined with input from the department manager. The goal is to perform the job at an average performance level within two months. For most of these situations, that goal should not be difficult. The MBA graduates are talented individuals and most of them should achieve this within the first month for a majority of the assignments.

Another application objective focuses on the project and has two parts: A project improvement recommendation must be submitted after three months, and if possible, it should have a monetary value assigned to it. Participants will be given instructions on how to formulate their project, complete it, conduct the analyses, and present it. They will also be asked to present the recommendation in a formal meeting with the department manager and any key employees.

Several objectives are developed at Level 4 (Business Impact). After the program is fully operational:

1. 80 percent of participants will receive a permanent assignment within one year.
2. A 90 percent retention rate will be achieved after two years.
3. At least 50 percent of participant projects are implemented in the rotational departments representing direct efficiency and effectiveness measures, with a $10,000 average target.

For Level 5 (ROI), the ROI objective is set at 20 percent, keeping it slightly above the minimum required for capital expenditures. This is only a minimum acceptable performance.

Monetary value would come from a reduction in turnover, participant performance in their job, and implementing improvements in the departments. The cost of the program would include administrative costs, the cost for the two weeks of training, and subsidized salaries in the department where the participants work. In those departments, salaries would be subsidized by 20 percent from the global talent team budget to entice department heads to use these participants in their work. The department absorbs the rest of their salary because the participants are performing an actual job. This is an important monetary contribution from the participant.

EVALUATION PLANNING

Data Collection Plan

Figure 16-1 shows the data collection plan for this program, which is quite comprehensive, involving a variety of data collection methods, including questionnaires and data monitoring. The challenge is to collect an appropriate amount of data without significantly burdening the participants to provide too much. At the same time, participants know they are proving themselves and will take these assignments seriously. A major part of the evaluation is the promotion to permanent assignment, followed by retention and the implementation of individual projects.

Figure 16-1. Data Collection Plan

Program: MBA Onboarding   Responsibility: _____   Date: _____

Level	Broad Program Objective(s)	Measures	Data Collection Method/ Instruments	Data Sources	Timing	Responsibilities
1	**REACTION AND PLANNED ACTION** After completing this program, participants will: • Perceive this program as relevant to their individual needs • Perceive this program as important to their own career success • Recommend this program to other participants After participants visit each department, section manager will: • Perceive this program as necessary • Perceive this program to be important to the company's success	• Achieve 4 out of 5 on 5-point rating scale	• Questionnaire	• Participants • Section managers	• After two months and every two months • After each rotation	• Talent development team
2	**LEARNING AND CONFIDENCE** After completing the two-week program on 12 knowledge and skill areas for banking, participants will: • Demonstrate successful acquisition of knowledge and skills After completing each rotational assignment participants will: • Demonstrate their knowledge of the department's function, processes, and activities • Assess the extent to which the visit met their learning needs	• 90% of participants score successful • 80% Score • Achieve 4 out of 5 on 5-point scale	• Quizzes • Exercises • Department quiz	• Participants • Questionnaire	• At the end of two-week program • After each assigned area	• Talent development team

Figure 16-1. Data Collection Plan (continued)

Level	Broad Program Objective(s)	Measures	Data Collection Method/Instruments	Data Sources	Timing	Responsibilities
3	**APPLICATION/IMPLEMENTATION** During the rotational assignments: • Participants achieve average performance in two months in an existing job in the department • Participants submit a process improvement project to the section manager no later than three months into the assignment. • Participants complete at least four assignments in the program	• Rating of performance 3 out of 5 on 5-point scale	• Rating form • Report submitted	• Section manager • Participants	• After each assignment • Three months into assignment	• Talent development team
4	**BUSINESS IMPACT** After completing the program: • 80% of participants receive a permanent assignment in one year • Annualized turnover rate of MBA graduates will be less than 18% after one year and two years of operation • A least 50% of process improvement projects will be implemented realizing at least $10,000 of direct effectiveness and efficiency measures	• Transfer complete • Voluntary turnover rate • Monetary value of improvement	• Job transfer form • Performance monitoring • Project report summary	• HR records • HR records • Project documents	• Program completion • One year, two years • End of assignment	• Talent development team
5	**ROI** • The project will deliver at least a 20% ROI	Baseline Data: Comments:				

The ROI Analysis Plan

Figure 16-2 shows the ROI analysis plan for data analysis techniques and information. For isolating the effects of the program, expert estimates would need to be used. Sometimes the expert is the participant and at other times the expert is the talent management staff. For converting data to monetary values, the turnover reduction is the critical impact. An accepted value taken from previous studies is used where the cost of turnover is 1.5 times the annual salary. For these projects the availability of monetary value will depend on the extent that the participants have already tackled the issue. If they have, then the number is used, subject to credibility tests and potential further analysis.

The costs are fully loaded, including 20 percent of the salaries of the MBA participants while they are on the rotational assignments. A variety of intangibles is perceived to be linked directly to this program. The executives will need this information along with other audiences. Communication of results is a critical part of the plan.

Timing and Sampling

The program was developed and ready to go in January 2013 for MBA graduates recruited for the year. The target was to recruit about 125 MBAs who would be cycled through the program. The largest group would join the company after spring graduation (during May and June). The talent development team decided that the evaluation would be for the first year, but only for the 54 graduates that were recruited in the spring. Essentially, this becomes the sample of graduates that measures impact and ROI.

The graduates participated in a two-week learning program as their first assignment in the organization. Because they were available in May or June, three separate two-week learning sessions were organized for these graduates and all 54 attended.

Although data were collected from the other graduates during the year, the analysis was confined just to these 54, and their performance was traced for one year, or until their first permanent assignments. The tracking would include the participants' performance in the potential assignments. Although the sample size was small, it represents almost half of the graduates for the year and was the appropriate size for the executives who wanted to see the effects of the program as quickly as possible.

Figure 16-2. ROI Analysis Plan

Program/Project: MBA Onboarding   Responsibility: _____   Date: _____

Data Items (Usually Level 4)	Methods for Isolating the Effects of the Program/Process	Methods of Converting Data to Monetary Values	Cost Categories	Intangible Benefits	Communication Targets for Final Report	Other Influences/ Issues During Application	Comments
Job Assignment	• Expert Estimation	• Estimation	• Needs Assessment • Design Development • Coordinated Administration • Participant Salaries • Classroom • On-the-job and Classroom Training • Facilities • Evaluation	• Job Satisfaction • Job Engagement • Recruiting Image • Leadership Succession • Operational Efficiency	• Senior Executives • Department Managers • Section Managers • MBA Participants • Talent Development Team • Prospective MBA Students • All Employees		
Voluntary Turnover Rate	• Participant Estimation	• Standard Value					
Project Implementation	• Expert Estimation	Variety: • Standard Values • Expert Input • External Consultants					

Execution

As the new program was implemented, a full-time program director was assigned to be part of the talent development team. Initially, this person was responsible for the design and development of the program using external vendors. Then after implementation, she was responsible for administering the program effectively. This person had a full-time assistant, and the cost of both of these individuals would be included in the overall cost. These two individuals worked through placements in rotational assignments; addressed performance issues; assisted with data collection, coordination, and administration; provided performance feedback; and tackled other issues that surfaced during the program.

Time for Payout

Although this plan required tracking the graduates' performance until the permanent assignment, which would usually be about one year, an important question had to be addressed during the planning process—is this a long-term or short-term solution? Following the guiding principles of the ROI Methodology, if it is a short-term solution, only one year of benefits are used in the analysis. It was clear to the team that this was not a short-term solution because it involves at least a one-year commitment for each individual and much planning, preparation, and cost. Some could argue that the benefits of the program should be monitored for several years (or at least the data should be extrapolated for several years). After some discussion, it was decided to use a two-year payout, which was a very conservative approach. On a practical basis, the team would monitor the turnover for one year and extrapolate it for a second year. The monetary value from the participants' process improvement projects would be extrapolated for two years. This was considered to be ultraconservative, as a case could be made for extrapolating this data for three or four years. The important point is that the decision was made to stick with a two-year analysis before data collection began.

RESULTS

The results are presented in this section, arranged by levels of data, from reaction to ROI. In addition, the intangibles are presented to make a complete set of six types of outcome data sets.

Reaction Data

Table 16-1 shows the reaction data from both the participants and the managers. For the participants, the numbers exceeded the target of an average of four-out-of-five, but for the managers it was slightly less. Although the managers seem to support the program, there was some concern about how necessary and important the program was to company success. This early feedback allowed the talent development team to work with the section managers to continuously explain the importance of the program.

Table 16-1. Reaction Data

Participant's Perception	Rating
1. Relevant to Needs	4.3
2. Important to Career	4.4
3. Recommend to Others	4.2
Manager's Perception	
4. Program Is Necessary	3.9
5. Program Is Important to Company Success	3.7
Scale: 1 = Not at All; 2 = A Little; 3 = Moderate Amount; 4 = Much; 5 = Very Much	
N = 54 MBA Participants 100% Response	

Learning Data

Table 16-2 shows the learning data, which have several important parts. Data were collected for the 16 modules of the two-week program. Through a variety of exercises, quizzes, and simulations, evidence was available to the faculty that the participants were completing the program. Of the 54 individuals, only one was unsuccessful, leaving a 98 percent completion rate. The unsuccessful individual was allowed to make up extra time and continue the program.

Table 16-2. Learning Data

Learning Component	Successful Completion
Two-Week Workshop	98%
Rotational Assignment Quiz	96%
Rotational Assignment Self-Rating	4.4 of 5
N = 54 MBA Participants 100% Response	

The departmental quiz administered at the end of the rotational assignment tested the participants' knowledge of the activities, processes, and functions of the departments. All but two MBA participants successfully completed the quiz, and those two individuals stayed a little longer in the department and verbally passed the assessment.

At the end of the assignment the participants provided feedback, including the amount to which the assignment met their learning needs. Collectively, they scored a 4.4 out of a five-point scale.

Application Data

Table 16-3 shows the application data. As this table reveals, there were several components to application. The first, and perhaps most important, was the performance rating of the individuals performing an actual job in each rotational assignment. The goal was for the individual to assume the job as quickly as possible and reach an acceptable level of performance within two months. Ninety-six percent, representing 52 out of 54, achieved average performance within that timeframe, with the average time being 1.2 months. The other two were counseled and allowed to spend more time. One of those individuals left the organization. Collectively, 93 percent provided process improvement projects, which represented 50 out of the 54. The individuals who did not provided acceptable reasons for not being able to complete that assignment and they were allowed to continue the program.

Table 16-3. Application Data

Application Component	Success
Achieved Average Performance Average Time to Performance	96%
Submitting Process Improvement Project	1.2 months 92% (50)
N = 54 MBA Participants 100% Response	

Impact Data

Table 16-4 shows the impact data for this program, which involved several issues. The first issue was the time for permanent assignment. The goal is to secure an assignment quickly, with an objective for 80 percent to have a permanent assignment in one year. That objective was exceeded, with 84 percent landing assignments in that time period. The average time to permanent assignment was 13.2 months, indicating that several individuals remained in the program for more than one year. This is acceptable considering that the pressure is on to find a permanent assignment as soon as possible.

Table 16-4. Impact Data

Impact Component Permanent Assignment	Success
Secure Assignment in One Year	84%
Average Time to Permanent Assignment	
Turnover and Retention	13.2 months
Voluntary Annualized Turnover Rate One Year	4%
Previous Annualized Turnover Rate One Year	
Process Improvement Projects	22%
Process Improvement Projects Submitted 50	93%
Process Improvement Projects Implemented 24	48%
Average Value of Process Improvement Projects	$7,340
Highest Value of Process Improvement Projects	$40,000
Lowest Value of Process Improvement Projects	$1,200
Total Monetary Value	$176,160
Percent Attributed to This Program	81%
Confidence in the Estimation	78%
Adjusted Monetary Benefits	**$111,298**

In regard to turnover, the annualized voluntary turnover rate for this group was 4 percent (two individuals left) in one year, as compared with the previous turnover rate of 22 percent. The team concluded that no external conditions could have lowered this number aside from the new approach of the program. Thus, the difference in these turnover rates would be attributed to the program. Essentially this is a trend analysis, in which the team suggested that the 22 percent turnover trend would have continued if the new program had not been implemented. The difference in the two, which is the 18 percent, is attributed to this program.

Process improvement is the next area for adding value. Fifty participants, representing 93 percent, submitted projects. However, only 24 projects (48 percent) were implemented, which was slightly less than the goal of 50 percent. The average monetary value for these projects was disappointing ($7,340), which is less than the $10,000 goal. The largest value of $40,000 was a surprise to the team. They felt that some individuals' projects would have a much higher cost savings.

Other factors could have caused these projects to be implemented and other factors could have influenced the results. In some cases, the projects would probably have been implemented anyway because they were opportunities that needed to be addressed, or problems that needed solving. Participants were asked, along with the section manager, to estimate the percent of this improvement as related to the program. For many projects, 100 percent of the improvement was allocated to this program, suggesting that this project would probably not have been attempted otherwise and that there were no other variables influencing the savings.

To make it more credible, the individuals were asked to indicate their confidence in the percentage, and the confidence ranged from as low as 60 percent to as high as 100 percent, with an average of 78 percent. When these adjustments are made, the total monetary value, attributed to the program, with adjustments for confidence in the allocation, is $111,298.

Converting Data to Money

Table 16-5 shows the process of converting data to money. The turnover rate conversion was straightforward. First, the number of turnovers was calculated. Basically, 18 percent turnover (10 turnovers), annualized, was prevented by this program. There were two turnovers by the end of the program (4 percent); however, previously it would have been 12 turnovers, so the improvement is 10. The cost of turnover, which is usually a multiple of an annual salary, is readily available in the literature and generally accepted within the talent development team. The team used a value of 1.5 times the annual salary to represent the cost of turnover. This is a conservative amount because when an individual leaves there is a tremendous loss of effort and time into the processes, as well as cost of recruiting and selection. The average MBA salary was priced at $80,000 for this group. It is interesting to note that most of the graduates came from three schools that seemed to have the best record at Global Bank. These were not the highest-ranked MBA schools, but rather those that stressed leadership as an important component, and prepared their MBA students to take leadership roles. Had Global Bank recruited at the top-tier schools, this salary would have been higher. So the cost of a single turnover is determined by $80,000 times 1.5 yields $120,000. By avoiding 10 turnovers, this provided a monetary benefit of $1.2 million.

Table 16-5. Converting Data to Money

For Year One	
Turnover Data	
Improvement 22% – 4% = 18%	
Cost of Turnover = 1.5 x Annual Salary	
Annual MBA Salary = $80,000	
Cost Avoided $80,000 x 1.5 x 10 =	$1,200,000
Process Improvement Projects	
From Table 16-4	$111,298
Early Job Assignment	
The Value Is Not Very Credible	N/A
Total Monetary Benefits (First Year)	$1,311,298
For Year Two (Extrapolated)	
Turnover Data	$1,200,000
Process Improvement Projects	$111,298
Total Monetary Benefits (Second Year)	1,311,298
Total Monetary Benefits Two Years	**$2,622,596**

Regarding the process improvement projects, the projects themselves required the individuals to show the monetary value possible with the improvement. Multiple years were included when it was appropriate and most of the projects contained second, third, and in one case even 10 years of revenue stream. From those implemented projects, $111,298 was claimed for the first year, and the same amount was claimed for the second year.

The early job assignment, which is very critical in the new design, had some obvious value. Having a person in a leadership role quickly adds value to the bank, sometimes even preventing an external hiring into the job. Although the number could have been estimated, it was not pursued because the value is not credible enough to include. This left a total monetary value for the first year of $1,311,298. When this is extrapolated for the second year, it leaves $2,622,596 for the total monetary value.

Program Costs

Table 16-6 shows the cost of this program. All the costs for needs assessments and program development were included, although there would be value for this for the next few years. The workshop development, workshop materials, facilitation, and facilities for the workshop were also included. The workshop materials are used beyond the two-week assignment, and included some other reading assignments that were required during rotational assignments. The coordination and administration, which involved two full-time people, were also included. The salaries of participants were indicated completely from the two-week assignment, recognizing that there is no direct value to the organization while they are in the two-week class. Therefore, the total salaries fully loaded using a 40 percent benefit factor realized a total of $232,615. A 40 percent benefit factor is suggesting that the total benefits package represented about 40 percent of the annual pay.

For the rotational assignment, the talent development department assumed 20 percent of their pay, and the visiting department absorbed the remaining 80 percent. When this 20 percent is calculated on a one-year basis, the total is $1,209,600. A salary of $80,000 was used with a 40 percent adjustment for the benefits (80,000 x 54 x 1.4 x 20% = $1,209,600). Executives at different levels were involved in the program, reviewing data, helping to plan, reviewing consequences, having discussions, and serving as mentors. This total time was estimated to be $55,000 by the talent development team. The cost of evaluation was $50,000 as an external firm conducted it. This gave a one-year total cost of $1,902,215.

Table 16-6. Total Cost of Program

For Year One	
Needs Assessment	$10,000
Program Development	5,000
Workshop Development	20,000
Coordination	93,000
Facilitation of Workshop (3 Groups)	150,000
Facilities, Food, and Refreshments	45,000
Administrative Expense	16,000
Workshop Materials	16,000
Participants (Salaries)	
Two-Week Workshop	232,615
Rotational Assignments (20%) 12 Months	1,209,600
Executive Time (Salaries)	55,000
Evaluation	50,000
	Total $1,902,215

Table 16-6. Total Cost of Program (*continued*)

For Year Two (Extrapolated)	
Coordination	16,000
Administration	5,000
MBA Participants Salaries 20%, 1.2 months	120,960
Executive Time	5,500
	Total $147,460
	Two-Year Total $2,049,675

For the rotational assignment, the talent development department assumed 20 percent of their pay, and the visiting department absorbed the remaining 80 percent. When this 20 percent is calculated on a one-year basis, the total is $1,209,600. A salary of $80,000 was used with a 40 percent adjustment for the benefits (80,000 x 54 x 1.4 x 20% = $1,209,600). Executives at different levels were involved in the program, reviewing data, helping to plan, reviewing consequences, having discussions, and serving as mentors. This total time was estimated to be $55,000 by the talent development team. The cost of evaluation was $50,000 as an external firm conducted it. This gave a one-year total cost of $1,902,215.

When the year-two costs were calculated, they are not repeated for those who were placed into assignments. Some costs were still there for any MBA students who were not yet assigned. They represent coordination and administration time and salaries for 1.2 months, the average length of time beyond the 12 months included in the first-year monetary costs. The executive time is now down to $5,500, leaving a total of $147,460 for the second year. The two-year total cost of this program, fully loaded and being ultraconservative, is $2,049,675.

BCR and ROI Calculations

Table 16-7 shows the benefit-cost ratio and the ROI calculations for this program. Using the total benefits for two years and the total costs for two years, the benefit-cost ratio is 1.28 and the ROI is 28 percent, exceeding the minimum acceptable performance of 20 percent. Using two years of costs and benefits is very conservative. If a third-year framework is used, the total costs do not change from the second year because all students are assigned and in their permanent assignment. However, the benefits continue as these individuals remain on the job. If there is still only a 4 percent turnover in the third year, the ROI calculation would be almost 100 percent. This would not only meet the objective, but is an impressive payoff for the program.

Table 16-7. BCR and ROI Calculations

$$\text{Benefits} = \$2,622,596$$
$$\text{Costs} = \$2,049,675$$

$$\text{BCR} = \frac{\$2,622,596}{\$2,049,675} = 1.28$$

$$\text{ROI} = \frac{\$2,622,596 - \$2,049,675}{\$2,049,675} \times 100 = 28\%$$

Intangible Benefits

Table 16-8 shows the intangible benefits derived from this program. The most obvious one is the early job assignment. There is no calculation of this benefit, although it should be very substantial. Because it was not converted to money, it is considered to be an intangible. This allows the bank to use the talents of these graduates to fill key jobs sooner. The program is also building a leadership team, efficiently and effectively, which is a major purpose of the team. The individuals were asked on a follow-up questionnaire to indicate the extent to which certain intangible measures are connected to the program. The table lists those intangible benefits in the order of the strength of their connection to this program. They all were rated at least 3.5 out of a five-point scale, with four as an average. The strongest is career satisfaction, and the weakest is recruiting image, which is perhaps more difficult for them to see.

Table 16-8. Intangible Benefits

	Rank
Early Job Assignment	
Build Leadership Team	
Job Satisfaction (Career)	1
Job Engagement	2
Leadership Succession	3
Operational Efficiency	4
Recruiting Image	5

At least 3.5 out of 5-point scale

CONCLUSIONS AND RECOMMENDATIONS

From all indications, this is a successful program with few minor adjustments that need to be made. It appears that the analysis has yielded the proper solution—having an early assignment is critical, and having detailed training to build capability, knowledge, and thinking in Global Bank was important. The focus on the rotational assignments to learn the job and achieve success was a critical component that seemed to work extremely well.

The disappointing part is that the process improvement projects had less than expected monetary value, which is an opportunity for improvement. In addition, some work is still needed with the managers and executives who did not have the benefit of this type of program. Many of them came up the hard way, starting at the bottom without an MBA and without the comprehensive focus of the program. It is difficult for them to see how critical this program is to the success of the organization.

The conclusion is to continue to administer the program as planned, with the exception of placing more focus on process improvement. Another module should be added to the two-week program to focus on the work projects in each rotational assignment using data from this study, in which the individual topics and how they are calculated are outlined. The participants are encouraged to examine big-picture items as well as small process improvement opportunities. The goal is to have the benefit of an external view from a highly trained individual to see improvements in the processes. This ultimately may be one of the biggest benefits of this program.

Lessons Learned

Ultimately, the talent development team was very pleased with this program, and there were some lessons learned in the process.

1. **Conduct a very thorough needs assessment to understand what is needed to make this program work.** The principal problem was excessive turnover. The nominal group process seemed to reveal many of the key issues that were causing the participants to leave during the program. This enabled a very focused solution that seemed to work extremely well.
2. **Create expectations and plan the process very appropriately.** Individuals must know that they are being evaluated at each rotational assignment, not because of punitive issues, but just to ensure that they are learning what they need to learn. This created expectations

that the MBA graduates met. Regarding the process improvement, the success that was achieved was because of the early planning dedicated to that process. With more planning, it will be much better.

3. **The number of years of benefits is an important issue.** This project was negative for only one year of monetary benefits. But clearly, this is not a one-year, short-term solution. It is a solution that could easily expect to pay off in a three-, four-, or five-year timeframe. Two years were used to keep it extremely conservative, and it may be too conservative. So the lesson learned is to make sure that this is addressed properly, so that it is not too short for the monetary benefits tabulation.

Questions for Discussion

1. Is this study credible? Please explain.
2. Critique the methods used to isolate the effects for the program.
3. Should a monetary benefit be placed on achieving early assignments? Please explain.
4. Should a longer period of time be used for monetary benefits? Please explain.
5. How should this be communicated to the senior executives?

Chapter 17

Measuring ROI in a
Mobile Learning Solution for Sales

Transoft Inc.

by Jack J. Phillips and Patti P. Phillips

This project involves a mobile learning application for sales associates of a large software firm specializing in software solutions for the trucking industry. Sales associates were provided a mobile learning solution for their iPads, designed to describe and sell an upgrade to its most popular software product. Although the release occurred at the same time for all sales associates, not all of them logged onto the learning portal through their iPads, which allowed an opportunity for a comparison group. This case study highlights the key issues in calculating the impact and ROI of a mobile learning solution on business results. The case is arranged in a multiple part format to allow readers to experience the issues and recommended actions and solutions.

BACKGROUND

Organizational Profile

Transoft is one of the largest software companies for the trucking industry. With more than 12,000 users, Transoft dominates the trucking landscape. Transoft provides software solutions for carriers, brokers, logistics companies, and shippers. A variety of software solutions are available, including products for financial operations, fleet management, document systems, dispatch operations, freight management, and broker management. Its most popular software, ProfitPro, integrates a variety of software solutions, all aimed at improving the efficiency and profitability of the trucking company. The trucking industry is highly competitive, often producing low margins. Having an efficient operation is usually the difference in profit or loss. ProfitPro has a reputation for helping trucking companies meet profit goals.

Situation

Transoft has an extensive network for sales and marketing, with more than 200 sales associates serving all of North America. Sales associates are strategically located across the United States and most work from their homes. Bringing sales teams into three regional offices for training has become a thing of the past, unless extensive formal development of new sales associates is needed.

Transoft has just completed an upgrade on its most popular software, ProfitPro, and has released it to the sales team to begin selling the upgrades. An upgrade costs the client from $1,000 to $3,000, depending on the scope of operations. For the client, the upgrade provides some new features and streamlines some of the previous processes. It should help make clients more profitable by reducing the time to complete certain documents, ensuring on-time filing, reducing invoicing errors, and improving other operating efficiencies.

Solution

The learning and development team agreed on a solution that would involve a mobile learning application directly accessible on an iPad. Previously, sales teams were furnished with iPads for work. With five modules, the program would take about two hours to complete, which would prepare a sales rep to sell the upgrade. The specific modules include:

- Rationale for the upgrade
- Key features of the upgrade
- How the upgrade will increase profits (time savings, quality improvements, and productivity)
- Pricing options
- Implementation and support

Each module contains tools to check learning and to encourage and plan for application. In addition, brief summaries of each module are produced for review just before meeting a client. The program provides an integration with Salesforce.com to set up appointments with customers to discuss the upgrade. This feature identifies the target clients, listed by potential sales volume. It also develops the pricing options based on the client's use of ProfitPro. Modules were designed to develop an understanding of the upgrades and to assist, encourage, and even require a sales associate to sell the upgrade.

A mobile solution was selected because of its flexibility, convenience, and cost. It was not feasible to train the sales force in face-to-face workshops. A half-day workshop would have required sales associates to lose an average of a day at work, and more than 80 percent of them would have incurred travel costs. A mobile solution was not only ideal for this type of program, but it was the only way to go from an economic and convenience perspective.

Rationale for ROI

Although mobile learning appeared to be the only feasible solution in terms of cost, time, and convenience, the management team wanted to know whether it was working, perhaps at the same level as a face-to-face workshop. Executives wanted an evaluation that would show how well the program was working, how quickly it was working, and what issues were inhibiting the success of this type of learning. While executives were convinced that this approach was necessary for a diverse sales force scattered around the country, there was still a nagging concern about the effectiveness of mobile learning programs. Although they would see the sales numbers, they wanted to know more in terms of costs versus benefits. The learning team was challenged not only to secure data but also to evaluate the program up to and including the financial ROI. They insisted that the analysis should be credible, separating the influence of this program from the special promotion for the upgrade.

Exercise

1. Is this level of accountability typical? Please explain.

   _____

   _____

   _____

2. What do you think the broad objectives should be at each level?

_____

_____

_____

Reaction

_____

_____

_____

Learning

_____

_____

_____

Application

_____

_____

_____

Impact

_____

_____

_____

ROI

_____

_____

_____

PLANNING

Objectives

After the decision was made to go with the program, the next step was to develop the detailed objectives at all five levels. This step was completed with input from a project manager, a sales manager, and subject matter experts. At Level 1, it was decided that participants should see this program as relevant to their work and important to their success. It should have content that they intended to use and that they would recommend to others.

In terms of learning, a self-assessment on the five modules included a simple true/ false quiz at the end of each module. Each module had five questions, representing 25 questions total. A participant should score at least 20 out of 25, allowing for one missed question for each module. The score would not be punitive as there would not be any consequences for missing the desired score. This was only a gauge for participant success, as they immediately saw the correct answers with an explanation. Sales associates were encouraged to repeat the exercise if they scored less than four out of five correct answers for each module.

For application, the objectives focused on sales associates using the skills quickly and to make the first scheduled call within a week of completing of the program. By the end of the month, the goal was to see routine use of each of the major tasks, actions, or skills from the five modules.

For business impact, sales should occur within three weeks of program completion, and the associates should reach $10,000 in sales per month within three months. This was suitable to the management team and should result in success for the program.

For the Level 5 objective, a 20 percent ROI was set. This is slightly above what Transoft would use for capital expenditures (for example, the headquarters building), and it would seem reasonable to executives. The objective was the minimum acceptable performance, not only for this level of ROI, but for the other levels as well.

Exercise

Based on these objectives, what is your recommended approach for data collection and analysis? Please complete the data collection plan and the ROI analysis plan for this program. See Figures 17-1 and 17-2.

Data Collection Plan

The evaluation planning meeting was conducted with the program manager, the designers and developers who were on contract, and the project manager for the program. In addition, the evaluator moderated the meeting.

Figure 17-1. Data Collection Plan

Program: _____ Responsibility: _____ Date: _____

Level	Broad Program Objective(s)	Measures	Data Collection Method/Instruments	Data Sources	Timing	Responsibilities
1	REACTION & PLANNED ACTION					
2	LEARNING & CONFIDENCE					
3	APPLICATION & IMPLEMENTATION					
4	BUSINESS IMPACT					
5	ROI	Baseline Data:				
		Comments:				

Figure 17-2. ROI Analysis Plan

Program: _____   Responsibility: _____   Date: _____

Data Items (Usually Level 4)	Methods for Isolating the Effects of the Program/ Process	Methods of Converting Data to Monetary Values	Cost Categories	Intangible Benefits	Communication Targets for Final Report	Other Influences/ Issues During Application	Comments

In this case, the evaluator was an external consultant who was conducting the ROI study. Figure 17-3 is the data collection plan, which details the methods, source, and timing for collecting data at four levels. Level 1 and 2 data were captured in the system as the participants completed five modules in the mobile learning program. Level 3 was a web-based questionnaire with simple questions. To achieve a good response rate, 20 techniques were used, which are shown in Table 17-1. Level 4 impact data were retrieved directly from the Salesforce.com system at Transoft.

Table 17-1. Techniques to Increase Response Rates

1. Provide advance communication.
2. Communicate the purpose.
3. Identify who will see the results.
4. Describe the data integration process.
5. Let the target audience know that they are part of a sample.
6. Design for simplicity.
7. Make it look professional and attractive.
8. Use the local manager's support.
9. Build on earlier data (Level 1 and 2).
10. Pilot test the questionnaire.
11. Recognize the expertise of participants.
12. Have an executive sign the introductory letter.
13. Send a copy of the results to the participants.
14. Report the use of results.
15. Introduce the questionnaire during the program (first and last module).
16. Use follow-up reminders.
17. Consider the appropriate medium for easy response.
18. Estimate and report the necessary time needed to complete the questionnaire.
19. Show the timing of the planned steps.
20. Collect data anonymously and confidentially.

ROI Analysis Plan

Figure 17-4 shows the ROI analysis plan, which is straightforward for this type of analysis. The two business measures collected were the monthly sales per associate for the upgrade and the time for the first sale. The method of

Figure 17-3. Completed Data Collection Plan

Program: <u>Product Upgrade With Mobile Learning</u>   Responsibility: _____   Date: _____

Level	Broad Program Objective(s)	Measures of Success	Data Collection Method/ Instruments	Data Sources	Timing	Responsibilities
1	REACTION & PLANNED ACTIONS Achieve positive reaction on: • Relevance to my work • Recommend to others • Important to my success • Intent to use	Rating of 4 out of 5 on a composite of four measures	LMS survey, built into program	Participant	End of program	Program manager
2	LEARNING Learn to use five concepts to sell new upgrade: • Rationale for upgrade • Features of upgrade • How upgrade will increase client profit • Pricing options • Implementation and support	Achieve 4 out of 5 correct answers on each module Achieve 20 of 25 total correct answers	True/False quiz	Participant	End of program	Program manager

Figure 17-3. Completed Data Collection Plan (*continued*)

3	APPLICATION/ IMPLEMENTATION Use of five skills: • Explain rationale for upgrade • Identify key features of upgrade • Describe how upgrade increases client profit • Identify pricing options • Explain implementation and support • Make the first call in 5 days	Rating (4 of 5) on a 1-5 scale System check	Questionnaire, web- based Performance monitoring	Participant Salesforce. com	1 month after program 1 month after program	Evaluator
4	BUSINESS IMPACT • Increase in sales to $10,000 per month • Sell first upgrade in 3 weeks	Monthly sales per associate Actual sale	Business performance monitoring Business performance monitoring	Salesforce. com Salesforce. com	3 months after program 1 month after program	Evaluator
5	ROI 30%	Comments:				

Figure 17-4. Completed ROI Analysis Plan

Program: Product Upgrade With Mobile Learning   **Responsibility:** _____   **Date:** _____

Data Items (Usually Level 4)	Methods for Isolating the Effects of the Program/Process	Methods of Converting Data to Monetary Values	Cost Categories	Intangible Benefits	Communication Targets for Final Report	Other Influences/Issues During Application	Comments
• Monthly sales per associate	• Control group analysis • Participant estimates (both measures)	• Direct conversion using standard profit contribution	• Needs assessment • Design • Content development • Mobile device • Participants' salaries plus benefits (time) • Cost of coordination and administration (time) • Project management (time) • Evaluation	• Customer engagement and satisfaction • Job satisfaction of sales associates • Stress reduction • Reputation	• Program participants • Sales managers • Product manager • Senior executives—regional and headquarters • Learning coordinators, designers, and managers • All sales associates	• No communication with control group	
• Time to first sale	• Control group analysis • Participant estimates (both measures)	• N/A					

isolation was a comparison group method—a classical experimental versus control group method. As a fallback, participant estimates would be used to sort out the effects of this program. During the evaluation meeting, there was discussion about the possibility of setting up the comparison group. Based on previous experience, some of the sales team might not use the module for several weeks, or at all, depending on their schedules, their interest in the upgrade, and their eagerness to learn through mobile technology. At the same time, some will get involved immediately. Given this situation, there could be an opportunity for a comparison group. Also, it is helpful to know that some, if not all, would sell the upgrade without taking part in the mobile learning program. They would flip through the brochure and attempt to make the sale—and succeed in doing so. The challenge was to match the first 25 users with a corresponding group of nonusers. Because of timing (when they might have started the program) the matching group would be larger so that, as users logged in, they would be dropped out of the control group. This was the best shot at having a comparison group, and the planning team realized at the onset that it might not work. Consequently, participant estimates were used as a backup, adjusted for error.

Converting data to money was very easy. The sales were adjusted with the profit margin for the new product. This was developed by the product launch team and was actually known to the sales force. For this upgrade, the margin was 20 percent. The time for sale was a measure that was monitored but not converted to data. This sales data actually would be included in the overall sales and to include them again would be double counting the sales. The cost categories are routine and listed in the figure, including a small prorated cost for the iPads and the design and development cost prorated for the 25 participants. The expected intangibles included customer satisfaction and engagement, job satisfaction for the sales team, brand awareness, reputation of the company, and stress reduction for sales associates. The individuals who needed to see the results were the complete sales team, sales managers (including the vice president of sales and vice president of marketing), the participants who provided the data, and their immediate managers.

RESULTS

Reaction, Learning, and Application

The first 25 people signed up within three days of the program's announcement. Level 1 reaction data were collected at the end of the fifth module and are presented in Table 17-2. Reactions were as expected, with the exception of intent to use, which was very high.

Level 2 learning seemed appropriate, and quiz scores were above targets, as shown in Table 17-3. Scores were slightly lower than desired for the quiz for implementation and support. This was not a huge concern, as this information is clearly in the documents and the product brochures.

Level 3 application data seemed to be on track as shown in Table 17-4. Identifying pricing options and explaining implementation and support were off a little, but overall the objectives were met. The time for the first call was below the objective, which was very good. As expected, there were some barriers and enablers to success, as shown in Table 17-5. The barriers were minimal. However, there was a concern that 9 percent of sales associates were not encouraged by their managers to use the program. As expected, the number one enabler was management encouragement.

Table 17-2. Reaction Results

Rate the Following	Rating
Relevant to my work	4.3
Important to my success	4.1
Intent to use	4.7
Recommend to others	4.2
Target: 4.0	Average: 4.3

(Scale: 1 = not at all; 2 = some; 3 = average; 4 = above average; 5 = very much)

Table 17-3. Learning Results

Module	Quiz Categories	Avg. Number of Correct Responses
1	Rationale for the upgrade	4.3
2	Key features of the upgrade	4.2
3	How upgrade will increase client profit	4.3
4	Pricing options	4.1
5	Implementation and support	3.9
Possible score: 25		Average: 20.8
Target: 20		

Table 17-4. Application Results

Extent of Use in One Month	Rating
Make the first call (target: 5 days)	3.5 days
Explaining the rationale for upgrade	4.2
Identifying key features of upgrade	4.3
Describing how the upgrade increases client profit	4.1
Identifying pricing options	3.9
Explaining implementation and support	3.8
Target: 4.0	Average: 4.06

(Scale: 1 = not at all; 2 = some use; 3 = moderate amount of use; 4 = significant amount of use; 5 = very significant amount of use)

Table 17-5. Barriers and Enablers

Barriers	% Reporting
Lack of time to be involved	12%
Lack of management encouragement	8%
Took too long to complete	8%
Technology issues	4%
Other	4%
Explaining implementation and support	3.8
Enablers	**% Reporting**
Management encouragement	60%
Easy to use	52%
Timely	48%
Convenient	40%
Relevant	36%
Other	16%

Isolating the Effects of the Program

An important and perhaps the most challenging issue was to determine the effects of this program from other influences. The best way to do this was to use a classic experimental versus control group, although that became tricky with this program and it was questionable whether or not it would work throughout the program. At first, 25 sales associates were selected based on the first 25 to complete the modules. This was accomplished within the first three days. This group of 25 was matched to a group of other sales associates. The first challenge was finding an appropriate match; the second was to have enough remaining in the control group, since they drop out of the experiment when they complete the program. Some people would wait weeks or months to take the program, or they would choose not to take it at all. And some dropouts are a reality when mobile learning is left entirely up to the individual. Instead of forcing participants to use the program, the team wanted the program to be taken voluntarily. The communication for the program, which emphasized that learning is needed in order to sell this upgrade properly, was presented in hopes that this plea would cause them to sign up.

To select the control group, the factors that should affect sales were considered. The four most important considerations were:

1. Current sales level, on an annual basis
2. Tenure with the company
3. Performance rating in human resource system
4. Total selling experience

Although the fourth item was a little more difficult to determine because it counted selling experience in other companies, a quick review of human resource records revealed the total number of years of selling experience. Given these factors, more than 80 associates matched with the 25 in the trial group. Fifty of those were selected randomly as the control group, recognizing that some of them may drop out of the control group when they started this mobile learning program.

Impact Results

Table 17-6 shows the impact data comparing the experimental group of 25 sales associates with the control group of 22. As expected, almost every one of the control group (19 of 22) was actually selling the upgrade though not participating in the program, but the difference of the two groups was very impressive. The difference for that second month is then annualized, producing an annual improvement of $1,140,000. The time of the first sale was impressive for the group involved in the program—11 days compared to 21 days for the control group.

Table 17-6. Sales Data in Three Months After Launch

Group	Avg. Sales (Month 3)	Avg. Time to First Sale
Trial (Experimental) group: 25 sales associates	$7,500	11 days
Comparison (Control) Group 19 sales associates (out of 22)	$3,700	21 days
Difference =	$3,800	
Annualized = $3,800 x 12 x 25 = $1,140,000 20% profit = $228,000		

Converting Data to Money

Converting data to money was easy. As outlined on the ROI analysis plan, the profit margin had to be used. This new upgrade had a predicted profit margin of 20 percent, and this value was used in the analysis. This yields a monetary value of $228,000. The time of the first sale was not converted to money, as that sale was actually already in the total sales number.

Cost

As shown in Table 17-7, the fully loaded costs were included to make the ROI calculation credible. The initial needs assessment represented very little cost, because the need was precipitated by the new product and the solution was dictated by the time and cost constraints. A charge of $3,000 was estimated for the time to pin down needs. The design and development cost was estimated to be $56,000. This amount was prorated over the evaluation for the 25 participants. To be conservative, it was assumed that half the sales team (110) would not use the program. The design and development cost per participant was $509, resulting in $12,725 for 25 participants. The project manager's time was included, as was time for participant involvement. Although many sales associates complete technology-based learning on their own time, this program was planned for use during regular work hours between calls or just before calls. In sales, work hours can be anytime. A conservative estimate was two hours per associate, recognizing that some of them completed the program on their own time. Some cost was prorated for the use of the iPad, albeit minor as the iPad is used for other purposes. An external evaluation was used in order to ensure objectivity, which created a high evaluation cost. Still, this evaluation will suffice for the entire sales force, although it's for the sample. Also, internal evaluation would have cost about $5,000. When costs and monetary benefits are combined, the cost-benefit ratio and ROI can be calculated.

Table 17-7. Costs

Needs assessment (est.)	$3,000
Design and development ($56,000/110 x 25)	$12,725
Mobile device (prorated)	$1,700
Sales associate time	$2,524
Administration time (est.)	$6,000
Project management (est.)	$14,500
Evaluation	$15,000
Total	**$55,449**

Exercise

1. Calculate the BCR and ROI below.

    BCR =

    ROI =

2. What should the approach be to communicate the results to the appropriate audiences?

Figure 17-5 shows the benefit/cost ratio and the ROI calculation. As anticipated, results exceed the ROI objective.

Figure 17-5. BCR and ROI Calculations

$$BCR = \frac{\$228,000}{\$55,449} = 4.11$$

$$ROI\ (\%) = \frac{\$228,000 - \$55,449}{\$55,449} \times 100 = 311\%$$

Intangible Benefits

In addition to the tangible sales increase converted to money, several intangibles were connected to the program, as presented in Table 17-8. Receiving the first sale within the time period is intangible, because it was not converted to money and used in the calculation (this would be double counting). In addition, the other intangibles are connected to the program as indicated on the questionnaire distributed for Level 3 data. This questionnaire contained an extra question about the extent to which this program influenced these measures. At least five participants had to rate 3 or more on a 5-point scale. There is no neutral point on a scale.

Table 17-8. Intangible Benefits

• Made the first sale in 11 days, average
• Customer satisfaction
• Brand awareness for ProfitPro
• Job satisfaction of sales associates
• Stress reduction for sales associates
• Reputation of company

Communicating Results

Because this project was very successful, communicating its results was not difficult. At first there was a briefing with an executive who asked for the ROI study. The 30-minute briefing provided an opportunity to see the power of mobile learning technology and how it could affect business measures.

Data were sent to the 25 participants, along with their immediate managers, within three weeks of data collection. Also, some minor adjustments were made to the program as a result of the evaluation. These were announced in the same communication.

An executive summary of the evaluation was provided to all sales associates to show them the success of the program and to entice others to get involved in this and future programs.

A brief article (about 1,000 words) was placed in the company newsletter for all employees to read. Results were presented at a technology-based learning conference as a case study. All sales and support managers received an executive summary. The learning and development team received a full copy of the study, along with a two-hour workshop.

Recommendations

Some barriers to success were underscored. These barriers led to minor adjustments to the program, including a reduction from four hours to three hours and 15 minutes. Also, support for the program was strengthened.

Lessons Learned

This study results in several important lessons.

1. Early planning was crucial, before any design and development took place. Had the team waited until the program was designed, developed, and implemented before planning the evaluation, it would have been incomplete.
2. The objectives gave the designers, developers, and participants the proper focus. There was no mystery about what was expected of participants.
3. The control group versus experimental group method was the best one for isolating the effects of the program; however, there were some concerns about the matching of the groups. The problem with the approach of matching groups was that the evaluation team was at the mercy of the time when participants signed up for the program. If everyone were required to participate, the matching group technique would not work, and other processes would be involved.

Questions for Discussion

1. Is this study credible? Please explain.
2. What other methods might be used to isolate the effects of the program? Please explain.
3. What other ways could data collection be accomplished? Please explain.
4. Is the three-month follow-up for impact data appropriate? Please explain.
5. Was a year of impact data appropriate? Please explain.
6. How should this data be presented to management in terms of sequencing, emphasis, and approach?
7. Could this study be replicated? Please explain.

Chapter

Measuring ROI in a
New Selection Process

International Premium Hotel Group

by Jack J. Phillips and Patti P. Phillips

This case study shows the ROI in a new comprehensive selection process, which includes a new recruiting source, instruments to measure the engagement of candidates, a simulation to measure customer engagement approaches, and a realistic job preview. This upscale hotel chain needed new employees to fit into their engagement culture and be prepared to provide the ultimate customer experience. After experiencing problems with turnover of new employees when they could not adjust to the engagement culture, the recruiting and selection system was changed to include improvements in retention, the time

BACKGROUND

International Premium Hotels (IPH) owns more than 70 upscale hotels operating in 12 countries. Through its different brands, IPH prides itself on providing excellent guest satisfaction delivered by employees who have superb hospitality skills. The hotel business is a very competitive market and guest satisfaction is a critical measure. IPH charges a premium price, and for that, it wants to offer a premium service. Providing a less than desired service level will impact the company's image, ultimately leading to reduction in revenue. At the same time, IPH must also be efficient.

The Situation

The cost of high staff turnover in the first 60 days of employment has been increasing hotel costs. Management is concerned that the quality of the new staff is not where it should be in terms of being engaged with the work and customers. The IPH executives asked the HR team to experiment with new recruiting and selection processes to decrease the turnover of employees early in their tenure and while also improving guest satisfaction and employee performance. The first pilot program would be for 24 hotels in the United States. If the concept proved effective, it would be adapted to different cultures in other countries and implemented globally.

Needs Analysis

The first step was for the IPH HR staff to examine why the company was facing unusually high turnover in the first 60 days. Focus groups were conducted using a nominal group technique to arrive at the cause of turnover (Phillips and Edwards 2009). The team found that the top reasons for early turnover were that employees were:

- Not adapting to the engagement culture
- Lacking hospitality experience
- Not providing the level of engagement needed
- In a job that wasn't what they had expected

The definition of the turnover measure is avoidable turnover. In addition to voluntary turnovers, other turnovers could be avoided if actions were taken to prevent terminations. These could be prevented through counseling or improved selection processes.

SOLUTION

Armed with the information from the focus groups, the following solutions were developed and approved:

- Change the recruitment efforts to a website and recruiting source that would attract experienced hospitality candidates.
- Administer an engagement preference instrument that matches the candidate's value systems with the hotel's value systems.

- Conduct customer engagement exercises where the candidates would view a variety of videos and make a decision about what to do in each case. The assessment is designed to pinpoint a candidate's attitude toward customer engagement and customer satisfaction.
- Provide a realistic job preview. The last stage in the selection process assigns a new candidate to a brief rotational process lasting about two hours to provide a sense of the customer engagement culture in the hotel. This was designed to have candidates self-select out of the process if they are not comfortable with the engagement culture.

Recruiting Method

The first solution is a change in the recruiting method, which involved using a website that serves as a job match for the hospitality industry. Employers can advertise jobs and include the requirements and necessary qualifications on the site. Candidates can apply and provide background information; they are forwarded to the company if their credentials meet the requirements the company requires. IPH had previously used local recruiting sources, job ads, and other online services to recruit the candidates. This new website was expected to provide more experienced candidates for the hospitality industry.

Engagement

The second solution was an engagement fit instrument that checked validity and reliability. The instrument assesses what candidates want and need at work and compares them to the engagement profile of successful employees to see if their profiles match. If a profile doesn't match, the candidate should be rejected. The data show that this instrument can prevent early turnover because it ensures a proper match between the engagement culture of the organization and the work values of the candidate. A partial listing of the statements candidates agree or disagree with using a five-point scale includes:

1. I prefer to work in a stress free environment.
2. My work is not successful until the customer is satisfied.
3. I work best when I can control my schedule.
4. I take full responsibility for my results.
5. There is a limit to what we can do to satisfy a customer.

6. I work best in a supportive team environment.
7. A customer referral is more important than having a satisfied customer.
8. My work must be important.
9. My pay increases should be in proportion to my contribution.
10. I need to be recognized for my work.
11. I prefer individual rewards to team rewards.
12. I need clear expectations for my work.
13. Every customer service issue can be resolved.
14. I need opportunities to grow at work.
15. Quality of work is more important than quantity of work.
16. I need routine feedback on my progress.

Customer Service

The third solution was a customer service simulation, where the candidates view a variety of customer service videos and are asked to indicate a course of action. The situations require a person to use judgment, knowing when and how to respond to a customer as they are empowered to take that action. At the same time, they must not be too extreme with customer wishes. IPH struggles with this issue because it wants customer service staff to be empowered to take care of the customer at almost any cost, but know when the requests and issues are on the unreasonable side.

Realistic Job Preview

A fourth solution was the realistic job preview. This is based on the assumption that individuals need to see the actual job or some parts of it in operation. That way they can self-select out of the process if it isn't a good fit. In this situation, the individual observes as many issues as possible in a two-hour period in a real-life setting. This is not a new concept and has a history of minimizing early turnovers.

Figure 18-1 shows the concept of this new selection process, where the pool of applicants is initially very broad but then the hospitality source reduces that number considerably. The engagement instrument narrows it even more, and the customer service exercise even reduces it further. Finally the realistic job preview allows some participants to self-select out of the process. The result is the eligible list of candidates.

Figure 18-1. New Components of Recruiting and Selection Process

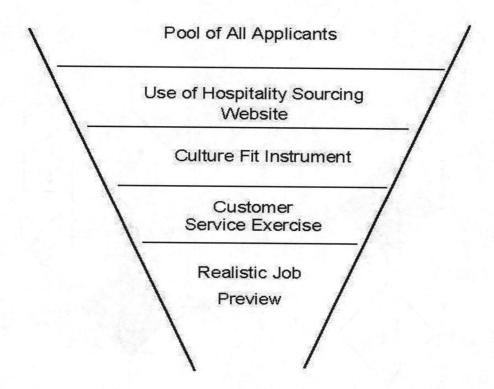

Pool of All Applicants

Use of Hospitality Sourcing Website

Culture Fit Instrument

Customer Service Exercise

Realistic Job Preview

Figure 18-2 shows the selection system and what has been added. The process is comprehensive, systematic, and can easily be administered by each hotel's HR staff. The goal is to process as many qualified candidates through the system as quickly as possible, ensuring that those candidates fit in the organization properly and remain for a longer period of time.

IMPLEMENTATION CHALLENGES

Cost

The new processes will increase the cost of recruiting and selection. The challenge is to keep these costs to a minimum while, weighing the cost verses the monetary benefit of the change. This situation created the desire to conduct the ROI analysis.

Figure 18-2. The Revised Recruiting and Selection System

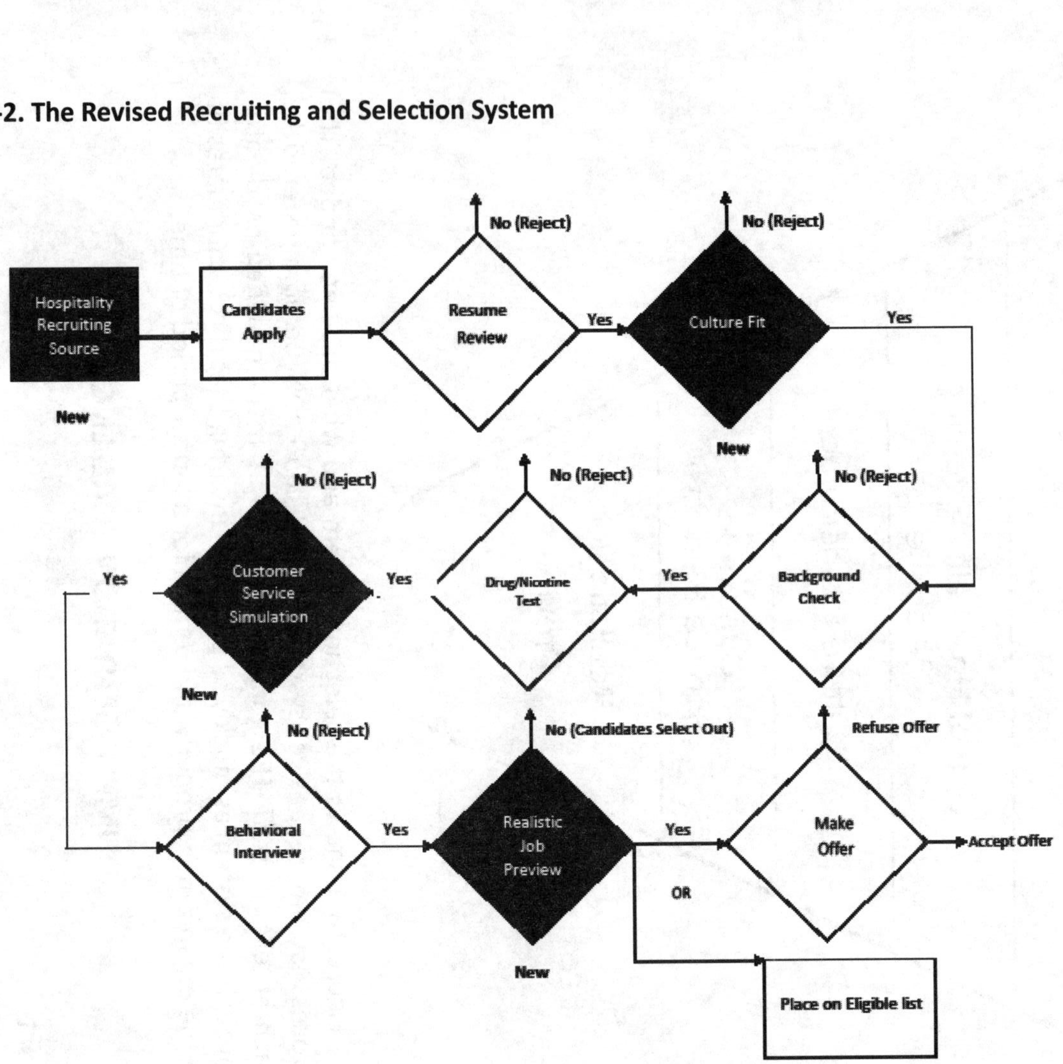

Time to Start

This new process must be implemented efficiently so that it does not add to the time to start, which is an important measure at the hotel. The time to start is a measure of time from the point that a particular job opening has been identified and a requisition has been signed to the day when the new candidate is on the job. Time to start is currently averaging 30 days and this measure needs to be at the same number (or less), even though the extra steps of the new system are extending the selection process.

Reaction to Hotel Staff

It is important for the HR staff and executives at each hotel to see the need for the change in recruitment and selection. They must see it as important to the success of the hotel and necessary to enhance guest satisfaction. They must also see the need to make the change based on the current level of performance and retention, linked to the selection of improper candidates.

Consistent Implementation

This process must be administered consistently and efficiently. One of the requirements of having a valid selection system is that the recruiting and selection process is always consistent. There is no option to administer some parts of the process but not others. For example, the same amount of time should be allocated for the realistic job previews each time a candidate participates in this step. But, candidates must also proceed efficiently through the selection system.

OBJECTIVES

The program's objectives are critical to maintain the focus on the solutions. The objectives were set at five levels.

Reaction

Based on the analysis and implementation issues described already, the following objectives were developed for reaction. After implementing this program, the HR recruiting and selecting team will see this program as important to the company's success, important to guest satisfaction, necessary for recruiting qualified candidates, and a program they intend to implement properly.

Learning

After initiating this project, the stakeholders will be able to properly use the new recruiting source, the engagement assessment instrument, a simulation on customer service, and the realistic job preview.

Application

When the project is implemented:

- The new recruiting source will be used appropriately and routinely to attract candidates.
- The engagement survey will be administered timely and consistently for each applicant.
- The customer service simulation will be administered under consistent conditions.
- The job preview will be implemented each time under the same conditions.

Impact

After the program is fully implemented:

- The avoidable turnover rate (annualized) in the first three months of employment will be reduced from 28 percent to 18 percent, which is a reduction of 10 percentage points.
- Guest satisfaction will be maintained or improved.
- The performance of new employees will be improved one half of one point on a five-point scale.
- The time to start measure will not exceed 30 days. Employee job engagement will improve.

ROI

The ROI objective for this project is set at 20 percent, which is the minimum acceptable performance.

DATA COLLECTION

Figure 18-3 shows a data collection plan for this project. First a questionnaire will be administered to the HR team that is involved in the recruiting, testing, assessment, and selection processes. This questionnaire

Figure 18-3. Data Collection Plan

Program/Project: <u>RECRUITING/SELECTION PROJECT</u>   Responsibility: _____   Date: _____

Level	Broad Program Objective(s)	Measures	Data Collection Method/ Instruments	Data Sources	Timing	Responsibilities
1	**SATISFACTION/ PLANNED ACTION** • Participants must see it is important to hotel success • Participants must see it is important to guest satisfaction • Participants must see it is necessary to recruit • Participants must intend to use	• 4 out of 5 on a 5-point rating scale	• Questionnaire	• HR Team	• Just After System Is Implemented (3 weeks)	HCA Team
2	**LEARNING** Participants must be able to: • Describe and use recruiting source • Describe and use culture fit instrument • Describe and use customer service simulation • Describe and use realistic job preview	• 4 out of 5 on a 5-point rating scale	• Questionnaire	• HR Team	• Just After Implementation (3 weeks)	HCA Team

Figure 18-3. Data Collection Plan *(continued)*

3	**APPLICATION/ IMPLEMENTATION** The Use Of: • Recruiting Source • Culture Fit Assessment • Customer Service Simulation • Realistic Job Preview	• 4 out of 5 on a 5-point rating scale	• Questionnaire • Interview • Performance Monitoring	• HR Team • HR System Records	• 2 Months After Implementation	HCA Team
4	**BUSINESS IMPACT** • Reduce early turnover by 10 percentage points • Enhance Guest Satisfaction • Time to start will not exceed 30 days • Enhance Employee Performance • Enhance Employee Engagement	• % Leaving (avoidable) • 4 of 5 on a 5 point scale	• Performance Monitoring • Questionnaire	• HR System Records • HR Team	• 4 Months After Implementation	HCA Team
5	**ROI** • 20% ROI	Comments:				

captures reaction and learning data three weeks after the new system is implemented, using self-assessment input that explores any issues that are surfacing at this point. Two months after implementation, another questionnaire is administered to ensure that all the four processes are operating properly.

For Level 4 assessments, the source of turnover and time to start data will be in the records. The rest of the impact measures will be in a questionnaire administered in four months. By then, the impact should materialize and this questionnaire will also be used to isolate the effects of this program on the impact data. Figure 18-4 shows the data integration by level.

ROI ANALYSIS PLAN

Figure 18-5 shows a completed ROI Analysis plan. The plan starts with business impact data identified from the data collection (Level 4) and presents a method of isolation. For this project, an experimental versus control group would not be possible because immediate implementation was planned for all U.S. hotels. American executives didn't want to withhold the processes for some hotels to see the effect on the control group because they wanted to resolve the problem as quickly as possible. Hotels outside the United States would not necessarily be a good match for use as a control group because of differences in global cultures. Instead, the HR team decided to use two other methods: trend line analysis and estimates from the stakeholders involved in the process. The trend line would work only if no other new process was implemented that would affect the impact measures during the four-month period. The estimations were a fallback approach.

The team relied on an acceptable standard value for the cost of turnover to convert the data to money. Regarding guest satisfaction, the hotel had some data that indicated the monetary pay-off of improving guest satisfaction, but it was not considered to be credible. Employee performance, time to start, and employee engagement were not converted to money because of the difficulty of developing a credible value.

The costs of the four new processes are fully loaded. Some additional intangibles are anticipated, which means that some information must be collected to see the extent in which these intangibles are connected to the program. The groups for communicating results are typical, with particular emphasis placed on briefing with hotel executives and providing information to the key stakeholders.

Figure 18-4. Data Summary and Integration

	REACTION	LEARNING	APPLICATION	IMPACT	BARRIERS / ENABLERS	COSTS
Questionnaire Just after Launch (3 weeks)	X	X				
Questionnaire After Launch (2 months)			X		X	
Hotel Records (2 months)			X			
Follow-Up Questionnaire (4 months)				X		X
HR Systems (4 months)				X		X
HR Records Manager Assessment (4 months)				X		

Figure 18-5. Completed ROI Analysis Plan

Data Items (Usually Level 4)	Methods for Isolating the Effects of the Program/ Process	Methods of Converting Data to Monetary Values	Cost Categories	Intangible Benefits	Communication Targets for Final Report	Other Influences/ Issues During Application	Comments
Early Turnover	• Trend Line Analysis • Participants Estimates	• Accepted Value (Standard)	• Needs Assessment • Development • Purchase/Lease • Time for Meetings/ Training • Time to use the New Processes • Evaluation	• Employee Engagement • Time to Start • Employee Performance • Guest Satisfaction • Reputation • Recruiting Image	• Recruiting and Selection Team • Hotel HR Managers • Hotel GM's • VP Operations (Corp) • VP HR (Corp) • Analytics Team	This is a Short-term solution- Need to collect ASAP	Implementa-tion will be in the 24 USA Hotels
Time to Start	• Trend Line Analysis • Participants Estimates	N/A					

RESULTS

The results are presented by the different levels, beginning with Level 1 and moving through to Level 4 and 5 analyses and ending with intangibles.

Reaction

The reaction results are presented in Figure 18-6. The reaction was satisfactory except for one issue: The individuals who are involved in recruiting and selection didn't see how the project would affect guest satisfaction. Because of this, the project team put some extra effort into communications with the recruiting and selection staff to show them the connection between having a staff with a culture of customer service and the guest satisfaction. Although the solution may prevent turnover in the early stages of employment, a mismatch early on in the hiring process can create problems with guest satisfaction. Having an employee with a longer tenure also provides continuity and continues to build client satisfaction.

Figure 18-6. Reaction Results

Reaction Results Participants rate the Following:	Score
This program is important to hotel success	4.0
This program is important to guest satisfaction	3.2
This program is necessary for recruiting qualified candidates.	4.5
This team intends to implement processes properly	4.1

Scale: 1. Not at all **2.** A Little **3.** Some **4.** Much **5.** Very Much   Average response = 4.0

Learning

Learning was obtained using a simple self-assessment on a questionnaire. The results are captured in Figure 18-7. The participants indicated that they could describe each of the new processes and use them properly. While there were no surprises at this level, the lowest ratings were for the customer service simulation and the realistic job previews. These were a little more complicated than the change in recruiting source and the engagement survey assessment. The excellent results at this level may be a reflection of the fact that the objectives were clearly defined.

Figure 18-7. Learning Results

Learning Results Participants are able to:	Score
Describe the new recruiting source and website	4.2
Use the new recruiting source and website	4.1
Describe the culture fit assessment	4.4
Use the culture fit assessment	4.3
Describe the customer service simulated	3.9
Use the customer service simulated	4.0
Describe the realistic job preview process	3.8
Use the realistic job preview process	3.9

Scale: **1.** Not at all **2.** Some **3.** Moderate Amount   **Average response = 4.**
4. Significant Amount **5.** Very Significant Amount

Application, Barriers, and Enablers

Figure 18-8 shows the application data and reveals that the new steps were being operated properly and consistently, except for the realistic job preview.

Figure 18-8. Application Results

Application Results Participants are able to:	Score
The new recruiting source is being used properly	4.2
The new recruiting source provides a steady stream of candidates	4.6
The culture fit survey is administered for every candidate	4.7
The culture fit survey is administered under the same conditions for each remaining candidate	4.6
The customer service simulation is administered	4.0
The customer service simulation is administered under the same conditions	4.1
The realistic job preview is administered for each remaining candidate	3.7
The realistic job preview is administered under the same conditions	3.8
The four new processes are successful	4.3

Scale: 1. Not at all **2.** Occasionally **3.** Sometimes **4.** Often **5.** Always

Figure 18-9 shows the barriers to use and Figure 18-10 shows the enablers that support the use. The barriers reveal that the realistic job preview is a problem, with nearly 70 percent having difficulty with it. The issue is also connected to the second barrier. ever, the enablers were very positive and encouraging.

Figure 18-9. Barriers to Effective Use

Barriers to Use	Percent Responding
The realistic job preview is difficult to execute	39%
The process takes too much time	28%
Candidates resist the two assessments	17%
It's difficult to be consistent each time	8%
Others	14%

Figure 18-10. Enablers to Effective Use

Barriers to Use	Percent Responding
The realistic job preview is difficult to execute	39%
The process takes too much time	28%
Candidates resist the two assessments	17%
It's difficult to be consistent each time	8%
Others	14%

Figure 18-11 shows the efficiencies that are coming through the system with these changes. Previously, only 54 percent of applicants made it through the resume review. With this new system 81 percent are making it through the resume review, underscoring that the recruiting source is providing more qualified candidates. Thus, out of 100 initial applications, 81 move on to the engagement assessment round, which eliminates another 29 applications. The customer service simulation drops another 10, but the realistic job preview only removes 1. So in essence, this process provides better candidates in the beginning, eliminating 40 percent of applicants that would potentially have left the organization in the early stages of employment. These are impressive results, with the engagement survey having the most impact thus far. In total, 79 of the 100 candidates who applied were eliminated from consideration. The engagement survey accounted for 29 (37 percent) of the total eliminations.

Figure 18-11. Recruiting/Selecting Efficiencies

| | For Every 100 Candidates Apply | | |
	These Remain		After
	81	81%	Resume Review (previously 54)
New	52	64%	Culture Fit Assessment
	44	84%	Background Check
	39	89%	Drug/Nicotine Test
New	29	74%	Customer Service Simulation
	22	76%	Behavioral Interviews
New	21	95%	Realistic Job Previews
	18		Make Offer
	3		Move to Eligible List
	17	94%	Accept Offer

Business Impact

The early turnover data are presented in Figure 18-12 for the four months prior to the program and four months after the program. As expected, the annualized turnover data are reduced.

The isolation by trend line analysis seems to work for this data set. It shows that 28 percent turnover would be expected, but after four months the actual turnover is 16 percent. The HR team indicated that the pre-program trend would probably have continued if nothing had changed in the system. More importantly, the HR team could not identify any other new influences that would have caused this improvement. Therefore it is safe to use the trend line analysis as a method of isolation.

Time to start is an important measure and Figure 18-13 shows the details. The program reduced the time to start to 27 days, compared to about 30 days prior to the program. However, there was already a downward trend in place the when the program started, and the projected trend line shows that time to start may have hit 27 days even without the program. This means that the program may have actually added more days to what the time to start could have been.

However, the team could not explain the downward trend on the program data, or the fact that it would have continued. Consequently, the HCA team suggested that the objective had been met.

Figure 18-12. Trend Line Analysis for Early Turnover

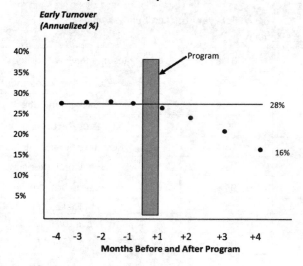

Figure 18-13. Trend Line Analysis for Time to Start

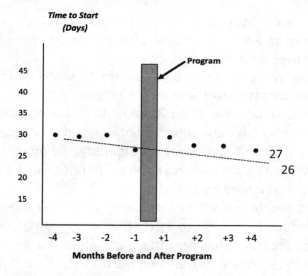

Converting Data to Money

In total, the company was expecting to hire 255 employees in the 24 U.S. hotels during the year of this study. To calculate the cost of early turnover, the hotel had been using 40 percent of annual pay, which was a number accepted by the management team. This is for early turnover, where the investment in new employees is not as much as for longer-term employees and the loss of knowledge and experience is not very high. However, there are still upfront variable costs related to replacements, so 40 percent is a conservative number that covers the cost of recruiting, selection, employment, onboarding, and initial training before new employees become productive. It also includes the cost of the disruption and the bottlenecks caused by turnover, as well as the time involved in addressing the turnover situation. Figure 18-14 shows the calculation for the cost savings of the reduction in turnover.

Figure 18-14. Turnover Analysis

Turnover Analysis
255 Employees
Turnover Improvements 28 -16 = 12% Annual
255 x 12% = 31 Employees
Average Salary $36,000
Turnover Cost 40% of Salary
36,000 x .4 = 14,400
Annual = 14, 400 x 31 = $446,400

The time to start decreased slightly but wasn't converted to monetary value. It is left as an intangible.

Cost

The fully loaded cost of these four solutions, including the solution and purchase instruments, is shown in Figure 18-15. The team was very anxious to make sure all cost were included, both direct and indirect. Some of the costs included ongoing cost in the future because these services are being used for the recruiting database, instrument, and customer service simulation. The question that surfaced was how much cost to include. In the very beginning of the project, it was determined that this would be considered a short-term solution, which means the benefits would be accumulated for one year and the early turnover would be extrapolated for an entire year when the impact was actually determined. In other words, after four months, the change in turnover rate would be extrapolated for the year to arrive at the benefits in the previous section.

A case could easily have been made for this to be a longer-term solution, which would allow two or even three years of benefits to be used. However, the team decided to use one year to increase the credibility of the data.

Figure 18-15. Fully Loaded Costs of Four Solutions

Cost of Four Solutions at 24 Hotels (Annualized and Prorated)	
Needs Assessment	
- Prorated over 5 years	$1,200
Development/Purchase	
- Customer Service	15,000
- Realistic Job Previews	8,000
Lease/ Royalties	
- Recruiting Source (*Annual*)	20,000
- Culture Fit (*Annual*)	17,200
- Customer Service Simulation(*Annual*)	23,500
Learning Session for Recruiting	
and Selection Team	4,300
Time to Use the Processes	
- Recruiting Source	Less Than Previous
- Culture	2,200
Administrative Issues	
- Coordination, Supplies, etc.	15,800
- Customer Services	4,400
- Realistic Job Preview	22,000
Evaluation	4,500
Total	$138,100

Finally the BCR and ROI were calculated, as shown below in Figure 18-16. Monetary benefits for one year were determined to be $446,400, whereas the cost for one year of the program was $138,100.

Figure 18-16. BCR and ROI Analysis

Monetary Benefits (1 year) = $446,400
Costs (1 year) $138,100

$$BCR = \frac{\$446,200,400}{\$138,100} = 3.23 \text{ to } 1$$

$$ROI = \frac{\$446,400 - \$138,100}{\$138,100} = 223\%$$

The benefits cost ratio and the ROI are extremely high, making it difficult for people to accept. However, the impact data are credible because they come right out of the system. The high early turnover rate was substantially reduced, and the monetary benefits are realistic since management agreed on the cost of turnover. In addition, the program was not very expensive, particularly when considering that all of the costs for the four processes are included. The HCA team felt good that this could be defended in the communication of results.

Intangibles

As it turned out, this study influenced some important intangibles, with three measures that were initially identified as impact turning out to be intangibles. The time to start was not converted to money, as mentioned earlier, although there were certainly some costs avoided with improvement in that measure. Time to start was left intangible because it could not be developed credibly with a reasonable amount of resources. The records of the individuals participating in the program were reviewed to determine employee performance. The performance was higher and actually slightly exceeded the requirement for one-half of one point in performance improvement. The average performance improvement rating increased from 3.8 to 4.4 on a 5-point scale, where 3 is average performance rating. It was impossible to connect guest satisfaction directly to this group of employees.

Although each hotel has guest satisfaction measures, those numbers aren't broken down by individual person or even function. However, on the questionnaire the HR team asked employees to indicate the extent to which the program had improved guest satisfaction; they were able to connect the ranking of 4.1 out of a 5-point scale to guest satisfaction. Other intangible measures included reputation of the hotel, brand awareness, and recruiting image (Figure 18-17).

Figure 18-17. Intangible Benefits Connected to this Program

Intangible Benefits	
Time to Start	Slight Reduction
Employee Performance	3.8 to 4.4 out of 5
Guest Satisfaction*	4.1
Recruiting Image*	4.3
Brand Awareness*	3.8
Hotel Reputation*	3.2
*Scale 1. No Influence 2. Some Influence 3. Moderate Influence 4. Significant Influence 5. Very Significant Influence	

CONCLUSIONS AND RECOMMENDATIONS

This program was a success in terms of its overall connection with the impact measures. However, the realistic job preview doesn't seem to be adding value, which is addressed in the recommendation. Data collection was smooth and efficient, participation was high, barriers were minimal, and enablers were very strong. On a conservative basis, the program adds tremendous value, with most of the improvement coming from the engagement survey. The program also underscores the fact that management support was extremely high, because the HCA team was handed a problem, but not the specific solution. Although management hinted at the solution— something had to be changed in the assessment, selection, and sourcing process to stem the turnover—the specific solution was left up to the team to uncover. This works much better, instead of having the management team implement or bring a predetermined solution, only to find out later that it was not the right one. By planning for the ROI in advance, this project brought a tremendous focus on the outcome, provided for early detection of problems, and helped achieve the results that were ultimately delivered.

In terms of recommendations, the HCA team recommended that this concept be applied to hotels in other countries, but in the context of the culture of that country. This may be more expensive because of language, labor laws, and the cultures of the different countries. For some, it might not even be worth it. However, each country would be evaluated individually and at least some parts of the process should be considered.

Also as it turns out, the realistic job preview did not have a significant effect, with only one person self-selecting out in the four months of operation results. Given the cost of this process, the difficulties the hotel HR team is having with this task, and the amount of time it takes for other hotel staff to be involved, the HR team recommended that this part be dropped from the process going forward.

Communication Plan

With results in hand, the first stop was the executive group. The HR team gave the U.S. hotel executives a briefing during one of their regularly scheduled meetings. This 30-minute briefing gave the team the opportunity to explain the methodology that was used, describe their results, and gain approval for their recommendations. This briefing was carefully planned and orchestrated and was successful in meeting the agenda and achieving its purposes. Beyond that, a summary and full report was sent to the HR team involved in the project. This was followed with a webinar briefing, which used the same set of slides as the executive group briefing. In addition, all the hotel general managers were given a summary, a complete report, and a webinar on the results, with opportunities for Q&A. This hour and a half session accomplished the same goals as the executive briefing, but included a little more detail about operational issues at the hotel.

In addition, the team wrote a brief article for the employee newsletter explaining the study, what was done, and results that were achieved. A complete study was also made available to the HR managers at all the hotels in the United States and internationally. A webinar was offered to this complete group and was conducted in two sessions, one with the U.S. HR managers, and the other with those outside the United States, with some discussion around the applicability and feasibility of the same process in their country.

Finally, a brief paragraph of this study was included in the quarterly financial report that was released the quarter following the executive briefing. This was designed to alert investors of the progress being made to make the organization more successful in terms of guest satisfaction and controlling cost.

Lessons Learned

The lessons learned from this program are very straightforward:

1. It is best to have a problem to work with so the team can find the right solution. This is in contrast to many requests when the solution is brought to the HR team.
2. The decision to measure the impact and ROI was made early, at the time of the analysis: This helped in planning the study, making it more focused, and keeping the attention on results throughout the implementation. This approach actually enhanced the results that were achieved.
3. Excellent support of the management group made it successful. The hotel general managers saw the problem, knew it was expensive, and were pleased to see the solution.
4. This type of analysis does take a little bit of time, but when it is all considered, it is worth it. The extra efforts are actually necessary steps in the process.

Questions for Discussion

1. Is this study credible? Please explain.
2. Are there other potential solutions to this problem? Please explain.
3. Critique the data collection. Are there other ways to collect data? If so, explain.
4. What others ways could be used to isolate the effects of the program?
5. Could the effects of the engagement be isolated from other parts of the solution? If so, how could this be accomplished?
6. Could the ROI from the engagement survey be calculated? If so, how?
7. Should this be a long-term or short-term solution? Explain.
8. Could you defend this study with your executives? Please explain.

Reference

Phillips, J.J., and L. Edwards. 2009. *Managing Talent Retention: An ROI Approach.* San Francisco: John Wiley.

Chapter 19

Measuring ROI in Safety Leadership

Global Engineering and Construction Company

by Jack J. Phillips

This case study shows the power of a safety leadership program for project safety leaders on construction sites. These are large construction sites and the safety project leader is a full-time safety and health professional. Responding to disappointing safety performance, a thorough needs analysis was conducted, yielding a variety of actions that needed to be taken through the project safety leaders. These managers are responsible for safety for their large projects. They need to take leadership actions to improve a variety of measures. This program involved a two-day workshop with action plans to drive business performance measures. Each participant selected three measures to improve, using the content of the program and the detailed action planning process provided. The results are very impressive, underscoring the benefit of having an action plan built into the program and the power of the program's focus on results.

BACKGROUND

Global Engineering and Construction Company (GEC) designs and builds large commercial projects such as chemical plants, paper mills, and municipal water systems. The company employs 35,000 full-time associates. In addition, another 200 to 1,500 contract workers are involved during each project's peak construction phases. During a typical year, contract workers account for another 100,000 at construction sites. Safety is always a critical matter at GEC and usually commands much management attention.

From a corporate perspective, safety is managed by a safety and health team composed of specialists and managers who report to the director of environment, health, and safety (EHS). Each project has at least one person responsible for safety who functions as a project safety leader.

The Need

During the previous two years, safety performance has deteriorated or remained flat at unacceptable levels. Because of this disappointing and sometimes erratic safety performance, the chief operating officer (COO) asked the EHS director to explore the causes of the unacceptable performance and to offer a remedy. The department reviewed the safety records, safety procedures, and safety administration, searching for common threads of causality. Questionnaires were sent to all the project safety leaders at each site, and a select group of safety leaders were interviewed in an attempt to pinpoint what could be done to improve safety. From this initial needs assessment, the following conclusions were made:

1. There is still a lack of knowledge about the different tools and techniques available for the project safety leaders to use to improve safety performance.
2. There is clear evidence that project safety leaders are not operating on a proactive basis, but merely reacting to events and issues as they happen.
3. Routine safety meetings need more content, better planning, and improved coordination.
4. Project safety leaders need to use available tools for investigation, causation analysis, and corrective action.

With this in mind, the EHS Team recommended a two-day safety leadership workshop for all the project safety leaders. This workshop would focus on the gaps defined in the needs assessment and would provide the motivation, knowledge, skills, and tools to improve safety performance.

The program was designed for project safety leaders, who usually had the title of safety manager, safety engineer, or safety superintendent. The program focused on safety leadership, safety planning, safety inspections and audits, safety meetings, accident investigation, safety policies and procedures, safety standards, and safety problem solving. The objectives for the program are listed in Table 19-1.

Table 19-1. Objectives for Safety Management Program

Level	Measurement Focus
1. Reaction	Obtain favorable reaction to program and materials on: • Need for program • Relevance to project • Importance to project success Identify planned actions.
2. Learning	After attending this program, participants should be able to: • Establish safety audits. • Provide feedback and motivate employees. • Investigate accidents. • Solve safety problems.
3. Application and Implementation	• Use knowledge, skills, and tools routinely in appropriate situations. • Complete all steps of action plan.
4. Business Impact	• Improve at least three safety and health measures.
5. Return on Investment	20%

These topics were fully explored in a two-day safety leadership program. Safety leaders (the participants) were expected to improve the safety performance of their individual construction projects. The safety performance measures used in the company were also reviewed and discussed in the workshop. This particular program would be expensive, because it would be necessary for all the project safety leaders to travel, and they would miss two days of work while participating in the program. The COO wanted to make sure that this was the right solution and that it represented a good investment. He asked for success measures that would show how safety performance has improved. Ideally, he wanted to see the ROI for conducting this particular program.

Business Alignment

The program facilitator asked participants to provide limited needs assessment data before attending the program. Participants were asked to review the safety performance of their projects and identify at least three safety measures that, if improved, should enhance safety performance. Each measure selected should be important and have the possibility of being improved using the topics covered in the safety management program. Some possible business impact measures include disabling injury rate, accident severity rate, first aid treatments, OSHA citations, OSHA penalties, property accidents, hazardous material incidents, or near misses. Each participant could have different measures, but it is important to avoid selecting measures that cannot be enhanced through the team's efforts and the content covered in the program.

As the participants register for the program, they are reminded to complete the action plan. This requirement is presented as an integral part of the program, not as an add-on data collection tool, because action planning is necessary to show actual improvements generated from the program.

Why Evaluate This Program?

Although the COO had suggested the ROI calculation, the EHS director was convinced that this program would add value and he wanted to show top executives that investments in safety and health had high payoffs. The safety team decided at the outset to collect and present improvement data to the C-suite, so the evaluation and action plan steps were built into the program. This decision was based on three issues:

- This program is designed to add value at the construction-project level and the outcome is expressed in project level measures that are well known and respected by the management team. The evaluation should show the actual monetary value of improvement.
- The application data enable the team to make improvements and adjustments.
- The data also help the team gain respect for the program from the operating executives and project managers.

The ROI Process

The safety and health team staff used a comprehensive evaluation process to develop the ROI. The ROI Methodology generates six types of data: reaction, learning, application and implementation, business impact, ROI, and intangible measures.

To determine the contribution the program makes to the changes in business impact measures, a technique to isolate the effects of the program was also included in the process. Figure 19-1 shows the ROI process model used. Data collection plans and an ROI analysis plan were developed before data collection actually began. Four levels of data were collected, which represents the first four types of data listed above, and the process also included techniques to convert data to monetary value. The ROI is calculated by comparing the monetary benefits with the cost of the program. The intangible measures, the sixth type of data, are those impact measures not usually converted to monetary value, such as job satisfaction and image. This comprehensive model allows the organization to follow a consistent standardized approach each time it is applied to evaluate safety programs.

Figure 19-1. ROI Methodology ™ Process Model

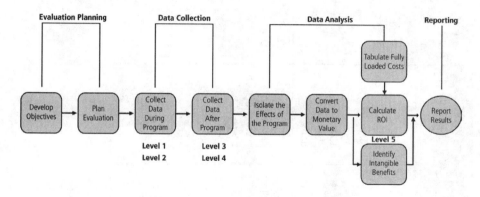

PLANNING FOR EVALUATION

Planning for the evaluation is critical to save time and improve the quality and quantity of data collection. It also provides an opportunity to clarify expectations and responsibilities and shows the client group—in this case, the senior operating team—exactly how this program is evaluated. Two documents are created: the data collection plan and the ROI analysis plan.

Data Collection Plan

Figure 19-2 shows the data collection plan for this program. Program objectives are detailed along the five levels of evaluation, which represent the first five types of data collected. As the figure illustrates, the typical reaction and learning data are collected at the end of the program by the facilitator. Learning objectives focus on the major areas of the program.

Figure 19-2. Data Collection Plan

Level	Broad Program Objective(s)	Measures	Data Collection Method/Instruments	Data Sources	Timing	Responsibilities
1	**REACTION** • Obtain favorable reaction to program and materials on – Need for program – Relevance to project – Importance to project success • Identify planned actions	• Average rating of 4 out of 5 on feedback items • 100% submit planned actions	• Standard questionnaire	• Participant	• End of program	• Facilitator
2	**LEARNING** After attending this session, participants should be able to: • Establish safety audits • Provide feedback and motivate employees • Investigate accidents • Solve safety problems • Follow procedures and standards • Counsel problem employees • Conduct safety meetings	• Achieve an average of 4 on a 5-point scale	• Questionnaire	• Participant	• End of program	• Facilitator

Figure 19-2. Data Collection Plan *(continued)*

Level	Broad Program Objective(s)	Measures	Data Collection Method/ Instruments	Data Sources	Timing	Responsibilities
3	**APPLICATION/IMPLEMENTATION** • Use knowledge, skills, and tools in appropriate situations • Complete all steps of action plan	• Ratings on questions (4 of 5) • The number of steps completed on action plan	• Questionnaire • Action plan	• Participant • Participant	• Two months after program • Three months after program	• Safety and health team
4	**BUSINESS IMPACT** • Improve three safety and health measures	• Varies	• Action plan	• Participant	• Three months after program	• Safety and health team
5	**ROI** 20%					

Comments: Several techniques will be used to secure commitment to provide data on the questionnaire and action plan.

Through application objectives, participants focus on two primary broad areas. The first is to use the knowledge, skills, and tools routinely in appropriate situations, and the second is to complete all steps on their action plans. A follow-up questionnaire was selected to measure the use of knowledge, skills, and tools. This was planned for two months after the program. For the second area, action plan data are provided to show the actual improvement in the safety measures planned.

Business impact objectives vary with the individual, as each project safety leader identifies at least three safety and health measures needing improvement. These are detailed on the action plan and serve as the basic principal document for the safety and health team to tabulate the overall improvement. The ROI objective is 20 percent, which was higher than the ROI target for capital expenditures at GEC.

ROI Analysis Plan

The ROI analysis plan, which appears in Figure 19-3, shows how data are analyzed and reported. Safety performance data form the basis for the rest of the analysis. The effects of the program were isolated using estimations from the safety project leader. The method to convert data to monetary values relied on three techniques: standard values (when they are available), expert input, and participant's estimates. Most of the costs of safety measures were readily available. Cost categories represent a fully loaded profile of program costs, including direct and indirect costs; anticipated intangibles are detailed and the communication audiences for the results are outlined. The ROI analysis plan represents the approach to process business impact data to develop the ROI analysis and capture the intangible data. Collectively, these two planning documents outline the approach for evaluating this program.

ACTION PLANNING: A KEY TO ROI ANALYSIS

Figure 19-4 shows the sequence of activities as the action planning process is introduced to participants and reinforced throughout the program. The requirement for the action plan is communicated prior to the program along with the request for needs assessment information.

Figure 19-3. ROI Analysis Plan

Program: <u>Safety Management Program</u>   Responsibility: _____   Date: _____

Data Items (Usually Level 4)	Methods for Isolating the Effects of the Program/Process	Methods of Converting Data to Monetary Values	Cost Categories	Intangible Benefits	Communication Targets for Final Report	Other Influences/Issues During Application	Comments
• Three safety and health measures identified by project safety leader	• Participant estimation	• Standard values • Expert input (Safety team) • Participant estimation	• Needs assessment • Program development • Program materials • Travel and lodging • Facilitation and coordination • Participant salaries plus benefits while in the program • Extra project expenses related to program • Evaluation	• Job engagement • Job satisfaction • Stress • Image • Brand	• Construction project general manager • Participants • Director, environment, health and safety • Corporate safety and health team • Operating executives • Senior VP human resources		

Client Signature: _____   Date: _____

Figure 19-4. Sequence of Activities for Action Planning

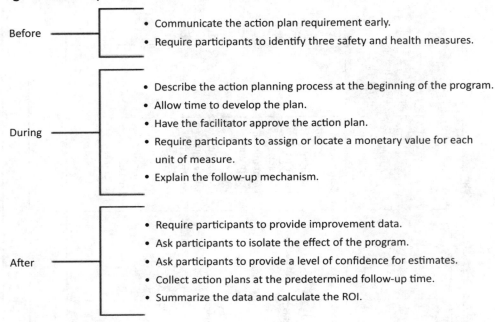

Before
- Communicate the action plan requirement early.
- Require participants to identify three safety and health measures.

During
- Describe the action planning process at the beginning of the program.
- Allow time to develop the plan.
- Have the facilitator approve the action plan.
- Require participants to assign or locate a monetary value for each unit of measure.
- Explain the follow-up mechanism.

After
- Require participants to provide improvement data.
- Ask participants to isolate the effect of the program.
- Ask participants to provide a level of confidence for estimates.
- Collect action plans at the predetermined follow-up time.
- Summarize the data and calculate the ROI.

Teaching and Explaining the Plan

On the first day of the program, the facilitator described the action planning process in a 15-minute discussion. The guidelines for developing action plans were presented using the SMART (specific, measurable, achievable, realistic, and time-based) requirements. The participants were given five blank action plans (three of which they needed to complete). The facilitator also presented examples to illustrate what a complete action plan should look like. This discussion reinforced the need for action plans and the importance of the tool to participants.

Developing the Plan

At the end of the second day, the booklets were completed in a session that lasted about 90 minutes. Participants worked in teams to complete three action plans, which took 20 to 30 minutes each. Figure 19-5 shows a blank action plan. During the session, participants completed the top portion of the action plan; they listed the action steps in the left column and parts

Figure 19-5. Action Plan Form

Name: _____ Facilitator Signature: _____ Follow-Up Date: _____

Objective: _____ Evaluation Period: _____ To: _____ Improvement Measure: _____

Current Performance: _____ Target Performance: _____

Action Steps	Analysis
1. _____	A. What is the unit of measure? _____
2. _____	B. What is the value (cost) of one unit? $ _____
3. _____	C. How did you arrive at this value? _____
	D. How much did the measure change during the evaluation period?
4. _____	(monthly value) _____
	E. What other factors could have caused the improvement?
5. _____	1. _____
	2. _____
6. _____	3. _____
7. _____	F. What percent of this change was actually caused by this program?
	_____ %
8. _____	G. What level of confidence do you place on the above information?
	(100%=Certainty and 0%=No Confidence) _____ %
9. _____	H. How many months to project completion? _____
	Other benefits and consequences _____
Comments: _____	
_____	
_____	

A, B, and C in the right column. The remainder of the form was completed during a three-month follow up. A facilitator monitored the session and several operations executives were present. Involving operations executives not only keeps participants focused on the task, it usually leaves executives impressed with the program and the quality of the action planning process.

The action plan could focus on any specific steps, as long as the steps are consistent with the program's content and are related to the safety and health improvement measures. The most important part of developing the plan is to convert the measure to a monetary value (B and C). Three approaches were offered to the participants. First, standard values, which are values already known to the project safety leaders, are used if they are available. In this case, standard values were available for most of the EHS measures because the safety and health team had previously assigned a cost to particular measures for use in controlling costs and developing an appreciation for their impact. If a standard value was not available, the participants were encouraged to use expert input, such as from a corporate safety and health team member who may know the value of a particular item. The program facilitator encouraged participants to call the expert and include the given value in the action plan. If a standard value or expert input was not available, participants were asked to estimate the cost or value using the knowledge and resources available to them. It was important to require this value to be developed during the program.

ROI FORECAST WITH REACTION DATA

At the end of the two-day leadership program, participants completed a customized questionnaire to evaluate the safety leadership program. Participants were asked to provide a one-year estimated monetary value of their planned actions, explaining the basis for and placing a confidence level on their estimates. Table 19-2 presents these data. Data were supplied by 19 of the 25 participants. The estimated cost of the program, including participants' salaries for the time devoted to the project, was $120,000.

The monetary values of the planned improvements were extremely high, reflecting the participants' optimism and enthusiasm. As a first step in the analysis, extreme data items were omitted (one of the guiding principles of the ROI Methodology). Data such as millions, unlimited, and $4 million were discarded, and each remaining value was multiplied by the confidence value and totaled. This adjustment is a way to reduce highly subjective estimates.

Table 19-2. Level 1 Data for ROI Forecast Calculations

Participant No.	Estimated Value ($)	Basis	Confidence Level	Adjusted Value ($)
1	80,000	Reduction in accidents	90%	72,000
2	91,200	OSHA reportable injuries, OSHA Fines	80%	72,960
3	55,000	Accident reduction	90%	49,500
4	10,000	First-aid visits/visits to doctor/DIR	70%	7,000
5	150,000	Reduction in lost-time injuries, OSHA Fines	95%	142,500
6	Millions	Total accident cost	100%	—
7	74,800	Workers' compensation, Injury	80%	59,840
8	7,500	OSHA citations, Accidents	75%	5,625
9	50,000	Reduction in accidents	75%	37,500
10	36,000	Workers' compensation (lost time)	80%	28,800
11	150,000	Reduction in total accident costs	90%	135,000
12	22,000	OSHA fines/accidents	70%	15,400
13	140,000	Accident reductions	80%	112,000
14	4 Million	Total cost of safety	95%	—
15	65,000	Total workers' compensation	50%	32,500
16	Unlimited	Accidents	100%	—
17	20,000	Accidents	95%	19,000
18	45,000	Injuries	90%	40,500
19	200,000	Lost-time injuries	80%	160,000
			Total:	**$990,125**

The resulting tabulations yielded a total improvement of $990,125. The projected ROI, which was based on the feedback questionnaire, is:

$$ROI = \frac{\$990,125 - \$120,000}{\$120,000} \times 100 = 725\%$$

Although these projected values are subjective, the results were generated by project safety leaders (participants) who should be aware of what they could accomplish. The follow-up study will determine the true results delivered by the group.

Collecting this type of data focuses increased attention on project outcomes. This issue becomes clear to participants as they anticipate results and convert them to monetary values. This simple exercise is productive because of the important message it sends to participants—they will understand that specific action is expected, which produces results. The data collection helps participants plan the implementation of what they are learning.

Because a follow-up evaluation of the program is planned, the post-project results will be compared with the ROI forecast. Comparisons of forecast and follow-up data are helpful. If there is a defined relationship between the two, the less expensive forecast may be substituted for the more expensive follow-up in the future.

IMPROVING RESPONSE RATES

Data were collected at Level 1 and 2 (Reaction and Learning) at the end of the two-day workshop. As expected, the facilitator was able to secure a 100 percent response rate directly from the participants. However, not everyone completed the forecast of results, with only 19 of the 25 providing data. A follow-up questionnaire, which was completed two months after the program, had an impressive response, with 22 out of the 25 providing data.

This response rate was achieved by taking on the following techniques:

1. The questionnaire was reviewed at the workshop, with the expectation that the data would be provided in two months.
2. The questionnaire was positioned as a tool for participants to see the progress they were making.
3. The questionnaire was designed for ease of response, with the expectation that it would take only about 20 minutes to complete.
4. The COO signed the memo to the participants, asking for the data and encouraging them to reflect over what they were actually doing as a result of this program. The participants were promised a summary of the questionnaire results, and were assured that actions would be taken to improve the program as a result of their comments.
5. Two follow-up reminders were provided: an email and a phone call directly from the facilitator.
6. Participants were given a new book on the importance of safety as an incentive for responding—this was an exchange, the questionnaire for the book.

Action plans were collected three months after the program, providing an opportunity for the participants to show the impact of their work. Because of their commitment and ownership of the data, a response rate of 92 percent was achieved. The facilitators also used several techniques similar to those used with the questionnaire to obtain the action plans.

In summary, the data collection was extremely effective with high levels of commitment and participation by the individuals.

RESULTS

The safety and health team reported results in all six data categories developed by the ROI Methodology, beginning with reaction and moving through ROI and the intangibles. Here are the results in each category with additional explanations about how some of the data was processed.

Reaction and Learning

Reaction data, collected at the end of the program using a standard questionnaire, focused on issues such as relevance of and intention to use the content. The delivery and facilitation also are evaluated. Table 19-3 shows a summary of the reaction data with ratings. Learning improvement was measured at the end of the program using self-assessment. Table 19-4 shows the summary of the learning results. Although these measures are subjective, they provide an indication of improvements in learning.

Table 19-3. Reaction Measurements

Topic	Rating
Need for the program	4.3
Relevance to construction project	4.5
Importance to project success	4.5
Delivery of the program	4.2
Facilitation of the program	4.2
Planned actions developed	100%

1= Unsatisfactory   5 = Exceptional

Table 19-4. Learning Measurements

Topic	Rating
Establish safety audits	4.2
Provide feedback and motivation to employees	4.0
Investigate accidents	4.9
Follow safety procedures and standards	4.2
Counsel problem employees	3.9
Conduct safety meetings	4.8

1 = Cannot do this   5 = Can do this extremely well

Application and Implementation

To determine the extent to which the knowledge, skills, and tools are actually being used and to check the progress of the action plan, a questionnaire was distributed two months following participation in the program. This two-page, user-friendly questionnaire evaluated the success of the program at the application level. Table 19-5 provides a summary of the results, which show progress in each of the areas and success using the content. The safety leaders also indicated that this program was affecting other safety measures beyond the three selected for action planning. Typical barriers of implementation they reported included lack of time, understaffing, changing culture, and pressures to get work done. The highest ranked enabler was support from the project general manager. This follow-up questionnaire gave project safety leaders an opportunity to briefly summarize progress with the action plan.

Table 19-5. Application Results

Success With:	Rating
1. Conducting safety audits	4.1
2. Providing feedback to employees	3.9
3. Investigating accidents	4.8
4. Solving safety problems	4.9
5. Following safety procedures and standards	4.7
6. Counseling problem employees	4.2
7. Conducting safety meetings	4.6
1= Unsuccessful 5 = Very Successful	

In essence, it served as a reminder to continue with the plan, as well as a process check to see if there were issues that should be explored.

Business Impact

Project safety leaders provided safety improvement data specific to their construction projects. Although the action plan contained some Level 3 application data (the left side of the form in Figure 19-6), the primary value of the action plan was business impact data obtained from the documents.

In the three-month follow up, participants were required to furnish the following items:

1. The actual change in the measure on a monthly basis (included in part D of the action plan). This value is used to develop an annual (first year) improvement.
2. A list of the other factors that could have caused the improvement (part E), which is the only feasible way to isolate the effects of the program. As they monitor the measures and observe their improvement, the project safety leaders probably see the other influences driving a particular measure.
3. The percent of improvement resulting from the application of the content from the safety management program (the action steps on the action plan). Each project safety leader was asked to be as accurate as possible with the estimate and express it as a percentage (part F).
4. The level of confidence in their allocation of the contribution to this program. This reflects the degree of error in the allocation and is included in part G on the action plan, using 100 percent for certainty and 0 percent for no confidence.
5. An estimate of the number of months to project completion. This allows for the calculation of the duration of the benefits.
6. Input on intangible measures observed or monitored during the three months that were directly linked to this program.
7. Additional comments, including explanations if necessary.

Figure 19-6 shows an example of a completed action plan. The example focuses directly on first-aid visits from participant number five. This participant was averaging 22 incidents per month, and the goal was to reduce it to 10. Specific action steps are indicated on the left side of the form. The average cost of a first-aid visit is $300, an amount that represents a standard value. The actual change on a monthly basis was 11 visits, which was slightly below the target. Three other factors contributed to the improvement. The participant estimated that 60 percent of the change was directly attributable to this program, and is 80 percent confident in this estimate. The confidence estimate frames a range of error for the 60 percent allocation, allowing for a possible 20 percent (plus or minus) adjustment in the estimate. To be conservative, it is adjusted to the low side, bringing the contribution rate of this program to a 48 percent reduction:

$$60\% \times 80\% = 48\%$$

Figure 19-6. Action Plan

Name: <u>Roger Gerson</u>   Facilitator Signature: _____   Follow-Up Date: <u>1 July</u>   Objective: <u>Reduce first-aid treatments</u>

Evaluation Period: <u>January</u> To: <u>April</u>   Improvement Measure: <u>First-aid visits</u>

Current Performance: <u>22 / Month</u>   Target Performance: <u>10 / Month</u>

Action Steps	Analysis
1. Review first-aid records for each employee—look for trends and patterns.	A. What is the unit of measure? <u>One first-aid visit</u>
2. Meet with team to discuss reasons for first-aid visits—using problem-solving skills.	B. What is the value (cost) of one unit? $ <u>300</u>
3. Counsel with "problem employees" to correct habits and explore opportunities for improvement.	C. How did you arrive at this value? <u>Standard Value</u>
4. Conduct a brief meeting with an employee returning to work after a visit to first aid.	D. How much did the measure change during the evaluation period? (monthly value) <u>11</u>
5. Provide recognition to employees who have perfect accident records.	E. What other factors could have caused the improvement?
6. Follow-up with each discussion and discuss improvement or lack of improvement and plan other action.	<u>1. Required OSHA training</u> <u>2. Project leadership (General Manager)</u>
7. Monitor improvement and provide recognition when appropriate.	<u>3. Safety-first program for all employees</u>
	F. What percent of this change was actually caused by this program? <u>60</u> %
Other Benefits: <u>Greater Productivity</u>	G. What level of confidence do you place on the above information? (100%=Certainty and 0%=No Confidence) <u>80</u> %
Comments: <u>The action plan kept me on track with this problem.</u>	
	How many months to project completion? <u>18</u>
	OPTIONAL: Calculate the value: (B x D x 12 x F x 9) 11 x 300 x 12 x 60% x 80% = <u>$19,008</u>

The actual improvement value for this example can be calculated as follows:

11 visits x $300 per visit x 12 months = $39,600

The number of months to project completion is 18, making it appropriate to use the one-year rule for benefits. In the last three months of a project, most of the employees have left the job. Consequently, a project has to have at least 15 months remaining to use one year of data. Otherwise, an adjustment must be made. For example, a project with 14 months remaining would use 11 months of benefits instead of one year.

Table 19-6 shows the annual improvement values on the first measure only for the first 25 participants in this group. Similar tables are generated for the second and third measures. The values are adjusted by the contribution estimate and the confidence estimate. For participants, the $39,600 is adjusted by 60 percent and 80 percent to yield $19,008. This same adjustment is made for each of the values, with a total first-year adjusted value for the first measure of $320,309. The same process is followed for the second and third measures for the group, yielding totals of $162,310 and $57,320, respectively. The total benefit is $539,939.

Program Cost

Table 19-7 details the program costs reflecting a fully loaded cost profile. The estimated cost of the needs assessment ($5,000) is prorated over the life of the program, which will be with three sessions. The estimated program development cost ($7,500) is also prorated over the life of the program. The program materials and facilitators are direct costs, and the program also includes a book on safety management. Travel and lodging are estimates using an average for each participant. Facilitation and coordination costs were estimated, too. Time away from work represents lost opportunity and is calculated by multiplying two days by daily salary costs, adjusted for 40 percent employee benefits factor. The average hourly rate for these leaders is about $50. When adjusted for benefits, the rate is $70, which is $560 per day or $1,120 per participant for the two days. That brings the total to $28,000 for 25 participants, which is the second-largest cost item after travel. The cost for the evaluation was estimated. The total costs of $106,087 represent a very conservative approach to cost accumulation.

Table 19-6. Business Impact Data

Participant	Annualized Improvement ($ Values)	Measures	Other Factors	Contribution Estimate From Safety Project Leaders	Confidence Estimate	Adjusted $ Value
1	5,000	Medical treatment	2	40%	90%	23,400
2	5,500	Property damage	4	25%	70%	963
3	32,800	Disabling injuries	2	70%	60%	13,776
4	21,800	First aid	1	80%	80%	13,952
5	39,600	First aid	3	60%	80%	19,008
6	19,800	Disabling injuries	2	70%	90%	12,474
7	25,000	OSHA citations	3	30%	70%	5,250
8	23,000	Property damage	4	30%	40%	2,760
9	34,500	Medical treatment	1	75%	800%	20,700
10	50,000	Near miss	0	100%	100%	50,000
11	75,000	Disabling injury rate	2	45%	75%	23,313
12	42,350	Medical treatment	3	50%	75%	15,881
13	40,000	OSHA fine	4	25%	80%	8,000

Total this page $209,477

Table 19-6. Action Plan (continued)

Participant	Annualized Improvement ($ Values)	Measures	Other Factors	Contribution Estimate From Safety Project Leaders	Confidence Estimate	Adjusted $ Value
14	59,000	Disabling injuries	3	40%	85%	20,060
15	75,000	Disabling injuries	2	20%	90%	13,500
16	missing					
17	24,900	Hazmat violations	2	40%	70%	6,972
18	25,000	Property damage	5	20%	80%	4,000
19	missing					
20	39,000	OSHA citations	2	60%	95%	22,230
21	13,500	OSHA citations	2	70%	90%	850
22	15,000	First aid	0	100%	90%	13,500
23	1,000,000	Near miss	0	100%	100%	
24	54,000	Hazardous materials	3	60%	70%	22,680
25	22,000	Property damage	3	40%	80%	7,040

*Extreme data was omitted from this analysis.

Total Annual Benefit for Second Measure is $162,310

Total Annual Benefit for Third Measure is $57,320

Total this page	**$110,382**
Total First Measure	**$320,309**

ROI Analysis

The total monetary benefits are calculated by adding the values of the three measures, which total $539,939. This leaves a benefits-cost ratio (BCR) and ROI as follows.

$$BCR = \frac{\$539,939}{\$128,067} = 4.22$$

$$ROI = \frac{(\$539,939 - \$128,067)}{\$128,067} \times 100 = 322\%$$

There is a significant difference between the actual ROI as compared to the forecasted ROI. The return is 54 percent less than the forecast, but this is expected because of the optimism experienced at the end of the workshop.

Table 19-7. Program Cost Summary

Needs Assessment (Prorated over three sessions)	$1,667
Program Development (Prorated over three sessions)	2,500
Program Materials—25 @ $100	2,500
Travel and Lodging—25 @ $2000	37,500
Facilitation and Coordination	50,000
Facilities and Refreshments – 2 days @ $700	1,400
Participants Salaries Plus Benefits	28,000
ROI Evaluation	4,500
Total	**$128,067**

Credibility of Data

This ROI value of more than 300 percent greatly exceeds the 20 percent target value. However, despite being extremely high, the ROI value was considered to be credible. This is because of the principles on which the study was based.

1. The data came directly from the participants.
2. The data could be audited to see if the changes were actually taking place.
3. To be conservative, only the first year of improvements was used.

With the changes reported in the action plans, there should be second and third-year values which were omitted from the calculation.

4. The monetary improvement was discounted to account for the effect of other influences. In essence, the participants only took credit for the part of the improvement related to the program.
5. The estimate of contribution was adjusted for error, which represents a discount, adding to the conservative approach.
6. The costs are fully loaded to include both direct and indirect costs.
7. The business impact does not include value obtained from using the skills to address other problems or to influence other measures. Only the values from three measures taken from the action planning projects were used in the analysis.

The ROI process develops convincing data connected directly to project construction costs. From the viewpoint of the chief financial officer, the data can be audited and monitored. It should be reflected as actual improvement at the project site.

Intangible Data

As a final part of the complete data profile, the intangible benefits were itemized. The participants provided input on intangible measures at two timeframes. The follow-up questionnaire provided an opportunity for participants to indicate intangible measures they perceived to represent a benefit directly linked to this program. In addition, the action plan provided an opportunity to add additional intangible benefits. Collectively, each of the following benefits was listed by at least five individuals:

- Improved productivity
- Improved teamwork
- Improved work quality
- Improved job satisfaction
- Improved job engagement
- Enhanced image
- Reduced stress.

To some executives, these intangible measures are just as important as the monetary payoff.

The Payoff: Balanced Data

This program drives six types of data items: satisfaction, learning, application, business impact, ROI, and intangible benefits. Collectively, these data provide a balanced, credible viewpoint of the success of the program.

Communication Strategy

Table 19-8 shows the strategy for communicating results from the study. All key stakeholders received the information. The communications were credible and convincing and the information helped build confidence in the program. The CEO and CFO were pleased with the results. The data given to employees, shareholders, and future participants were motivating and helped to bring more focus on safety.

Table 19-8. Communication Strategy

Timing	Communication Method	Target Audience
Within one month of follow-up	Executive briefing	Regional exectives CEO, CFO
Within one month of follow-up	Live briefing	Corporate and regional operation executives
Within one month of follow-up	Detailed impact study (125 pages)	Program participants Safety and health staff • Responsible for this program in some way • Involved in evaluation
Within one month of follow-up	Report of results (1 page)	Project general managers
Within two months	Article in project news	All employees
As needed	Report of results (1 page)	Future participants in similar safety programs
End of year	Paragraph in annual report	Shareholders

Lessons Learned

It was critical to build evaluation into the program, positioning the action plan as an application tool instead of a data collection tool. This approach helped secure commitment and ownership for the process. It also shifted much of the responsibility for evaluation to the participants as they collected important data, isolated the effects of the program on the data, and converted the data to monetary values—the three most critical steps in the ROI process. The costs were easy to capture and the report was easily generated and sent to the various target audiences.

This approach had the additional advantage of evaluating a program in which a variety of measures were influenced. The improvements were integrated after they were converted to monetary value. Thus, the common value among measures was the monetary value, which represented the value of the improvement.

Questions for Discussion

1. Is this approach credible? Explain.
2. Is the ROI value realistic?
3. Were the differences in the ROI forecast and the actual revenue per inquiry expected? Explain.
4. How should the results be presented to the senior team?
5. How can the action planning process be positioned as an application tool?
6. What type of programs would be appropriate for this approach?

Chapter

Measuring ROI in a
Work-at-Home Program

Family Mutual Health and
Life Insurance Company (FMI)

by Patti P. Phillips and Jack J. Phillips

This case study shows the power of a work-at-home project designed to ease the environmental problems of traffic and congestion caused by the long daily work commute of more than 300 employees. The project cut average daily commute times from one hour and forty-four minutes to 15 minutes, saving each participating employee the cost of 490 gallons of fuel per year and keeping an estimated total 1,478 tons of carbon emissions out of the air. Employees taking part in the project also reported significant intangible benefits, including reduced stress and absenteeism and increased job satisfaction and engagement. The company not only got a boost in its image as an environment-friendly concern, it saved money through increased productivity, lower office expenses and less employee turnover. From an environmental perspective, the study shows how an important project can have significant impact by lowering carbon emissions. It represents a win-win project for participants, their initially reluctant managers and the organization. Perhaps the greatest winner is the environment. While this type of project may not be suitable for every organization, this is an example of how such a project can be implemented for many organizations.

BACKGROUND

Family Mutual Health and Life Insurance Company (FMI) has enjoyed a rich history of serving families throughout North America for almost 80 years. Their focus has been on health and life insurance products and they are regarded as a very innovative and low-cost health insurance provider. The executives are proud of their cost control efforts and the low prices they can offer. Company advertisements regularly highlight their low-cost approach, quality of service and ethical practices.

FMI has grown significantly in recent years due to increased healthcare concerns in North America, particularly in the USA. Rising healthcare cost has forced the company to raise premiums several times in recent years, while still maintaining a cost advantage over other suppliers.

The Challenge

Lars Rienhold, CEO, is proud of the accomplishments of FMI and is perhaps its biggest fan. A man of considerable and contagious personality, he is continually trying to offer affordable health and life insurance policies, provide excellent customer service and be a responsible citizen. As part of this effort, Lars wanted to ensure that FMI was doing all it could to help the environment. While FMI's carbon footprint is relatively low compared to manufacturing companies, its headquarters was located in a congested area. Lars became concerned about helping the environment in as many ways as possible. During a recent trip to Calgary, Canada, he saw a television report about a local company that had implemented a work-at-home program. The report presented the actual amount of carbon emissions that had been prevented with this project. Lars thought that FMI should be able to implement a similar program, including the possibility of employees working from home. He brought this idea to Melissa Lufkin, executive vice president of human resources. The message was short. "I want us to make a difference. I think this is the way to do it." Although her team already had examined the work-at-home issue, Melissa agreed to explore the possibility in a more formal way.

Exploring the Situation

Melissa began her investigation by discussing the issue with the operations chief. Although there was some resistance, John Speegle, executive vice president of operations, was interested in exploring the idea. John was concerned about the lack of a productivity increase in the past three years with the largest segment of employees, the claims processors and the claims examiners. There were 950 employees involved in processing or examining claims submitted by customers or healthcare providers. Claims examiners reviewed claims that were disputed or when an audit sparked a review of a particular claim. The number of claims processors and examiners had grown to the point that the office space they occupied in Building 2 was overflowing. This impeded productivity, not to mention made it an uncomfortable environment in which to work. Given the company's continued growth, it was likely that a new building space or perhaps a new facility was needed to manage the growth.

John concluded, "I'm interested in the possibility of employees working from home if it can be managed properly. Let's explore the possibility if all parties are in agreement to pursue it." John was interested in lowering the real estate cost of new office space, which averaged about $17,000 per person per year and improving productivity, which was at a rate of 33.2 claims processed and 20.7 claims examined per day.

Melissa discussed the issue with Linda Green, the vice president of claims, to identify her concerns about processors and examiners working at home. Although this issue had been discussed in previous meetings and many people had said that these jobs could be easily managed remotely, Melissa had never received direct communication on the topic. Linda was supportive but raised several concerns. "Some of our managers want to keep tabs on what is going on and they feel like they have to be there to resolve issues and problems and they want to see that everyone is working and busy. I am afraid it is a matter of control, which they may have a hard time giving up if people work remotely." Melissa realized that it would take some extra effort with these managers, who would have to view this initiative as necessary and feasible in their world. Linda added, "I realize that the right approach might make their jobs easier, but right now they may not be at that point."

Next, Melissa met with the IT department and discussed how they could equip workstations at home with the latest technology. She found a supportive audience in Tim Holleman, senior vice president and chief information officer, who thought that employees could be setup with adequate security and technology to work at home in the same manner as they were working onsite. Tim added, "They can have full access to all databases and they could be using high-speed processes. It would cost FMI a substantial amount the first year, but may not represent a very significant cost in the long run."

Melissa later discussed potential issues with the legal department. Margaret Metcalf, chief legal officer, was cautious, as expected and said several legal issues would have to be addressed from a liability perspective. She asked about other companies that were pursuing this route and Melissa agreed to furnish examples and make contacts with them to discover what problems they had encountered.

Melissa then contacted Anne Burson, executive vice president of sales and marketing, to uncover any customer service issues that might arise. Anne was in favor of the move as long as customer service would not suffer. She remarked, "The claims examiners are in direct contact with the customers and I want to make sure that acceptable customer service is maintained. Also, many of the processors have to make routine direct contact with healthcare suppliers, as well as patients, and we want to maintain these contacts at an acceptable level. Other than these concerns, I can see that this would probably help morale and might even improve our service. Let's give it a try."

Finally, Melissa met with her chief financial officer, Rodrick Harper, to discuss the project and the plan to measure its success. Melissa previously had talked with Rod about measuring success and he expressed some desire to show the value of major human resources initiatives. Melissa was eager to show the value of HR programs and had challenged her staff to measure success, even using ROI. Rod volunteered a member of his team to work with Melissa on these types of projects. When Melissa discussed the project with him, including the measurement plans and a financial ROI, Rod's interest really piqued. He said, "Let's make sure this is very credible analysis and that it is very conservative. Frankly, I think we want to be involved when you discuss ROI. I think it's proper that we use a standard approach to analysis and we would like to be involved in this every step of the way, if you don't mind." Melissa was pleased with the support, but somewhat anxious about working with the Finance and Accounting Team to evaluate a program that she ultimately would own. However, she felt the project was necessary and would be advanced by the very good relationship she and her team had with the Finance and Accounting Group.

Melissa and her staff explored the attitudes of the employees to determine how they would perceive a work-at-home program. She was not sure how many would take advantage of the opportunity, but she was certain most would be interested. The staff conservatively estimated that at least a third would opt to participate in the program. For many in this group, working at home would be a huge motivator and would probably make a difference in retaining them at FMI. From that perspective, the staff suggested that it be explored. Melissa cautioned, "They may have issues at home that they want to address, but we must be able to get eight hours of work out of them. They cannot discontinue daycare, trying to manage childcare and work as well. If they have an elderly or disabled person at home, this cannot be a way for them to deal with both situations. We must have full productivity, and that is essential."

With this positive reaction (and a few concerns), Melissa and her team decided to undertake this substantial project. After much discussion, the group decided to engage a consulting group, Workforce Solutions International (WSI), to manage the project. WSI had considerable experience in implementing alternative work systems, particularly work-at-home programs. They knew what questions to ask and what situations were going to occur and more importantly, they were able to anticipate the problems that could derail the project.

THE ANALYSIS AND INITIAL ALIGNMENT

After some discussion, the group asked WSI for a proposal. Included in the request for proposal (RFP) to WSI was a forecasting component for the project. Essentially, WSI was asked to bid on analyzing the need for the project to determine its feasibility, forecast its value, design the appropriate program and implement and monitor the success of the program. Success would be measured at the ROI level. Armed with this information, WSI was prepared to begin work on the proposal.

The Consultants

Deborah Rousseau was selected by WSI as the lead consultant for this project. Deborah had previous experience with flexible work systems, had managed many successful projects and was an outstanding consultant. Deborah believed in showing the value of their work and she guided the proposal process toward an agreement to deliver the four components:

1. Clarifying that the solution is needed and connecting it to the appropriate business measures

2. Forecasting the impact and ROI of the project
3. Implementing the program with claims processors and examiners
4. Showing the value of the project using the ROI Methodology

With this focus on results, Deborah knew that she had to skillfully present the best proposal and the most focused implementation possible. There was no room for error. WSI was obligated to deliver the value desired by the clients.

To make the proposal meaningful, Deborah asked the client if they could forecast ROI after they verified the solution. The client agreed. In essence, the proposal was developed in two parts. The first proposal validated the solution and provided a forecasted ROI. The forecast would be developed and approved by the client before the program would be implemented. The second proposal focused on implementation and an impact study with ROI. This seemed reasonable because the analysis required to develop the forecast was part of the analysis that would verify the proper solution to drive the business measures. WSI proposed $31,000 for the first proposal ($21,000 for the initial analysis and assessment and $10,000 for forecasting ROI), which included a briefing to senior executives.

The Analysis

When the first contract was awarded, Deborah began meeting with appropriate individuals from the HR Team, including representatives from employee relations, learning and development, recruiting, compensation and HR planning. She examined records, conducted employee focus groups and conducted a survey of a small, selected group of employees to understand their desire, need and intentions to work at home if the option was available. In this survey, employees were asked about benefits from this type of arrangement. The focus groups and the survey revealed that this solution should drive business measures.

Part of this analysis involved the examination of other case studies of work-at-home projects, to understand the payoffs of those projects and the barriers to success. This analysis focused on potential improvements in productivity, reduction in absenteeism, improvements in healthcare costs and a reduction in real estate costs. The potential effect on healthcare costs was weak and it was removed as a potential impact measure that could be influenced by this new arrangement. By using the employee feedback, analysis of other studies and examination of internal records, Deborah and the HR Team agreed that this solution could drive important business measures.

Alignment

Deborah's next task was to identify specific business measures. Her key input for this task was provided by the executive vice president of operations (EVP), who thought that this program could reduce real estate and productivity costs. It was obvious that the real estate costs could be improved, unless the cost of maintaining an at-home office proved to be excessive or the same office space for each participant continued to be maintained at FMI. Deborah worked with the EVP to set clear objectives for office space and productivity. After some discussion, the EVP suggested that processors and examiners could both process an average of at least one more claim than they had been producing and the office expense should be dramatically reduced, in the neighborhood of 20 percent for the first year. When discussing the actual ROI of the study, the EVP was reluctant to set an objective. However, when Deborah suggested that the ROI should be more than an investment in a building, for example, the EVP agreed to set a goal. Given that FMI would average about 15 percent for capital expenditure investments, Deborah suggested that an ROI of about 25 percent would be appropriate and the EVP agreed.

The vice president of claims confirmed the objectives regarding productivity and real estate costs with Deborah and then focused on turnover reduction. The annual turnover rate at the time was 22.3 percent and they felt that an improvement rate of at least 5 percent to 17.3 percent should be achievable if the project was successful. They also reviewed the absenteeism rate and thought it could drastically improve from a current level of 7.3 percent to a new level of 4.0 percent. Deborah addressed the critical issues regarding implementation during this discussion.

Deborah met with Ginger Terry, environmental coordinator in the procurement function, to collect data about carbon emissions from automobiles and set a goal to show the actual reduction in carbon emissions that could be realized by eliminating the office commute. Ginger had compiled data about the commute time of employees for these two groups and the average time was estimated to be one hour and forty-four minutes each day. In a work-at-home arrangement, this time could be reduced to about 15 minutes, assuming a visit to the office every seven days. Deborah realized that the environmental benefits would not add to the ROI in monetary terms, but would be a substantial intangible for the citizens of this city and of the country as a whole.

Finally, she met with the CFO, chief legal counsel, chief information officer and the HR Team. The principal focus of the meeting with this group was to review the tentative objectives for additional refinement and concurrence.

Deborah's meeting with the HR team generated some important information, in terms of what employees and managers must learn to make the process effective and successful. Several questions surfaced about working without distractions, such as childcare issues, other people in the residence or elder parent care. Associates also would have to adjust their working habits from an office to a home environment. They would need to adopt the discipline and structure necessary to be effective, by following consistent rules, regulations and working hours. It was also noted that managers must be able to effectively provide coaching and counseling along the way and be there for associates to address particular issues.

Deborah also explored the issues of perception and desired reaction with the executives. The executives expressed their belief that the process was needed and ultimately would be motivational and rewarding for participants. With this data, Deborah began to develop the objectives that would lead to the ROI forecast.

Questions for Discussion
1. Critique the way in which the analysis has been conducted.
2. Are there additional questions or issues you would explore? If so, what are they?
3. Write the objectives for all five levels.
4. Complete the V-model showing the connection between the upfront assessment, objectives and evaluation at five levels.

OBJECTIVES AND ALIGNMENT
From the discussions, subsequent analyses and potential solutions, Deborah, Melissa and the HR Team could develop all of the objectives at different levels. The objectives are developed from the needs at different levels.

Objectives

Table 20-1 shows the objectives for the project by different levels, ranging from reaction to ROI. Deborah secured agreement on the objectives from those stakeholders involved.

Alignment

The alignment model is shown in Figure 20-1. It shows the connection between the upfront needs assessment, the objectives and the evaluation. Deborah found it helpful to construct this model to clearly determine whether any pieces were missing. She worked through the analysis in order beginning with Level 5. The project's value became obvious early in discussions. She then clearly explored the business needs with different stakeholders. Job performance needs were revealed in concerns voiced by the senior vice president of claims. The learning needs evolved from that conversation and the reaction needs were consequently developed from these discussions. Previous studies in which Deborah and her firm had been involved dictated some of the learning and reaction needs, e.g., projects sometimes fail because people do not fully understand the rules, do not understand the work process or have the incorrect perception of the process. The objectives came directly from the needs assessment and were specifically developed based on each need. At this point, evaluation was tentative in terms of how the data would be collected. More detail on the evaluation side would be provided as the project unfolded, but the V-model provides the alignment necessary at the different levels of needs assessment, objectives and evaluation.

Questions for Discussion

1. What is the value of having objectives at all five levels? Please discuss.
2. Is it helpful or necessary to develop a V-model on a program that is destined for implementation? Please explain.

ROI FORECAST

With a clear understanding of the solution and the connection to the business impact measures, a forecast was now possible. Although Deborah could have forecast reaction, learning and application, she limited her forecast to impact and ROI. This essentially is what was requested in the RFP, with most of the emphasis on the ROI number itself. Deborah developed the forecast, following the assumptions from the various involved stakeholders.

Figure 20-1. Project Alignment

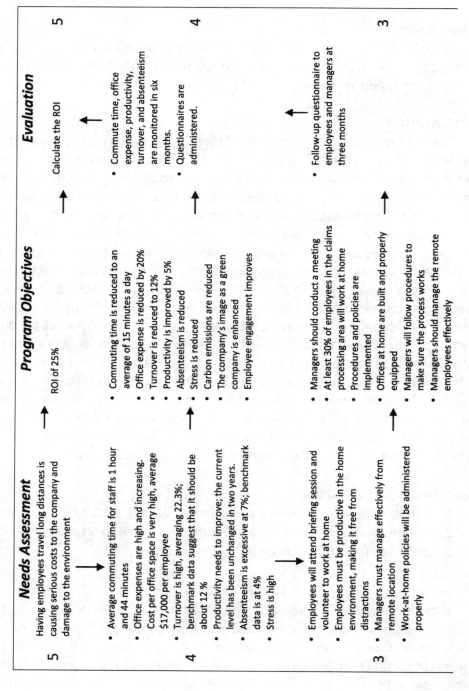

Needs Assessment

5   Having employees travel long distances is causing serious costs to the company and damage to the environment

4
- Average commuting time for staff is 1 hour and 44 minutes
- Office expenses are high and increasing. Cost per office space is very high, average $17,000 per employee
- Turnover is high, averaging 22.3%; benchmark data suggest that it should be about 12 %
- Productivity needs to improve; the current level has been unchanged in two years.
- Absenteeism is excessive at 7%; benchmark data is at 4%
- Stress is high

3
- Employees will attend briefing session and volunteer to work at home
- Employees must be productive in the home environment, making it free from distractions
- Managers must manage effectively from remote location
- Work-at-home policies will be administered properly

Program Objectives

5   ROI of 25%

4
- Commuting time is reduced to an average of 15 minutes a day
- Office expense is reduced by 20%
- Turnover is reduced to 12%
- Productivity is improved by 5%
- Absenteeism is reduced
- Stress is reduced
- Carbon emissions are reduced
- The company's image as a green company is enhanced
- Employee engagement improves

3
- Managers should conduct a meeting
- At least 30% of employees in the claims processing area will work at home
- Procedures and policies are implemented
- Offices at home are built and properly equipped
- Managers will follow procedures to make sure the process works
- Managers should manage the remote employees effectively

Evaluation

5   Calculate the ROI

4
- Commute time, office expense, productivity, turnover, and absenteeism are monitored in six months.
- Questionnaires are administered.

3
- Follow-up questionnaire to employees and managers at three months

Figure 20-1. Project Alignment (*continued*)

- Employees need to understand the reality of working at home, the conditions, roles, and regulations
- Employees must have the discipline and the tenacity to work at home

2
- Mangers must understand how this can work
- Managers must know how to manage remotely

→

- Employees must have the discipline and tenacity to work at home
- Employees will know the realities of working at home, the conditions, roles, and regulations

2
- Managers must know how to explain the policies and regulations for working at home
- Managers must know how to manage remotely

↑

- Checklist
- Questionnaire

→

- Participants must see this offer as satisfying to their jobs, important to their own success and needs, rewarding, and motivational

1
- Managers must see this as a necessary, appropriate, and important to their own organization's objectives

↑

- Employees will find satisfaction with, and see the importance of, working at home
- This work arrangement will be rewarding and motivational
- Managers will view this new work arrangement as important and appropriate
- Managers will see the need for the new work arrangement

→

- Reaction questionnaire at the end of the meeting to announce the program

1

Table 20-1. Detailed Objectives

After implementing this project:

Reaction
- Employees should see the work-at-home project as satisfying, important, rewarding, and motivational.
- Managers must see this project as necessary, appropriate, and important to FMI.

Learning
- Employees must know the realities of working at home, the conditions, roles, and regulations.
- Employees must have the discipline and tenacity to work at home.
- Managers must be able to explain company policy and regulations for working at home.
- Managers must be able manage remotely.

Application
- Managers should conduct a meeting with direct reports to discuss policy, expected behavior, and next steps.
- At least 30% of eligible employees should volunteer for at-home assignments within one month.
- At-home offices are built and should be properly equipped.
- Work-at-home employees should work effectively at home.
- The at-home workplace should be free from distractions and conflicting demands.
- Managers should properly administer the company's policy.
- Managers should manage the remote employees effectively.

Impact
For those involved in the program:
- Commute time should be reduced to an average of 15 minutes per day.
- Office expense per person should reduce by 20% in six months.
- Productivity should increase by 5% in six months.
- Employee turnover should reduce to 12% in six months.
- Unplanned absenteeism should be reduced.
- Stress should be reduced.
- Carbon emissions should be reduced.
- The company's image as a green company should be enhanced.
- Employee engagement should improve.

ROI
- The company should achieve a 25% return on investment.

Impact Forecast

The first important input to the forecast was the expected number of employees who would participate. This was a voluntary program for which both the advantages and disadvantages were clearly laid out for employees, along with conditions and regulations. Not everyone would be willing to go down this path. As stated earlier, Deborah and the HR Team thought that about one-third of employees would sign up for this program. One-third of 950 is 317, so the forecast is based on 317 participating employees. Based on the percentage makeup of the two groups, this translates into 237 and 80, respectively, for processors and examiners.

Figure 20-2 shows the development of the monetary forecast, following estimated improvement in business measures. The estimated business impact was obtained directly from the chief of operations and the vice president of claims. The monetary value of a claim also was obtained by these stakeholders, estimated to be $10 cost for processing a claim and $12 for review of a claim. The office expenses were estimated to be $17,000 and the cost of a turnover taken directly from a similar study (where the cost of turnover was pegged as a percent of annual pay) was provided at $25,400. With this in mind, the calculations are listed below:

Figure 20-2. Forecast of Monetary Benefits

Anticipated Participation

- Target Group: 950
- Predicted Enrollment: 1/3
- 950 x 33 1/3% = 317
- Allocation: 237 processors
            80 examiners

Estimated Impact

- Productivity: 1 additional claim processed
            1 additional claim examined
- Office expenses: 20% reduction
            $17,000 x 20%=$3,400
- Turnover reduction: 22.3% to 12%=10.3% improvement

Converting Productivity to Money

- Value of one claim=$10.00
- Value of one disputed claim=$12.00
- Daily improvement=1 claim per day
- Daily improvement=1 disputed claim per day
- Annual value=237 x 220 work days x 1 x 10.00= $521,400
- Annual value=80 x 220 days x 1 x 12.00=$211,200

Office Expense Reduction

- Office expenses in company office: $17,000 annually per person
- Office expenses at home office: $13,600 first year per person
- Net improvement: $3,400, first year
- Total annual value=317 x 3,400=$1,077,800

Converting Turnover Reduction to Money

- Value of one turnover statistic = $25,400
- Annual improvement related to program=10.3%
- Turnover prevention: 317 x 10.3% = 33 turnovers prevented
- Annual value=$25,400 x 33= $838,200

Estimated Costs and ROI Forecast

The costs of the project were estimated to be about $1 million. This estimate is the total cost including the amount of the initial analysis to determine whether this was the proper solution and the development of that solution. The majority of the charges were in the IT support and maintenance, administrative and coordination categories. When the monetary benefits are combined with the cost, the ROI forecast is developed, as shown in Figure 20-3.

Figure 20-3. Forecasted ROI

Total Forecasted Monetary Benefits

Benefits =
$521,400	Processor Productivity
211,200	Examiner Productivity
1,077,800	Office Costs
838,200	Turnover Reduction
$2,648,600	

Costs = $1,000,000

$$BCR = \frac{\$2,648,600}{\$1,000,000} = 2.65$$

$$ROI = \frac{\$2,648,600 - 1,000,000}{\$1,000,000} \times 100 = 165\%$$

Presentation of Results

Although this number is quite impressive, Deborah cautioned the team not to make the decision solely on the ROI calculation. In her presentation to the senior executives, Deborah stressed that there were significant intangibles, first and foremost being the contribution to the environment, which is not included in this calculation. Other factors such as job satisfaction, job engagement, stress reduction and image were huge intangibles that should be directly influenced from this. However, because these projects need to be based on good business decisions, the ROI forecast is credible and conservative and based on only one year of value. Much more value will be realized after the first year, because most of the office setup expenses will occur in the first year.

Deborah also cautioned that for these results to materialize, the program would have to be implemented with a focus on results and the objectives set for the program. One by one, she presented each of the objectives and stressed that they would be communicated to all the stakeholders, including the employees. This would ensure that everyone would clearly grasp his or her responsibilities to make the program successful. While it should deliver a significant ROI, most of the emphasis should be placed on the intangibles.

Questions for Discussion
1. What value does a forecast add to the situation? Is it needed in today's climate?
2. How helpful would it be to include reaction, learning, application and intangibles in the forecast?
3. What prevents credible forecasts from being an option pursued by consultants and clients?

THE SOLUTION
The details of the solution were developed with proper input. For this program to be successful the design had to be acceptable and the execution must be flawless.

Design
The design of the program followed the traditional work-at-home model, in which employees work a full 40-hour week in a home office designated for this work. The office was equipped with the appropriate interconnectivity to the company, databases and functions, much like an office in one of FMI's buildings. The pertinent ground rules for this arrangement included the following:

1. The office must be free of distractions. For example, it is recommended that a television not be located in the room.
2. Employees must work on a set schedule, if they are required to have direct contact with customers, which most are. Employees must log on at the time they begin their work and log off when they have completed work for the day.
3. The system has mechanisms for monitoring the work being accomplished. Each activity can easily be tracked to provide a user performance profile. In essence, the system determines if a person is working and records the results.
4. The home office must be designed for efficiency, good health and safety.
5. Employees were urged to take short breaks and re-energize as necessary and to always take a lunch break. The total amount of expected actual work time was 40 hours.

6. Employees were required to negotiate expectations and agreements with the family and significant others.
7. When employees must take time off for personal errands, visits to the doctor or other breaks, this time will be subtracted from their time worked. The employees will be required to make up that time during the week.
8. Employees must stay in touch with the office and periodically make contact with the immediate manager.
9. Employees must sign a work-at-home pledge and attend a session on "working at home."
10. Because there was an initial investment in equipment, computers and connections, employees were required to sign a two-year commitment to continue to work for FMI, with certain conditions. If they were to leave the company before the end of two years, they would be required to pay back the setup charges, estimated to be about $5,000.

The principal stakeholders agreed on the design. It was reviewed by a group of employees in a focus group and then modified to produce the final set of regulations.

Execution

With the design finalized, the program was launched via communications to the target group of 950 employees. Employees received memos explaining the program and were asked to attend briefing sessions during formal working hours to discuss the work-at-home arrangement. In all, 21 employee meetings were held for the 950 employees and managers held meetings with their respective teams to discuss the advantages and disadvantages of the process. Employees were given three weeks to make a decision and to enroll in the program.

Questions for Discussion
1. Critique the design of the work-at-home arrangement.
2. Discuss the implementation and execution.
3. What precautions must be taken in an experiment involving only one segment of the company?

ROI PLANNING

The next logical phase of the process was to plan for the ROI Study. This involved completing the data collection plan and the ROI analysis plan. This phase emerged from the objectives and the input that went into the V-model.

Data Collection Plan

The starting point for the data collection plan, shown as Figure 20-4, are the objectives listed in Table 20-1. The measures are further defined along with those objectives. Methods of data collection are identified, sources of data are pinpointed and the timing for data collection is determined. The plan concludes with the responsibilities for collecting the data. The data collection is comprehensive and primarily focused on interviews, questionnaires and monitoring the data in the system.

ROI Analysis Plan

Figure 20-5 shows the ROI analysis plan, which details the analysis for the impact study. This document begins with the impact measures planned for analysis. The first column lists each of the data items, followed by the method of isolating the effects of the program on the data and the method of converting data to money. The intangibles anticipated from the project are listed after the particular cost categories. The individuals or groups targeted for the results are then identified, along with any influences that might make a difference in this evaluation.

When completed, the data collection plan and the ROI analysis plan provide a road map to conduct the study. The various stakeholders approved these documents, allowing the work to begin.

Data Collection and Integration

Data collection followed the data collection plan using interviews and questionnaires. The interviews were few in number but they did provide an opportunity to explore the issues that were included on detailed follow-up questionnaires. All participating employees and their managers received the questionnaires. In total, 342 questionnaires were distributed to employees and 45 managers. Figure 20-6 shows the data integration plan and how the data was collected and integrated to form the results.

Figure 20-4. Data Collection Plan

Evaluation Purpose: Measure Success of Program

Program: FMI Work-at-Home Project

Responsibility: HR/Consultants

Date: March 30

Level	Broad Program Objectives(s)	Measures	Data Collection Method/ Instruments	Data Sources	Timing
1	*Reaction* • Employees should see the work-at-home project as satisfying, important, rewarding, and motivational • Managers must see this project as necessary, appropriate, and important to FMI.	• Rating scale (4 out of 5)	• Questionnaires • Interviews	• Participants • Managers	• 30 days • 30 days
2	*Learning* • Employees must know the realities of working at home, the conditions, roles, and regulations • Employees must have the discipline and tenacity to work at home • Managers must be able to explain company policy and regulations for working at home • Managers must be able to manage remotely	• Rating scale (4 out of 5)	• Questionnaires • Interviews	• Employees • Managers	• 30 days • 30 days

Figure 20-4. Data Collection Plan (continued)

3	**Application** • Managers should conduct a meeting with direct reports to discuss policy, expected behavior, and next steps • At least 30 percent of eligible employees should volunteer for at-home assignments within one month • At-home offices are built and properly equipped • The home workplace should be free from distractions and conflicting demands • Managers will properly administer the company's policy • Managers should effectively manage the remote employees	• Checklist • Sign Up • Rating Scale (4 out of 5)	• Data Monitoring • Data Monitoring • Questionnaires	• Company Records • Company Records • Participants • Managers	• 30 days • 30 days • 90 days • 90 days
4	**Impact** • Commute time should be reduced to an average of 15 minutes per day • Office expense per person should reduce by 20 percent in six months • Productivity should increase by 5 percent in six months • Employee turnover should reduce to 12 percent in six months • Unplanned absences should be reduced • Stress should be reduced • Carbon emissions should be reduced • The company's image as a green company should be enhanced • Employee engagement should improve	• Direct costs • Claims per day • Voluntary turnover • Rating scale (4 out of 5) • Rating scale (4 out of 5)	• Business Performance Monitoring • Survey	• Company records • Participants • Managers	• 6 months • 6 months • 6 months • 90 days • 90 days
5	**ROI** • Achieve a 25% return on investment	Baseline Data:			

Figure 20-5. ROI Analysis Plan

Program: FMI Work-at-Home Project   Responsibility: HR/Consultants   Date: _____

Data Items (Usually Level 4)	Methods for Isolating the Effects of the Program/Process	Methods of Converting Data to Monetary Values	Cost Categories	Intangible Benefits	Communication Targets for Final Report	Other Influential Issues during Application
• Office expenses	• Control group • Expert estimates	• Standard value based on costs	• Initial analysis and assessment • Forecasting Impact and ROI • Solution development • IT support and maintenance • Administration and coordination • Materials • Facilities and refreshments • Salaries plus benefits for employee and manager meetings • Evaluation and reporting	• Reduced commuting time • Reduced carbon emissions • Reduced fuel consumption • Reduced sick leave • Reduced absenteeism • Improved job engagement • Improved community image • Improved image as environmental friendly company • Enhanced corporate social responsibility • Improved job satisfaction • Reduced stress • Improved recruiting image	• Participants • Managers • HR team • Executive group • Consultants • External groups	• Must observe marketing and economic forces • Search for barriers/obstacles for progress
• Productivity	• Control Group • Participant estimates	• Standard values				
• Turnover	• Control Group • Participant Estimates	• External studies				

Questions for Discussion
1. Critique the data collection plan.
2. Critique the ROI analysis plan.
3. How helpful is the data integration figure?
4. What improvements would you recommend for data collection and analysis?

Figure 20-6. Data Collection Methods and Integration

Method	Level 1 Reaction	Level 2 Learning	Level 3 Application	Barriers / Enablers	Level 4 Impact	Costs
Initial Participant Questionnaire	X	X	X		X	
Initial Manager Questionnaire	X	X	X		X	
Participant Interviews	X	X	X		X	
Follow-up Questionnaire: Participants	X		X	X	X	
Follow-up Questionnaire: Managers	X		X	X		
Company Records			X		X	X

RESULTS
The data were collected following the data collection plan. The levels of data present the results.

Reaction Data
Reaction data was collected early in the program and focused on both reactions from the employees involved in the project and their managers. Although open verbal and informal positive reactions were detected early in the process, four particular measures were collected on the questionnaire directly from the employees.

1. The satisfaction with the new work arrangement.
2. The importance of this approach to their success.
3. The rewarding effect of this opportunity for them.
4. The motivation effect of this arrangement. The company anticipated this new work arrangement would provide a more motivated employee who would produce more.

These four measures scored high numbers and Table 20-2 shows the results. The reaction from the employee perspective averaged 4.4 on a 5-point scale.

Table 20-2. Reaction Data

<u>From Participating Employees</u>
- Rating of 4.6 out of 5 on satisfaction with new work arrangement
- Rating of 4.7 out of 5 on importance of new work arrangement to their success
- Rating of 4.2 out of 5 on the rewarding effect of the new work arrangement
- Rating of 4.1 out of 5 on motivational effect of new work arrangement

<u>From Managers</u>
- Rating of 4.2 out of 5 on importance of the work alternative
- Rating of 4.1 out of 5 on appropriateness of the work alternative
- Rating of 4.3 out of 5 on the need for the work alternative

From the managers' perspective, it was important to understand how managers perceived this new work arrangement. Although there were many aspects of this issue, the objectives focused on three points: how managers perceived this program to be necessary, appropriate and important to the company. Managers must see the necessity of this program in today's work climate when considering problems encountered with commuting and the environment, as well as the desire for the flexibility of working from home. Table 20-2 shows the managers' reactions, which exceeded expectations. The ratings averaged 4.2 out of 5 on the three items. In summary, the reaction surpassed the expectations of the implementation team.

Learning Data

Although this project is not a classic learning solution, where significant skills and knowledge must be developed for the program to be successful, there is still a learning component. Employees must understand their roles and responsibilities and managers must understand the policies of working at home. They also must have the ability to explain the policies and successfully address any performance issues that can develop in the unique environment of a remote workforce. The managers and employees provided self-assessment input on their questionnaires, which typically show the learning from the two groups. The managers were given an opportunity during meetings to practice the performance discussions so they would be able to address the issues effectively. The facilitator of the meeting was required to confirm that each manager could successfully address those issues and that every manager involved in the program properly demonstrated their ability to do so. As Table 20-3 shows, the self-assessment ratings exceeded the expectations on five measures from employees, averaging 4.3 out of 5. Managers averaged 4.1 out of 5 on two measures. The confidence to explain the policy was 3.9 out of 5, just short of the goal of 4.0. Still, there was confidence that learning had occurred so that the program could be properly implemented. Also, each manager successfully demonstrated four types of performance discussions through role playing.

Table 20-3. Learning Data

<u>From Employees</u>
- Rating of 4.0 of 5 on the discipline and tenacity to work
- Rating of 4.1 of 5 on the tenacity to work at home
- Rating of 4.3 of 5 on roles and responsibilities
- Rating of 4.3 of 5 on conditions and regulations
- Rating of 4.2 of 5 on the realities of working at home

<u>From Managers</u>
- Rating of 4.2 of 5 on key elements of the policy for working at home
- Rating of 3.9 of 5 on the confidence to explain policy
- Successful skill practice demonstration on performance discussions – all checked

Application Data

These types of programs can easily go astray if employees are not following the policies properly and the managers are not managing the process appropriately. Consequently, application and tracking the implementation of the process became a very important data set. Table 20-4 shows the key items monitored which are directly connected to objectives. In all, 93 percent of managers conducted meetings with employees to discuss the work-at-home arrangement. Although 100 percent would usually be expected, a few managers either did not have direct employees or had no employees who were interested in working at home. The possibility remained that some managers did not conduct the meetings when they should have. Because of this, a complete briefing involving all employees covered most of the issues that the managers were exploring in the meeting. The meeting with the managers represented reinforcement and showed their connection to the project.

Table 20-4. Application Data

- Ninety-three percent of managers conducted meetings with employees to discuss working at home.
- Thirty-six percent of eligible employees volunteered for at-home work assignments (342 participants).
- In total, 340 home offices were built and equipped properly (two employees changed their minds before establishing an office).
- Work-at-home employees rated 4.3 out of 5 on working effectively at home.
- Ninety-five percent of employees reported the workplace was free of distractions and conflicting demands.
- Managers rated 4.1 of 5 on administering policy properly
- Managers rated 3.8 of 5 on managing remote employees effectively

After all the briefings and information sharing, 36 percent of eligible employees volunteered for work-at-home assignments, representing 342 participants. This participation was better than expected and left the project team pleased. In the follow-up data, the participants rated 4.3 out of 5 on working effectively at home; in addition, 95 percent of the employees reported that the workplace was free of distractions and conflict. The managers rated themselves 4.1 out of 5 on properly administering policy. However, some had difficulty when it came to the rating of managing employees remotely, which was 3.8 out of 5.

Barriers and Enablers

With the recognition that many issues could derail the success of this program, the barriers and enablers were captured. Table 20-5 shows the barriers and enablers to success and as expected, there were some classic barriers; however, the barriers did not prove to be very significant. The greatest obstacle was the lack of manager support, with 18 percent of participants indicating this as a concern. Following closely behind was lack of necessary support from staff that would normally support them in their office work. Additionally, 15 percent indicated communication breakdown, while 11 percent thought this program would limit their career progression. A few felt that they would be left out of decision-making and that IT support would be lacking, while some indicated that they were concerned about the lack of social interaction.

Table 20-5. Barriers and Enablers to Success

Barriers	Percent Indicated
Managers support is lacking	18%
Lack of support staff	16%
Communication breakdowns	13%
Career progression is limited	11%
Left out of decisions	9%
IT support is lacking	7%
Lack of social interactions	5%
Enablers	**Percent Indicated**
Personal cost savings	89%
Flexibility to schedule	71%
Convenience of work	71%
Work-life balance	64%
I have all the tools	54%
Support of manager	31%
Support of staff	14%

Regarding the enablers, the number one enabler on this list is the personal cost savings. Many employees signed up for this arrangement as a way to save costs by not paying to commute. Next was the flexibility of having some adjustments in their work schedule and taking time for personal activities to be made up. After that was the convenience of working in a home setting and improved work-life balance. Most said they had all the tools to make it work. Only 31 percent said the support of the managers helped to make it more successful. Finally, 14 percent said staff support helped them. These barriers and enablers provided an opportunity for process improvement.

Isolating the Effects of the Program

As the impact data were collected, the key question was how much of this improvement actually was connected to this specific project. While several methods were considered, a classic approach was used. The work-at-home group was considered an experimental group and compared to a matched group that would serve as a control group. The comparison group was matched with the experimental group on job category, length of service with the company, gender, age, and marital and family status. With these multiple variables it was difficult to get a perfect match, but the team felt that there was a very good comparison between the two groups. As a backup, expert estimates were used.

Impact

The impact data were monitored and included three measures: productivity, office expense and turnover. The team decided not to value this program on absenteeism and instead left it as an intangible. Although absenteeism is probably connected to the program, the HR team thought it would be best to avoid absenteeism as a measurable objective. If there is too much focus on this measure, some employees may decide to work while sick. Table 20-6 shows the impact data of both the experimental group and comparison group six months after the project began. The differences are significant, representing distinct improvements in the three measures and exceeding the objectives of the project. Having the data identified and isolated to the project, the analysis moves to the next step, converting data to money.

Table 20-6. Impact Data

Business Performance	Work-at-Home Group	Comparison Group	Change	Number of Participants
Daily Claims Processed	35.4	33.2	2.2	234
Daily Claims Examined	22.6	20.7	1.9	77
Office Expense Per Person	$12,500	$17,000	$4,500	311
Annualized Turnover* (*Processors and Examiners)	9.1%	22.3%	13.2%	311

Converting Data to Money

Table 20-7 shows how each of the data sets was converted to monetary value. As the table explains, the method for converting the productivity improvement to value was using standard values. The value previously was developed by a group of experts and analysts in finance and accounting. The number was rounded to $10 for claims processing and $12 for claims examination. The calculation shows the annual cost saving.

Office expenses were rounded numbers taken directly from the procurement function. The projected cost for at-home employees was $13,600. However, the actual cost was rounded to $12,500 for the first year. This was compared to the annual cost to maintain the office for all employees, $17,000 per person. The first-year value included cost of a computer, desk and other items that would certainly be there as long as that person works at home. The net improvement was $4,500. The second-year value shows a cost reduction of $3,600. To be conservative, only the first-year value was used in the comparison.

Table 20-7. Converting Data to Money

<u>Productivity Improvement</u>
• Cost (value) of processing one claim=$10.00
• Cost (value) of examining one disputed claim=$12.00
• Daily improvement=2.2 claims per day
• Daily improvement=1.9 disputed claims per day
• Annual value=234 x 220 work days x 2.2 x 10.00= $1,132,560
• Annual value=77 x 220 days x 1.9 x 12.00=$ 386,232

<u>Office Expense Reduction</u>
• Office expenses in company office: per person $17,000 annually
• Office expenses at home office: per person $12,500 first year; $3,600 second year
• Net improvement: $4,500, first year
• Total annual value=311 x 4500= $1,399,500

<u>Turnover Reduction</u>
• Value of one turnover statistic= $25,400
• Annual improvement related to program=41 turnovers prevented, first year
• Annual value=$25,400 x 41= $1,041,400

<u>Total Annual Benefits</u>
• Productivity—processing one claim $1,132,560
• Productivity—processing one disputed claim $386,232
• Office expense reduction—$ 1,399,500
• Turnover reduction—$1,041,400

Total $3,959,692

For turnover reduction, several turnover cost studies were performed on jobs in the insurance industry, using the ERIC database. The cost ranged from 90 percent to 110 percent, which seemed consistent and credible to the project team. The 90 percent figure was used and when multiplied by the average salary, yielded $25,400. In all, 41 turnovers were prevented in the first year based on six months of experience. The total annual benefits for the program equal $3,959,692.

Costs

The costs of the entire project as developed and monitored were estimated and are shown in Table 20-8. These costs include the initial analysis to determine whether this was the proper solution, the ROI forecast and the actual development of the solution. Most of the charges are for IT support and maintenance, administration and coordination categories.

Table 20-8. Project Costs

Initial Analysis and Assessment	$ 21,000
Forecasting Impact and ROI	$ 10,000
Solution Development	$ 35,800
IT Support and Maintenance	$ 238,000
Administration and Coordination	$ 213,000
Materials (400 @ $50)	$ 20,000
Facilities and Refreshments – 21 meetings	$ 12,600
Salaries Plus Benefits for Employee and Manager Meetings	$ 418,280
Evaluation, Monitoring and Reporting	$ 23,000
Total First Year Costs	**$ 991,680**

Questions for Discussion

1. Calculate the benefit-cost ratio and ROI for this project.
2. Interpret these two calculations and what they mean.
3. Are the results of this study credible? Explain.

ROI Calculations

The ROI is calculated when the costs are totaled and the monetary benefits are tallied. Table 20-9 shows the calculation of the benefit-cost ratio and the ROI. The ROI calculation at 299 percent greatly exceeds the initial objective of 25 percent. However, important results are not included in the calculation. The intangibles are critical to this study.

Table 20-9. ROI Calculations

$$BCR = \frac{Consulting\ Monetary\ Benefits}{Consulting\ Costs} = \frac{\$3,959,692}{\$991,680} = 3.99$$

$$ROI = \frac{Net\ Consulting\ Benefits}{Consulting\ Costs} = \frac{\$3,959,692 - \$991,680}{\$991,680} \times 100 = 299\%$$

Intangible Benefits

Table 20-10 shows a list of the intangible benefits connected to the project. A list of expected intangibles is included on the participants' and managers' questionnaires. To compile these results, at least 10 percent of respondents had to indicate a 3, 4, or 5 on a 5-point scale where 3 is moderate influence, 4 is significant influence and 5 is very significant influence. These are powerful intangibles, including those connected to the environment. Participants and managers can clearly see the connection. These may be the most important data sets in the minds of some executives, because it is the intangible image of helping the environment that often drives these types of projects. When these data sets are combined with the very high ROI, it is easy to see the tremendous payoff of this program.

Table 20-10. Intangible Benefits

- Reduced commuting time
- Reduced carbon emissions
- Reduced fuel consumption
- Reduced sick leave
- Reduced absenteeism
- Improved job engagement
- Improved community image
- Improved image as an environmental-friendly company
- Enhanced corporate social responsibility
- Improved job satisfaction
- Reduced stress
- Improved recruiting image

Fuel Savings

Because the individuals involved in this program have eliminated their commute, with the exception of an occasional required visit to the office, the fuel savings were significant. The average daily commute time reduced from 104 minutes to 15 minutes. When considering the average speed (30 mph), the average miles per gallon of gasoline (20 mpg) and the cost of fuel ($3 per gallon), a savings of $1,470 per year is realized in fuel costs alone.

Carbon Emissions

From the perspective of the top executive, the principal motivating factor of this program was to reduce carbon emissions. With reduced fuel consumption, carbon emissions were consequently reduced. A total of 490 gallons of fuel per person was saved, for a total of 152,390 gallons each year. This translates into 1,478 tons of carbon emissions.

What Makes the Results Credible

It is important to understand what makes this data credible. It is impressive in terms of the numbers, but some specific things make it very credible.

1. The impact data improvements were taken directly from the records and are not estimated.
2. The effects of the program were isolated from other factors using a comparison group.
3. Several impact measures were not converted to money, although they have significant value.
4. All the costs were included, including the very heavy start-up cost.
5. Only the first-year values are used in the analysis. This program will have a lasting effect as long as each individual is employed with FMI.
6. When estimates were used, they were taken from the most credible sources.
7. All of the data sets and methods have buy-in from the appropriate operating executives and key managers.

There is no reason to dispute the results presented in this process.

Questions for Discussion

1. Which audiences should receive the results of this study?
2. What specific methods should be used to communicate results?
3. What specific improvements could be made to this program going forward?

Chapter

Measuring ROI in a Blended Learning Solution for Engagement

PolyWrighton

by John Kmiec, Sandra Dugas, Cyndi Gaudet,
Heather Annulis, Mary Nell McNeese, and Susan Bush

This case study describes the evaluation of a blended learning program designed to enhance the capabilities of immediate managers to positively influence line employees' work engagement. The study used quasi-experimental research design to analyze changes in work engagement for line employees assigned to two of 14 business units at PolyWrighton, a manufacturer of high-quality, lightweight plastics. The test group of immediate managers in the production business unit received the learning initiative. The maintenance business unit managers did not receive the initiative. Also evaluated were the production unit's participant reaction, learning, application, and business impact data. Production's adjusted return on investment estimate was 598 percent, or $1,265,565.

BACKGROUND

PolyWrighton makes high-quality, lightweight plastics used to package a wide variety of food, beverage, and personal care products. Meeting rigorous hygienic, chemical, and environmental safety standards and specifications for these products requires constant monitoring and testing, state of the chemicals used in the manufacturing process are both toxic and flammable. The plant machinery is very complex, massive in size, and hazardous in its own right. The product itself is processed under high heat and pressure. These conditions combine to demand heightened operational and safety awareness by all employees.

Adding to the complexity of the operation are the costs associated with product waste and rework. In a highly competitive market where raw materials are expensive and frequently in short supply, it is imperative that PolyWrighton generate as little waste and rework as possible. Rework is defined as product that fails to meet customer expectations for quality, and therefore must be reprocessed. Product waste is unusable, because it cannot be reprocessed and must be discarded. The costs associated with rework and waste result in an additional $35,000 for every 1 percent of product rework and $245,000 for every 1 percent of waste per total product produced. The larger of the two expenses, product waste, costs PolyWrighton about $600 per minute for every minute waste is generated.

As with many manufacturing processes, most waste and rework can be prevented, although a smaller amount cannot be prevented and may be considered normal. Controllable waste and rework, for instance, are the result of assignable causes. That is, their causes are identifiable, can be eliminated, and prevented from reoccurring. For example, some controllable waste in the production business unit may represent the cost of a single human error in judgment or decision making that occurred during the manufacturing process. The waste in this example can be traced to the specific cause, and the cause can be diagnosed and eliminated by appropriate intervention. The same holds true for an unexpected equipment failure that must be diagnosed and repaired by the maintenance unit. If the breakdown is preventable, it is controllable. Depending on the nature of the problem, the cause of the mechanical breakdown may be assignable to the maintenance unit (such as improperly performed or neglected servicing procedure), the production unit (for example, operating the equipment improperly), or both. On the other hand, common waste and rework are random and their causes are unknown. Common waste and rework are considered normal byproducts of production, as long as they remain within normal limits of the manufacturing process.

The Need

The blended learning program was designed to prepare the production business unit's immediate managers to more effectively create and sustain a motivational work environment to increase the level of engagement in direct reports. The program supposed that, by providing a more motivational work environment, the production business unit managers would have a positive impact on the work engagement of their 32 line employees. The program would evaluate the extent to which any improvements in work engagement led production to higher performance, productivity, business results, and/or profitability.

Work engagement is a positive psychological state of mind that researchers have linked to employee satisfaction and superior job performance. Research suggests that higher levels of work engagement are associated with positive feelings of individual well-being (vigor); a strong sense of commitment to the organization and its mission, goals, and objectives (dedication); and the employees' full concentration and involvement with the work itself, where time passes quickly (absorption). Work engagement is measured by the frequency an employee experiences the three psychological substates of vigor, dedication, and absorption at work. The self-coaching skills taught during the learning program were intended to help the participating managers create and sustain a more favorable environment for work engagement to positively affect employee motivation and performance.

Program Objectives

Five self-coaching skills were taught to production business unit managers during a rigorous 90-day blended classroom and online learning program that included on-the-job skills practice, journaling, and peer interaction. The objectives of the program were for each participant to 1) describe, relate, and apply the concepts of motivational work environments, work engagement, and organizational performance; 2) effectively employ the five skills to create and sustain a motivational environment that positively impacts work engagement and organizational performance; and 3) develop a habit of continuous self-coaching for the personal development in, and the practice of, the five skills.

A Summary of the Five Skills

Rooted in self-coaching, or the personal practice of monitoring and assessing one's own job performance, the five skills are self-managing, reflecting, acting consciously, collaborating, and evolving. *Self-managing* refers to clearly knowing one's self and practicing self-discipline and control in one's actions, communications, and interpersonal relations. Self-managing requires managers to understand how they are perceived by others, and how these perceptions can affect the business unit's overall performance. *Reflecting* is the practice of silent observation, or detaching one's self from emotionally charged situations to view these situations with much greater clarity. Helping the manager avoid ineffective or harmful courses of action, reflecting suspends judgment to consider the environment, situation, and possible decision outcomes. When *acting consciously,* managers are more deliberate in their decision making. Because they take the time to understand the facts and nuances of a situation, these managers have a heightened awareness of the consequences and desired outcomes of alternative courses of action. By engaging in informed, conscious decision making, these managers deliberately and decisively act to achieve optimal performance and results. *Collaborating* managers invite team contributions, not just the opinions of a chosen few. Promoting a spirit of inclusion and abundance, these managers fully use the talents of their employees so they can more effectively achieve organizational goals and objectives. *Evolving* managers continue to purposefully grow and develop themselves, both personally and professionally. These managers are open and eager to learn, and they are quick to see work challenges as opportunities for improving their own capabilities and performance.

Basis for Linking Skills to Performance

Research suggests that immediate managers who consistently and effectively practice the self-coaching skills of self-managing, reflecting, acting consciously, collaborating, and evolving play a significant role in shaping motivational work environments that positively affect individual and group performance. Motivational work environments more effectively engage the talents and abilities of employees in ways that positively influence their behavior on the job. Specifically, because motivational work environments lead to greater levels of employee satisfaction, work engagement, and productivity, the more highly engaged employees outperform their lesser-engaged peers. Effective managers afford their people the opportunity to perform well by providing them with critical resources and information needed to do an excellent job. These managers also provide meaningful professional development and growth opportunities, recognition and rewards, and other support valued by their employees. Superior managers build trust, treat people fairly, genuinely appreciate the contributions of their employees, and respect each person as a highly valued member of the team. By clearly communicating organizational plans, goals, and objectives, and by setting and enforcing high standards of performance, these managers successfully align the personal aspirations and efforts of their people with the mission, goals, and objectives of the organization.

Purpose of Evaluation

This study focused primarily on the production business unit's performance, as measured by the four participating immediate managers' reaction, learning, and application of the five skills taught during the program. Also evaluated were the work engagement levels of the production managers' 32 line employees compared to the control group's 31 line employees assigned to the maintenance business unit. Moreover, the study evaluated the impact and return on investment (ROI) of the initiative in terms of the production unit's controllable waste and rework. The program was evaluated to provide information for PolyWrighton decision makers considering whether to extend the blended learning program to the remaining 13 business units, to make improvements to the program, or to abandon the program altogether.

EVALUATION METHODOLOGY

The ROI Methodology was used to determine five levels of value, including participant reaction, learning, and on-the-job skills application. Also measured were business impact, intangible benefits, and return on investment in the production unit. That is, the evaluation focused primarily on the unit's performance, as measured by the four immediate managers' reaction, learning, and application of the five skills taught during the program. Using the extensively studied and validated Utrecht Work Engagement Scale (UWES), the evaluation also compared the work engagement of the production managers' 32 direct reports to the 31 direct reports assigned to the maintenance unit. The impact and ROI of the program were evaluated in terms of the production unit's controllable waste and rework.

Planning the initiative and its evaluation required a thorough needs assessment to ensure it aligned with organizational priorities. The results of the needs assessment are shown in Figure 21-1.

For the production unit, aligning the initiative with organizational needs meant increasing employee work engagement and reducing controllable product waste and rework. The production unit's work engagement was compared to the maintenance unit's work engagement using the UWES. In a quasi-experimental research design format, work engagement comparisons were generated by taking repeated UWES measurements of both production and maintenance units. Product quality was measured in terms of costs associated with the production unit's monthly percentages of controllable product waste and rework. Trend analysis and participant and management estimates were used to isolate the effects of the initiative. The fully loaded costs of the program were included in the ROI calculation to ensure the monetary benefits were not overstated. PolyWrighton provided standard values for converting controllable waste and rework data into monetary values. At PolyWrighton, rework and waste result in an additional \$35,000 for every 1 percent of product rework and \$245,000 for every 1 percent of waste per product produced. Data not converted to monetary values, including work engagement, were listed as intangible benefits.

The participating managers' on-the-job application, learning, and reaction data were also collected. The on-the-job application of participant skills was measured using immediate manager self-assessment surveys and UWES data collected from their direct reports after the program. During six of the seven sessions, learning was measured by the participants' summarizing how they practiced the previous session's content on-the-job, and by their completed assignments and skill development journal entries. Learning was also measured using a pre- and post-program skill assessment inventory, and by UWES data collected from the direct reports during the course of the program. Participant reaction data pertaining to program content relevance and importance, as well as the participants' planned implementation actions, were collected at the end of each of the seven learning sessions.

Categories/Levels of Data

Corresponding to the ROI Methodology, the categories, or levels, of data included those listed in Figure 21-1. Level 1 Reaction data measured participant satisfaction and planned actions for implementing the learning. The organizational need was for the participants to perceive that the learning

Figure 21-1. Business Alignment and Forecasting

Level	Needs Assessment	Program Objective	Measurement and Evaluation
5	**Payoff Needs** ⇨ Avoid costs associated with Controllable Waste and Rework ⇩	**ROI Objectives** ⇨ Target Return-On-Investment of 15% ⇧	**ROI** Calculate ROI ⇧
4	**Business Needs** ⇨ Reduce Controllable Waste and Rework Increase Work engagement ⇩	**Impact Objectives** ⇨ Monthly Percentages of Controllable Product Waste and Rework Decline Increase Work Engagement ⇧	**Impact** Percentages of Controllable Product Waste and Rework at 8-months after completion of the program compared to the same measurements taken before the program UWES of direct reports at 6-months ⇧
3	**Job Performance Needs** ⇨ Immediate manager effectiveness in the areas of leadership, setting and maintaining standards, and developing and motivating employees ⇩	**Application Objectives** ⇨ Effectively and continuously apply the five self-coaching skills at work Effectively create and sustain motivational work environments that increase engagement ⇧	**Application** Participant self-assessment at 3-months after completion of the program UWES of direct reports at 3-months ⇧
2	**Learning Needs** ⇨ Increase success skills of immediate managers in the areas of leadership, setting and maintaining standards, and developing and motivating employees ⇩	**Learning Objectives** ⇨ Immediate managers learn to effectively apply the five self-coaching skills of self-managing, reflecting, acting consciously, collaborating and evolving Learn how to foster motivational work environments that increase engagement ⇧	**Learning** Session content summaries, participant assignments, and Skill Development Journal entries during the program Pre/Post Self-Assessment Profile Utrecht Work Engagement Scale (UWES) of direct reports during the program ⇧
1	**Preference Needs** ⇨ Learning that is relevant and important to successful job performance ⇩	**Reaction Objectives** ⇨ Program content receives favorable rating of 4 out of 5 in relevance and importance 80% of participants identify planned actions	**Reaction** Reaction and planned action questionnaires at the end of each session of the program

was relevant and important to successful job performance, and plan to use the learning on the job. The program objectives, in this case, included a mean rating of 4 out of 5 points for content relevance and importance, based on participant reaction surveys, and 80 percent of participants' identifying planned actions.

Level 2 Learning measures participant acquisition of knowledge and skills, as well as changes in attitude. The need was for the immediate managers to learn how to effectively apply the five skills on the job, as determined by facilitator assessments of participant discussions, responses to questions, and completed assignments. Also, the facilitator administered pre- and post-program self-assessment profiles to gauge the participants' perceptions of changes in key behaviors related to the five skills. UWES surveys of the production unit direct reports were taken before and at day 45 and 90 of the initiative and compared to those of maintenance unit workers.

Level 3 Application measured on-the-job use of the skills taught in the program. The organizational need was for the immediate managers to consistently and effectively apply the five skills, measured through participant self-assessments taken three months after the program. UWES data of production and maintenance direct reports also was taken at three months to assess changes in work engagement.

Level 4 Impact measures changes in business impact. The organizational need was to reduce the percentage of controllable waste and rework generated by the production unit. Monthly percentages of controllable rework and waste were used to determine whether program objectives had been met. Also, one last UWES comparison of direct reports was taken six months after the program.

The Level 5 ROI calculation compared the program's benefits to its costs. In this case, a conservative 15 percent target ROI for the reduction of the production units' controllable rework and waste was established.

Data Collection Strategy

The data collection plan in Figure 21-2 shows the level of evaluation, broad program objectives, measures/data collected, collection methods, data sources, timing, and responsibility. Level 1 reaction data collected at the end of each session gauged the participants' perceptions of the program and their intent to apply what they had learned. In addition to Level 2 participant pre- and post-self-assessment profiles and facilitator appraisals

Figure 21-2. Data Collection Plan

Level	Broad Program Objectives	Measures/Data	Data Collection Methods	Data Sources	Timing	Responsibility
1 Reaction	• Program content receives favorable ratings from participants • Participants plan to apply the learning on the job	• Program content receives average favorable rating of 4 out of 5 for relevance and importance • 80% of participants identify planned actions	• Questionnaires	• Participants	• End of each session during the program	• Facilitator
2 Learning	• Learn to effectively apply the five self-coaching skills of self-managing, reflecting, acting consciously, collaborating, and evolving • Learn to foster motivational work environments that increase engagement	• Participants demonstrate successful completion of program learning objectives outlined in the facilitator and participant guides • Self-assessment • Work engagement	• Observations of performance, guided discussions, questioning, and assignments • Skill development journals • Pre/post self-assessment profile • Utrecht Work Engagement Scale (UWES)	• Facilitator • Participants • Participants • Direct reports	• Throughout the 90-day learning program • Day 0, Day 90 • Day 0, Day 45, Day 90	• Facilitator

3 Application	• Apply the five self-coaching skills at work • Foster motivational work environments that increase engagement	• Self-assessment • Work engagement	• Questionnaires • UWES	• Participants • Direct reports	• 3 months after program completion	• Program manager
4 Impact	• Reduce product waste and rework • Increase work engagement	• Percentage of controllable waste and rework generated by the Production business unit • Work engagement	• Organizational records/databases • UWES	• Business unit manager • Direct reports	• 8 months after program compared with pre-program • 6 months	• Program manager
5 ROI	Target ROI 15%	Comments: ROI = (Net Program Benefits ÷ Program Costs) X 100				

of learning, the evaluation used work engagement data collected from the production business unit during the program, and compared it to the work engagement of the maintenance unit. Participant self-assessment profiles and work engagement data taken three months after the program gauged the Level 3 on-the-job application of participant skills. Level 4 data included work engagement measurements taken six months after the initiative and the percentage of controllable waste and rework generated by production at eight months. Level 5 ROI was a calculation of net program benefits over costs.

ROI Analysis Strategy

The ROI analysis for this project, shown in Figure 21-3, depended on tracking the percent of controllable waste and rework for the production business unit before, during, and after the learning initiative. Monetary values were calculated directly, based on the percentage of total product waste and rework generated each month. The researcher used two methods to isolate the effects of the program on controllable waste and rework. The strategy called for trend analysis of the monthly percent of controllable waste and rework per total product, less those outliers identified by PolyWrighton management as nonattributable to the production business unit. Management and participant estimates of the impact of the program and the level of confidence in those estimates were also taken and adjusted. Work engagement was not converted to a monetary value, but was listed as an intangible benefit. Fully loaded costs were calculated and verified by management to ensure the most conservative ROI possible.

Isolation Techniques. Participant and management estimates of the impact of the initiative on business results, corrected for estimate error, were used in conjunction with trend analyses of controllable waste and rework. Outliers identified by PolyWrighton management as nonattributable to the production business unit were removed from the trend analyses.

Data Conversion Techniques. The conversion from percent controllable waste and rework to monetary values was direct. As previously noted, it costs PolyWrighton $35,000 for 1 percent of product rework and $245,000 for 1 percent of product waste. Data not converted to monetary values, including work engagement, were listed as intangible benefits.

Figure 21-3. Data Analysis and ROI Plan

Data Items	Methods for Isolating the Effects of the Program or Process	Method for Converting Data to Monetary Values	Cost Categories	Intangible Benefits	Communication Targets for Final Report
• Percentage of controllable waste • Percentage of controllable rework • Work engagement	• Participant and management estimates • Trend analysis	• Percentage of controllable waste X $245,000 • Percentage of controllable rework X $35,000 • Work engagement not converted to a monetary value	• Consulting fees (needs assessment, program design and development, learning delivery, and program evaluation) • Printing and supplies • Participant salaries • Facilities • Facilitator travel	• Increased work engagement • Employee satisfaction • Improved teamwork and communications • Better decision making	• Management • Participants • Training • Human Resources

Cost Summary. The program cost categories shown in Figure 21-3 included the consulting fees for the learning needs assessment, program design and development, learning delivery, and program evaluation. Printing and supplies, participant salaries, facilities, and travel were also planned costs of the program. In actuality, all fees and expenses were waived, leaving only the cost of participant salaries for PolyWrighton to bear. However, in order to provide the most conservative ROI figure for decision makers, all costs were included in the calculation.

EVALUATION RESULTS

Level 1, Reaction Results

The four participating immediate managers from the production unit completed reaction questionnaires at the end of each of the seven learning sessions. The areas surveyed were content relevance to the job, content importance to job success, intent to use the material on the job, facilitator effectiveness, material effectiveness, likelihood the participant would recommend the program to others, and overall satisfaction. Participants rated these items on a scale of 1 (strongly disagree) to 5 (strongly agree). They also indicated planned actions. Evaluation targets were set for a mean rating of 4 out of 5 points for content relevance and importance, and at least 80 percent of participants' identifying planned actions. The targets set for content relevance and importance, and for planned actions were met. Content relevance and importance scored mean ratings of 4.16 and 4.07, respectively. Also, all participants developed plans to apply what they learned during the program.

Level 2, Learning Results

Production unit managers were taught the self-coaching skills of self-managing, reflecting, acting consciously, collaborating, and evolving during seven learning sessions over 90 days. Facilitator observations, participant self-assessments, and UWES measurements of the participant's direct reports were used to evaluate learning.

The pre-and post-program self-assessment profile asked participants to rate how consistently they practiced 25 specific work behaviors anchored to the five skills. Each behavior was rated on a scale of 1 (never) to 5 (always).

Administered at Day 1 of the learning initiative, the pre- program self-assessment mean score for all 25 behaviors was 105.0 points. The Day 90 self-assessment mean score was 107.6 points. An increase of 2.6 points for the mean, while statistically inconclusive, suggests the possibility that at least a modest amount of learning occurred during the program. The project team deemed this acceptable, since the learning was designed to become participant self-directed and to continue after the formal program ended. This evolution from facilitated instruction to self-coaching required that learning be evaluated as it was practiced on-the-job. With this in mind, work engagement levels would help evaluate participant skill acquisition during the program.

Taken in the context of the organizational setting, work engagement readings of the production test group and maintenance control group line employees provided additional insight into the participants' on-the-job skill development. A highly disruptive plant fire that occurred toward the end of the learning program produced a significant gap between these two groups; a slight drop in production work engagement compared to a much steeper decline in maintenance.

A thorough assessment of the situation found that the fire should have had no more of an adverse impact on maintenance (control group) compared to production (test group). According to the senior human resource manager, the lead training manager, and the business unit and line managers at PolyWrighton, both groups experienced the same extended period of excessive overtime and intense physical labor. While work engagement was more negatively affected in maintenance compared to production, no apparent reason could be identified. This may suggest that the production immediate managers had been better equipped to deal with the plant fire and its consequences than their maintenance business unit counterparts. In other words, it is possible that the five skills helped keep the production unit from being as negatively affected.

Level 3, Application Results

Self-assessments suggested the self-coaching participant managers from production appeared to be applying their newly acquired knowledge and skills more frequently at Day 180, with a mean score of 112.6, than they were at Day 90, with a mean score of 107.6. While work engagement in both business units was on the increase three months after the program, production maintained a higher response from its direct reports than did maintenance. Managers at PolyWrighton have suggested that the gain in the control group, the maintenance unit, probably was the result of supervisory changes made during that period.

Barriers to Application. Engaged leadership by the lead manager in production and closer communication among all managers in that business unit prevented any notable barriers to application.

Enablers to Application. Production unit leadership was a driving force in enabling the transfer of learning by the participating managers to the job. The lead manager participated in the learning program and practiced the five skills alongside her direct reports, the four line managers. In addition, regular meetings of these managers to discuss application of the five skills, and an improved system of tracking unit performance initiated by these managers, supported the continued use and development of the learning.

Level 4, Business Impact Results

The business impact measures included production's controllable rework and waste summarized in Table 21-1. Also measured were production's work engagement levels compared to those of the maintenance unit. Work engagement data were not converted to monetary values but were treated as intangible benefits.

Pre-program monthly percentage and cost averages, based on data collected during the eight-month period preceding the program, projected trends for controllable waste and rework through the end of the eight-month period following the initiative. A linear trend line returned the projected percentages shown in Table 21-1. The projected trend values through the end of the post-program period were 0 percent for rework and 1.5 percent for waste.

All rework and waste data, the cause of which was not assignable to the production business unit, were treated as outliers and removed from calculation of the pre- and post-program eight-month averages. PolyWrighton management made the final determination of which data points would be treated as outliers. Examples of causes not assignable to production included new product specifications, ongoing technical issues stemming from the plant fire recovery, an unexpected line freeze attributable to severe weather, and worse-than-usual supplier material shortages. Controllable rework during the pre-program period averaged 2.69 percent. At a cost of $35,000 for every 1 percent, pre-program rework averaged $94,000 per month. The projected trend value through the end of the post-program period was 0 percent for rework. The post-program monthly average for rework, however, was 1.87 percent, for a cost of $65,450.

Controllable waste during the pre-program period averaged 0.73 percent. At a cost of $245,000 for every one percent, pre-program waste averaged $178,850 per month. The projected trend value through the end of the post-program period was 1.5 percent for waste, or $367,500. The post-program monthly average for waste was $53,900, based on 0.22 percent. The difference between the post-program average and the projected trend represented an average monthly cost decrease of $313,600 for product waste.

Combined, the cost of rework and savings on waste totaled an average monthly cost savings of $248,150, before factoring in participant and management impact estimates and correcting for confidence error, for a total projected annual cost savings of $2,977,800.

Isolation. Also shown in Table 21-1, the combined participant and management estimates of the impact of the initiative on business results, corrected for estimate error, were used in conjunction with the trend analyses of controllable waste and rework. In this case, the 12-month total program benefit (expressed as a positive value of $2,977,800), multiplied by the adjusted estimate of the program's impact on program benefits (expressed as a decimal value of 0.425), returned an annual cost avoidance of $1,265,565 before expenses. This is the total benefit, adjusted for impact, before subtracting total program costs.

Data Conversion to Money. PolyWrighton provided standard monetary values for waste and rework. The company estimated the value of 1 percent of rework at $35,000, and 1 percent of controllable waste at $245,000. The average monthly percentages were multiplied by these values to determine monetary value.

Table 21-1. Production Controllable Rework and Waste

	Pre-intervention 8-month Average[3,6]		Projected Trend[4]		Post-intervention 8-month Average[5,6]		Percent Change[7]	Average Monthly Cost[8,10]	12-Month Cost Projection[9,10]
	Percentage	Value	Percentage	Value	Percentage	Value			
Controllable Rework[1]	2.69	$94,000	0.0	$0	1.87	$65,450	+1.87	+$65,450	+$785,400
Controllable Waste[2]	0.73	$178,850	1.5	$367,500	0.22	$53,900	-1.28	-$313,600	-$3,763,200
Total Program Benefits (Controllable Waste and Rework Combined)[11]								-$248,150	-$2,977,800

Isolation of Impact on Total Program Benefits	Impact Estimate[12]	Confidence[13]	Adjusted Estimate[14]	Total Benefit Adjusted for Impact[15]
	50%	85%	42.5%	$1,265,565

[1] $35,000 is the monetary value of 1 percent of controllable rework per total product produced. Monetary values provided by PolyWrighton.

[2] $245,000 is the monetary value of 1 percent of controllable waste per total product produced. Monetary values provided by PolyWrighton.

[3] Pre-intervention monthly percentage and cost averages are based on the data collected during the 8-month period preceding the intervention.

[4] The projected trends are based on the pre-intervention percentage waste and rework data collected during the 8-month period preceding the intervention. A linear trend line, generated in Microsoft Excel and extended through the end of the post-intervention period, returned the projected percentages shown. The dollar values referenced in notes 1 and 2 were then multiplied by the trend percentages to return the projected values.

[5] Post-intervention monthly percentage and cost averages are based on the data collected during the 8-month period following the intervention.

[6] Data points, whose causes were not assignable to the Production business unit, were treated as outliers and removed from the calculation of the pre- and post-intervention 8-month averages. PolyWrighton management made the final determination of which data points would be treated as outliers. Examples of causes not assignable to Production included new product specifications, ongoing technical issues stemming from the plant fire recovery, an unexpected line freeze attributable to severe weather, and worse than usual supplier material shortages.

[7] Percent change is the post-intervention percentage minus the projected trend percentage for both controllable rework and waste.

[8] Average monthly cost is the post-intervention value minus the projected trend value for both controllable rework and waste.

[9] Average monthly cost multiplied by 12 months for both controllable rework and waste.

[10] Negative values represent PolyWrighton cost avoidances.

[11] Total benefit before factoring in participant and management impact estimates corrected for confidence error.

[12] Combined manager and participant estimate of the intervention's impact on improvement.

[13] Combined manager and participant confidence of their estimate of the intervention's impact on improvement.

[14] Combined adjusted impact estimate based on combined manager and participant estimate and confidence.

[15] (12-Month Total Program Benefit expressed as a positive value)X (Adjusted Estimate expressed as a decimal value) = (Total Benefit Adjusted for Impact): $2,977,800 X 0.425 = $1,265,565

Program Costs. The learning program was provided free-of-charge to the company, but the estimated cost for the program was calculated at $253,761. While the firm's actual cost for the initiative was $3,360, this study provided the more conservative return on investment calculation to allow PolyWrighton managers to make a better-informed decision when considering whether to extend the program to the other 13 business units.

Level 5, ROI

The total projected annual benefit adjusted for impact, before subtracting total program costs, was $1,265,565. The $1,265,565 benefit less the program cost of $253,761 was $1,011,804. The net benefit of $1,011,804 divided by the total program cost of $253,761 was 3.99. Multiplied by 100, the Level 5 ROI calculation was 399 percent.

$$ROI = \$1,265,565 - \$253,761/ \$253,761 \times 100 = 399\%$$

Intangible Benefits

Work engagement was studied throughout the program plus six months afterward. Work engagement is a positive psychological state of mind that researchers have linked to employee satisfaction and superior job performance. Higher levels of work engagement are associated with positive feelings of individual well-being (vigor); a strong sense of commitment to the organization and its mission, goals, and objectives (dedication); and the employees' full concentration and involvement with the work itself (absorption). Work engagement is measured by the frequency an employee experiences the three psychological sub-states of vigor, dedication, and absorption at work. The self-coaching skills taught during the learning program were intended to help the participating production managers create and sustain a more favorable environment for work engagement to positively affect employee motivation and performance. A series of statistical tests examined work engagement in the production and maintenance units using the UWES in a quasi-experimental research design.

An independent sample t-test for differences between the production (test group) and maintenance (control group) means was not statistically significant at Day 1 of the program; the difference between the two groups' work engagement was too small to matter. However, the gap between these two business units widened considerably by the end of the program. By

Day 90, mixed-design analysis of variance statistical testing indicated that the difference between production and maintenance work engagement was statistically significant and powerful. Further, Cronbach's alpha testing showed the statistical reliability of the UWES was high. Given the organizational context, including a disruptive plant fire during the final 30 days of the study, the program can perhaps be seen as more preventive in nature. That is, it may be the production managers learned to handle the high stress situation more effectively than their maintenance counterparts.

By Day 270, six months after the program, work engagement in both business units was on the rise. Managers at PolyWrighton indicated the gain in the control group, maintenance, was probably the result of key supervisory changes made after the plant fire that occurred in the last 30 days of the program. While the post-program gap continued to narrow, production maintained high enough levels of work engagement to remain statistically significant at Day 180 and Day 270. In essence, production managers held that increased work engagement led to greater employee satisfaction, improved teamwork and communications, and better decision making.

COMMUNICATION AND IMPROVEMENT STRATEGY

Results Reporting

Face-to-face meetings with members of the PolyWrighton management team, the participants, the training function, and the director of human resources ensured the results were fully understood and reconciled prior to issuing the final written report.

Stakeholder Response

PolyWrighton had a positive reaction to the results and requested the initiative extend to the 13 remaining business units.

Program Improvement

Stakeholders remained engaged throughout the entire data collection, analysis, and reporting process and offered suggestions to improve future iterations of the learning initiative. PolyWrighton agreed to collaborate with the design team to reduce the 90-day learning period, without sacrificing quality and transfer of skills to the job.

LESSONS LEARNED

Process Learning

Researchers should conduct additional research into programs, particularly in the context of organizational settings and individual business units. For instance, exploring a wider variety of applications for the UWES, including longitudinal studies that link work engagement to tangible business results indicators, may prove useful in assigning monetary values to calculate return on investment. Also, using program research to move toward a more common and practical engagement construct that links the preconditions, psychological factors, behavioral outcomes, and business results may enhance the evaluation of such programs in an organizational setting.

The study confirmed that practitioners should first take the time and effort to assess relevant business and learner needs in the context of organizational objectives and environmental conditions, before selecting a program. In this case, the blended self-coaching learning initiative was designed to meet the needs of PolyWrighton, and to link program objectives and measures to meaningful business outcomes. The integration of measurement and evaluation into the initiative from the start proved invaluable, because it helped shape a more successful implementation. Finally, programs firmly grounded in research are more likely to succeed.

Organizational Response

Organizational response was favorable and positive. The key element in the overall success of the project was the highly engaged leadership by PolyWrighton managers to ensure the program was implemented on-the-job, as intended. Regular team meetings in production enhanced communications among participating managers, and an element of accountability for implementing the self-coaching skills on the job were leadership-driven enablers of success.

Questions for Discussion

1. How critical do you think the business alignment and forecasting plan in Figure 21-1 was to the success of the program? Explain.
2. Given the time invested into the program, would this online and classroom program be practical to try in your organization? Why was it successful at PolyWrighton?

3. How might the close coordination with the PolyWrighton stakeholders serve as a model for implementing similar initiatives in other organizations?
4. Besides the UWES and self-assessment profiles taken three months after the termination of the program, how would you have measured on-the-job implementation of the five skills? Explain.
5. Guiding Principle 8 states, "Extreme data items and unsupported claims should not be used in ROI calculations." How would you relate that principle to the elimination of nonassignable outliers from production's waste and rework calculations? What about the use of the estimated total cost instead of the actual amount paid for the program? Explain.
6. The authors state that a key element in the overall success of the project was the highly engaged leadership by PolyWrighton managers to ensure the program was implemented on the job, as intended. In what ways do you believe that level of involvement impacted the outcome, and how can it be nurtured in other organizations, where the environment isn't as user-friendly?

Chapter 22

Measuring ROI in a Sales Training Program

Multinational Automotive Company

by Emma Weber

This case study describes how an automotive company evaluated a sales training process to demonstrate value, using data that were already available in the organization. This approach is powerful. The key to success was building trust in the process to enable a high level of response to the surveys. Multinational Automotive Company (MAC) had been operating a sales training program for at least five years. With the business becoming increasingly competitive and budgets for learning being squeezed, it was important to be able to demonstrate the ROI of the training program. The program was usually conducted five to six times per year and this evaluation runs for the total year. The programs included in the analysis were conducted in a one-year period, with each full program typically lasting 10 weeks. Lever Learning was contracted to perform an ROI analysis on the sales training program.

PROGRAM DESCRIPTION

A four-day sales training is run for MAC sales executives. It is essential for the skills to be transferred to the workplace, so the four-day training program is accompanied with a Turning Learning Into Action® program, which includes four 45-minute telephone coaching sessions to secure the learning transfer to the workplace. In total, the program and the telephone follow-up take place over a period of 10 to 12 weeks.

For each program the Level 1, Level 2, and Level 3 data are already collected. The program receives good feedback and change occurs in the business consistently. However, to be able to show some financial benefit conclusively would be valuable for the training department to maintain support and funding.

PLANNING FOR ROI EVALUATION

Figure 22-1 shows the completed data collection plan. It was decided that data would be leveraged that had already been collected by the business. Focus groups, interviews, and observation in the field were considered too expensive or inappropriate. Questionnaires at different stages of the program, including three months after the participants had completed the classroom element of the program, were used.

Access to sales data at a participant level was available, but because it was preferable to compare the before and after data and many of the participants were new to the business, a comparison could only be created for some of the attendees. For those that were new to the business it was impossible to isolate the data on the program.

As data were collected, an ROI analysis plan was developed, as shown in Figure 22-2.

DATA COLLECTION TOOLS

Reaction and Learning

Level 1 data (Reaction) and Level 2 data (Learning) are consistently collected for every program. A 100 percent response rate was achieved for the Level 1 survey, as this is completed at the end of the four-day training program before the participants leave the training venue.

The Level 2 data (knowledge and demonstration of new skills) are tested twice during the program, during role-plays observed by coaches. Coaches complete the Level 2 data forms. If a participant is not able to demonstrate the skills, he receives additional coaching to bring him up to the required standard. The role-play evaluation form is shown in Figure 22-3.

Figure 22-1. Data Collection Plan

Sales Training Program for Sales Executives

Level	Broad Program Objectives	Measures	Data Collection Method/Instruments	Data Sources	Timing	Responsibilities
1.	**Reaction, Satisfaction and Planned Action** • Positive reaction to the program • Recommend improvements collected	• Average rating of at least 4 on a 5-point scale • Percent of people who completed an action plan	• Reaction/feedback questionnaire • Action plan document	• Participants	• End of day 4 of the program	• Reaction/feedback questionnaire: Lead facilitator • Action plan: Consultant to collate
2.	**Learning** • Acquisition of skills including AUSS, WWW, using customer profiles	• Scale of 1 to 5 for each skill observed in live role-plays	• Coaches recording on an observation feedback form • Videos of role-play shared with participants to verify ratings	• Coaches observing participants	• During role-plays, days 2 and 4 of training	• Role-play coaches
3.	**Application/ Implementation** • Use of skills learned • Application of skills learned	• 4 telephone coaching conversations discussing progress, end valuation form collected 3-4 months after the 4-day program • Aim for 60% of participants to offer feedback	• Evaluation form including scale of meeting objectives, what changes have you made, what benefits have you made	• Participants	• After the final coaching call typically 2-3 months after the 4-day program	• Telephone coach to distribute • Consultant to collate info on to dashboard

Figure 22-1. Data Collection Plan (*continued*)

#						
4.	**Business Impact** • Sales increase • Changes made for business benefits	• Percent sales increase in units 6 months after the 4-day program compared to the 6 months before the 4-day program. Analysis completed for any participant who was in the business for 6 months before attending the program • Impact questions one valuation form re: changes and benefits, estimated completed by 60% of people	• Sales taken from reports	• Reports	• 6 months after the end of the 4-day program	• Consultant to collate report on dashboard
5.	**ROI** • Target ROI	• Target ROI is greater than 20%				
	Baseline Data: Comments:					

Figure 22-2. ROI Analysis Plan

Data Items (Usually Level 4)	Methods for Isolating the Effects of the Program	Methods of Converting Data to Monetary Value	Cost Categories	Intangible Benefits	Communication Targets for Final Report	Other Influences/ Issues During Application	Comments
• Sales per participant • Questionnaire 3 months post program: "What benefits have the program brought for the business?"	• Trend-line analysis • Comparing pre-program and post-program uplift compared to companywide uplift	• Use an average gross per vehicle to convert sales to money. • Only convert if specific numbers are included by participant; otherwise move to intangible and show in word cloud.	• Facilitator costs • Turning learning into action costs • Travel costs (flights/ accommodation) • Administrative costs • Participant time	• Recorded through questions on questionnaire • Examples: NPS word clouds, changes in Level 3, and benefits in Level 4	• Create dashboard and distribute to senior teams • ROI figures to distribute to key stakeholders during stage 1	• Due to many of the participants having no historical sales, the pre- and post-program comparison cannot be made and therefore benefits are only available for some participants.	• Using the pre and post and comparing to overall business should discount seasonal changes.

Figure 22-3. Role-Play 2: Qualification/Objection Handling/Close

Name: _____ Coach: _____

Role-play: _____

Negative Behavior	Rating	Positive Behavior
Clearly unaware of customer pace/focus type. Does not change pace or focus to customer type. Continues "on a track" in spite of verbal/nonverbal signals. Speaks down to customer. Clear lack of 'customer type' understanding. Frequently uses 'motor trade' jargon.	Establishing pace and focus - - - + + +	Establishes customer pace/focus type. Demonstrates behavior appropriate to customer's pace/focus. Adapts qualification process to customer's stated needs. Speaks customer language. Avoids jargon.
Asks lots of closed, long, or assumptive questions. Does not probe when questioning. Changes subject abruptly. Never summarizes or paraphrases. Fails to record answers. Frequently asks for the same information. Clearly has no pattern or theme to questions.	Understanding needs - - - + + +	Seeks to obtain information at early stage of the process. Uses range of questions to establish need. Identifies key information, e.g., current vehicle, buying plans. Summarizes what customer has said to check understanding. Logically builds on line of questioning.
Stiff or stilted conversation. Disinterested or detached manner. Rambles; ignores questions; talks over customer. No indication of active listening. Poor body language and ignores nonverbal signals. Fails to indicate positive and personalized benefits. 'Feature dumps.'	Building rapport - - - + + +	Easy and natural conversation style. Attentive, calm, confident, and polite. Displays interest in customer. Observes and actively listens. Positive body language throughout. Matches benefits of product to customer need. Relates to customer's hobbies, interests, or family.
Unstructured in approach to objections. Shows a lack of sensitivity to points raised by the customer. Ignores/overrides objections. Does not establish cause of objection. Interrupts or contradicts the customer. Does not offer options. Leaves customer unhappy with outcome.	Handling objections - - - + + +	Effectively deals with customer objections. Uses a process. Always acknowledges objections. Asks probing questions. Paraphrases. Never directly disagrees/contradicts customer. Explores options. Seeks mutually agreeable outcome.

Fails to close or gain a commitment. Does not ask direct questions to close sale/ gain commitment. Gets upset, irritated, or put off if rebuffed. Lacks variation in approach. Unclear on agreement/next steps. Makes excessive, unwise, or no concessions.	Gaining commitment - - - + + +	Attempts to close at an appropriate point in the conversation. Asks direct questions to close sale/gain commitment. Reacts calmly and confidently if rebuffed. Shows subtle persistence in rebuilding another closing opportunity. Precise and accurate about agreement reached. Acts commercially.
Customer feels uncomfortable/unwelcome. Salesperson clearly lacks basic knowledge of products and brand. Fails to summarize. Conversation finishes abruptly. Salesperson is not someone you would want to go back to or recommend to another person.	Overall - - - + + +	Helps customer feel relaxed and natural. Credible and knowledgeable about products. Summarizes agreed results. Ends on a positive note. Salesperson is someone you 'want to do business with.' You would recommend a friend to this salesperson.
☹	🙂	

Fell below ☒   **Met** ☒   **Exceeded** ☒

Observations regarding attitude/behavior/representing the brand:

_____
_____
_____
_____

Figure 22-3. Role-Play 2: Qualification/Objection Handling/Close *(continued)*

For Accreditation Summary:	
Role-play 2:	
😐	😊
Attitude/behavior/representing the brand:	
😐	😊
Delegate Action Plan	
_____	
_____	
_____	
_____	

The Level 1 data are collected, but are only used to highlight major challenges or disenchanted participants. On a regular basis, over 85 percent of responses to questions are at a five on a five-point scale. While this is rewarding for the trainer and the program content, it does not indicate business outcomes. It communicates that the program is of high quality, and that if a return is not realized, it is because of a problem further down the line, probably in the transfer of the learning. Figure 22-4 shows the questionnaire used for collecting data at Levels 1 and 2.

Figure 22-4. Level 1 and Level 2 Course Evaluation

Name: _____	Course Title: __MAC Sales Training__
Dealership: _____	Instructor: _____
Position: _____	Date: _____

We would appreciate your evaluation of this course. Please tick the relevant rating boxes.

Objectives: As a result of this training course I am able to:	Strongly Disagree 1	Mostly Disagree 2	Neither Agree nor Disagree 3	Mostly Agree 4	Strongly Agree 5
Make a clear distinction between premium selling and other forms of selling.					
Describe the expectations of a customer buying a MAC brand.					
Explain the skills required by a successful sales consultant.					
Give and receive feedback and use feedback for self-development.					
Explain to others my personal strengths and development areas.					
Show how to make a good first impression and its importance in sales.					
Demonstrate the range of questions and techniques that can be used in sales.					
Explain the difference between emotional and rational focus of the customer.					
Practice active listening.					
Use positive body language and other nonverbal signals.					
Deliver a variety of closing techniques.					
Instructor evaluation	**1**	**2**	**3**	**4**	**5**
The instructors demonstrated a thorough knowledge of the subject(s).					
The instructors' explanations were easy to understand.					
Course evaluation	**1**	**2**	**3**	**4**	**5**
The course content was relevant to my role in the dealership.					
The course materials were easy to understand.					
The course provided me with adequate opportunity for involvement.					

Figure 22-4. Level 1 and Level 2 Course Evaluation *(continued)*

What changes, if any, should we make to this training course?
What did you find to be of the most value in this training course?
General comments:
Action Plan: When you return to the dealership, what initial steps will you take to apply your knowledge/skills?

Application

The Level 3 and Level 4 data are of most interest to the head office executives. These data describe the changes in terms of what participants have achieved after returning from the training program. Level 4 captures the impact this has had on the business. Specifically for this program, a sales increase is the goal, but the open questions on the survey will capture intangible benefits also. An 85 percent response rate for the survey was attained. The survey was conducted two to three months after the initial four-day training and at the end of the Turning Learning Into Action telephone coaching process.

This high response rate is achieved because the telephone coaching process is one-on-one and the coach builds rapport and trust with the participants and stresses the importance of responding. The script used for the phone conversation is as follows.

"Because everything that we have covered in the past four telephone coaching sessions is confidential, it is essential that the feedback forms are submitted to the automotive company. It is the only opportunity the automotive company has to know that you and I haven't just discussed the weather during our conversations. It should only take five minutes to complete and I will send it across to you by email this afternoon. It is an online form."

The survey is online and is created via a survey design program in our own bespoke system. It enables generation of Excel spreadsheets with the collected data for easy analysis. Also included are some Level 1 data on the coaching program itself and the NPS (Net Promoter Score), which is widely acknowledged to be useful in assessing client satisfaction, a Level 1 measure. This is interesting but does not contribute to the evaluation of program outcomes.

Information is collected on progress toward the goals that the participants have set at the end of training program and the level to which they have achieved them. In terms of commentary the following questions are asked:

- What changes have you put into place?
- What benefits or results have the changes created for the business?

Impact Dashboards

Figure 22-5 illustrates an impact dashboard, which Lever Learning uses to display data at the impact level. The dashboard represents the program between May 2010 and May 2011 with 78 participants. It includes the detail of the sales; however, certain information was removed as it was too commercially sensitive to distribute across the business.

Clients enjoy the dashboards that are created. The dashboard gives them a tangible way to illustrate results even though it doesn't actually generate the results. Turning Learning Into Action, the learning transfer process, generates the results and the dashboard allows a manager, CEO, or learning and development professional to showcase the results. Until the creation of the impact dashboard, the person going through the changes knew how well the program worked, and sometimes the manager did as well, but results were not reported across the TLA program. When the dashboard was introduced, it gave the CEO or manager a birds-eye view of just how effective the program had been collectively. Figure 26-6 shows the questionnaire used for creation of the dashboard.

PROGRAM DETAILS AND RESULTS

The program details box in the top left box of the dashboard offers the reader an immediate overview of the program the results relate to. As shown in Figure 22-5, 78 participants went through the TLA program and were asked to complete survey feedback. Of the 78 requested feedback forms, 53 people completed the feedback and the results in the impact dashboard relate to that feedback. Where the client is familiar with Net Promoter Score

(NPS), the dashboard also includes this popular metric. The NPS is the score derived from asking customers one question: "How likely is it that you would recommend our company to a friend or colleague?" The theory is that the more "promoters" a company has, the greater the loyalty and impact and ultimately the greater the growth. It is a standardized way to gauge customer satisfaction.

Figure 22-5. Impact Dashboard

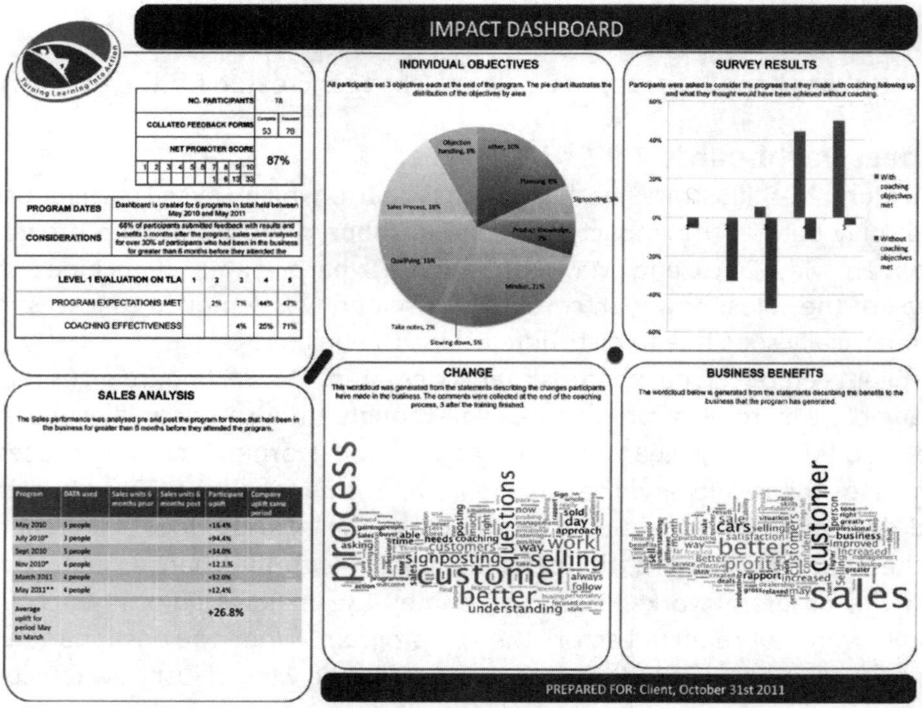

The program details box also specifies the dates of the TLA programs and any considerations that need to be appreciated to interpret the dashboard effectively, such as people who have left the business or had extended leave.

This section also provides Level 1, reaction-based evaluation data. The data allow the reader of the dashboard to establish on a scale of 1–5 whether the participant's expectations of the program were met. It also demonstrates on the same scale of 1–5 whether participants considered the coaching effective in supporting their transfer of learning.

Remember, Level 1 evaluation is only interested in the reaction of participants to the process. While the most useful evaluations are Level

3 (application), Level 4 (impact), and Level 5 (ROI), this measure is a good indication to a manager what his or her people actually thought of the program. It gives a sense of participants' first impressions of the program and flushes out any major problems.

Figure 22-6. Questionnaire for Creation of Dashboard

Name:
Program:
Date program completed:
1. Your calibration for goal 3 at the end of training program was:
2. For goal 3, where do you calibrate yourself now, at the end of the coaching? (Scale: 1 low—10 high)
3. Given your goals above—To what degree were your expectations of coaching as a transfer of training tool met? (1 low—5 high)
4. Given your goals above—To what degree have the objectives you set at the end of the training program been met? (1 low—5 high)
5. Given your goals above—To what degree, do you believe, would the objectives in your Action Plan have been met WITHOUT coaching? (1 not met—5 fully met without coaching)
6. Effectiveness of coaching—How useful was the coaching in ensuring that you followed through on your Action Plan? (1 not useful—5 essential)
7. What changes have you already made specifically as a result of the program and follow-up?
8. What benefits or results have these changes created for you or the business?
9. In an ideal world, what specifically would you like in the future to help you develop further in your role?
10. Any additional comments?

Individual Objectives

At the end of a training program everyone in the program commits to three actions that they detail in their TLA plan. The pie chart in the top middle box of the dashboard is a visual representation of the distribution of objectives by topic or area. Everyone's objectives are then grouped under relevant subheadings to create relevant categories. When this square is coupled with the top right box it becomes a Level 3 measure, as it captures what the participant puts into place back in the business by recording the goals set and the progress that they have made.

This offers managers a quick snapshot of the key themes or types of actions that participants have focused on during the change process, and most of the time these key themes will relate to the content of the training program. This is a quick way to see what issues were the most popular for participants to implement and work on during the TLA process.

Facilitators find this information useful because it tells them what parts of the training the participants think is most relevant to their daily job responsibilities. It offers insights about how to improve the training for maximum impact and it may even offer insights on how to create future training solutions. This information is also very useful for the head of learning and development for similar reasons. If this pie chart indicates that participants are using one topic or section of the training more than others, it may influence future content.

Survey Results

In the feedback process, all participants in the TLA program are asked to answer the following two questions:

1. On a scale of 1–5, to what level did you meet the objectives that you set at the end of the program?
2. On a scale of 1–5, what level do you think you would have met those objectives without coaching?

These questions allow participants to reflect on how far they have come in the TLA process and what they think would have happened had they not had that coaching support.

This box in the top right of the dashboard represents all actions for all participants, so it offers a big picture view of how effective participants have considered the process, and shows the manager how relevant the participant considers the TLA process to be. It has been determined over many years that when people are asked to self-score from 1–5, they view themselves in three ways:

- Low level of objectives met (1–2)
- Average level of objectives met (3)
- High level of objectives met (4–5)

If a participant gives herself a three, she is saying she is average, and we know that average in the context of learning transfer is about 20 percent implementation. If someone self-scores a one or a two, it means he is going to do nothing.

Around 10 percent of people believe they would have met their goals without coaching, which is generally true, as 10 percent of learners are typically focused enough to create their own change. This section in the impact dashboard provides the first Level 3 evaluation and indicates whether or not real behavioral change has occurred, if objectives have been met, and what knowledge people have applied.

Sales Analysis/Results Section

This is the box that is most tailored to each client, and the information that appears here will often depend on the type of training that was undertaken. In our example, it was sales training. This box details the results of the training and TLA program on sales uplift for each group of participants who went through the program.

For some clients, this dashboard results section looks at the individual goals set in the program and how far the participants have come in achieving those goals during the coaching. Participants are asked to rate themselves on a score of 1–10 on their objectives when they set that objective and then again after the coaching. For example, if a participant set a goal of generating more leads, he would be asked to rate himself on generating leads before the coaching and again after the coaching, and this results section would illustrate those improvements.

Much of the feedback displayed in this section of the impact dashboard is received from the TLA participants themselves. This is because it is the participant who knows her role best and therefore knows what she has achieved (or not). In Phillips' terms, we are using expert estimation, with the participant as the expert.

To add an additional level of validity to these results so that managers and leaders can be confident that they reflect real-world results and are not just wishful thinking by the participant, this section can include a manager's corroboration score. When the participants send the feedback on how they have done on the program and what changes they have made, the information is relayed to their manager, who is asked to verify their score. The manager is asked, "On a scale of 1–10 how confident are you that you have seen this level of change?" The answer is documented on the impact dashboard as the manager's corroboration score. The higher the score, the more the managers agree with the participants' assessments of their performance.

This section of the impact dashboard provides more in-depth Level 3 evaluation by exploring the real-world changes that have occurred in the business as a result of the training and TLA process.

Change

In the bottom middle section, the word cloud is generated around all the anecdotal information received in the feedback forms. Participants are asked, "What changes have you put into place?" and their responses generate the word cloud.

Word clouds or tag clouds were developed in the mid-1990s. They are a basic visualization method for text data; originally they were used to depict keyword metadata on websites. The importance of each "word" is shown in terms of size or color. Software developed in 2008 is used more widely to visualize word frequency in free-form natural language sets, which are great for analysis of individual changes made due to training. For purposes of creating the word cloud, www.wordle.net is used.

In the example shown, the words "process," "customer," "better," "questions," and "selling" are larger than "listening" or "positive" because the larger words appeared more often in the way the participants described the changes they had implemented following the TLA process.

This information can be useful to get a sense of what participants are really taking from the experience and what is actually changing. The larger words will reflect the content of the training and the genuine real-world changes that the participants have made in the workplace.

This section of the impact dashboard provides an additional perspective on Level 3 evaluation by describing the changes that have occurred as a result of the training and TLA process.

Business Benefits

The last section of the impact dashboard, the bottom right, contains another word cloud. This time it is generated using all the answers received from participants to the question, "What benefits have your changes created?"

Again, the larger words represent the words or descriptors most often used to describe the business benefits achieved as a result of the TLA process. This business benefits word cloud provides a Level 4 evaluation and explores the impact the training and TLA process has had on the business.

Intangible Benefits

Intangible benefits are those benefits that cannot be converted to monetary values credibly, with a reasonable amount of resources. Many intangibles were realized through the development of the word clouds such as better rapport with customers, improved customer satisfaction, better understanding, better focus and attitude, and enhanced knowledge.

Collecting The Level 4 Sales Data

Seventy-eight participants completed the program between May 2010 and May 2011. The program was run six times with the average participants per program being 13. For each individual program, the sales history and data for the year, by month, needed to be collected.

When examining the participants' reasons that the data were not available or could not be used, explanations included:

- **Not in a sales role:** Some of the participants in the program were not in a direct sales role. They could have been sales managers who did not have sales directly attributed to themselves or they could have been cadets who were not yet fully selling but were being trained to sell. Their sales figures, therefore, had no pre-and post-sales and could not be used.
- **Left the business:** Likewise, sales managers who have left the business part of the way through the program cannot have the data included in the analysis.
- **No comparison data:** Those sales executives who had just joined the business before they attended the training program had no sales before the training program and therefore could not be included in the analysis to create the business uplift comparison, or be included in the total benefits of the program.
- **Exceptions:** For some sales executives, even though they had been within the business for three months before and after the training program, their roles had significantly changed during the time period

and they had not had an opportunity to use the new skills in their roles. The roles had changed to special vehicles in one case, and from used cars to new cars in the other case, where the volumes are completely different and therefore would skew the comparison.

Finally, the data were being collected from the incentive rewards program for the company. On investigation, one of the dealerships was not included in the incentive rewards program and therefore they had inaccurate data on the system. For the data from this particular dealership, the dealership was contacted directly and asked to manually collate the data for the two sales executives involved in the program.

Isolating the Benefits

To isolate the benefits of the program for each individual participant, we collected the total sales for the six months before the program and the total sales for the six months after.

Using the total number of people per sample, we calculated the average sales per consultant for six months before and then the six months after the program, enabling calculation of the additional cars sold per participant after the program. The company sales trend for the same period was then calculated for the six months before and six months after the program. For each program, those that had attended training had a higher uplift than the company average, as Table 22-1 shows. This difference illustrates a business benefit. The technique is often labeled control group analysis, where the trained group is the experimental group and the rest of the sales team is the control group.

Table 22-1. Participant and Company Sales Uplift

Program	Data Used	Sales Units 6 Months Prior	Sales Units 6 Months Post	Participant Uplift	Company Uplift Same Period
May 2010	5 people	176	205	+16.4%	+11.7%
July 2010	3 people	77	150	+94.4%	+3.6%
Sept. 2010	5 people	120	161	+34.0%	+3.6%
Nov. 2010	6 people	178	190	+12.3%	+3.2%
March 2011	4 people	107	142	+32.0%	+5.4%
May 2011	4 people	113	127	+12.4%	-32.7%

Having demonstrated business impact to create the ROI for the program it is important to convert the additional sales to money and then compare this to the cost of the program. This was accomplished by:

- Using the percentage uplift from the program, calculate this to the additional number of units sold.
- Using the percentage uplift from across the business at this time, calculate which of these sales were additional sales due to the sales training program.
- Using an average gross margin per unit, calculate the additional sales for the six months.

Costs

Fully loaded costs for the program were calculated by considering expenses for flights and accommodations, participants' salaries, trainer costs, administrative costs, and others, as shown in Table 22-2.

Table 22-2. Fully Loaded Costs

Category of Spend for Participants	Amount	For 13 Participants	% of Participants	Total Cost
Accommodation per person	$200	$2600	70%	$1820
Flights per person	$350	$4550	67%	$3048
Average wage package per	$2200 per person	$28,600	100%	$28,600
TLA cost per participant	$931	$12,103	100%	$12,103
Admin per participant	$50	$650	100%	$650
Other Categories of Spend				**Total Cost**
Cost for trainer		$2250 per day x 4 days		$9000
Program development costs*				
TOTAL				$55,221
Total cost for 6 programs				$333,326

ROI Calculation

$$\text{ROI (\%)} = \frac{\text{Monetary Benefits} - \text{Total Program Costs}}{\text{Total Program Costs}} \times 100$$

$$\text{ROI (\%)} = \frac{\$469,397 - \$333,326}{\$333,326} \quad 40.8 \times 100 = 40.8\%$$

Remembering the 40.8 percent ROI is generated:

- Only using the monetary benefits accrued in the six months immediately after the program, for each participant
- Only 27 out of the 78 participants had data available to contribute to the ROI analysis

From this, the business can easily see that the benefits from the program have been realized and the investment is worthwhile.

This can also be expressed as a benefit-cost ratio:

$$\text{BCR} = \frac{\text{Monetary Benefits}}{\text{Total Program Costs}}$$

$$\text{BCR} = \frac{\$469,397}{\$333,326} = 1.40:1$$

Communication Strategy

Due to an internal change in the head of the training department, it was important that ownership was taken for communicating the results to the business. The thoroughness and commitment of the training department to take the program to the level of ROI demonstrated that they were serious in wanting to make a real return to the business and were very conscious of business costs.

The department head communicated the results on a one-on-one basis to the key stakeholders involved and got their buy-in for the figures and the process. The report was received positively; but more importantly, the commitment to measurement set a new benchmark for the department.

Post-ROI Analysis

Another automotive company department that is running a new recruitment process has asked for an ROI project to measure the effectiveness of the new process to be rolled out during the second half of 2012.

Lessons Learned

The client was pleased with the study and outcome; however, with the benefit of hindsight two changes would be made for similar studies in future:

1. The comparison control group of the total company comparison wasn't ideal; for future programs we would try and isolate a smaller control group of a similar size and geographic location of the group attending the program. In addition, where sales consultants didn't have any sales history prior to attending the program, these participants would be matched with those of equal tenure in a control group.
2. In the costs section of the analysis, no costs were attributed to the ROI analysis itself; in future programs this would need to be budgeted for and included in the fully loaded costs.

Questions for Discussion

1. What, if anything, could have been done to make the control group arrangement more reliable?
2. Telephone coaching was used in this study and helped achieve a high response rate. Could this be feasible in your organization? Why or why not?
3. Why do you think the clients had such a favorable reaction to the dashboards? To whom should these dashboards be presented?
4. Only six months of data were used in the analysis. Should a year of data be used? Why or why not?
5. Do you have enough data to fully understand the monetary benefits? If not, what do you need?

Chapter 23

Measuring ROI in Simulation-Based Sales Training

Future-Tel

by Claude MacDonald and Louis Larochelle

Future-Tel, a national telecom company in Canada, invited TalentPlus, a professional services firm specializing in business development, to develop and deploy a unique simulation-based training program. The one-day training activity, called The Solution Challenge, was aimed at enhancing the way Future-Tel's 560 sales professionals go about selling solutions to their clients. Specifically the training program had to enhance three key competencies: 1) the ability to create value through skillful questioning; 2) the ability to qualify major opportunities and decide if they are worth pursuing; and 3) the ability to build strong business proposals.

The training program was also aimed at testing, honing, and developing people's knowledge of Future-Tel's solution portfolio as well as the key vertical markets their clients evolve in.

To evaluate the effect and profitability of the project, Future-Tel asked TalentPlus to conduct a Level 5 ROI study. Therefore, data on reaction, learning, application, business impact, as well as intangible benefits were collected during and after the training activities. After isolation of the effects and conversion of data to monetary value, the ROI study showed that each dollar invested in the training program brought back $1.42 in sales revenues for Future-Tel.

BACKGROUND

Future-Tel is a major Canadian telecommunications company offering a wide variety of IT and telecom solutions to private and public organizations across the country. Future-Tel has also developed industry-leading telecom consulting expertise and has adopted industry-recognized assessment tools in order to measure, understand, refine, and fully implement "best practices."

Thirty years of experience has enabled Future-Tel to build strong alliances with all major hardware and software manufacturers, including IBM, HP, Cisco, and Microsoft. The company has also forged partnerships with smaller, more specialized IT companies. Those partnerships allow Future-Tel to offer a broad solutions portfolio through its sales force.

Program Description

After observing a decline in sales results, Future-Tel initiated a major reorganization that led to the creation of a new entity: The Future-Tel Business Market Group. The strategic objective of this new group was to improve operational efficiency and enhance customer intimacy.

As part of the overall strategy to accomplish this goal, Future-Tel decided to enhance the competencies of its sales professionals. In this context it was decided to provide all sales professionals with a Solution Selling Training Program.

A survey was conducted by the sales effectiveness team to understand what Solution Selling meant for Future-Tel's professionals. Most expressed the importance of understanding and meeting the requirements in their specific vertical markets, such as health, government, financial services, retail, and others. The data from this survey allowed the sales effectiveness team to identify the following key learning objectives with regards to the training program:

- Improve teamwork among sales representatives.
- Develop people's business acumen.
- Develop and refine vertical market knowledge.
- Improve knowledge of the Future-Tel solutions portfolio.
- Develop skills to understand the client's business challenges.
- Develop skills regarding the design and delivery of complex solutions.

In light of Future-Tel's requirements and challenges, TalentPlus was chosen to develop a one-day program, called The Solution Challenge Sales Simulator, a game-based approach that allows acceleration of learning and increases the retention rate of participants.

Three hundred twenty-one (321) individuals, including 308 sales professionals, took part in the program. The training was structured as follows:

Part 1 (2 hours):
- Vertical forum:
  - Most important drivers (four or five) of the vertical markets clients evolve in
  - Identification of current projects that focus on such drivers
  - Presentation by each team

Part 2 (5.5 hours):
- The Solution Challenge Sales Simulator, as shown in Figure 23-1

Figure 23-1. The Solution Challenge Sales Simulator

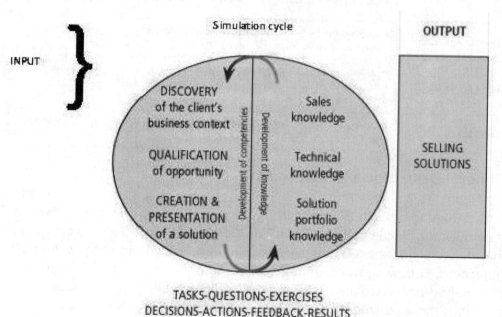

Evaluation Methodology

In order to validate the relevance and profitability of the training program offered to Future-Tel's sales representatives and solutions specialists, TalentPlus suggested conducting an impact study.

The Phillips ROI Methodology was selected due to its proven and documented use. This approach produces six types of data: reaction, learning, application, business impact, ROI, and intangible benefits.

Also, the methodology uses a systematic logic model to collect, analyze, and report data. Along the way, the process is guided by 12 conservative standards.

The levels of data captured by the ROI Methodology are listed in Table 23-1.

Table 23-1. Levels of Data

Level 1: Reaction	• Measures the participants' reactions to training. • Data captured at the end of the session.
Level 2: Learning	• Measures the participants' level of retention. • Data captured at the end of the session and validated in the application survey.
Level 3: Application	• Assesses the frequency of use of what was learned. • Data captured via an online survey, 60 to 90 days after the training.
Level 4: Impact	• Measures variations on KPIs (revenues, margins, etc.) • Data captured via an online survey and through client database, 120 to 180 days after the training.
Level 5: ROI	• Measures the actual ROI, by comparing the net monetary contribution of the training program against its fully loaded costs.

General Description Of Approach

Figure 23-2 shows that the ROI Methodology was integrated into the entire training project. Before starting the design of the training content, a meeting took place between TalentPlus CRP's and Future-Tel's stakeholders in order to align (phase 1) the client business objectives and the evaluation objectives. Following the alignment meeting, a data collection plan and an ROI analysis plan were produced and then validated by Future-Tel. Table 23-2 describes the assessment levels.

During the skill-building phase, 24 training sessions (one day) took place. At the end of each training session, the participants, the most credible source of data, had to complete two questionnaires to assess Levels 1 and 2.

Sixty days after the completion of data collection at Levels 1 and 2, each sales professional who attended the one-day training session had to complete a Level 3 survey. The collected data allowed assessment of what extent the salespeople were using the knowledge acquired during their one-day training session. In addition, after 120 days, the sales professionals were given a business impact questionnaire (Level 4) to verify if the changes in terms of attitude and behavior were maintained. This questionnaire also allowed collection of information on predefined key performance indices (KPI).

Figure 23-2. Evaluation Methodology

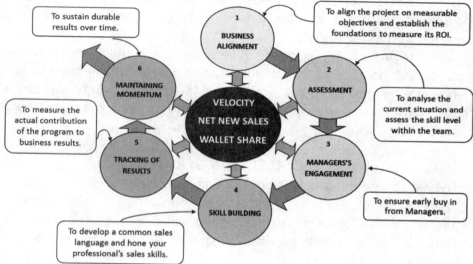

Table 23-2. Desired Outcomes

Level 5	Desired ROI	What kind of ROI is required from this project?
Level 4	Desired business impact	To achieve the ROI target, what business impact is required?
Level 3	Behavior outcomes	To get business impact, what kind of behaviors need to change?
Level 2	Learning outcomes	To change those behaviors, what must people learn?
Level 1	Reaction outcomes	To drive learning, what kind of reactions must we provoke?

At the end of the training program, Future-Tel granted TalentPlus access to its business results database. Performance indicators such as average revenue per closed sale, number of opportunities closed with their dollar amounts, and sales cycle duration were observed.

To calculate a conservative and precise ROI, one KPI was selected: revenue increase. It was decided to measure the difference between the total sales revenues won by Future-Tel nine months before the training sessions and nine months after the training program.

In order to isolate the effects of the program, the participants were asked to estimate in percentage the actual impact of the training on their sales results as well as their level of confidence in their evaluation. This provides the actual contribution of the program.

The revenue increase measured was then multiplied by the actual contribution to assess the portion of revenue increase that could be associated to the training program.

Finally, in order to be as conservative as possible, the ROI was measured by comparing the costs of the program to the net profit generated through the revenue increase. The net profit considered in this study was chosen based on the lowest net margins observed in Future-Tel's annual reports over the last three years.

DATA COLLECTION STRATEGY

The data collection plan was developed following the alignment meeting between TalentPlus CRP's and Future-Tel stakeholders. Table 23-3 shows an abstract of the data collection plan, which details objectives at all levels, the measures, source, and collection method of data, as well as the timeline and responsibility for collection.

Level 1 data were captured through a satisfaction questionnaire completed at the end of the training session. Figure 23-3 shows an example of the questionnaire. Participants were asked to rate each statement from one to four, with one being "strongly disagree" and four being "strongly agree."

ROI ANALYSIS STRATEGY

Table 23-4 shows the ROI analysis plan for the project, which gives a guideline for measuring ROI. It features the Level 4 Impact measures, the method used to isolate the effect on the data, the method of converting the data to monetary values, categories of costs, intangible benefits, and the targets for communication of results.

Figure 23-3. Satisfaction Questionnaire (*continued*)

Trainer: _____   Date: _____

Name (Optional): _____

Title (Optional): _____

Thank you for taking the time to complete this questionnaire. The information we collect will enable us to assess the real impact of this training activity on the business objectives.

Your Reactions:

Indicate on a scale of 1 to 4 if you agree with the following staatements
(4=Strongly Agree, 3=Agree, 2=Disagree, 1=Strongly Disagree)

Statement		Score			
		4	3	2	1
1	I have acuired new knowledge or additional information in this training activity.				
2	I intend to use what I learned in this training activity.				
3	I would recommend this training activity to my colleagues.				
4	I will be able to apply what I learned in this training activity				

Enablers

Among the following, identify at least three elements that could facilitate or help you with the implementation of the knowledge and skills acquired during the training activity.

- Support from my supervisor to sustain the implementation of my knowledge
- Additional training on the same subject
- Coaching
- Increased support from the specialist in charge of my vertical
- Better teamwork
- Other: _____

_____

_____

Your comments and suggestions are appreciated: _____

_____

_____

Table 23-3. Data Collection Plan

Level	Program Objectives	Measures	Data Collection Method	Data Source	Calendar	Responsibility
1	**Reaction and Perceived Value** • Check whether the participants said they gained additional knowledge and information through the training (target=80%).	• Percentage of participants who report having gained new knowledge. Scale of 0 to 100%.	• Satisfaction questionnaire	• Participants	• End of each training session	• TalentPlus
	• Estimate the number of participants intending to use the knowledge gained (target=80%).	• Percentage of participants who said they plan to use the knowledge gained. Scale of 0 to 100%.	• Satisfaction questionnaire	• Participants	• End of each training session	• TalentPlus
	• Assess how many participants intend to recommend the activity to others.	• Percentage of participants who intend to recommend the activity. Scale of 0 to 100%.	• Satisfaction questionnaire	• Participants	• End of each training session	• TalentPlus
	• Identify elements that could prevent participants from implementing the objectives of the activity.	• Percentage of participants who indicate that the activity is highly relevant. Scale of 0 to 100%.	• Satisfaction questionnaire	• Participants	• End of each training session	• TalentPlus
2	**Learning and Confidence** • Assess whether the participants know how to apply what they learned (target=80%).	• Percentage of participants who know how to apply what they learned. Scale of 0 to 100%.	• Satisfaction questionnaire	• Participants	• End of each training session	• TalentPlus
	• Evaluate the level of retention of key concepts by participants (target = average results of 80%).	• 5 questions measuring the level of understanding of 5 key concepts.	• Learning questionnaire	• Participants	• End of each training session	• TalentPlus
	• Evaluate the level of concepts by participants (target = average results of 80%).	• 3 questions measuring the level of retention about 3 key concepts.	• Application questionnaire	• Participants	• 45-60 days after the training session	• TalentPlus

Table 23-3. Data Collection Plan (*continued*)

3	Application and Implementation				
	• Check if participants use recently learned techniques such as 6P methodology, the 5 strategies, and the MARS methodology (target = 80%).	• The percentage of participants who use techniques they learned. Likert scale going from strongly agree to strongly disagree.	• Application questionnaire	• Participants	• 45-60 days after the training session	• TalentPlus
	• Evaluate to what extent the training has helped develop the participants' skills to hold professional conversations that enhance their business acumen and their industry knowledge (target = 80% agreeing).	• Percentage of participants who say that the training helped develop this skill. Likert scale going from strongly agree to strongly disagree.	• Application questionnaire	• Participants	• 45-60 days after the training session	• TalentPlus
	• Evaluate to what extent the training has prompted the participants to offer comprehensive solutions (multiple products or services) to their customers (target = 80% agreeing).	• The percentage of participants who say that the training prompted them. Likert scale going from strongly agree to strongly disagree.	• Application questionnaire	• Participants	• 45-60 days after the training session	• TalentPlus
	• Identify which training content has the greatest impact on the respondents' ability to hold quality business conversations, to qualify opportunities, and to prepare high-quality business presentations.	• Multiple choices related to key training concepts.	• Application questionnaire	• Participants	• 45-60 days after the training session	• TalentPlus
	• Identify the factors that could prevent the implementation of knowledge and skills acquired during the training activity.	• Multiple choices, with "other" option.	• Application questionnaire	• Participants	• 45-60 days after the training session	• TalentPlus

Table 23-3. Data Collection Plan (continued)

	• Identify the factors that could facilitate the implementation of knowledge and skills acquired during the training activity.	• Multiple choices, with "other" option.	• Application questionnaire	• Participants	• 45-60 days after the training session	• TalentPlus
	• Assess the frequency of use of the newly acquired knowledge (at least a few times a month = 80%).	• The frequency of use of the new knowledge. Likert scale: never, once per month, a few times per month, multiple times per week.	• Impact questionnaire	• Participants	• 90 days after the training session	• TalentPlus
4	**Impacts and Consequences** • Assess the variation of sales revenues before and after the training program.	• $ values	• CRM	• Finance department	• Monthly reports for 2009 and 2010	• Future-Tel: Steve Thomas
5	**ROI** 25% ROI					

Table 23-4. ROI Analysis Plan

Data Element	Isolation Method	Conversion Method	Costs Categories	Intangible Benefits	Communication Target	Other Influence or Problem
Sales revenues	1. Participants' estimate: • A. How much impact did the Solution Challenge training activity have on your sales funnel since the training activity? (Scale 0 to 100%) • B. How much confidence (in %) do you have in your estimate? Average of A x B = Project's Level of Impact 2. Seasonality: Historic of variation of sales per month in percentage	• Standard • Value – profit margin • Internal experts	• External services • Salaries and benefits of the project team, participants, and other employees • Introduction video • Printing and reproduction	• Better preparation for business presentation • Better team work • Greater capability to discover client's concerns	• Project team • Executives	N/A

OBSERVATIONS AND CAPTURED DATA

Reaction (Level 1) Data

Reaction and learning data were captured immediately following each training session. The participants were first given a satisfaction questionnaire. The overall results obtained for all 312 participants (sales representatives) are shown in Table 23-5. The reaction results from the 312 participants surpassed expectations. The objective had been set for each question at 80 percent.

Table 23-5. Reaction Data: Percentage of Participants Who Agree or Strongly Agree

Questions	Score
I have acquired new knowledge or additional information in this training activity.	98%
I intend to use what I learned in this training activity.	98%
I would recommend this training activity to my colleagues.	96%
I will be able to apply what I learned in this training activity.	98%

Here are a few examples of comments received during the reaction level evaluation:

- "The course was challenging and exceeded expectations. We were challenged to think on our feet and provide responses to situations in 10 or 15 minutes. That was a great way to make the course relevant to real life."
- "I believe the 6Ps can be an effective tool for pre-call planning."
- "Great training session! I really enjoyed the 6P approach—very thorough and applicable."

Learning (Level 2) Data

As shown in Table 23-6, a knowledge assessment questionnaire was used immediately following the training to measure the participants' level of retention of the key concepts.

Table 23-6. Learning Data (Immediately Following the Training)

Number of Questions Answered Correctly	% of Teams that Answered Adequately
5/5	93%
4/5	7%
3/5	
2/5	
1/5	

In order to verify the participants' retention of the key concepts 60 days after the training, three knowledge assessment questions were included in the application questionnaire. Note that 312 questionnaires were sent and 164 of them were completed. Table 23-7 presents the overall results obtained from the respondents in percentage.

Table 23-7. Learning Data (60 Days after the Training)

Questions	Results
Name at least 4 key drivers related to your market that have been presented during the Sales Simulator training session.	79% of respondents gave 4 good answers out of 4 for this question.
Name the 5 strategies that can be adopted to push forward an opportunity.	89% of respondents gave 5 good answers out of 5 for this question.
Name the 4 components of the MARS method that allow preparing a strong business presentation.	92% of respondents gave 4 good answers out 4 for this question.

Application (Level 3) Data

As shown in Table 23-8, the application level data were gathered 60 days after each training session. The questions asked were identical for all respondents.

Table 23-8. Application Questionnaire

Questions	Results
The Sales Simulator training activity has helped develop my skills to hold professional conversations that show my business acumen and my industry knowledge.	24% Strongly agreed 64% Agreed **Total in agreement 88%**
The Sales Simulator training activity prompted me to offer comprehensive solutions (multiple products or services) to my customers.	17% Strongly agreed 56% Agreed **Total in agreement 73%**
I have used or I intend to use in the near future the 6P Methodology (Perspective and Planning, Projects and Preoccupation, etc.) to improve the way I uncover my clients' business concerns and expectations.	15% Strongly agreed 61% Agreed **Total in agreement 76%**
I have used or I intend to use in the near future one or several of the 5 strategies (frontal, lateral, etc.) to move forward one or many opportunities.	24% Strongly agreed 52% Agreed **Total in agreement 76%**
I have used or I intend to use in the near future the MARS Methodology (Message, Audience, etc.) to prepare one or more business presentations.	29% Strongly agreed 49% Agreed **Total in agreement 78%**

The application questionnaire also identified which key concepts taught to participants had the most impact on their ability to hold quality business conversations, to qualify opportunities, and to prepare high quality business presentations, as shown in Table 23-9.

Table 23-9. Key Concepts with the Most Impact

Rank	Content
1	Increased knowledge of my vertical market's key drivers
2	Opportunity qualification evaluation grid
3 - Tie	5 strategies related to the pursuit of opportunities
3 - Tie	6P Methodology
5	MARS Methodology
6	VCC principle (Value Creation Capability)

Barriers and Enablers

The application questionnaire also captured potential barriers that could hinder the use of the training content. Multiple answers were allowed. Potential enablers were also captured, such as elements that could facilitate the implementation of knowledge and skills acquired during the training activity. Multiple answers were allowed. Note that 96 people out of 185 respondents to this precise question gave the answer "none" (meaning no barrier).

Figure 23-4. Barriers to Implementation

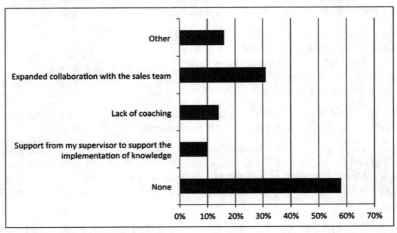

Potential enablers were also captured, such as elements that could facilitate the implementation of knowledge and skills acquired during the training activity. Multiple answers were allowed. Note that 216 people out of 312 participants gave the answer "better teamwork."

Figure 23-5. Enablers to Success

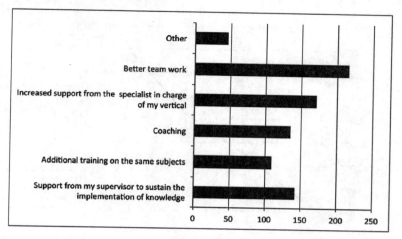

Business Impact (Level 4) Data

The business impact of the project was measured using three methods:

- A questionnaire to isolate the effects of the training solution
- A questionnaire on actual usage of the training content
- An in-depth study of Future-Tel's customer relationship management (CRM) database.

Isolating the Effects of the Program. To assess the contribution the program had on sales revenue, each respondent had to answer two questions:

- How much impact did the Sales Simulator training activity have on your sales since the session (e.g., 20%)?
- How much confidence do you have in your estimate (e.g., 60%)?

Both answers were multiplied (20% x 60% = 12%) for each participant and then an average was calculated using the results from all participants. This approach is recognized by ROI Institute as an effective method to isolate the effects of a training solution. Overall, 312 questionnaires were sent and 227 were returned, representing a 65 percent response rate.

The collected data shows that participants who confirm the program significantly contributed to their sales are those who most often use the techniques learned. Figure 23-6 shows that the more a sales representative uses the techniques, the higher the contribution percentage was.

Figure 23-6. Content Usage Frequency

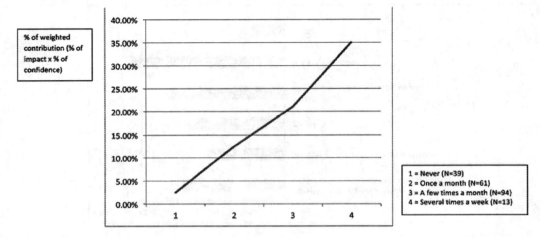

% of weighted contribution (% of impact x % of confidence)

1 = Never (N=39)
2 = Once a month (N=61)
3 = A few times a month (N=94)
4 = Several times a week (N=13)

After the calculation of the contribution given by each participant, it appeared that the average contribution was 15.6 percent.

The application/impact questionnaire shown in Table 23-10 was used to obtain each participant's estimate regarding the contribution of the Sales Simulator program to their sales. It also assessed the usage frequency of specific techniques taught during the training. Please note that 312 questionnaires were sent and 204 of them were completed.

The CRM database was analyzed using the following methodology:

- Sales volume (opportunities closed and won revenues) analysis according to Table 23-11.
- Investigation of the seasonality in the sales cycle over the course of a complete year and reduction of the contribution accordingly.

Since the actual contribution of the Sales Simulator training program on revenue is 15.6 percent, the actual contribution of the Sales Simulator training program is:

$39,870,785.68 x 15.6% = $6,299,584
in additional revenue attributed to the program.

Table 23-10. Application/Impact Data Questionnaire (120 Days after the Training)

Questions	Results
How often have you used the 6P Methodology (Power and People, Projects and Preoccupation, etc.) to uncover your clients' concerns and expectations?	80% of respondents use the 6P Methodology at least once a month to discover their customers' requirements and challenges.
How often have you used the MARS Methodology (Message, Audience, etc.) to prepare a business presentation?	79% of respondents use the MARS Methodology at least once a month to prepare a business presentation.
How often have you used the 5 commercial strategies (frontal, lateral, etc.) to move an opportunity forward?	78% of respondents use the 5 commercial strategies at least once a month to move opportunities forward.

Table 23-11. Won Revenues: Before vs. After (from CRM database)

Director of Sales	CRM Closed Won Revenues Before	CRM Closed Won Revenues After	Variation
Director 1	$26,868,761.85	$15,377,730.51	($11,491,031.34)
Director 2	$13,747,394.63	$28,988,430.62	$15,241,035.99
Director 3	$13,900,757.10	$15,333,933.34	$1,433,176.24
Director 4	$22,071,110.74	$20,908,274.90	($1,162,835.83)
Director 5	$18,118,868.35	$18,497,932.45	$379,064.10
Director 6	$15,172,906.14	$30,115,566.87	$14,942,660.74
Director 7	$6,816,578.26	$10,948,935.45	$4,132,357.19
Director 8	$22,068,795.45	$33,949,732.24	$11,880,936.79
Director 9	$17,142,327.16	$23,464,606.08	$6,322,278.91
Director 10	$9,887,337.21	$7,528,824.48	($2,358,512.73)
Director 11	$19,220,684.40	$31,978,905.88	$12,758,221.48
Director 12	$17,425,731.21	$20,029,077.99	$2,603,346.78
Director 13	$10,938,664.41	$12,620,177.63	$1,681,513.23
Director 14	$40,183,349.32	$22,054,822.13	($18,128,527.19)
Director 15	$10,082,033.32	$11,719,134.64	$1,637,101.33
TOTAL	$263,645,299.53	$303,516,085.21	$39,870,785.68

Conversion Methodology. In order to be as conservative as possible, it was decided with Future-Tel's CFO to use the net contribution of the project as the number to be compared to costs.

Using Future-Tel annual reports of the last three years, the lowest net profit over the three years was 9.8 percent.

- 2009 Operating Revenues: $17.735 million
- 2009 Net Earnings: $1.738 million
- 2009 Net Profit Margin: 9.8 percent

Therefore the real contribution of the Sales Simulator program is:

additional revenues attributed to the program x net profit margin
$6,299,584 x 9.8% = $617,359

Fully-Loaded Costs

In order to calculate a credible ROI, all costs associated to the program were calculated. Table 23-12 provides a detailed description of these costs.

Table 23-12. Fully Loaded Costs of the Sales Simulator Program

Analysis Cost	
Salaries and benefits – Future-Tel team members	$4,125
Total Analysis Cost	**$4,125**
Development Cost	
Salaries and benefits – Future-Tel team members Salaries and benefits –	$8,000
Other Future-Tel employees	$10,000
Printing and reproduction	$200
Introduction video	$5,300
Total Development Cost	**$23,500**
Delivery Cost	
Salaries and benefits – Future-Tel team members	$30,000
Salaries and benefits – Participants	$150,000
Salaries and benefits – Other Future-Tel employees	$800
Meals, travel, and incidental expenses – Participants	$15,125
External services	$160,000
Facility costs	$4,500
Total Delivery Cost	**$360,425**
Evaluation Cost	
Salaries and benefits – Future-Tel team members	$4,125
Printing and reproduction	$50
Total Evaluation Cost	**$4,175**
Total Program Cost	**$392,225**

The fully loaded cost that will be used to calculate the ROI of the program will therefore be $392,225.

ROI Calculation

The ROI calculation requires several data. Here are the different variables calculated until now:

- Total variation (before and after) of opportunities closed and won revenue = $39,870,785.68
- Estimated contribution by participants = 15.6%
- Additional revenues attributed to the program = $39,870,785.68 x 15.6% = $6,299,584
- Profit added = $6,299,584 x 9.8% = $617,359
- Fully loaded cost of the Sales Simulator training program = $392,225

ROI calculation based on real monetary benefits and fully loaded cost:

$$\text{BCR (Benefit-Cost Ratio)} = \frac{\text{Benefits}}{\text{Costs}} = \frac{\$617,359}{\$392\ 225} = 1.57:1$$

$$\text{ROI (Return on Investment)} = \frac{\$617,359 - \$392,225}{\$392,225} \times 100\% = 57.4\%$$

Consequently, each $1 invested in the Sales Simulator program created a return on investment (ROI) of $1.57.

To compensate for seasonal variations in sales, we also calculated the ROI based on adjusted revenues. Using financial data provided by Future-Tel's CFO, a negative variation rate of 9.7 percent was calculated. Consequently, the real contribution of the Sales Simulator program becomes:

$$\$617,359 \times (1 - 0.097) = \$557,475.$$

ROI calculation with adjusted revenue according to sales seasonality:

$$\text{BCR (Benefit-Cost Ratio)} = \frac{\text{Benefits}}{\text{Costs}} = \frac{\$557,475}{\$392,225} = 1.42:1$$

$$\text{ROI} = \frac{\$557,475 - \$392,225}{\$392\ 225} \times 100\% = 42.1\%$$

Consequently, each $1 invested in the Sales Simulator program created a return on investment (ROI) of $1.42 (adjusted for seasonal variations).

Intangible Benefits

The intangible benefits were also captured throughout the impact study. Figure 23-7 presents the intangible benefits identified by the participants (multiple answers were allowed).

Note that four of the intangible benefits obtained over 40 percent of support. They are:

- Better preparation for business presentation
- Better teamwork
- Greater capability to discover clients' concerns
- Higher capacity to create value for clients

Figure 23-7. Intangible Benefits

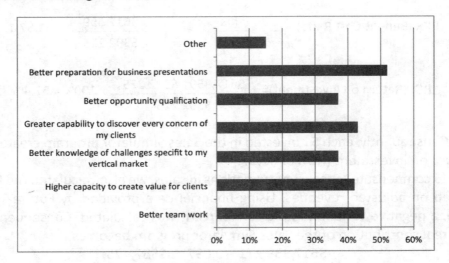

CONCLUSIONS

A High Retention Level Yields a High Impact on Sales

Some learning level questions were included in the application level questionnaire, in order to verify the participants' level of retention regarding specific concepts. The results obtained were very revealing. As proof, it appears that the questions that received the highest scores overall were about market knowledge and business opportunity development strategies.

In addition, the same application questionnaire revealed that both of these concepts were identified by the respondents as having had the greatest impact on their work. As shown in Table 23-13, it can be concluded that there is a strong correlation between the elements that had the greatest level of retention and those that had the most impact on business development.

This shows the importance of measuring the retention level immediately after the training sessions as well as other amounts of time after. Both sets of data show a strong correlation with the content elements that have the most impact for the participants.

Table 23-13. Retention of Key Concepts

Rank	Key Concepts with Highest Impact	% of Retention About Key Concepts
1	Increased knowledge of my vertical market's key drivers	79% of sales representatives gave 4 over 4 good answers regarding 4 key drivers related to the vertical market
2	Opportunity qualification evaluation grid	N/A
3 -Tie	5 strategies related to the pursuit of opportunities	89% of sales representatives gave 5 over 5 good answers regarding 5 strategies to push an opportunity
3 -Tie	6P Methodology	N/A
4	MARS Methodology	92% of sales representatives gave 4 over 4 good answers regarding 4 MARSs communication method components allowing to prepare a business presentation
5	VCC principle (Value Creation Capability)	N/A

A Strong Correlation Exists Between Actual Usage and Contribution to Sales

The application level questions verified to what extent the participants had used or planned to use the key techniques and strategies taught during the training session. It appears that more than three fourths (75 percent) of the respondents confirm they use or plan to use these techniques.

In addition, the objective of the impact level questionnaire was to assess the usage frequency of the same techniques found in the application questionnaire. The analysis results indicate that more than 50 percent of respondents confirm that they use these techniques at least once a month.

As demonstrated in Figure 23-8, there is a strong correlation between the use of acquired knowledge and usage frequency.

Figure 23-8. Content Usage Frequency

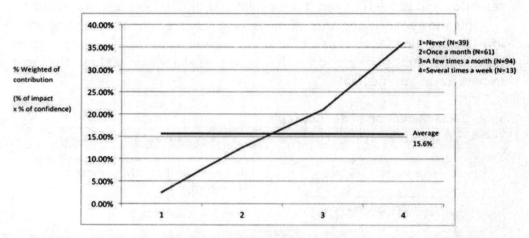

Several Teams Have Taken Ownership of The Content Elements

The results of the Level 4 questionnaire show that the Sales Simulator program contributed a 15.6 percent increase in sales. A more in-depth analysis of the contribution percentage for each director of sales reveals that the contribution percentage varies greatly among them. The assumption can therefore be made that certain senior managers have assumed ownership of key techniques and strategies taught and have integrated them in their business processes more than others.

The assumption can also be made that certain groups felt that the contents of the program were more applicable to their situation (specifically when all the participants were from the same vertical market and worked only in this vertical market).

The Data Show a Clear Chain of Impact

The analysis carried out on the Sales Simulator program has a very clear chain of impact between the reaction, application, and impact levels.

- The results from the reaction questionnaire revealed that 98 percent of the participants confirm having the intention of using the knowledge acquired during the training in conjunction with their work.

- The results from the application level questionnaire indicate that a high proportion (about 78 percent) of the participants use or plan to use three of the most important techniques taught during Sales Simulator.
- The results from the impact level questionnaire reveal that the majority of respondents confirm they use these same techniques at least once per month (79 percent).

In spite of a high usage rate for the concepts taught, the chain of impact shows a gradual decrease in enthusiasm among the people trained regarding the training contents. It would therefore be important to examine the ways of maintaining momentum and encouraging the use of the training's contents.

The Absence of Barriers Correlates with Greater Use

The application level questionnaire reveals that 52 percent of respondents do not see any barriers to implementation of the knowledge acquired during Sales Simulator. Moreover, the impact level questionnaire shows that more than 79 percent of respondents use the key techniques taught during the training at least once a month. It is therefore very probable that those who do not see any barriers to implementation are those who actually use the knowledge acquired and who grant a higher percentage of contribution.

Teamwork: Mission Accomplished

One of the Sales Simulator program's objectives was to encourage teamwork. Consequently, multidisciplinary teams across specific vertical markets were formed in order to achieve this objective. The importance of teamwork was also answered in various questionnaires. The results obtained are quite revealing:

- The reaction level questionnaire reveals that 67 percent of the participants say that teamwork is a major facilitating element with respect to the implementation of the knowledge acquired.
- The results from the application questionnaire show that teamwork is the second highest intangible benefit (48 percent) resulting from the Sales Simulator training.

These two observations confirm the initial strategy regarding the formation of groups was good. Furthermore, should other similar business transformation projects be initiated, in our opinion Future-Tel would benefit, from repeating this strategy.

The Content Was Not Only Useful But Very Relevant

The analysis of results from the application rates reveals that 78 percent of respondents say they use or plan to use the 6P and MARS techniques. A few eloquent testimonials prove the usefulness of these techniques. In fact, the use of the MARS technique helped to reactivate and conclude an important multimillion project with a major account. According to the testimonial, the project had been dragging for a while and the MARS technique enabled implementation of the strategy needed to provoke action from the client. This kind of data shows the relevance and effectiveness of the techniques and strategies taught during the Sales Simulator program.

Application of Content Yields Business Results

The majority of participants confirm having acquired useful knowledge. This correlates with the application data that shows usage rates of up to 78 percent. When asked how much the program contributed to their sales results, overall contribution is 15.6 percent, which is considered very good for a one-day training program. Moreover, the 42 percent ROI shows that the techniques used contributed to improving sales within the Future-Tel business market group.

Finally, 73 percent confirm that it did contribute to increasing the number of offers of more complex solutions. Please note that the initial objective was set at 80 percent. It would therefore be important to offer effective means of encouraging the use of the techniques taught and of convincing the participants of their effectiveness.

Questions for Discussion

1. Should all training programs related to business development or sales be submitted to an ROI study?
2. To what extent is it important to adjust revenue variation according to seasonality of the business?
3. What is the actual impact on the study when scorecards are created and presented to senior management on a regular basis?
4. What is the correlation between the size of a company and the need to measure the outcome of projects?

Chapter 24

Measuring ROI in
Selling Skills

McArthur Sp. z.o.o.

by Malgorzata Mitoraj-Jarosek

This case study is a description of an ROI project based on sales training targeted at retail sales assistants in a chain of shoe stores in Poland. A trend analysis was used as a method of isolating the effects of training. The sales training brought overall positive results.

BACKGROUND INFORMATION

McArthur Sp. z.o.o. is a medium-sized trading company, with a network of several shoe shops in large shopping centers in Poland. The senior management felt that the current level of sales was unsatisfactory. In addition to implementing a sales training program, the company conducted a series of mystery shopper surveys to assess the level of customer service and found the results to be very negative.

The Solution

It was acknowledged that there was an obvious sales training need for store managers, assistant store managers, and sales assistants. The sales training was conducted in nine stores and included the following topic areas: customer service standards, making contact with prospective customers, diagnosing customer needs, offering a solution (i.e., making a shoe presentation), presenting benefits, handling objectives, and closing the sale. In addition, to support and encourage the development of selling skills, managers and assistant store managers took part in tailor-made coaching training. In all, there were 45 participants in the training. Fortnightly, managers were asked to complete a competency assessment sheet for each of their staff members, and send it to the head office for verification by the sales and marketing director. After completing the observation sheet, the managers were asked to conduct coaching meetings with each of their staff members. The whole coaching process took three months.

The Measurement Challenge

The guidelines from the senior management were very clear, the aim was to raise the level of sales. To measure the effectiveness of the challenge, the ROI Methodology from the ROI Institute was applied. The process consisted of six areas of measurement: reaction and planned action, learning, application and implementation, business impact, ROI, and intangible measures.

The process includes a comprehensive plan for data collection and analysis, as shown in Figure 24-1. It contains steps leading up to the calculation of ROI, starting from evaluation planning and including types of information needed at each level of evaluation. To complete the process at Level 4, an analysis of intangible benefits is also carried out.

PLANNING FOR ROI

One of the important elements of the ROI evaluation is evaluation planning. Two key documents were used: the data collection plan and the ROI analysis plan.

Data Collection Plan

Figure 24-2 shows a completed data collection plan for this project, including all stages of the planning process and data collection. The objectives at Level 1 were identified as: participants indicate a positive response to the training program and complete an action plan at the end of training. The satisfaction level for this objective was a rating between 4.0 and 5.0 on a 5-point scale.

The objectives at Level 2 aimed to check the level of sales skills acquired during the training. At the end of the training, the trainer assessed all participants by a means of a pass or fail aptitude test focusing on the skills practiced. Over 80 percent of the participants passed the test.

At Level 3, two means of evaluation were implemented. The sales assistants were evaluated every two weeks by their managers or by the assistant store managers with a yes-or-no observation checklist for a period of three months. The satisfaction level was set at the implementation level of 80 percent of learned skills in the sales assistants' daily work. In addition, information regarding the implementation of skills was also verified by a mystery shopper survey.

The business impact expected was sales growth, monitored throughout a period of three months after the training was completed. The results of the ROI calculation were expected to be 50 percent.

The data collection plan was a crucial part of the evaluation strategy. It allowed for a very clear outline in terms of the types of information needed, how the data should be collected, and when and by whom it should be collected.

ROI Analysis Plan

The ROI analysis plan was also important to the evaluation. As shown in Figure 24-3, the ROI analysis plan shows how to analyze data at Level 4 (business impact) and convert it to money so a credible ROI calculation can be achieved.

Figure 24-1. ROI Methodology ™

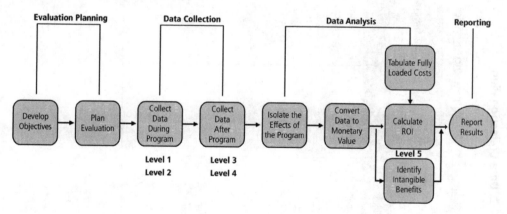

Figure 24-2. Data Collection Plan

Program: <u>Selling Skills</u>   Purpose: <u>Increase Sales Results</u>   Responsibility: <u>Malgorzata Mitoraj-Jaroszek</u>   Date: <u>15.04.2011</u>

Data Items (Usually Level 4)	Methods for Isolating the Effects of the Program/Process	Methods of Converting Data to Monetary Values	Cost Categories	Intangible Benefits	Communication Targets for Final Report	Other Influences/ Issues During Application
• Increase in Sales	• Trend Analysis	• Standard value/ profit margin	• Facilitators fees • Program materials • Meals and refreshments • Participant salaries and benefits • Cost coordination and evaluation • Mystery shopper	• Customer Satisfaction	• Program participants • Sales managers • Store managers • Training staff	• N/A

Figure 24-3. ROI Analysis Plan

Program: <u>Selling Skills</u>   Purpose: <u>Increase Sales Results</u>   Responsibility: <u>Małgorzata Mitoraj-Jaroszek</u>   Date: <u>15.04.2011</u>

Level	Program Objectives	Measures	Data Collection Method/Instruments	Data Sources	Timing	Responsibility
1	SATISFACTION/PLANNED ACTION • Positive reaction – four or five • Action plan for store managers	• Rating on a composite of five measures	• Questionnaire	• Participants	• End of program	• Facilitator
2	LEARNING • Shop Assistants: needs analysis skills, handling customer objectives, closing the sale, applying customer service standards • Store Manager: selling, coaching	• Pass or fail on skills practiced	• Test	• Participants	• End of program	• Facilitator
3	APPLICATION/IMPLEMENTATION • Use customer service standards on the job • 80% of shop assistants apply sales techniques • Shop managers apply and use coaching	• Yes-or-no scale • Checklist for observation	• Mystery shopper • Observation	• Manager • Mystery shopper	• Every 2weeks after the training or a period of 3 months • 3 months after the training	• Małgorzata
4	BUSINESS IMPACT • Increase in sales • Intangible measures: customer satisfaction	• Weekly average sales per store	• Business performance monitoring	• Company System	• 3 months after program	• Head of sales
5	ROI • 50%	Comments:				

RESULTS

Reaction and Learning

All of the participants (100 percent) who took part in the training completed the evaluation questionnaire. The results are shown in Table 24-1. During the training, participants were evaluated by the trainer using a yes/no test. Eighty percent of the participants received a positive evaluation.

Table 24-1. Reaction Questionnaire Results

Participants' Reactions	
This program met the objectives.	4.8
The program was relevant to my work.	4.7
The program was important to my job success.	4.6
The program provided me with new information.	4.4
I will recommend the program to others.	5.0
The program was good investment in me.	4.9
The program met my needs.	4.8
The program was a good use of my time.	4.8
I intend to use the material.	4.7
Overall result	4.7

Note: Participants rated the following on a scale of 1-5

Application and Implementation

Every two weeks from the end of the training, participants were assessed by their superiors. The process took three months. Managers evaluated the use of sales standards in the sales assistants' daily work. As a result, the study found that 70 percent of the participants used all of the acquired sales standards. Thirty percent did not use one of the acquired standards, closing the sale. Also, 80 percent of store managers effectively conducted on-the-job coaching.

An additional source of information was a mystery client survey. The results after this period were satisfactory. In six of the stores, there was visible improvement, and in three of the stores no changes were observed. (Note: During the evaluation process, staff changes occurred in three of the stores—store managers and sales assistants were dismissed, or resigned on their own.)

Barriers to Success

After completing the sales training program, a focus group was conducted concentrating on the barriers linked to the implementation and application of sales standards. The results of the focus group brought out that the greatest barriers were:

- Lack of time to practice some of the skills when there is an increased number of customers in the store (especially true during the weekend rush hours)
- Lack of support from immediate superiors, irregular and insufficient amount of constructive feedback

Store management pointed out that this type of training should be organized more frequently, at the same time stressing that a crucial element of further trainings was to allow the participants to practice in non-standard situations in which they apply the acquired skills. Another crucial observation that was made was that the participants still faced problems with closing the sale. This was the first sales training carried out for McArthur sales assistants, therefore the level of motivation and commitment in this case was extremely high.

Business Impact

It was decided that the business analysis would only take into consideration the results from six of the shops, due to the fact that in three of the stores there was a high employee rotation during the project (this group was excluded from further analysis). Shoe sales were studied in six of the stores for a period of three months after completing the training.

Isolating the Effects of the Program

A key element of the ROI Methodology is isolating the effects of the program on the data. It was decided that in order to do this effectively, a sales trend analysis for a period of three months after the training would be used to compare the results with the same period from the previous year. Actual average unit sales taken starting the week the trainings commenced, during the three-month period was 4,928 pairs of shoes sold. Forecasted average unit sales taken starting the week the trainings commenced, during the three-month period was 3,610.25 pairs of shoes sold, as shown in Figure 24-4.

Average "real" – average "forecast" = 1,317.75

A group of experts most familiar with the situation indicated that no additional new influences entered during the post-evaluation period. They also indicated that the pre-program influences are still present in the post period.

In all of the stores surveyed, a positive difference was observed between the actual results and the forecasted results. Conducting the same analysis in all of the stores at the same time strengthened the credibility for the increased results.

Figure 24-4. Trend Analysis

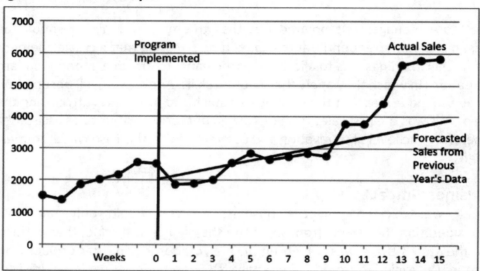

Converting Data To A Monetary Value

To calculate the monetary value of the benefits, the following steps were taken, as shown in Table 24-2. The average price of shoes is 79 PLN, of which 40.29 PLN is the net profit (data supplied by the Sales and Marketing Director). The increase in sales within the three months of the evaluated period was 1,318 units, giving an increase of 439 units per month. Annually, this gives an increase of 5,268 units x the net sales profit of 40.29 PLN. Which gives an overall sum of 212,247.72 PLN.

Table 24-2. Steps for Converting Data to Monetary Value

Step 1: Sale value of 1 pair of shoes
Step 2: V = Average price of 79 PLN for 1 pair = net profit 40.29 PLN
Step 3: ΔP = 1,318 units / 3 = 439 units
Step 4: Annual ΔP x12 = 439 x 12 = 5,268 units
Step 5: AΔP x V = 5,268 x 40.29 PLN = 212,247.72 PLN

Program Costs

Table 24-3 outlines all program costs. The costs take into account the cost of training for nine stores, although the benefits are calculated only on the results of six of the stores.

Table 24-3. Project Costs

Item	Total
Facilitators fees	20,000 PLN
Program materials	300 PLN
Meals and refreshments	11,000 PLN
Participant salaries and benefits	18,700 PLN
Cost coordination and evaluation	5,000 PLN
Mystery shopper	5,000 PLN
Total costs	60,000 PLN

ROI Calculation

The ROI and benefit-cost ratio (BCR) were calculated for the project as follows:

$$BCR = \frac{212,247.72}{60,000} = 3.5 \text{ or } 3.5{:}1$$

$$ROI\% = \frac{212,247.72 - 60,000}{60,000} = X\ 100 = 253.7\%$$

The ROI interpretation is as follows: each zloty invested returned 2.5 zloty (PLN) in benefits. The training proved to be a good investment and worthy of continuing in the future in order to develop staff sales competence. The whole process was consistent with the 12 Guiding Principles of the ROI Methodology:

1. When a higher level evaluation is conducted, data must be collected at lower levels.
2. When an evaluation is planned for a higher level, the previous level of evaluation does not have to be comprehensive.
3. When collecting and analyzing data, use only the most credible sources.
4. When analyzing data, select the most conservative alternative for calculations.
5. At least one method must be used to isolate the effects of the solution/project.
6. If no improvement data are available for a population or from a specific source, it is assumed that little or no improvement has occurred.
7. Estimates of improvements should be adjusted for the potential error of the estimate.
8. Extreme data items and unsupported claims should not be used in ROI calculations.
9. Only the first year of benefits (annual) should be used in the ROI analysis of short term solutions.
10. Costs of a solution, project, or program should be fully loaded for ROI analysis.
11. Intangible measures are defined as measures that are purposefully not converted to monetary value.
12. The results from the ROI Methodology must be communicated to all key stakeholders.

Intangibles

An intangible benefit that emerged during the training was an increase in customer satisfaction in six of the shops. A customer satisfaction survey was conducted and mystery shoppers evaluated salespeople for the same criteria. Table 24-4 shows the criteria being examined within the sales staff.

In addition, during the store management training sum up, it was discovered that one of the additional advantages of this training was a much higher level of commitment on the part of the sales assistants. The training also helped to improve communication between the head office and individual stores.

Table 24-4. Mystery Shopper Salesperson Evaluation

1. The sales assistant greeted me with a smile.
2. The sales assistant made eye contact with me.
3. The sales assistant offered help too soon (he was pushy).
4. The sales assistant said good morning.
5. The sales assistant offered to help me find the right shoes.
6. The sales assistant presented the benefits of the product.
7. The sales assistant handled the objections from my side concerning the product, offers, prices, etc.
8. The sales assistant comprehensively offered and presented alternative products.
9. The sales assistant suggested I purchase additional products.
10. The sales assistant informed me of the current promotion.
11. The sales assistant attempted to close the sale.
12. The sales assistant informed me about the possibility of refunds / exchanges.
13. The sales assistant encouraged me to re-visit the shop.
14. The sales assistant presented the company's loyalty program and encouraged me to take part in it.
15. The sales assistant was dressed neatly and aesthetically.

Communication of Results

The project results were presented at a meeting with the sales and marketing director and the chairman of the board. The six steps of assessment, the data collection plan, the method of isolating the effects of training, and proposals for the future were presented during the meeting. The overall results of the project were also presented to the participants of the project.

Lessons Learned

Conclusions which emerged during the discussion:

- The training time should be longer (one day is not enough to effectively practice sales competencies).
- The process of coaching should be continuous, not limited to specific projects.
- Before a decision is made about whether to implement training, the motivation level and commitment of participants should be examined (one needs to avoid situations in which the company invests in training employees who may be dismissed in the nearest future or may resign on their own).
- This first ROI project made me realize that this is an extremely practical methodology, which should be applied in companies on regular basis and function as part of their overall organizational process. The first step that is worth recommending is choosing individual training programs in order to evaluate them at various levels. My goals are

to propose the ROI Methodology to companies in Poland, conduct open training sessions on the ROI Methodology, and to consult and conduct research on the application of the ROI Methodology.

Questions for Discussion
1. How credible is this case study? Explain.
2. What other methods could be used to isolate the effects of the program on the data?

Chapter

Measuring ROI in Employee Engagement with a Broad Focus

Home Furnishing Stores, Inc.

By Jack J. Phillips and Patti P. Phillips

This large chain of home furnishing stores with popular brands is pushing for more growth, increased profitability, and more talent performance. Although the chain is very successful, top executives and the HR team believed that better performance was possible, particularly if employees were more engaged. The concept of engagement was pushed beyond just being engaged with work but also being engaged with customers and the community. With this broader definition of engagement, the chain implemented a comprehensive revised employee engagement program with impressive results. The combination of making adjustments in responsibilities, changing the definition of engagement, and utilizing the creativity, experience, and smart thinking of employees was what made this program successful. Store managers were involved, a new engagement survey instrument was developed, e-learning was used to focus on seven components of engagement, workshops were conducted for both the employees and managers, and online support helped to deliver a very positive ROI to the executives.

BACKGROUND

Home Furnishing Stores (HFS) is a large international retailer for several major brands. Some brands exist within their major store name and locations; other brands represent stand-alone stores for the brand and integrate with the overall products. HFS operates in more than 20 countries with more than 40,000 employees. Customers can purchase items in the store, have items delivered to their home, or have items delivered to a pickup center. As with many other retailers, HFS is shifting to an e-commerce option and the executives want to make sure the same excellent customer experience that is offered in-store is also felt online.

HFS, which is traded on the New York Stock Exchange, has been a good investment for shareholders. However, in a very competitive industry, and with the ups and downs of global markets, HFS wants to place additional focus on making the stores more profitable and growing both the number of stores and the e-commerce platform. While there are many facets that drive store profitability and growth, most of it rests with the talent in the organization. Their focus is on the employees who work directly with the customers and procure their products (procurement) and who distribute the products to the various customers and locations (distribution centers).

Vision

There is usually some debate on which stakeholder group is more important to the success of the organization. Some would indicate that the investors are more critical because, without them, there is no company. The goal of the company is to provide a good return on investment through share price growth and dividends. Others would say that the customers make the difference. Without the customers, there are no sales and the goal is to attract great customers and keep them for a long time. Still, others would say none of this occurs without great talent in the stores, distribution centers, and procurement function. Together they make it work. The executives at HFS have indicated that while all three groups are important, improvements in the organization have to focus on the employees. The vision for HFS is for it to be truly a great organization. In simple terms, executives want HFS to be a great place to work. This is where employee engagement becomes a critical issue: The company has been a great place to work, but the executives want to make it better. Recent years have seen an excessive rise in employee turnover; executives want to increase engagement to lower turnover and continue to make the company one of the best places to work and attract the best and brightest in the future.

In addition, executives want HFS to be a great place to shop by providing the best customer experience possible, whether customers are in the store or online. They want customers to feel respected, engaged, and nurtured along the way—the same online experience that Zappos has enjoyed and has been reported in several references (Heish 2010). For the in-store sales they want the experience to be extremely pleasant and helpful to make customers return often, purchase more, and stay with them for a long time.

At the same time, with great talent providing a great customer experience, financial performance should follow, increasing the profitability of the stores and allowing investors to receive more return on their investment through dividend and share price growth. From the investment perspective, executives want HFS to be a top performing company. Still, the top executives, and particularly the CEO, wanted to do more. They wanted to make HFS an important part of the community and a great company for the community. This would entail focusing on not only issues such as local health, education, and low-income challenges, but also environmental projects.

Collectively when these four goals are achieved, a very important sustainable enterprise is developed: the vision for the organization.

The Value of Engagement

This new vision places a tremendous focus on employee engagement. The perception is that employee engagement would drive all three subsequent issues: a great place to shop, a great place to invest, and a great company for the community. Figure 25-1 shows the connection. By revising the engagement process to focus on broader issues beyond the scope of the work of one individual, the company will be able to achieve several important changes. When employees become engaged with the customer and encourage and support them, the customers become more valuable to the organization. This customer experience will improve customer satisfaction, the net promoter score (NPS), customer loyalty, and customer complaints.

Figure 25-1. The Value of Employee Engagement

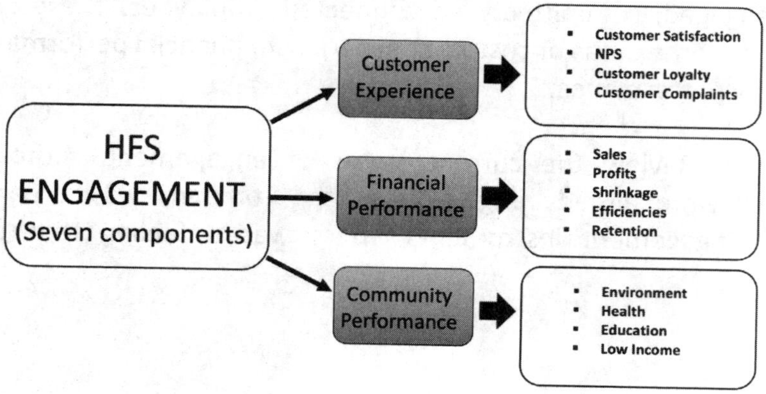

Engagement should connect directly to sales growth, profit improvement, shrinkage reduction, improved efficiencies, and increased retention. These are classic outputs from employee engagement and should be a substantial part of the process to improve the organization's financial performance.

Having employees become more involved and engaged in the community provides much support and assistance where stores are located and distribution centers are placed. Locally, they can help with education issues if employees volunteer for projects in school systems. They can work in low-income areas if the company sponsors projects aimed at uplifting people. And finally, HFS employees could help the environment by participating in recycling programs, efficient fuel consumption, energy conservation, and other important areas.

This perception of employee engagement provides a backdrop for major revisions in an employee engagement program in order to achieve these significant outcomes.

The Analysis

The HR team went about the process of making these changes. The team began with the end in mind, which were the goals shown in Figure 25-1, and asked a few questions, including "How can engagement make this improvement?" and "What must employees be doing in the future that they are not doing now that can have such an important impact on customers, financial performance, and the community?" This analysis involved several phases to make sure that an employee engagement program is the proper solution and is clearly connected to the business.

Stage 1: Review literature on engagement. Fortunately, there are many examples of outstanding companies that have been built on the shoulders of fully engaged, committed, and connected employees. These examples covered the three areas of customer experience, financial performance, and community performance.

Stage 2: Review the current status of engagement. Although HFS employees were already engaged and the company was already using standard engagement instruments, there was a feeling that this was not enough. This was because there wasn't a broad enough definition of engagement, some of the existing scores were not where they should be, and some of the issues needed to strengthened beyond just engagement to include accountability and responsibility for success.

Stage 3: Form focus groups with employees. Several focus groups were conducted to see what employees thought might be possible after reviewing the proposed concepts to strengthen engagement. The focus groups met with great excitement and enthusiasm, and suggested some changes and adjustments that would make them better. This created a lot of interest in the program.

Stage 4: Form focus groups with managers. Although the store managers would work together throughout the process, the company held separate focus groups to see how management team would react to the program and to see what was feasible. It also wanted to know what the managers would support and achieve in the demanding environment of retail stores. Again, great input was received, which led to more adjustments to the process to make it better.

Stage 5: Conduct interviews with senior executives. Several interviews were conducted to show the draft of the program and how it linked to the business. With these inputs, the team was ready to design and implement the program.

THE APPROACH

Once employee engagement was redefined with its many facets, the process was ready for execution. The challenge was to introduce the program in a way that was meaningful and timely, and with ample support along the way.

Engagement Defined

Figure 25-2 shows the seven components of engagement that fit the new definition desired by the company: my role, my team, my customer, my responsibility, my career, my leadership, and my community.

Figure 25-2. The Components of Engagement

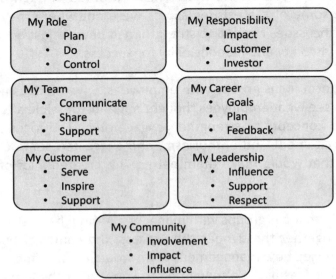

My Role: The beginning point is to redefine the role of work so that all employees can clearly see that they have many responsibilities in their work. They have to plan the work, they have to execute it, and they have to control that work. This involves checking progress, making decisions, and making changes. It is fundamental to engagement to have employees operating in a different way, being more involved in decisions, and checking their progress along the way.

My Team: The company had previously worked in teams in the stores, online, in distribution centers, and in procurement. Although all employees have individual responsibility, it is important for them to help one another and coordinate with the others. This involves continuous communication to share information with one another about the status of individual efforts. An important part of this process is supporting one another, filling in when necessary, and helping out when requested, which all works to make sure that the team functions extremely well as a unit.

My Customer: Here the focus is on working with customers. It is important for employees to provide great customer service in every way possible and inspire customers to have an amazing experience while they are in the store. This will encourage customers to refer others to the store, which will increase the net promoter score. Employees are also encouraged to show customers how to become more engaged. As customers become more involved in learning about products in the store, as well as providing input on new products and suggesting product changes, great things will happen. Customers will become a vast network of decision makers to help provide guidance in the future.

My Responsibility: Along with changes in work, team expectations, and customer expectations comes a change in responsibility and accountability. Here, the focus is not what they are doing as much as what the impact will be. The philosophy must be that the impact and not the activity is what makes a difference, whether it's with the employees closing a sale, the customer returning often, or the investors realizing an improving return on their investment. This requires the outcomes to be clearly focused on improvements that will help the customers, investors, and the community.

My Career: HFS wants to have more internal promotions. To achieve this, career opportunities are provided for individuals to move up in stores, the regions, and the distribution centers and procurement. Career paths had already been developed, but now the focus will be on the employee taking initiatives. This is action is voluntary, suggesting that it will be helpful for the employees to work on their career. This begins with setting clear goals and working toward those goals with a career development plan that is carefully followed and routinely monitored. The key will be the manager's role in providing feedback on progress and supporting employees in their career development efforts.

My Leadership: HFS recognizes that leadership is not just for those who are in leadership positions. Leadership is everywhere. Every person can exhibit leadership by influencing others and by serving as a role model of what should be done or the processes that should be completed. Leadership is also about supporting and serving others, earning respect along the way. Influence, support, and respect are an important part of everyone's leadership dimension.

My Community: To ensure that each HFS location is an important part of the community, employees are encouraged to get involved in an area they would like to pursue. In some cases, some time off may be provided. In others, it's a part-time responsibility. This will be coordinated by the corporate social responsibility team, with individual outcomes monitored along the way. The key is to be involved in some activity that will have an impact in the community that can be connected to their own efforts and influence.

Collectively these seven components provide a much broader definition of engagement, moving from typical engagement with the work itself to other dimensions of the team, the customer, the career, and the community.

Program Design

With a new definition of engagement, the challenge is to introduce the program to the entire team and make it successful in the organization. The program was designed in six steps, as shown in Figure 25-3.

Figure 25-3. Program Design

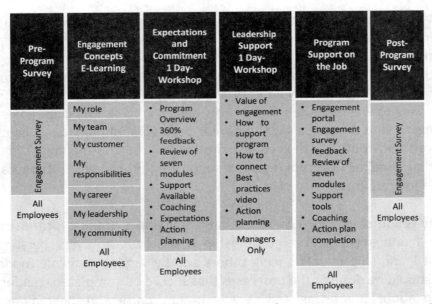

Before a program is rolled out in a new region or area, engagement data are collected using a preprogram survey. Following that, all employees take seven, 30-minute e-learning modules, each of which is aimed at one of the seven components of engagement.

Next, a full-day workshop for associates and managers is conducted. This is designed to provide an overview for the program, and provide feedback on the engagement survey data, which were collected from the employees and managers. It also serves as a quick review of the seven modules, ensuring that everyone has taken the e-learning modules and understands what is involved. Some limited skill practices are conducted, and the support that is available for them to use and reference is described, including the fact that their immediate manager will serve as a coach for the process. Expectations are defined and the concept of action planning is introduced. Action planning involves a particular team, usually led by a manager, and provides the associates and their managers with an opportunity to see how engagement is making a difference with customers, financial performance, and community performance.

The managers attend a second one-day workshop where the value of engagement is clearly outlined, along with tips on how to support the program and make it successful. They also learn how to be an effective coach to their employees. During the workshop they view best-practice videos that show some examples of the behaviors they need to support the seven modules. Some limited skill practices are also conducted with team managers. Finally, each manager selects a team and uses input from their team to choose two measures in the three areas to improve. This begins the action planning process.

The next component is on-the-job training, where the tools, information, and assistance is available to the participants through an engagement portal HFS developed. One-on-one coaching from the manager is available: It may be routinely scheduled or provided on an as-needed basis. Team meetings are often an important part of this program because they allow employees to discuss status, remove obstacles, and suggest enablers. The actions from the action plan are checked off as they are completed, until the desired impact is achieved.

Finally, two months after the program is introduced, a post-program engagement survey is conducted to show the difference between it and the preprogram version. Adjustments are made to the program as needed. Collectively, this design involves the key individuals who are required to make the program work, and it presents everything in a nonthreatening, unbiased way. The program is not focused so much on the performance of individuals, as it is on the performance of the program. Responsibilities and expectations are clearly part of the program and the focus is on having an impact, with engagement being the vehicle to achieve that impact.

EVALUATION APPROACH

HFS's comprehensive engagement program is highly visible, linked to key business objectives, and requires substantial resources. These critical factors, along with the need to identify program successes and improvement opportunities, led to the implementation of an ROI evaluation study using the ROI Methodology. In addition to determining the extent to which the program was increasing engagement capabilities and positively affecting key business measures, the evaluation was positioned to help identify opportunities for improvement for further implementation throughout the organization.

ROI Methodology

A robust evaluation was planned to identify:

- Reaction to the program by the associates and managers
- Knowledge and skills gained through participation in modules
- Success with the application of knowledge and skills in the workplace as associates are more engaged
- Barriers and enablers to the application of the knowledge and skills
- Business impact and return on investment of the engagement program

This provided insight into what was working well with the program and opportunities for improvement. Furthermore, evaluation results helped communicate the program's value to increase adoption once it becomes fully integrated into the organization.

The ROI Methodology serves as the structure for designing, planning, and implementing the evaluation study. This approach reports a balanced set of measures, follows a step-by-step process, and adheres to a set of guiding principles that are CEO- and CFO-friendly. These elements ensure a thorough and credible process for communicating the impact of the engagement program to key stakeholders.

The ROI Methodology approach begins with a fundamental framework of categorizing data, which represent measures that capture program success from the participant, system, and economic perspectives. Table 25-1 presents the definition of each level of evaluation data. When combined with intangible data, these five levels tell the complete story of the engagement program's success.

Table 25-1. Evaluation Framework

Level	Measurement Focus
1. Planned Action	Measures participant reaction to the program and planned action
2. Learning	Measures changes in knowledge and skills (engagement concepts)
3. Application and Implementation	Measures changes in actions and on-the-job behavior (engagement)
4. Impact	Measures changes in business impact measures
5. Return on Investment (ROI)	Compares the monetary benefits from the program to the costs of the program

Because the engagement program was comprehensive with many activities, the evaluation required careful planning. Detailed data collection and ROI analysis plans were developed and are presented as Figures 25-4 and 25-5.

Data Collection

Figure 25-4 shows the data collection plan for this program, which starts with the objectives and defines the measures, data collection method, source, timing, and responsibilities. This is a classic plan for ROI analysis.

ROI Analysis Plan

Figure 25-5 presents the ROI analysis plan for this program, and represents a very common approach to this type of analysis. It begins with the business impact measures that are influenced by the program, with each participant selecting at least two measures to improve using the engagement competencies and skills. The method of isolation is the participant's estimate of the program's influence on the impact data. While creating a comparison group would be the best way to show the impact of the program, the experimental versus control group comparison was not feasible because when participants select different measures, matching groups would be almost impossible. With participant estimates, the data are collected in a nonthreatening, nonbiased way, and there are adjustments for error in their estimates. Standard items (presented later) provided to participants in the workshop or through experts are used to convert data to money.

Figure 25-4. Data Collection Plan

Purpose of this evaluation: To show the value of engagement   **Program/Project:** Engagement
Responsibility: Engagement Team

Level	Broad Program Objective(s)	Measures	Data Collection Method/Instruments	Data Sources	Timing	Responsibilities
1	**SATISFACTION/PLANNED ACTION** Participants will rate the following reactions: • The program is important to my success • The program is important to HFS success • Content is relevant to our needs • The technology was user-friendly • The program was easy to follow • The classroom session was a good investment of my time • I would recommend this program to others • I will use the content in my work • The action plan was valuable	4 out of 5 on a 5-point scale	Questionnaire	Participants	2 to 4 months from start of program most items collected at the end of workshop	Employee engagement team
2	**LEARNING** Demonstrate successful knowledge of the following skill sets: • My role • My team • My customer • My Responsibilities • My career • My leadership • My community	Rating of 4 out of 5 on a 5-point scale Yes or No	Questioning Observation	Participants Facilitator	At the end of the E-learning At the end of the workshop	Program designer Facilitator

Figure 25-4. Data Collection Plan *(continued)*

3	APPLICATION/ IMPLEMENTATION	Checklist	Action Plan Questionnaire	Participants	2 months	Engagement team
	Participants will: •Complete the action plan items within 4 months •Use the coach					
	•Use the engagement portal					
	•Use the seven engagement concepts	4 out of 5 on a 5-point scale				
	•Use the engagement frequently	4 out of 5 on a 5-point scale				
	•Achieve success with engagement	4 out of 5 on a 5-point scale				
4	BUSINESS IMPACT	Definitions vary with the measure	Action plan	Participants	4 months after work-shop	Engagement team
	Participants will make improvements in at least two of the following measures: •New customers •Increased sales with current customers •Voluntary turnover •Store profit margin •Product returns •Inventory shrinkage •Store expenses •Customer complaints •Compliance Discrepancies •NPS •Customer Loyalty					
5	ROI 20%	Comments:				

Figure 25-5. ROI Analysis Plan

Purpose of this evaluation: <u>To show the value of engagement</u>   Program/Project: <u>Engagement</u>   Responsibility: <u>Engagement Team</u>

Data Items (Usually Level 4)	Methods for Isolating the Effects of the Program/Process	Methods of Converting Data to Monetary Values	Cost Categories	Intangible Benefits	Communication Targets for Final Report	Other Influences/ Issues During Application	Comments
At least two measures selected by team	Participant's estimate	Standard values or Expert input	• Initial analysis and assessment • Development of solutions • Implementation and application • Salaries/benefits for engagement team • Salaries/benefits for coordination time • Salaries/benefits for participants times • Salaries/benefits for coaches time • Program materials • Travel/lodging/meals • Use of facilities • Administrative support and overhead • Evaluation and reporting	• Teamwork • Career satisfaction • Net promoter score • Community image • Reputation • Brand • Customer loyalty • Reduction in carbon emissions • Community impact	• Top executives • Regional store managers • HR team • Participants • Engagement team • Prospective participants		

Sampling Approach

With the program in place, the team wanted to evaluate the early users to judge the success and make any adjustments. The program was rolled out globally, although the United States had a bit of a head start. Although the program was rolled out to the entire workforce, the sample evaluation was limited to 198 people, composed of store associates and managers, who formed 28 teams after participating in one of 12 workshops. They each took the survey engagement before attending the workshop. A team could be as small as two people working close together on a project or as large as 10 or 12 people. The key was to have the team focused on the action plan process to improve two measures, which would be individual or team-based.

RESULTS

Table 25-2 shows the data collection responses from all the planned data collection. The first part was the preprogram engagement survey, which targeted 210 people, of which 198 were in the first workshops. The pre-survey received 202 responses, representing 96 percent. During the workshop, several data sets were collected. First, reaction to the program and the concepts was collected, with 183 people providing the data (92 percent). For learning, the facilitator observed 198 associates and managers, and a subjective assessment was done to make sure the individuals were grasping the concepts and able to use them comfortably in their discussions.

In their workshop, the managers had more practice with the skills and were also observed by the facilitator, with a 100 percent "pass" rate. Although the end of each e-learning module captured some learning data, a questionnaire was used to capture learning data in the context of employee capability. While 160 of the associates received the survey, 147 of them completed it, for a response rate of 92 percent.

Two months later the post-program engagement survey was collected using the workshop participants as the target group. All 198 participants were sent the engagement survey and 169 people responded, for an 85 percent response rate. In addition, the same group received another questionnaire, which asked a few questions about the process; 174 people responded, representing 88 percent. Action plans were developed by 28 teams, with a total of 192 people participating. (Apparently, six people failed to connect with a team.) Four months later, 23 teams reported data with completed plans and five were either not available or did not provide the data. Thus, action plan data from 162 employees (84 percent) were provided, which represents 82 percent of the teams.

Table 25-2. Data Collection Responses

Data Collection Responses						
Level	Description	Method	Audience	Sent	Received	% Received
0	Input	Pre-program Survey	All	210	202	96%
1	Reaction	Questionnaire	All	198	183	92%
2	Learning	Observation	All	198	198	100%
		Observation	Managers	38	38	100%
		Questionnaire	Associates	160	147	92%
3	Application	Post-program Survey	All	198	169	85%
		Questionnaire	All	198	174	88%
4	Impact	Action Plan	Teams	192 (28 teams)	162 (23 teams)	82%

Level 1 (Reaction)

Table 25-3 shows how participants reacted to the program based on the data captured at the end of the workshop. This provided an opportunity for employees and their managers to clarify their reactions and provide responses. The group's average reaction met or exceeded expectations (four out of five on a five-point scale). A total of 183 responded to this questionnaire, representing a 96 percent response rate. The responses from managers and employees were similar and are reported together. The technology effectiveness question (question 4) had a lower-than-expected result, which may reflect several technology glitches; for example, some participants had difficulty following the different modules and processes. Otherwise, the reaction to the program was very good, with "intent to use" being the star measure.

Table 25-3. Reaction Results

	Average Reaction
• The program is important to my success	4.4
• The program is important to HFS's store success	4.4
• Content is relevant to our needs	4.4
• The technology was user-friendly	3.8

Table 25-3. Reaction Results (*continued*)

• The classroom session was a good investment of my time	4.1
• I would recommend this program to others	4.2
• The program was easy to follow	3.9
• I will use the content in my work	4.5
• The action plan was valuable	4.2
Using a 5-point scale, N-183	

Level 2 (Learning)

The first measure of learning was the observation of the skill practices. Because employees had to repeat practices if the skills were unsatisfactory, all participants scored satisfactory, as reported by the facilitators (all passed). For associates, role plays were minimal, whereas they were significant for managers. Additional learning results were connected by having the participants rate the extent to which they have the capability to use those skills. This observation was completed during the workshop, and a total of 147 people responded. "My Leadership" and "My Community" received the lowest ratings, which is understandable because some employees were uncomfortable with leadership issues and involvement in their community. The results are show in Table 25-4.

Table 25-4. Learning Results

	Average Reaction
• I am capable of using "My Role" concepts	4.8
• I am capable of using "My Team" concepts	4.7
• I am capable of using "My Customer" concepts	4.4
• I am capable of using "My Responsibilities" concepts	4.1
• I am capable of using "My Career" concepts	4.1
• I am capable of using "My Leadership" concepts	3.9
• I am capable of using "My Community" concepts	3.8
Using a 5-point scale, N=147	

Level 3 (Application)

Table 25-5 shows the application results collected two to four months after the workshop. It begins with the percent of teams completing action plans (82 percent), which was a very high number considering the detail involved in the actual planning process. The percent using coaching was a little less than expected, as well as those using the engagement portal. Although no objectives were set for portal use or coaching use, it was expected that almost all participants would use both. Pre- and post-engagement surveys (which each had 25 questions) showed gains, although the engagement skill sets were already there for many participants. The score of 3.6 is close to where it needs to be for success (four out of five). On the post-assessment, the results moved to a 4.5 for total skill assessment. The extent of use result just met the objective and was lower for frequency and success with use. The results shown are for a composite of all seven modules. The most valuable, least valuable, and most difficult engagement skills were what would be expected for this kind of process: career, leadership, and community, respectively.

Table 25-5. Application Results

	Percentage Responding
Percent completing action plans	82%
Percent using the manager in a coaching	51%
Percent using the engagement	61%
Average for engagement survey (8 skills):(24 Survey Items)	
Pre	3.61
Post	4.52
Using a 5-point scale	

Barriers and Enablers

Table 25-6 shows the barriers to use. As expected, there were not many barriers. The greatest barrier was not enough time, which was anticipated given the time constraints for the e-learning and virtual modules. The other noted barriers were minor, ranging from technology to lack of support, although lack of support was in the acceptable range.

Table 25-6. Barriers to Use

	Percent Responding
Not enough time to make it work	21%
Program was too comprehensive	14%
Lack of support from regional manager	8%
Technology issues	9%
Doesn't fit the culture	7%
Too difficult to use the concepts	6%
Other	8%

Also, as expected, the enablers were present with many of the participants, as shown in Table 25-7. This is encouraging because of the high use of the skill and follow-through on the action plans. The greatest enabler was the value of the engagement concepts, which was relevant to managers and employees. Following this was manager support. However, it was anticipated that the engagement portal would be rated higher than it was.

Table 25-7. Enablers to Success

	Percent Responding
Not enough time to make it work	21%
Program was too comprehensive	14%
Lack of support from regional manager	8%
Technology issues	9%
Doesn't fit the culture	7%
Too difficult to use the concepts	6%
Other	8%

Level 4 (Impact)

Table 25-8 shows the impact results in terms of the particular measures chosen by teams. Each team was asked to select at least two measures to improve using the engagement skills, concepts, and competencies in the program. By design, the measure should have a monetary value attached to it (or one that could be located easily). This eliminated the community measures, NPS, and customer loyalty.

Table 25-8. Impact Results

	Percent Responding
Valuable concepts	77%
Manager support	71%
Motivation	62%
Easy to use	52%
Team support	31%
Engagement portal	24%
Customer feedback	19%
Community response	12%
Other	21%

As expected, the most often used measure was acquiring new customers. HFS provided mechanisms to reach out to individuals who were not current clients, which was important for the teams, who selected that measure for improvement 21 percent of the time. The number 2 measure was increasing sales with current customers— including taking extra effort to up-sell, cross-sell, and entice current customers to visit the store more often and provide excellent service to make them buy more (17 percent of the managers selected this measure).

Increasing store profit margins was the next measure (13 percent), which was improved by controlling expenses, limiting waste, and avoiding price discounting or the need to give discounts to compensate for problems. Staff turnover came in fourth with 12 percent, although turnover at HFS is lower than a typical retail store. Product returns were reduced and 8 percent selected this measure. Returns occur when customers aren't fully satisfied with the product they have purchased or the product has not lived up to expectations. Good customer service can reduce returns. Inventory shrinkage was another important measure for consideration with 6 percent. Controlling costs and reducing customer complaints were the next two measures (6 percent and 4 percent, respectively). Finally, some managers addressed the compliance discrepancies measure (4 percent). There were several other miscellaneous measures that were either unique to a particular store or an unusual problem that was not one of the key measures. A few ambitious managers selected more than two measures.

Isolating the Effects of the Program

To have a credible analysis, initial steps had to be taken to isolate the effects of the program from other influences. Given the sales and marketing metrics that were used, many other factors will affect these measures, which often leaves a program like this with only a minor part of the improvement. While several processes were considered, such as setting up a control group or using simple trend line analysis, the team settled on using estimates from the participants.

The estimates were collected on the action-planning document (see Figure 25-6), with explanation in the workshop as to what was involved in the estimate and how important the issue was to the final analysis. In addition, the estimate was adjusted for error using a confidence estimate. Research has shown that estimates taken from credible people in a nonthreatening way are accurate and conservative.

Figure 25-6. Action Plan Focused on Obtaining New Accounts

Action Plan

Team: _____ Manager: _____ Engagement Team: _____

Objective: <u>Increase new accounts by 20%</u> Evaluation Period: <u>Jan – April</u>

Improvement Measure: <u>Monthly Sales</u> Current Performance: <u>118 for team of six</u> Target Performance: <u>142</u>

Action Steps		Analysis
Use engagement concepts	Routinely	A. What is the unit of measure?
Meet with team to discuss issues, concerns, opportunities.	Jan. 31	<u>One new account</u>
Encourage store visitors to go to website	Feb.2	B. What is the value (cost) of one unit? <u>$650</u>
Review customer NPS data—search for trends and patterns.	Feb. 5	C. How did you arrive at this value? <u>Market Research</u>
Counsel with current customers to identify potential customers.	Feb. 8	D. How much did the measure change during the evaluation period (monthly value)? <u>29</u>
Develop a plan for use of free samples.	Feb.10	E. What other factors could have contributed to this improvement? <u>Customer referral or new promotion</u>

Figure 25-6. Action Plan Focused on Obtaining New Accounts *(continued)*

Provide recognition to clients with long tenure. Ask for referral	Feb 15	F. What percent of this change was actually caused by this program? <u>40%</u>
Schedule appreciation actions for key clients. Ask for referrals	Feb.17	G. What level of confidence do you place on the above information? (100% = Certainty and 0% = No confidence) <u>80%</u>
Follow up with each discussion and discuss improvement and plan other action.	Routinely	
Monitor improvement, provide support when appropriate.	March 15	
Intangible benefits: <u>Client satisfaction, loyalty</u>		Comments: <u>Excellent program</u>

Converting Data to Money

To determine the monetary benefits, each individual data item has to be converted for use to money. This has to be profit-added, costs reduced, or costs avoided. Table 25-9 shows the measures that are driven in this program, along with the monetary value. These values were provided to the participants in the program, which means that it took almost no effort on their part to locate and use them in their action plan.

For new accounts, the marketing analytics section calculated the value based on the profit from the customer over the lifetime of the customer. In essence, if the customer stays active with the company for an average of five years, the company will make $650 in profit during that time. For the second measure, sales to current customers, the store operating profit margin is the value-add, which is averaging 20 percent.

Table 25-9. Converting Data to Money

Data Item	Value
New account	$650
Sales with existing customers	20% margin
Store profit margin	All is value add-profit
Staff turnover	60% of annual salary
Product returns	10% of average sale
Inventory shrinkage	All is value add-profit
Store expenses	All is value add-profit
Customer complaints	$500 per complaint
Compliance discrepancies	$500-1500

The store profit margin is already converted to money and any increases in value are benefits. The staff turnover figure comes from external studies about the cost of turnover for the retail industry—it totals 60 percent of annual pay and is accepted within the company as a credible, conservative number. This figure includes all costs of recruiting selection and onboarding, as well as the disruption cost of voluntary turnover. The customer care center uses 10 percent of the average sale to calculate product return. The cost is based on assumptions that the items may be damaged and cannot be resold, the items always need to be restocked, and an adjustment may need to be made. Inventory shrinkage is reported as money lost because of lost inventory.

Store expenses are direct cost reductions and are value-added directly into the calculation. Customer complaints come from the customer care center and are investigated locally, regionally, and globally, if needed. The group uses a model that estimates a cost of $500 per complaint. This assumes the time to address the complaint, the cost of satisfying the customer (which sometimes includes waiving part or all of the charge), and the ill will caused by the complaint.

The cost of a compliance discrepancy varies depending on the compliance and issue. These involve store compliance regulations from the city, county, state, and federal government. It could involve safety, environment, labor, or other issues. The team was asked to contact the compliance department for the estimate.

Monetary Benefits

When changes in the impact measures identified in Table 25-8 are adjusted for the effect of the program and converted to monetary values using the data in Table 25-9, the monetary benefits are developed. The improvement is different from one store to another—23 teams comprising 162 people completed the action plans and every team's task was to improve at least two measures. Unfortunately, five teams did not provide an action plan in four months. Although would be helpful to find out what happened, in terms of the analysis there is a very specific rule for addressing missing data: Guiding Principle 6 indicates that missing data get a zero in the process. Thus, the total benefits are adjusted based on the 23 teams and 162 individuals who provided data, but the cost is based on all 28 teams and 193 employees.

Table 25-10 shows a one-page sample of 12 pages of data showing the improvements connected to this program. While it only represents 12 measures, it illustrates the variety of data represented in the program, and shows how the adjustments are made. Three other tables complete the 52 measures for the 23 teams.

Next, the first-year value of this measure is developed using the data conversion numbers in Table 25-9. Although there could be some argument to suggest that this is a long-term program and that the benefits should be considered for a longer period, only the first year of benefits are calculated. This means that after the impact occurred, the amount was extrapolated for the entire year. Some may suggest that this is not credible because the data might not continue at that level for the entire first year.

However, when considering that the vast majority of the team members will still be in their jobs the second, third, and perhaps even fourth year, there should be some benefit from this program as long as they are in that job. A multiyear benefit also could be used. However, because it is possible to take the pre-work, attend the workshop, and work the virtual process in a few weeks, this was considered a short-term solution, so only one year of impact was used. This is to be conservative, which is reflected in Guiding Principle 9. Table 25-10 shows the monetary value for one year.

The contribution factor is the allocation to this program, because the team members provided a particular percent of the improvement that is directly related to the program. The next column is the confidence, which reflects the error in the allocation. Following the process, using Guiding Principle 7, the three values are multiplied to provide an adjusted value. When these are calculated for all 162 participants, including both measures, the total is 52 measures improved by at least some amount. With all of these totaled, the improvement is based on 52 measures valued to be $1,386,024.

The Costs

Table 25-11 shows the costs allocated to this program, some of which were prorated just to this sample size. For example, the needs assessment cost was estimated to be approximately $25,000, which includes reviews, focus groups, and interviews. This amount involves the up-front analysis necessary to decide on the specific need for this program. This value is divided by the total employees to yield a cost per employee, and then multiplied by 192, which is the total in the sample.

The most significant cost was the development. Some content was purchased from a major supplier, an outside production company produced the videos, and other content was developed under contract with freelancers or by the L&D team. In total, the development and production costs for the materials and videos totaled $425,000. Separately, the development of the two workshops cost $35,000.

The content for the engagement portal was developed for approximately $75,000, and developing the seven e-learning modules was about another $84,000. These costs were prorated over the 40,000 employees to develop a cost per participant. The total costs allocated to this sample of 192 represent the cost per participant multiplied by 192. Table 25-11 shows the prorated costs for these items. The cost of equipment and components were estimated to be around $12 per participant.

Table 25-10. Business Impact Data

Team	Annualized Improvement ($Value)	Measures	Other Factors	Contribution Estimate from Program	Confidence Estimate	Adjusted ($ Value)
1	142,400 Profit	Sales-Current	4	30%	60%	25,632
2	178,000 Profit	New Accounts	3	40%	85%	60,520
3	218,000 Costs	Voluntary Turnover	2	50%	70%	76,300
4	72,500 Profit	Sales-Current	3	40%	80%	23,200
5	68,000 Costs	Product Returns	1	70%	65%	30,940
6	226,200 Profit	New Accounts	2	40%	80%	72,384
7	7,000 Costs	Compliance	0	100%	100%	7,000
8	65,000 Costs	Store Expense	0	100%	95%	61,750
9	26,000 Costs	Inventory	2	40%	80%	8,320
10	21,400 Costs	Customer Complaints	2	40%	70%	5,992
11	99,000 Costs	Turnover	2	30%	70%	20,790
12	52,300 Profits	Store Profit	3	40%	85%	17,782

Total this team $410,610

Three other tables $975,414

Total $1,386,610

The coach's time was allocated at a half day per participant, because not all participants used their coach, and others used the coach for more than half a day total. For participants, the costs were calculated by their time for a day, the time away from work for the e-learning modules, and any other virtual activities. A total of three days of time was used. Most participants also required a travel expense, although minor. The cost of trainers, facilitation and coordination, and facilities and refreshments were easily available.

Table 25-11. Program Costs Summary

eLearning Programs (Prorated over all sessions) $84,000/40,000 = 2.1 x 192	403
E-Learning components used by participants $12 x 192	2,304
Program Materials $35 x 192	6,720
Travel & Lodging – Participants $390 x 192	74,880
Facilitation & Coordination $6,000 x 12 Days of Facilitation, Trainer, and Coordination	72,000
Facilities & Refreshments 12 days at $220 per day	2,640
Participants Salaries Plus Benefits $734 x 192	140,928
Coaches' Salaries Plus Benefits $520 x 192	99,840
Overhead	4,200
ROI Evaluation $40,000	40,000
Total	**$446,603**

In addition, an overhead cost for the total employee engagement team, including the L&D leadership not directly involved in the program, was estimated to be $4,200. The cost of the evaluation, which comprised the planning, data instrument design, data collection, analysis report writing, and briefings, was $40,000, including the cost of the briefings with travel. With all costs included, the total as indicated in Table 25-11 is $446,603.

ROI Calculation

When the total monetary benefits from Table 25-10 are compared with the total fully loaded costs from Table 25-11, the calculations are as follows:

$$\text{BCR} = \frac{\$1,386,024}{\$446,603} = 3.1$$

$$\text{ROI} = \frac{\$1,386,024-\$446,603}{\$446,603} \times 100 = 210\%$$

This is a very impressive ROI that greatly exceeds the objective of 20 percent. For every dollar invested in this program, it is returned plus another $2.10 in monetary benefits.

Intangible Benefits

The list of the intangibles connected with this project included teamwork, career satisfaction, net promoter score, customer loyalty, community image, reputation, brand, and reduction in carbon emissions. The participants were asked to indicate the extent to which these intangibles were influenced by the program. In order for a suggested intangible benefit to be included on this list, at least 10 percent of participants had to identify the influence as at least three out of five on a five-point scale. These intangibles represent an important data set for executives. If they were converted to monetary value, there would be even more value from this program and a higher ROI.

Credibility of the Data

When employee engagement is connected to the business in a program like this, there are always questions about the credibility of data. Here is what makes these data credible:

1. The business impact, which drives the ROI, represented actual store measures. They can be identified directly to the store and tracked and validated if necessary.
2. The participants selected the measures that were important to them with input from their immediate manager.

3. Participants had a desire to improve the measure, and took ownership in the program as they connected the skills of engagement to those important measures.

4. For participants who did not provide data (five teams in this case), there was an assumption that they received no value from the program. In reality, some of these individuals changed stores, either through promotion or transfer, and actually gained value despite not completing the project. However, the conservative approach is to use zero for them.

5. Only one year of improvement was recognized in the calculation. In reality, the significant change in engagement, which was validated with the data collection at Level 3, should provide value for a second, third, and even fourth year. However, to be conservative, only the first year was used.

6. All the costs were tabulated including time away from work. Some of these costs are debatable, but to be credible, every cost category was included.

7. Using participant estimates to isolate the effects of the program was not the most favored approach, but it is credible. The estimation was collected in a nonthreatening, unbiased way, and was adjusted for error.

8. A balanced profile of financial and nonfinancial, quantitative and qualitative data was presented. This provided executives with a great data set to make decisions about future implementation of the program.

COMMUNICATION OF RESULTS

With the results in hand, the data were communicated to the groups according to the communication plan. First, a live briefing was conducted with top executives and those responsible for the implementation of the program. In addition, briefings were conducted with regional executives during normal meetings and with the HR team. A three-page summary was sent to all store managers. The participants received a summary of the results shortly after they submitted them, as well as a summary of the changes made as a result of the program.

Based on the briefings with the executive team, the following adjustments were made:

- Improvements were made to make the technology easier and more reliable.
- The role of the participant's manager was strengthened to make sure that proper measures were selected and any needed support was provided.
- The role of the coach was diminished.
- Some efforts were taken to strengthen the link between the engagement survey and the rest of the program. There was concern that the engagement survey was not tightly integrated into the program.
- Another group of participants (teams) would be monitored in six months to ensure that the programs were still working.

Questions for Discussion

1. How did the company's new definition of engagement influence the design of the employee engagement program?
2. Discuss the importance of getting participants committed to provide quality data.
3. Critique the evaluation, design, and method of data collection.
4. Is this case study credible? Explain.
5. How can this type of process be used to build support for programs in the future?
6. How can the outcomes of engagement be linked to your organization's business objectives?

Reference

Hsieh, T. 2010. *Delivering Happiness: A Path to Profits, Passion, and Purpose.* New York: Business Plus.

ROI INSTITUTE®

Origin/Development/History

- The ROI Methodology™ was developed by Dr. Jack J. Phillips in the 1970s, refined through application and use in the 1980s, and implemented globally during the 1990s.
- First impact study – 1973, Measuring the ROI in a Cooperative Education Program, for Lockheed-Martin
- First public presentation on the methodology – 1978, ASTD Annual Conference
- First book published to include methodology – 1983, *Handbook of Training Evaluation and Measurement Methods,* Gulf Publishing (this was the first USA book on training evaluation)
- First one-day public workshop –1991, Birmingham, Alabama
- First two-day public workshop –1992, Johannesburg, South Africa
- First case study book published – 1994, *Measuring Return on Investment,* ASTD
- First international partnership established – 1994, Indonesia
- First public certification workshop – 1995, Nashville, Tennessee
- ROI Network organized - 1996
- First ROI Network Conference –1997, New Orleans, Louisiana
- First international ROI Network Conference – 2002, Toronto, Canada
- First ROI in Government Conference – 2003, Gulfport, Mississippi, Co-sponsored by The University of Southern Mississippi
- First ROI software release – 2003, Knowledge Advisors
- Distinguished Contribution to Workplace Learning and Performance awarded by ASTD to Jack Phillips for the work on ROI - 2005
- ROI Certification offered as part of Master's and Ph.D. degree – Capella University, 2006
- ROI Methodology adopted by the United Nations for system implementation- 2008
- One hundred books published with the ROI Institute founders as authors or editors- 2010
- ASTD celebrates 40th book written or edited by Jack and Patti Phillips- 2012
- ROI Institute celebrates 20th anniversary- 2013
- 10,000 participants involved in ROI Certification in 60 countries- 2014
- *Handbook of Training Evaluation and Measurement Methods,* 4th edition - 2016

Use

- More than 8,500 professionals are using the ROI Methodology, through planned implementation
- 4,000 professionals have achieved the CRP designation
- 5,000 organizations have formally implemented the methodology through ROI Certification™ conducted by the ROI Institute

- Approximately 5,000 impact studies are conducted annually in learning and development and human resources
- At least 300 public sector governmental units are using the methodology
- The ROI Methodology has been implemented in over 65 countries
- ROI implementation was first pursued in manufacturing, then moved to service, healthcare, non-profits, governments, and is now in educational systems

Applications

Typical applications include:

- Human Resources/Human Capital
- Training/Learning/Development
- Leadership/Coaching/Mentoring
- Diversity & Inclusion
- Knowledge Management
- Organization Consulting/Development
- Change Management/Culture
- Policies/Procedures/Processes
- Technology/Systems/IT
- Green Projects/Sustainability Projects
- Talent Retention Solutions
- Project Management Solutions
- Quality/Six Sigma/Lean Engineering
- Meetings/Events/Conferences
- Innovation/Creativity
- Marketing/Advertising
- Communication/Public Relations
- Public Policy/Social Programs
- Risk Management/Ethics/Compliance
- Healthcare Initiatives
- Wellness and Fitness Programs
- Recognition/Incentives/Engagement
- Safety and Health Programs

Articles and Publicity

- More than 200 articles have been published on the ROI Methodology in major publications in 30 countries
- The ROI Methodology has been a cover story on at least 15 publications, magazines, and journals
- At least 100 interviews in major global business and professional publications
- More than 25 radio and TV interviews in different countries

Books

- 75 books have been published on the ROI Methodology and its application (www.roiinstitute.net)
- Primary reference – *Return on Investment in Training and Performance Improvement Projects*, 2nd Edition, Jack J. Phillips, Butterworth-Heinemann, Woburn, MA, 2003 (originally published in 1997)
- Award winning book – *The Bottomline on ROI*, Patricia Pulliam Phillips, CEP Press, 2002 (received ISPI Award of Excellence for Outstanding Instructional Communication)
- General application – *Show Me the Money*, Jack J. Phillips and Patricia Pulliam Phillips, Berrett-Koehler, 2007
- Most comprehensive work – *Measurement and Evaluation Series*, Jack J. Phillips and Patricia Pulliam Phillips, Pfieffer, 2008

Case Studies

- More than 400 case studies published in books, journals, and industry publications
- Four-volume set published by ASTD in 1994, 1997, 2001, and 2005
- First public sector case book – 2002, published jointly by the International Personnel and Management Association and the American Society for Training and Development
- First International case book – 2005, Ireland published by Skillnets
- International case studies under development in 12 countries

Workshops (One-Day, Two-Day, and Three-Day)

- Approximately 200 one-day workshops conducted with more than 8,000 participants
- Approximately 500 two-day workshops conducted with more than 25,000 specialists and managers attending (offered in almost every major international city)
- Routine schedules of one-day, two-day, and three-day workshops offered in the USA and through partners around the world

ROI Certification™

- Five-day workshop plus two work products lead to certification for ROI implementation
- More than 10,000 professionals have attended certification, representing more than 5,000 organizations in at least 65 countries
- Certifications offered routinely about 50 times per year both internally and publicly by the ROI Institute (www.roiinstitute.net)
- On-line and self-study options for certification are available (www.roiinstitute.net)

Global Implementation

- First implementation of the ROI Methodology outside the USA – 1992, South Africa
- First certification in non-English language – 1995, Italy
- Implementation is accomplished through partners in various countries
- Implementation is currently occurring in 65 countries, with additional implementations planned in other countries
- Books published in more than 38 languages
- Regional ROI Institutes established in different continents

ROI INSTITUTE®

☎: 205-678-8101
✉: info@roiinstitute.net
www.roiinstitute.net

Special Offer from ROI Institute

Send for your own ROI Process Model and Application Guide, two indispensable tools for implementing and presenting ROI in your organization. ROI Institute is offering this exclusive gift to readers of this collection of case studies. The 11" x 25" multicolor foldout shows the ROI Methodology model and the key issues surrounding the implementation of the ROI Methodology. This easy-to-understand model has proven invaluable to professionals when implementing the ROI Methodology. The 20 page application guide provides more detail on each step in the model. Please return this page or email your information to the address below to receive your free foldout (a $6 value) and Application Guide (a $12 value). Please check your area(s) of interest in ROI.

Please send me the ROI Process Model and the Application Guide. I am interested in learning more about the following ROI materials and services:

☐ Workshops and briefing on ROI   ☐ Books and support materials on ROI

☐ Certification in the ROI Methodology   ☐ ROI software

☐ ROI consulting services   ☐ ROI Speakers Bureau

☐ ROI benchmarking   ☐ ROI online workshops

Name _____

Title _____

Organization _____

Address _____

_____

Phone _____

E-mail Address _____

Functional area of interest:

☐ Human Resources/ Human Capital   ☐ Learning and Development   ☐ Performance Improvement

☐ Consulting   ☐ Sales/Marketing   ☐ Technology/IT Systems

☐ Project Management   ☐ Quality/Six Sigma/LEAN   ☐ Technical/ Engineering Training

☐ Innovation and Creativity   ☐ Coaching & Mentoring   ☐ Organizational Development and Change

☐ Diversity and Inclusion   ☐ Leadership Development   ☐ Other (Please Specify) _____

Organizational Level

☐ Executive   ☐ Management   ☐ Consultant   ☐ Specialist

☐ Student   ☐ Evaluator   ☐ Researcher   ☐ Advisor

Return this form or contact: **ROI Institute**
P.O. Box 380637
Birmingham, AL 35238-0637
www.roiinstitute.net